Henry Truro Bray

Reason and Dogma

Or Footprints of a Soul. Third Edition

Henry Truro Bray

Reason and Dogma
Or Footprints of a Soul. Third Edition

ISBN/EAN: 9783337251642

Printed in Europe, USA, Canada, Australia, Japan

Cover: Foto ©Thomas Meinert / pixelio.de

More available books at **www.hansebooks.com**

REASON AND DOGMA

OR

FOOTPRINTS OF A SOUL

By Rev. HENRY TRURO BRAY, M. A., B. D., LL. D.

Author of

"*GOD AND MAN,*"
"*THE EVOLUTION OF A LIFE,*" *etc.*

Third and Revised Edition

CHICAGO
TRURO PUBLISHING COMPANY
1899

Entered according to Act of Congress in the year 1894.
BY HENRY TRURO BRAY,
In the office of the Librarian of Congress, at Washington.

THE REGAN PRINTING HOUSE, CHICAGO

Pluris est oculatus testis unus quam auriti decem.
(*Plautus.*)

Multos puto ad sapientiam potuisse pervenisse nisi putassent se pervenisse. (*Seneca.*)

Speak a word in season to him that is weary.
(*Isaiah.*)

NOTE FROM THE AUTHOR.

Although certain portions of the present work appeared in one of the author's former publications, "THE EVOLUTION OF A LIFE," a work of which only a small edition had been sold when the author, for personal reasons, stopped its further publication; nevertheless, the present work is so different in substance, and so wholly different in method and arrangement, from "THE EVOLUTION OF A LIFE," that it is absolutely necessary it should have a new title, one indicative of its true character and contents.

HENRY TRURO BRAY.

Chicago, Ill., Aug., 1894.

CONTENTS.

	PAGE
CHAPTER I.	
The Foundation and Limits of Dogma.............	13-23
CHAPTER II.	
Heredity and Environment.............................	23-30
CHAPTER III.	
Fruits of Study..	30-42
CHAPTER IV.	
Credulity..	42-53
CHAPTER V.	
Knowledge and Belief..................................	53-62
CHAPTER VI.	
Self-Deception..	62-71
CHAPTER VII.	
The Greatest Is Charity...............................	71-87
CHAPTER VIII.	
The Curse of Avarice..................................	87-99
CHAPTER IX.	
Lamps without Oil.....................................	99-104
CHAPTER X.	
Faith without Works...................................	104-114
CHAPTER XI.	
Imputed Righteousness.................................	114-126
CHAPTER XII.	
Brotherly Love..	126-137

CONTENTS.

CHAPTER XIII.
False Spirits...137–146

CHAPTER XIV.
Debasement of Religion..146–156

CHAPTER XV.
Unreasonable Dogmas...156–164

CHAPTER XVI.
Loyalty to Truth..164–170

CHAPTER XVII.
The Call of Duty..170–178

CHAPTER XVIII.
Clerical Skepticism...178–184

CHAPTER XIX.
Words and Works...184–191

CHAPTER XX.
Dishonorable Conduct..191–202

CHAPTER XXI.
The Dogma of Creation...202–221

CHAPTER XXII.
Thoughts of an Honest Priest..................................221–233

CHAPTER XXIII.
Divine Conceptions..233–240

CHAPTER XXIV.
The Judge's Statement of the Case.............................240–247

CHAPTER XXV.
The Judge's Conclusion..247–259

CHAPTER XXVI.
Husk and Kernel...259–268

CHAPTER XXVII.
Discussion of a Priest and a Warden...........................268–276

CONTENTS.

CHAPTER XXVIII.
Quieting a Mother's Anxiety.............................276-282

CHAPTER XXIX.
Law and Ecclesiasticism......................... 282-294

CHAPTER XXX.
One God—One Humanity.............................294-308

CHAPTER XXXI.
A Priest and a Physician on Ecclesiasticism..............308-318

CHAPTER XXXII.
The Resurrection...318-338

CHAPTER XXXIII.
The Heavenly Adversary...............................338-346

CHAPTER XXXIV.
Happiness and Virtue..346-356

CHAPTER XXXV.
Death and Immortality....................................356-374

CHAPTER XXXVI.
An Inquisitive Visitor........................... 374-386

CHAPTER XXXVII.
God and the World............................. 386-397

CHAPTER XXXVIII.
Reason Prevails................... 397-407

CHAPTER XXXIX.
The Barriers Are Broken............................. 407-418

CHAPTER XL.
The Old and the New.....................................418-436

" For he knew that no man is an orphan; but that there is an eternal Father who careth continually for all."

(*Epictetus, referring to Hercules.*)

PREFACE.

This work may be called a religio-philosophical novel; although the matter of the book is fact, not fiction.

Between reason and dogma there has always been waging a most deadly strife, which has never been more universal than to-day. In these pages are set forth truly and fully, with all the attendant circumstances, causes, reasons, and results, the origin and growth of this strife, in the soul of an honest and scholarly clergyman. Henry Merton was a real man among men; and the mental labors, spiritual sufferings, heart bereavements, and whatever else is related in this work, are real experiences, and not the work of imagination.

The incidents and occurrences of the average novel, while they may, or should, be possible, are scarcely ever actual; in other words, while they may not be contrary to human experience, they are hardly, and perhaps never, experienced by one and the same person. But in this work there is nothing made for the occasion. Neither art nor imagination has been allowed to run wild, or frame words not in themselves living realities. With the exception of a few fictitious names, every sentence in this work is but the footprint of a human soul, and that too of a soul burning with a love of truth and righteousness.

Here we have portrayed, as they actually occurred, the doubts and fears of an honest mind equipped, as but few are found to be, with abundant means for thorough investigation; and possessing, to a very rare degree, a firm resolution to probe these doubts and fears to the very bottom, at whatever costs. First, we see the causes that gave rise to these doubts and fears; secondly, their growth and development; and, thirdly, their reasons and results.

Henry Merton sought the truth as only the few ever seek it, for the great host of mankind follow their leaders; and the latter, sad to say, are in general bound by the three forces, prejudice, custom, and self-interest, to established usages and customs; and what these three forces fail to accomplish, ignorance for the most part perfects.

Thus there is but little opportunity for the birth and growth of Truth. Should Truth happen to be conceived, it is probably blighted in gestation; should it fortunately pass this stage, it will likely perish in infancy for the lack of sufficient nourishment; but should it marvelously reach maturity, then will it be exposed to the blandishments of ten-thousand false-hearted lovers, or tread Gethsemane alone, drink the bitter cup of persecution prepared by Superstition and Bigotry, and probably finally lay its life down as the reward of its own spotless virtue, and as a sacrifice for the good of humanity.

If the conclusions at which Merton arrived, and which are in this book worked out, are true, then is the religious nature of man grievously burdened with dogmas no less pernicious than unnecessary; and if these conclusions are not true, then is all reason astray, and science deceptive. But if reason be astray, and science deceptive, humanity can believe in nothing, trust in nothing, hope for nothing; for whether wrong or right, we have only the lamp of reason to go by, and the foundation of reason to stand upon; for even if we admit a divine and infallible revelation, we admit it only because we believe it to be reasonable. Nor is there any person to be found in the whole world, who will admit that his beliefs, however monstrous, are unreasonable in themselves. It is certain to all that, in the words of Locke, "Reason must be our last judge and guide in everything". It is not at all likely, therefore, that any person would be so rash as to assert that the reason of the world, for the last twenty-five hundred years, has been astray; and since science is nothing but objective reason, or reason's legitimate and necessary results, it can not be that the world of science is deceived. .

That the conclusions which Merton arrived at, and which are in this book worked out, are true therefore, we do not in the least doubt; and we are certain that the whole purely scientific world gives us its unqualified support as against the superstitions of the age.

Nor do we doubt but that, if the readers of this work accept the conclusions herein specified, they will be happier, more reasonable, more divine, and more god-like, enjoying more of heaven, and living more as Christ would have them live.

From whatever side we look at this book, it must result in a blessing to him who carefully reads and inwardly digests its contents. While, on the one hand, the incidents and experiences related are full of absorbing interests; on the other hand, the information the work contains on the Scriptures, theological dogmas, creeds, and other matters, is very great; the morals it inculcates are of the very highest order; and its theology is broad, elevating, reasonable, world-embracing.

But he who would derive the full benefit from the reading of this work, must, in the words of Huxley, "pluck the blessed fruit from the tree of knowledge, unconcerned whether these conquests trench upon the poetical imagination of faith or not". This may be hard in certain cases to do; but such fearless love of truth, of God, of humanity, never fails of its great reward: for above all other encouragements and blessings, is this one truth,

"*Die Unschuld hat im Himmel einen Freund.*"

THE AUTHOR.
Chicago, 1894.

REASON AND DOGMA
OR
FOOTPRINTS OF A SOUL.

CHAPTER I.
INTRODUCTION.

THE FOUNDATION AND LIMITS OF DOGMA.

Quid tam temerarium tamque indignum sapientis gravitate atque constantia quam aut falsum sentire aut quod non satis explorate perceptum sit et cognitum, sine ulla dubitatione defendere—What is so audacious or so unworthy the gravity and equanimity of the wise man, as to entertain a falsehood, or to defend unhesitatingly what is not sufficiently clearly understood and known. (*Cic.: De Nat. Deor. I. i.*)

The nature and destiny of man, the origin of the cosmos and how it is governed, are questions which have always interested the greatest that have ever lived, and can not fail to be of surpassing interest to all future generations. True, we have heard some say that they care nothing for these things; but certain it is that such an admission on the part of any person is conclusive proof of mental degeneration, or of a lack of those finer and more exalted powers essential to the highest development, or to harmony with nature and its laws.

It can not be denied, however, that thinking men have drifted away from the church, nor that in general they have become unbelievers, or radically indifferent. And although some may imagine that unbelief is worse than indifference, we are free to say that this is not true. Rather are we sure that of all states man can assume, that of indifference is the worst, the most inimical to his present and future welfare. Superstition is bad, a clog to the soul's development, and an impassable barrier to the highest mental progress; but indifference is much worse, for this gives no incentive to labor either for the present or future, but kills hope and deadens ambition. Shocked at the discovery of the fallacious character of their religious belief, it is not uncommon for persons most devotedly religious to cast aside gradually their former convictions, and finally assume a position exactly opposite to that which they formerly held. True religion is found between the lack and excess of religious faith, or between unbelief and superstition; but its discovery is not a very easy matter, for few are they with that equipoise of mind and heart necessary to their finding it. When once this golden mean is found, the universe seems more harmonious, the cosmos a unity, the earth brighter, and the future more hopeful; and he who loves truth for its own sake, who is willing to divest himself of prejudice, and follow the light of pure reason as it scatters the darkness of ignorance and error, can not seek this golden mean in vain; and, when found, he will be richly repaid for the energies he may have expended. It is for this golden mean that man should seek, that he may know more of God and man, more of the present, more of the future; that he may be blessed more and more with the freedom of reason, and liberated more and more from the shackles of ignorance and superstition.

When one, after having had unlimited faith in another, finds his confidence to have been misplaced, and himself to have been defrauded and maligned by the very person whom he had regarded as the dearest of all his friends, his faith in mankind receives a rude shock, and he probably becomes misanthropic, and distrustful of all. This is but natural, for man is a child of extremes. Thus is it in regard to man's religious faith. Rocked in the cradle of superstition, with his mind stored with everything but religious realities, and his imagination peopled with priestly creations, man is prone to rush to the extremes of unbelief and indifference, on discovering the untenable character of his childhood's faith. On finding the symbol of his faith irreconcilable with science, and repugnant to his own sense of justice and right, he concludes that there is no true faith, or declares with the fool "that there is no God." The foundations of his own temple having been washed away, built on the shifting sands, he can not readily believe that others may have been more fortunate, nor that there is a temple which abideth forever, founded deeply in the rock of eternal reason and truth. Happy are those who pause and think before they heedlessly cast themselves adrift to be beaten about by the ebb and flow of the tide, or to be driven about by the changing winds, without care, without purpose, an enigma to themselves, and a wonder to the gods. It may be that the weak-minded man must be either a drunkard or a total-abstainer, but the properly-balanced one will find rest in temperance. Thus it is true that the man unacquainted with nature and its laws, delights in myths, and finds pleasure in the dogmas of a coarse and bloody religious faith; and when by chance or endeavor he sees the error of his ways, he naturally goes to the opposite extreme, and finds himself without God, and without hope of a world to come. But the well-balanced mind will search earnestly for the truth until he finds it. Even the difficulties he may encounter in such search will not cause him to desist, for well he knows that no great prize is ever obtained unless ardently contended for. But when he finds the object of his search, his joy is great: religion is no longer the bane of civilization, but the purest and most exalted manifestation of God dwelling in man, sanctifying his life, and giving him hope in death—a religion consonant with reason, at one with nature, and comforting to the heart. While we hold that such a faith is not found in the symbols of the church, we do believe that it is unfolded in the pages of this book.

Calamity, distress, want, fear, praise, awe, and wonder are the foundation-stones of all early religious temples, and the chief impulses to all primitive devotional acts. Nor have these forces lost their sway to-day, for over minds of low degree they always have control. But as one advances in the scale of civilization, becomes acquainted with the laws of nature and his own being, he becomes more and more free from the tyranny of fear, yielding to the voice of reason only, or to the sweet commands of love and duty. The noble soul can never receive nor offer services given for the sake of reward, or with the hope of escaping punishment; but such a man yields his whole being to the drawings of love or to the sense of conscious duty. It is evident, therefore, that among all religious motives these two are incomparably the highest and noblest; and being highest and best, the soul that yields to them is doubly blest: he is happy in the service he renders, and the service itself ennobles his being. To get the noble man's service, therefore, he must be reasonably appealed to on the ground of duty or love, and not on those of fear or favor. The fact that the average appeal of the Christian pulpit is not made on the grounds of duty or love, shows in general the quality of the minds to whom the appeal is made, and the vicious character of the creed on which the appeal is founded.

As appeals founded on threats, or fear of punishment, must fail to move the noble soul, so equally ineffective are all appeals made on irrational grounds. What is contrary to reason the noble-minded can not, will not, believe; and what is founded on threats, he must instantly spurn. Can we wonder, then, why the brightest intellects and purest minds have not been, and are not, found in the church. How can such souls yield their assent to the great creeds of Christendom! They do not; they can not.

The two great creeds of Christendom are the Nicene and the Apostles', while a third form of faith is known as the Athanasian. As these forms of faith are the foundations of orthodoxy, we will here give them for the benefit of our readers:

THE NICENE CREED.

I believe in one God the Father Almighty, Maker of heaven and earth, and of all things visible and invisible: and in one Lord Jesus Christ, the only-begotten Son of God, begotten of his Father before all worlds, God of God, Light of Light, very God of very God, begotten, not made, being of one substance with the Father; by whom all things were made, who for us men, and for our salvation, came down from heaven, and was incarnate by the Holy Ghost of the Virgin Mary, and was made man, and was crucified also for us under Pontius Pilate. He suffered and was buried, and the third day he rose again according to the Scriptures, and ascended into heaven, and sitteth on the right hand of the Father. And he shall come again with glory to judge both the quick and the dead.

And I believe in the Holy Ghost, the Lord and Giver of life, who proceedeth from the Father and the Son, who with the Father and the Son together is worshipped and glorified, who spoke by the prophets. And I believe one Catholic and Apostolic Church. I acknowledge one baptism for the remission of sins, and I look for the resurrection of the dead, and the life of the world to come.

THE APOSTLES' CREED.

I believe in God the Father Almighty, Maker of heaven and earth: and in Jesus Christ his only Son our Lord, who was conceived by the Holy Ghost, born of the Virgin Mary, suffered under Pontius Pilate, was crucified, dead, and buried; he descended into hell; the third day he rose again from the dead, he ascended into heaven, and sitteth on the right hand of God the Father Almighty; from thence he shall come to judge the quick and the dead. I believe in the Holy Ghost; the Holy Catholic Church; the communion of saints; the forgiveness of sins; the resurrection of the body; and the life everlasting.

THE ATHANASIAN CREED.

Whosoever will be saved, before all things it is necessary that he hold the Catholic faith, which faith except every one do keep whole and undefiled, without doubt he shall perish everlastingly. And the Catholic faith is this: That we worship one God in Trinity, and Trinity in Unity; neither confounding the Persons nor dividing the Substance. For there is one Person of the Father, another of the Son, and another of the Holy Ghost. But the Godhead of the Father, of the Son, and of the Holy Ghost is all one, the glory equal, the majesty co-eternal Such as the Father is, such is the Son, and such is the Holy Ghost. The Father uncreate, the Son uncreate, and the Holy Ghost uncreate. The Father incomprehensible, the Son incomprehensible, and the Holy Ghost incomprehensible. The Father eternal, the Son eternal, and the Holy Ghost eternal. And yet there are not three eternals, but one eternal. As also there are not three incomprehensibles, nor three uncreated; but one uncreated, and one incomprehensible. So likewise the Father is Almighty, the Son Almighty, and the Holy Ghost Almighty; and yet there are not three Almighties, but one Almighty. So the Father is God, the Son is God, and the Holy Ghost is God; and yet there are not three Gods, but one God. So likewise the Father is Lord, the Son Lord, and the Holy Ghost Lord; and yet not three Lords, but one Lord. For like as we are compelled by the Christian verity to acknowledge every Person by himself to be God and Lord; so are we forbidden by the Catholic religion to say there are three Gods or three Lords. The Father is made of none, neither created nor begotten; the Son is of the Father alone, not made nor created, but begotten; the Holy Ghost is of the Father and of the Son, neither made nor created nor begotten, but proceeding. So there is one Father, not three Fathers; one Son, not three Sons; one Holy Ghost, not three Holy Ghosts. And in this Trinity none is afore or after other; none is greater or less than another. But the whole three Persons are co-eternal together, and co-equal; so that in all things, as is aforesaid, the Unity in Trinity, and the Trinity in Unity is to be worshipped. He, therefore, that will be saved, must thus think of the Trinity. Furthermore it is necessary to everlasting salvation that he also believe rightly the incarnation of our Lord Jesus Christ. For the right faith is that we believe and confess that our Lord Jesus Christ, the Son of God, is God and Man; God, of the substance of the Father, begotten before the worlds; and Man, of the substance of his mother, born in the world; perfect God and perfect Man, of a reasonable soul and human flesh subsisting; equal to the Father as touching his Godhead, and inferior to the Father as touching his manhood; who although he is God and Man, yet he is not two but one Christ; one, not by the conversion of the Godhead into flesh, but by taking of the manhood into God; one altogether, not by confusion of substance but by unity of Persons. For as the reasonable soul and flesh is one man, so God and Man is one Christ; who suffered for our salvation; descended into hell, rose again the third day from the dead; he ascended into heaven, he sitteth on the right hand of the Father, God Almighty; from whence he shall come to judge the quick and the dead. At whose coming all men shall rise again with their bodies, and shall give account for their own works; and they that have done good shall go into everlasting life, and they that have done evil into everlasting fire. This is the Catholic faith, which except a man believe faithfully he can not be saved.

The reader will find a sufficient discussion of the Nicene Creed in chapter XXXVIII of this work. The Apostles' Creed, exactly in its present form, is found for the first time in the writings of Pirminius, who is supposed to have lived in France, although he died about 758 in Germany. The substance, however, of this Creed is very clearly given by Rufinus, a priest of Aquileia, who died in Sicily in 410. But although the substance of this Creed occurs for the first time in the writings of Rufinus, it must not be supposed that he therefore believed in it, for he was bitterly attacked by Jerome for supporting the heretical tenets of Origen. The so-called Athanasian Creed is not the work of Athanasius, but is supposed to set forth the faith believed by him. There is much uncertainty about its date and authorship; but it is believed to have originated in France, somewhere during the fifth century. In written form it is found for the first time in 570; at which time Venantius Fortunatus, just before he became bishop of Poictiers, wrote a commentary on it. In the ancient English Church it was recited daily; in the modern English Church it is recited thirteen times a year, and in the Roman Church once a week. Waterland regards this creed as the work of Hilary of Arles; but notwithstanding the existing uncertainty attending its origin and authorship, it can not be doubted that in regard to the matters it sets forth, it fully and exactly embodies the Catholic faith, or that its definitions can be proved by "most certain warrant of Holy Scriptures." Almost every phrase of it can be found in the writings of St. Augustine; and the whole Western Church has accepted it for more than a thousand years, and does accept it to-day, as a most lucid, logical, and exact statement. Nor do we believe that any fair-minded person, competent to judge, can doubt that the Christian Church has come to this conclusion as a logical result of accepting the Christian Scriptures as inspired writings. In the words of a prominent teacher: "Just as Bacon, Kepler, Descartes, Leibnitz, Newton, had before them facts of nature, classified those facts, induced upon them certain general ideas, which seemed to explain them, and so by a process of careful verification arrived at the laws of nature—even so Athanasius, the two Gregories, Jerome, Augustine, and the other great theologians of the fourth and fifth centuries, had before them the facts of Revelation, carefully compared those facts, induced upon them certain general ideas which seemed to harmonize them, and so by a not less strictly inductive process arrived at the doctrines of theology; and these doctrines of theology which find expression in the Athanasian Creed, for instance, have been continually verified by succeeding ages, and have been found to explain the facts of Revelation so perfectly and satisfactorily, that they have come to be accepted by the whole Church with a confidence as justifiable as that with which astronomers accept the principles of Newton." (Norris: On the Prayer Book).

That the theologians referred to in this excerpt were just as rigidly logical in their inductions from the principles of Scriptures, as were Newton and others in their inductions from the facts of nature, we do not in the least doubt; but the absurd and repulsive doctrines of the Christian Church are not the result of vicious reasoning. A carpenter may use the best of skill in putting together the framework of a dwelling, but if the timbers be rotten, of what use is his skill? So with the theologians referred to: their logic is rigid enough, but the substance they use in their logical process, is not only not divine revelation, but the outgrowth of priestcraft and ignorance for thousands of years. The trouble, therefore, is not with the logic of the theologian, but is one much more radical than this. Whereas the premises of the scientist are based on the facts of nature, those of the theologian are based largely on superstition, mere assumption, ignorance, or the false notions of good men. The Creeds, with all their nature-contradicting assertions, are undoubtedly true photographs of the Scriptures. Should any person be inclined to doubt this assertion, let him take his Bible, and carefully examine the following references. While they are but few compared to the vast number which might be adduced, we doubt not that they are in themselves sufficient to establish every clause of the Athanasian Creed, the most lengthy symbol of orthodoxy: Isaiah vii. 14; Math. i. 18–25; xi. 27; xii. 31, 32; xxvii. 35; xxviii. 5, 6; Mark xvi. 15, 16; Luke i. 35; John i. 1, 3, 10; v. 22–29; xiv. 26; xv. 26; xvi. 28; xvii. 5, 24; Acts i. 22; ii. 24, 31; xiii. 37; Romans xi. 34; xiv. 10; II Cor. v. 10; I Eph. iv. 8, 9; Phil. ii. 6; Col. i. 15–17; I Tim. i. 16, 17; iii. 16; Tit. i. 3. ii. 10; iii. 4; Heb. ii. 14, 15; I Pet. i. 3; iii. 19–21; I John iv. 9; v. 7, 20; Jude 4, 25.

For many long years we repeated the Creeds, fully believing that they are truly expressive of the contents of the book upon which the Christian Church is founded; nor is our faith in these symbols, as exponential of the Bible, any less strong at this time than in those days when we stood a priest performing the functions imposed upon us. A more perfect epitome of Scriptural teaching than these three great Symbols of orthodoxy can not be produced nor imagined; and if a person would know the teachings of the Bible, we would certainly advise him to study the great Creeds of Christendom. If we refuse our assent to these Creeds, it is not because we question their accuracy as logical deductions, or as exponential of the Bible; but rather because we are unable in many cases to receive as truth the statements which form their premises. Let any person of average intellect, and fairly well acquainted with scientific facts, examine the following passages, and ask himself what conclusion he must come to: Gen. ii. 21, 22; iii. 8; vi. 1-7; Ex. iv. 24; vii. 3; xiv. 17; xxxii. 14; Deut. xx. 13-17; xxiii. 1, 2, 13, 20; xxxii. 41, 42; Judges i. 19; I Sam. xv. 32, 33, 35; II Kings xx. 1, 5; I Chron. xxvi. 27; II Chron. xviii. 20, 21; Ezek. xiv. 9; Rom. ix. 18-23. Surely, not a few theological deductions are founded on premises which are but vain creations of minds ignorant or superstitious or interested in forcing them on a credulous world. The scholar is willing to admit that the Church has no less a right, and that it may be no less expedient and proper for it, to declare a dogma than the philosopher a general law of nature; but neither the Church nor the philosopher has a right to violate the laws of the cosmos, nor transgress the bounds of reason.

CHAPTER II.

HEREDITY AND ENVIRONMENT.

(Μόρσιμα δ' οὔτι φυγεῖν θέμις οὐ σοφίᾳ τις ἀπώσεται
'αλλὰ μάταν ὁ πρόθυμος ἀεὶ πονον ἕξει)—

Everyone's fate is decreed, nor can one by wisdom ward it off; who tries to do so, will always only increase his pains.

(*Eurip.: Heraclidae, 614.*)

Among the many difficult problems which present themselves to the thoughtful soul, it can not be denied that there are some concerning which different minds will arrive at different conclusions,—in other words, concerning the correct solution of which man is in great uncertainty, and perhaps always will be; but in answering the question whether or not man to a large extent, is physically, mentally, and morally a necessary product of hereditary factors, we do not think there is any lack of unanimity. "Heredity," says the famous Weismann, "depends upon the germ-plasma. The minute molecular structure of the germ-plasma causes the egg-cell to develop into a duck or into a swan; it also causes the egg to develop into a Negro or into a European, into a Mr. Smith or into a Mr. Jones; in short, all qualities of the developed individual depend upon the constitution of the germ-plasma." Much less remote factors of descent are the mental and physical states of the parents at the time of conception, and of the mother during gestation. How fortunate the child whose qualities have been well beaten out in the forges of descent! how lamentable the wretched babe truly damned while yet its being was a cell, and before the spirit of nature had moved upon the chaos of its existence!

Henry Merton's deeply religious nature was a quality derived more especially from his father, who had been a most religious man, most affectionate, wholly unselfish, most assiduous in looking to the welfare of his children, always imparting such instructions as he could, and never ceasing to point them to God. He seemed to have been such a soul as the Divine Spirit must delight to dwell in. Henry was but little more than seventeen when he was bereft of this tender parent by death. Thenceforth, the word "father" had a different meaning to him: it brought thoughts of the grave, and sighs for the times that would come no more forever. It also took from him all hope of parental assistance in obtaining the education he sought, as well as his chief source of advice and encouragement. Thus so early left to his own resources, it would not have been possible for Merton to have achieved what he did were it not for the devotion of his youngest brother, and the large heartedness of a most benevolent gentleman who had become deeply attached to Merton in their church relations. In less than a year, however, this noble soul passed away, leaving Merton to himself and to his youngest brother.

The expense of Merton's early student-life at the university was somewhat lessened, from the fact that he was preparing for the ministry; for all ministerial students had dormitories, in the institution, free of rent. Such rooms were also larger, better situated, and more healthful than those, as a rule, obtained at private houses. Whether productive of good or evil, the young man preparing for the ministry is the recipient of very many favors. It is largely this fact, in all probability, that leads so many young men, weak in character, and of small ability, to choose the ministry as their profession in life. The many favors offered by the churches and educational institutions to young men preparing for the ministry, have undoubtedly great effect in filling the ranks of that profession with recruits; on the other hand, it is doubtful if young men, of great and noble parts, are likely thus to be attracted. And if they were attracted, there is generally no call for them; the crowds of less worthy applicants having already more than supplied the demand.

Among the very many assisted as we have said, there were some, as Merton knew, who were truly worthy in every respect; but the society of the average ministerial student, he soon found, was in no wise calculated either to make him purer in heart, or more polished in mind. Ignoble in conduct, and indolent in studies, many of the biblical students appeared to Merton more fitted to carry the hod than to build the temple. He also saw that the very worst characters among them were frequently the most demonstrative in prayer and profession.

At five o'clock on Sunday mornings, it was the custom for these students, aroused by some of the more active ones, to assemble for prayers. Great excitement would then prevail; much renewal of vows; great profession of faith and trust. At such times a student felt ashamed if he could not weep as much, and pray as loudly, as any other brother. Thus those of excitable temperament would shout, and sing, and pray, until they bordered on the very verge of frenzy.

Merton himself was of a very nervous temperament, and religious disposition; and it was not to be expected that a person of such nature could be long exposed to such and similar forces, without being greatly affected. Thus it was that Merton, who had never known a day without praying to God, nor without having faith in him, was greatly influenced by those who made the profession of sanctification; and in due time he made such profession himself, and continued in it for several years. Still he had every evidence for believing that it was not among those who made the greatest professions, that the purest characters were found; nor among those who professed to be nearest to Jesus, was the young man found who lived most like Christ. In illustration of this, we will give the following from his own journal:

"Last night I was awakened out of sleep by the most melodious strains of music nearly under my window. I listened in rapt delight for a time, when I heard the splashing of water, and a female voice saying: 'Goodness, gracious! That's my new dress.' The singing ceased, and the singers departed thinking they had been poorly paid for their intended kindness.

"In the morning there was a very bad feeling manifested among the boys at the occurrence, and a determination expressed to discover the student who had poured, from one of the dormitory windows, a bucket of dirty water upon the heedless heads of the unhappy serenaders. None appeared so much offended as a young man who was the son of a minister, and who professed sanctification. In giving his experience, he used to say that he wished to leave this wicked world to go and live with Jesus. In the course of a day or two, he was found to be the guilty party. He paid the young lady for a new dress; but the dirty act added to the feeling already prevailing against the theological students or the "bibs" as they were called."

At this time Merton was not without religious doubts and fears; but when thus troubled, he would fall on his knees in prayer, and there remain until such doubts and fears had passed away. The following extract, from his journal of this date, shows clearly enough the depth and earnestness of his religious life: "Glory be to thy name, dear Savior, for having taken me to be one of Thy sheep. O Lamb of God! may I never perish; but rule Thou in my soul every motive, every desire, and every action."

Nor was he less diligent in studies than devotional in

life. He sought to excel in whatever he undertook; and his superior ability and scholarship were readily acknowledged. The following instance may be given in proof of this. They were reading Antigone, a Greek play of Sophocles; and it was the professor's custom to translate for the class to-day what he would assign them as a lesson to-morrow. Merton protested against this custom, holding that it was ruinous for the professor thus to do the scholar's work. One morning at the recitation the professor hesitated in his translation, and finally told the class that, the passage being very obscure, he would excuse them for the day. In an instant Merton thoughtlessly replied: "Why professor? I am sure the passage is easy enough." With one voice the class cried out: "Read it, Merton. Get up, and read it." The professor blushed, but said nothing. Merton felt deeply the impropriety of his conduct, and longed to apologize, which he determined to do on the following day; but the next day the professor did not make his appearance; and Merton always thought that it was because of his deep mortification. On the second morning after the occurrence of the unpleasantness, as soon as he had opportunity, Merton arose in his seat, and apologized; for well he knew that although what he had said was true enough, his actions, as a student, were nevertheless very improper. The professor replied: "I recognized the impropriety of your conduct, Mr. Merton; but I willingly receive your apology. I also hope that in the future you will be as well prepared in your studies, as you have been in the past."

The daily life of many of the "bibs" was a great surprise to Merton, who had hoped to find in them examples of pure and holy living; but with their character, as a class, no person could be very favorably impressed. Among them there were not a few whose very exterior would condemn them anywhere, as worthless; and, taken as a body, they certainly did not appear to possess anything that should elevate them in the eyes of the world, or make them "chosen vessels," as they professed to be. Some of them whose worthlessness could not be easily covered, sought to turn it to their own advantage, by saying that God chose the weaker things of this world to confound the mighty.

It was the habit of the Greek professor to pray with his eyes wide open, whenever he led the devotional exercises in the chapel of the university. It was thought he had a good and sufficient reason for keeping his eyes open at such times; as Merton was told that at one time, when praying with his eyes closed, the professor's head had come into collision with an old shoe which had been thrown with unerring aim by one of the mischievous boys. This professor was not a favorite in the school; just why, Merton never learned.

Merton was quite a regular attendant at the meetings for holiness, held at the residence of a Mrs. Horton. Some very striking experiences were there related. At one of these meetings a Miss Mitchell said: "I see God face to face every day. He talks to me, and I talk to Him; and our conversation is full of heavenly things." Merton felt he saw an explanation of such experiences. The university was a great place for matrimonial alliances; and as there were many young men, either already preachers or soon to be, attending these meetings for holiness, it was, he thought, natural that young ladies should seek to attract their attention, and win their esteem. Nor is it to be doubted that such public profession of superior holiness, would appear a great attraction to those who were to be "watchmen in Zion."

In the month of April, Mrs. Maggie Varley, the great

revivalist, visited the university town. She labored hard to convert the young men; but the only effect of her work, as far as Merton could see, was the conversion, or frightening, of a few young girls. She had a good eye to business; for she sold her photographs to the "brethren." Being a very handsome woman, she found a ready market for them.

It is probable that Merton's philosophical tendency was derived from his mother. On her father's side she was of Hindu descent, her grandfather having been a wealthy Bengalese who, having come to England and been educated there, determined to remain in that country, and finally married a daughter of a Mr. Eddy, a clergyman of the Church of England.

The revival spoken of weakened Merton's faith in the sincerity of revivalists. Even in those days he began to suspect what he afterwards certainly knew, that to know them as they appear to be, is not to know them as they really are. How far reaching in its effects may a very small occurrence be! How unforeseen the forces and circumstances that produce man's character! It would seem that Huxley speaks not without reason when he says: In man as in brutes there is no proof that any state of consciousness is the cause of change in the motion of the matter of the organism. If this position is well based it follows that our mental conditions are simply the symbols in consciousness of the changes which take place automatically in the organism; and that the feeling we call volition is not the cause of a voluntary act, but the symbol of that state of the brain which is the immediate cause of the act.

(*Collected Essays, Vol. I, Essay v.*)

CHAPTER III.

FRUITS OF STUDY.

Profecto eos ipsos qui se aliquid certi habere arbitrantur, addubitare coget doctissimorum hominum de maxima re tanta dissensio.—So great a disagreement among the most learned concerning this, the most important of all questions, forces us to doubt the certainty of their information. (*Cicero: De Nat. Deor. I. i.*)

The great business of a man is to improve his mind. As for all other things, they are no better than lifeless ashes and smoke.
(*Marcus Aurelius.*)

Several of the young men at the university were known as "Conference Students." Such had been preaching for some years, but were now seeking a better education chiefly at the expense of their conferences. From the fact of having had experience in the ministry, their companionship was much sought by new matriculants at the schools; but one's esteem for them generally lessened as his acquaintance with them increased.

During the senior year Merton's room-mate was a young gentleman from Allentown. He had come to the school to prepare for the ministry. He was a most conscientious young man, and very sincere in his Christian life. In attending this school he had expected to find better means of obtaining purity of heart, and sound knowledge than he could find at home; but his treatment by the "brethren," and their conduct in general, soon dissipated his hopes. "Here," he said, "I felt sure I could know more of the height, and depth, and breadth of the love of God in Christ; but after a stay of about six months I find if I stayed much longer, Mr. Merton, I should be a first-class infidel. The actions of the brethren have been so disgraceful, that I have lost most of the honest faith I brought here with me. God help me to get home safe, and I'll promise not to come to this place again in a hurry, with the hope of receiving good from the society of young preachers! Look at what the Rev. Richter did to me! While I live I shall never forget the insulting act. For more than an hour I marched around in that cattle-show, carrying the tag which he had pinned to my back, and on which was written, 'This bull for sale;' and I should have continued walking with that insult there, were it not for that strange gentleman who asked me why I bore such a card. I was horrified at the discovery, and ashamed to be seen any longer among the people; and all this shame and mortification came to me from the hands of a minister of the Gospel. I have had enough of young preachers. By the help of God I will look for better society."

Merton's studies were bringing forth their fruit in him; but that fruit was the fruit of knowledge, of which if the student eats, his eyes will begin to open, his faith in dogmas to waver, his doubts to increase; and he will be a subject less and less affected by the innoculating virus of superstition. Such a mental state is well described in his journal of this date: "To-day my soul is sore, and my cry is going out to God: Hide not thyself for ever. O Lord, in thy mercy arise, and dispel the gloom; bind up Thou the broken-hearted.

"About a week ago I passed a night all in trouble and darkness. Sleep forsook my eyelids. I lay on my pillow from about half-past nine o'clock at night, till four in the morning, without slumber. I endured unspeakable distress of soul; and though I prayed continually that God would give me rest, my prayers seemed vain. I was in black despair. Last night I had a worse time, if possible. I sought slumber in vain till midnight, when I came out, and prayed to God to remove the agony of mind I was suffering. I seemed to be afraid of disease and death, and cried in the bitterness of my soul that God might show me the cause. A thousand fears seemed to flit through my mind; and my prayer has been, and still is, Lord be merciful to me." We copy these words because of their deep import. The state of mind spoken of induced such physical pain, and mental misery as made Merton's life for years almost unbearable. But he might have given us the reason for such a state. He might have written that it arose from the conscious conflict of reason with the superstition taught in the name of religion; and that its more immediate cause had been the reading of the posthumous essays of J. Stuart Mill, and other similar religio-philosophical writings. The argument of the great and truth-loving Mill had been too much for Merton. The taste for such writings once having been established, Merton's mind could find no rest until he had read almost everything he could find, bearing on the fundamentals of Christianity. Never was ground held more tenaciously; never was there a more unwilling tenant ousted; but, still, little by little was Merton obliged to surrender much that he had been accustomed to regard as essentials of Christian faith, and necessary to eternal life. This he had to do as reason forced the changes upon him. The fact also that from this date he made much less frequent entries in his journal, proves the change which was slowly but surely coming over him. He began to understand that states of mind, or experience, may result from faith in things that do not exist. A son rejoices in the hourly expectation of meeting his mother, although, unknown to him, she died yesterday while on her journey. Her death did not lessen his conscious joy, although the form which he was momentarily expecting to gladden his heart, was now cold in the embrace of death. His joy arose, not from the fact of his mother's existence, but from his faith in that existence,—in other words, from faith in something which he supposed had an existence, but which in reality had not. So with the Christian,—his ecstasy arising from belief in certain Christian teachings, is no proof that such teachings have any basis in reality. They may be dead, as the mother, though he rejoices in his belief that they are alive. So great is the faith of the sincere Mohammedan in Mahomet, as the great prophet of God, that his mind frequently enters into a state of ecstasy or even frenzy; so also is it with the Christian who, in a similar manner, trusts to Christ. Each declares that there is no other name given whereby a man may be saved; and each refuses to admit that the other can have salvation through the name in which he trusts. But it makes no difference to their happiness, for the reason, as we have seen, that a man may be as happy from hoping in a nonexistent thing, as in something so firmly established as the everlasting hills.

Man's religious principles are in general the slowly developed results of his early influences. During childhood Merton had lived in a deeply religious atmosphere; and, in due time, his imaginative nature seemed in touch with the spirit-world. The fact that that world was unknown to him, and the barriers separating the known from the unknown, impassable, could not deter him, in his waking hours, from forming conclusions concerning it and its inhabitants; nor, in his sleep, from mingling in their society. Thus when about nine years old Merton dreamt one night that father and mother, with the whole family, were seated around the fire. The father was telling stories, as was his custom, when some one was heard walking in the chamber above. They were all greatly surprised, and concluded, of course, that it was a spirit. In a short time steps were heard coming down the long stairway; and in a minute more, they beheld a beautiful spirit-child standing beside them. He said he had come from heaven, and that he wished one of them to accompany him. It was agreed that Merton should go. The beautiful spirit walked before him for some time, when he seized, and bore Merton into space, finally setting him down amidst a dazzling throng surrounding the throne of God, and praising Him who sat thereon. Here Merton was permitted to remain for some time, until he was so delighted with the many attractions of the beautiful place, that he wished to abide there; but the spirit was commanded to take and bear him away to the lower regions, that he might see himself the torments of the damned. In a twinkling they were whirling through space, and soon found themselves at the massive gates of the infernal regions. The doors were thrown open, and they were admitted. Here was every conceivable kind of torment which infinite power and skill could contrive. Wherever they looked were devils yelling, fires raging, and the lost groaning. Thousands of little dog-like fiends went hither and thither, snarling and biting; and Merton thought their bite was the bite of eternal death. Into the wound they made, they injected a poison which passed through and through the being bitten, vitiating more and more his nature, and leaving him irretrievably lost. Merton trembled; but the spirit said: "Stay near me, and they can not reach you."

Having seen the woes of the lost, burning in the fire that is never quenched, once more the gates of hell flew open; and Merton and the angel were rushing through space. Again they stood in the presence of God. Here Merton wished to remain forever; but God said: "It is not yet time; take him whence he came; let him finish the work I have given him to do." Unwilling as Merton was, he was taken by the spirit, and borne to his father's house.

At another time he dreamt he met the Devil, who challenged him to wrestle. At this time Merton was about fifteen years old, and enjoyed wrestling very much, and was considered very expert at it. Merton accepted his challenge, and soon threw him very heavily. This he repeated several times, when the Devil said to Merton: "You are a coward, nevertheless; why don't you take out those things you have in your pocket?" In his dream Merton had in his pocket a prayer-book and a Bible; and these he was unwilling at first to take out. Finally he said: "Although it is against my principles to wrestle without the prayer-book and Bible, still I am quite satisfied I can throw you with or without them; so to oblige you I will take them out."

No sooner had he taken them out than the Devil seized, and threw him so violently, that his very life seemed leaving him. He awoke in such screams that brought his father, who was some time before he succeeded in calming him. His nervous shock was a very severe one.

Again, when about sixteen, he dreamt that the Judgment-day had come. All mankind were passing, one by one, over a scales. Those who brought down the scales, went to the right; those who could not, went to the left. The pallid looks and trembling forms of the countless hosts awaiting their turns, revealed too plainly the awful anxiety pervading the silent breasts of all. Now had come the long expected moment for the final answer to the well known lines:

> "Where shall I find my destined place?
> Shall I my everlasting days
> With fiends or angels spend?
> Who can resolve the doubt
> That tears my anxious breast?
> Shall I be with the damned cast out
> Or numbered with the blest?"

The moments seemed years. Soon, however, Merton's fate had been decided; and he was praising God for being "numbered with the blest."

Such dreams show to a certainty the food Merton had been fed on, the books he had read, his mental state, and his deeply religious nature. It is a pity such books are ever printed. They are a curse to those who read them.

Merton found only one thing painful to him in the university. The students had a custom of "sloping" en masse, if the professor should be a few seconds late in coming into the recitation-room. By "sloping" is meant, leaving the room in a body, precisely as the hour for recitation arrives. By so doing the students could not have a new lesson assigned, and therefore would escape so much study. Against the practice of "sloping," Merton protested from the beginning. He felt every lesson missed was a loss to him, and that the professor owed him the recitation. He therefore would not leave, but await the professor's arrival. This brought the ire of the class down on Merton, and frequent threats of vengeance. One morning as he was passing under the university porch, coming from a recitation in French, which the class had "sloped," he narrowly escaped a bucket of water thrown from the window above, with the purpose of giving him a bath, because he would not "slope" with the other members of the class. After this the boys found him more obdurate than ever. It was not the way to gain their end. Merton held his own, and finally brought "sloping" into disfavor. The boys liked him the better in the end for what he did; although it seemed a little hard for him at first. He was very desirous of gaining the friendship of his class; but he could not think it right to possess that friendship, at the expense of losing his recitations. Some of his class tried, in every way, to make things as disagreeable for him as possible;

and none persecuted him so bitterly as the ministerial students.

The daily routine of college life soon becomes irksome and finally unbearable to a person not naturally studious, or not longing for a knowledge of nature as it really is, and of the great souls who have striven in the ages gone by to know it, and to give their thoughts to the world often at the sacrifice of their lives. To know such men as they really were, is to love and revere them as masters in the domain of thought,—as beacon lights of virtue and wisdom in a world engulfed in ignorance, wealth, and lust; and dark as the world is, and always has been, the earnest student searching for the truth, and not for some prop to support a cherished opinion, never finds it without some great souls, standing as rocks in mid-ocean, consecrated to their work, moved by the highest impulses, living as gods among men, and scattering seeds of justice and truth wherever they go. It was during the last two years at the college of arts that Merton became more especially acquainted with the thoughts of some of these men.

About this time he received a letter from his friend and college chum, R. B. Faye, who had been engaged in the active work of the ministry for some years; but at present was taking a course at the university, as a conference student. Merton and Mr. Faye confided to each other their inmost secrets. The religious doubts and fears of each were not unknown to the other. "Oh, friend Merton!" he wrote, "I have to inform you that my darling Lena is dead. Yes, dead, dead! My brightest earthly hopes are all crushed and withered. She was not only highly educated and accomplished, but naturally pure, virtuous, modest, gentle, and loving."

It is indirectly to the death of this excellent young lady, that Merton attributed, to no small degree, the great change that, a few years after, passed over the religious belief of this friend. Feeling his ignorance of those matters which ministers in general affirm as most certainly known, Mr. Faye determined on a course of post-graduate study. He went to Breslau, Germany, where he continued at work two years. He then returned, but not to preach. The result of his work so increased his conscious ignorance, that he resolved to assert no more, as known and true, what now he clearly saw was unknown and unreasonable. He took up the work of teaching, and, had he lived, would have become a well known educator. He died suddenly while experimenting at the laboratory of the college where he was teaching. He left behind him a widow and one or two little children. He was a hard-working student, a good man, and a true friend. He was the most intimate companion Merton ever had among all his college acquaintances; and he deeply regretted his death.

It is quite generally supposed that great affliction and sorrow tend to soften, and increase the religious spirit of the sufferer; but we have not found it so. On the contrary, we believe that it tends to increase the questioning spirit, and to make of the sufferer a more matter-of-fact man.

On Merton's return to the university, he chose the lake route. On board the steamboat there happened to be among the passengers an old gentleman by the name of Taggart. He had with him a charming and beautiful girl with whom Merton soon became well acquainted. It was through her that he was introduced to her father, who Merton discovered was, in popular language, an infidel. They frequently conversed on religious topics, at which times Merton would press upon him what he regarded as the most convincing proof of the deity of Christ. Having failed to satisfy his inquiring mind by argument, Merton spoke to him of the great pleasure derived from the feeling that God was our Father. To this he replied, "My dear sir! I never take a morsel of food, without thanking Him from whom all things come. That He is the Father of all, I doubt not; that I am his child, I confidently believe."

Here was a man called an infidel who Merton was forced to admit, had a faith far deeper, and a trust more complete than he, although a child of the orthodox faith. The knowledge of this fact set Merton to thinking, which in due time brought forth its abundant fruit.

The year now opening was to be his last at the college of arts; he was a member of the senior class. At such times young men's expectations are not so great as in preceding years. Fields at a distance look green; distance lends enchantment, distorts the reality. Like that of others, Merton's mind was tossed hither and thither, on the tempest of uncertainty. He was in the valley of indecision. At this time he could have well subscribed to the well known words of Vergil:

"*Rerumque ignarus, imagine gaudet.*"

There were very many obscure paths, but none so plain that he, a way-faring man, might not err therein.

As representing his religious faith at this time, we will quote from what Merton wrote, at this date, in his autograph album:

'Rerumque ignarus, imagine gaudet.'
And can the Infinite be known?
Is God the Father, God the Son?
Him whom no eyes have ever seen, whose fiat is the law,
Jehovah, Lord, God without end, man manifested saw!
What a conflict of words, unintelligible surds!
Who can extract their root?
More than reason affords, or history records.
Is the mystery of God's own book.

Every line of this original poem reveals deep doubt, a doubt ever widening and deepening as the consciousness grew in him, that reason and reason alone must be the ultimate judge in all things; and that whatever teachings did violence to reason, should not be accepted as true elements of faith. That not a few dogmas of Christianity did violence to reason, contradicted one another, and all ideas of the justice and goodness of God, Merton could not for one moment doubt.

Merton had now finished the course of study for the degree of B. A., and that, too, with great distinction; for of the many young men who had been contending with him for the gold medal, not one remained at the beginning of the senior year: he had outrun them all in the race. But his philosophical and scientific studies had served greatly to weaken his faith which once could receive the most unreasonable assertions, though based on the most incredible testimony. This effect is clearly manifested in a poem composed by Merton at that time, and with which we close this chapter. We give the poem not for its merit, but to illustrate the effect on Merton's mind of philosophical and scientific studies:

> Now rest my soul. Where wouldst thou go?
> I'd question thee of worlds unknown.
> Why sayest thou, 'let me alone,
> I'm doomed to linger here below?'
>
> The Hand that guides the starry host,
> And feeds for aye the cosmic flame,
> That gives to great and small a name,
> That moveth all and loveth most,—
>
> Whence came that Hand, if such there be?
> What powers produced the awful Cause?
> What are, who framed, the cosmic laws?
> Would'st thou by silence silence me?
>
> The link that binds thee to the sky,
> In substance what, in strength how great?
> When was it wrought? and why create
> A link whose substance some deny?

Still more I ask: whence comest thou?
Now, hold thy peace; I question fair.
If able, unto me declare
Where first thou dwelt, where dwellest now.

A friend sincere I've always been,
Would gratify thy least desire;
Yet know not I if earth or fire
Thou art; indeed, if anything.

I do not know thee who thou art,
And more, I'm ignorant of myself;
Of things below, e'en though but pelf,
Uncertain, too; yet love to mark—

Th' unfolding flower, the budding tree,
The march of time, th' expanding soul,
The atom, molecule, the whole,
E'en though thou ne'er canst answer me.

CHAPTER IV.

CREDULITY.

Wisdom and knowledge shall be the stability of thy times.
(*Isaiah.*)

THE summer in which he took his first degree in science and arts, Merton passed with his mother and youngest brother. During this time Merton was frequently with his brother's minister, the Rev. Mr. Tubbs, whose sermons appealed more to the reason than to the feelings. Many of Mr. Tubbs' people were displeased, and Merton wondered not; for of those who fill the churches, but few are they who relish reason. One said, "There is no food to be had in this church now." Said another, "He looks for all the world like an actor. If he has not missed his calling, then I am no judge of human nature."

"I can not help thinking," said Mr. Tubbs one day, "that I have some friends in this church; but I do not think, Mr. Merton, that I have ever preached a sermon in this place to what might be called an appreciative audience."

Merton replied that he was sorry to hear what Mr. Tubbs had said; and asked if the elder was not on friendly terms with him.

"The elder," said Mr. Tubbs, "is outwardly a professor of sanctification; but in his heart, Mr. Merton, he is an infidel."

Shortly after Merton's arrival the quarterly meeting of the church was held. The question came up whether or not Mr. Tubbs should be invited to return another year. At the first opportunity Father Sanctity arose, and said: "I have a large class, which as all know is the backbone of the church; and my class to a man is opposed to Mr. Tubbs' return. They know that Mr. Tubbs can not feed them with Gospel truth. They ask wheat, and receive chaff; they ask a fish, and receive a stone. I give my warning voice here in this meeting against inviting Mr. Tubbs to return here another year. Do so, brethren, and you do so at your own peril. I have been a Methodist all my life, and I know what Methodism is, and I know that Mr. Tubbs' new-fangled notions are not the good old-fashioned Methodism that I have been used to, and I want none of it. These are my sentiments and the sentiments of my class."

There were several other class-leaders present who felt highly offended at the manner in which Father Sanctity had extolled himself and his class. Seeing how their feelings were hurt, Merton arose, and said that Father Sanctity should not be misunderstood; that none better than Father Sanctity knew that the church did not stand on one man or one class; that Father Sanctity was a hard-working member of the church, and, as such, had a right to be heard; but that neither Father Sanctity nor his class could suppose that their judgment should overrule the combined judgment of the rest. Merton said that his own opinion was, that Mr. Tubbs should be invited to return to them another year; that it was desirable for Mr. Tubbs' future success, and that it was far from certain that any other man whom they might have in his place, would be any more acceptable to the people of Eudoxia. For this speech Father Sanctity could never forgive Merton. At the first prayer-meeting Merton attended on his return from school the next year, he saw many familiar faces. Father Sanctity was there, and was even invited by the Rev. Mr. Tubbs to make the closing prayer. He did so in a most familiar, boisterous manner. He prayed for a heart of love to God and man; a heart forgiving and kind; a heart at peace with the world and its God; a heart into which malice should never enter; a heart like unto the heart of Christ. His petitions were in general such as the pure-minded Marcus Aurelius might have made, and every child of man wish granted. The people having been dismissed, there was a general shaking of hands. Merton approached Father Sanctity, and offered him his hand. He refused to take it, saying Merton had hurt him the preceding year. Merton told him he was shocked at him, at the mockery of his prayer, and advised him to go home, enter his secret chamber, and come out no more until he had a better heart.

Here Merton had the most certain proof that man may use the words of prayer, yet never pray; that his lips may say, "the Lord be with you," while in his heart he may wish that you be possessed of a demon. Of this fact he became more and more convinced, as he watched more and more the lives of those who prayed. This knowledge increased the doubts already existing in his breast, and made him begin a more searching investigation of the fundamentals of Christianity. He felt more and more the uncertainty of things received without question, and determined not to enter on the work of the ministry, until he sought and obtained more information. He therefore made up his mind to complete a theological course. By so doing he felt sure he should get more light on those matters which now were so obscure to him. Surely, he thought, men whose sole work it is to teach theology, must know more than all others about the Being of whom they speak. So Merton thought, but so he found was not the case. Rather did he find in theology a mass of jarring words, and of unreasonable and conflicting statements; and in theologians, the bitterest antagonism to one another, and a general and profound ignorance concerning the subjects of which they speak. And after long continued and most earnest study, through the best and richest years of his life, Merton became convinced that theologians, as a class, are very fitly characterized by the words of Democritus:

> ὅσσον ἀλλοῖοι μετέφυν, τόσον ἄρ σφισν αἰεὶ
> καὶ τὸ φορνέ¨ν ἀλλοῖα παρίστατο—
> By as much as they differ in nature,
> Do they always differ in opinion.

The truth of these words may be doubted, but they can be doubted only by him who has not sufficiently investigated the subject. Merton was now again hard at work, studying for his degree in divinity. He found a great change from the atmosphere of a scientific school to that of a theological college. Everything was different. No more free discussion; no more study of nature; no more experimental inquiry. Even the very countenances of the professors had an appearance altogether different from that of teachers with souls at liberty to seek and speak the truth. They seemed all to have been cast in the same mold; and, as birds in a cage, all to act as if conscious of the narrow limits within which they were at liberty to move. Merton often thought, however, that as the captive bird, long confined, loses the power of flight; so, perhaps, those professors, having been so long schooled to act and teach under the restraint of their dogmas, may have been unconscious of their imprisonment, and even of the terrible ecclesiastical threat which always hung over them—"thus far shalt thou go and no farther, and here shall thy proud search after the truth be stayed." Merton clearly perceived that every theological professor had his premises provided him. With these he might labor to instruct his students, deducing such conclusions as seemed best to him, or as were generally drawn; but he would not dare question the premises, nor materially differ from other teachers, in the conclusions he arrived at. Should he be rash enough to attempt this, he would certainly lose his chair, and perhaps be exposed to want; and the student who should attempt it, would be advised to leave the school, as an unfit person to lead the flock of Christ. Students would often question among themselves the truth of this or of that dogma, or the genuineness of their episcopate; but they would not dare express such thoughts before their professors, nor too freely in the presence of one another. Should they do so, they would be told that such questions are asked by the infidel only, and that with such a person there was no time to waste in that school. Days, weeks, months, years might be spent in teaching what hymns to have sung, how the scriptures should be read, how best to raise money for parish expenses, how to prepare and deliver sermons, how to conduct prayer-meetings, how to work up revivals, how to intone, what vestments to wear, the origin of the creeds, the collects, or the rubrics; but not a moment to satisfactory inquiry into the nature of the foundation upon which all this super-incumbent, ecclesiastical structure is said to be founded. Still, the air of the school seemed healthier to Merton than that of most others; and the lectures of the professors, less conventional, and more full of research, than that of the average minister. The truth is that the professors under whom Merton sat, at this time, were not so creed-bound as such teachers in general; for some of them had imbibed deeply from the fountains of German rationalism, and had already acquired the name of being skeptically inclined. The lectures of the professor of systematic theology, if logically construed, would leave nothing standing of dogmatical Christianity; and many of the visiting lecturers taught what, in the parish minister, would be called rank infidelity. Merton often noticed that after having battered the walls upon which they stood, they would, just before leaving the rostrum, carefully patch up the breaks they had made, lest they might be overwhelmed in their temple's destruction; or lest the ecclesiastical powers might seize, and dethrone them from their exalted position. Especially liberal in his exegesis, was the professor of Hebrew. His sharp shears so pruned the Old Testament, that in Merton's judgment, not much of the Jewish tree remained; and at the fall of every branch, the professor would smile from a sense of satisfaction, as Merton thought, in having pruned a tree whose branches served as the resort of so many birds of prey. Among the many preparing for the ministry, was a young man named Pascoe. In proof of the untrustworthiness of "calls" in general, we here give what Mr. Pascoe considered the indubitable signs of his "call:"

"I was a superintendent of a mine in England, when I felt my 'call'; but, like Gideon of old, I wished a positive sign from God. I took a sample of ore, divided it into two equal portions, kept one for myself, and sent the other to a regular assayist. Not understanding the work of assaying, I promised God that if I determined correctly the percentage of metal in the ore, I would regard it as a positive sign that I was called to the work of the ministry. In due time I was surprised to know that the result of my assay agreed exactly with that of the regular assayist. For this I thanked God; but, still, I was undecided. Again I asked for a sign. I took some more ore, and, as before, divided it into two equal portions, keeping one myself, and sending the other to the assayist. This time I promised God that if I could find no metal in the ore as the result of my assay, I would not doubt that He had called me to preach the everlasting Gospel of the Son of God. To my great surprise, although the assayist found the same percentage of metal as before, I could not find even a trace. I thanked God for such a miraculous manifestation of his will concerning me, and from that time I have not doubted my 'call.' At the same time I was engaged to be married to a beautiful and accomplished young lady, who on finding my determination to enter the ministry, refused to become my wife. I was pained to give her up; but she drifted away with the world, while I am still clinging to the cross. Do you not think, Bro. Merton, that I had a wonderful experience?"

"However unfounded the reasons for a person's rejoicing may be, Mr. Pascoe, it is almost a pity to disturb his pleasant imaginations; but I am bound to confess that I have but little faith in the miraculous nature of your 'call.' As water will seek the lowest level, so must I always seek the most natural explanation of whatever occurs. I believe, if every one did this, there would be acknowledged no interference with the ordinary operations of nature. As I have never seen nor heard sufficient evidence for the acknowledgment of the occurrence of miracles in the past, so in your case I see nothing which I could not more reasonably explain without a miracle than with it. Besides, if you had a right to demand a miracle in proof of your mission, which you must confess is a very small matter, I certainly have a right to demand one in proof that the regular laws of nature have been violated, which we both must admit would be a stupendous thing to happen. As you can not give me such proof, I do not see how, as a reasonable man, I can believe that God gave you a miraculous sign. It seems to me it takes a miracle to prove a miracle, and that, too, without end; and this fact, it seems to me, makes belief in miracles impossible. In your case I find it much easier to suppose, first, that the crucible leaked, or, second, that the ore was non metallic, than in the occurrence of a miracle. Again, you must have been greatly excited, believing as you did in the visible interference of the hand of God. This itself would make you a very unsafe witness to testify in matters which, because of their very nature, demand the coolest reason, and most critical judgment. Lastly, by your own account, you were not a skilled assayist. Even in a common court of law, in proof of every-day occurrences, your testimony would be inadmissible, having admitted your own incompetency. What witness can testify about matters of which he himself admits his ignorance? I can not receive your testimony concerning the percentage of metal, as proving your case. I must conclude that you were deceived as to what you supposed was a miracle. It seems to me, to believe that in your case there was a miracle performed, would be like a man attempting to create a god to do a piece of work which a mouse could easily accomplish. No man should look to a miracle for the explanation of an occurrence which obviously offers a more ready explanation. Still, the proof you give for your miracle, is much superior to that for miracles in general, since it is given me at first hand, and by a man I know."

Mr. Gottlieb was the superintendent of the Methodist Sunday-school in Euphronia. Merton, while at his house one evening, was told the following in proof of miraculous interferences: "Not long ago," he said, "I lost my place on the New York Exchange. I tried every honest means to get back, but my enemies were too powerful for me. My family, used to luxury, was now threatened with want. In this state I sent a letter to one of the most prominent members, who, I knew, if he would, could have me re-instated in my former position. He answered my letter, saying: 'Ask me no favors; I have done with you. Never! never! never! shall you get back again, if I have the power to keep you out.' The letter gave me an indescribable feeling. I felt ruined, or as one who had lost all hope. With penury and disgrace staring me in the face, and the thought of a ruined family breaking my heart, I suddenly thought of my God. I went to the blessed book, opened its pages at random; and the first text I saw, was: 'Behold, I have set before thee an open door, and no man can shut it.' I took some letter-paper, wrote down the promise, and sent it to the man who before had answered me so cruelly. I waited some time.

fully believing that God would send his angel, and open the door, no matter how great the stone they had rolled against it. God kept his promise with me, Mr. Merton. In a short time I was back again in my old place; and, as far as the happiness of my family was concerned, I once more felt my feet upon a rock. From that time, Mr. Merton, I have never been able to doubt the Lord. He makes a way for his people, even though it be through the Red Sea."

Merton greatly wondered why a man of Mr. Gottlieb's intelligence, should seek a miracle, a supernatural cause, for the explanation of something the most natural in the world. Even were it true that without the words or promises sent to the person, Mr. Gottlieb would never have had his old place again, still it does not follow that a miracle was performed. On reading the words it would be but natural for his enemy to think, and, perhaps, reflect; and partly from the sense of justice, and partly from the feeling of pity, to relent, and move to restore the offending party. And, again, when we know that the mind of the most relentless enemy is subject to change, we should seek an explanation of such restoration here, a natural cause, rather than in something subversive of the order of nature, a supernatural cause. It is wonderful on what flimsy evidence the credulous-minded man admits the occurrence of miracles; but the reasonable man can not easily be induced to look beyond nature, as he knows it, for the explanation of things occurring in nature. Mr. Gottlieb had a very pleasant home, and quite a refined family; but very probably, had he given less attention to making corners in wheat, and gambling on Wall street, thus increasing the poor man's sweat, and decreasing his bread; and more attention to the proper cultivation of his intellect, he would have been able to find, even in his own village, a ready explanation of all that had occurred, and thus saved himself the trouble of going beyond the stars for it. But living in a world where superstition is planted in hot-beds, and cultivated with the most assiduous care, it is hard to free the uncultivated mind from the bands with which he is bound; even when you attempt to do so, you are in danger of being charged with atheism or infidelity.

Merton thought the country surrounding the theological school a most charming one; that no place of learning could have had a more delightful situation. It was surrounded with beautiful grounds covered with stately trees, among which stood the charming homes of the different professors whose work it was to teach the students the principles of their faith. Often would Merton saunter through those beautiful grounds, admiring the tall chestnut trees, the shady beech, the beautiful hickory, the graceful maple, and the noble oak; and when admiring them, their beauty and grandeur seemed to increase. There seems to be a bond of sympathy running through the whole creation. Often in his gloomy hours could Merton imagine that he heard the pine-tree groan; and when his heart was full of pleasure, he could not fail to see expand, as if with joy, the leafy branches of the beautiful maple, nor hear the laugh of the morning-glories. And why should this not be so? Are we not all children of the same mother, earth? And are we not all alike hushed to sleep on the same breast that nursed our life? Merton might well have felt his unity with nature, and nature's unity with him. Nor could he in those walks fail to think of the future. The time and place were fitting contemplation. "Building castles in the air," is all many have to live on; and while he had even then no small pleasure in acquiring knowledge, and increasing his information, he could still think of a time when he should be settled in life's work, building up on earth the kingdom of God the Father. His study-room was not a mansion. No lawns nor beautiful walks surrounded his humble dwelling-place; but peace reigned within and without, and the smile of his God was upon him. His heart was the temple of the Father, who was as near to him as to wrestling Jacob, or royal David; and his life was a unity of experience and hope. The aspect of the outer world seems determined by the state of the world within. To the heart contented and happy, all nature appears in festive attire; to the heart despairing and broken, she appears in mourning weeds. Thus it was with Merton: with all his doubts and fears he saw the image of God reflected in, to him, the living world; and he rejoiced in the thought of the nearness and fatherhood of God. Between nature and God, Merton could find no strife; for to him the former was but the visible manifestation of the invisible Deity. Conformity to the laws of nature was to him the highest evidence of conformity to the will of God; and this is most certainly true. As Schiller says:

"Wohl weiss ich dass man Gott nicht dient, wenn man die Ordnung der Natur verlaesst.--Well do I know that man can not serve God, and depart, at the same time, from Nature's order."

(*Mary Stuart, II. 2.*)

CHAPTER V.

KNOWLEDGE AND BELIEF.

> When you hear a discourse, make your understanding keep pace with it; and reach as far as you can into events and their causes. (*Marcus Aurelius.*)

MERTON was now pursuing the studies of the last year in the divinity school. In the autumn of this year, he made a visit to the great city. Having found a conspicuous place, he watched the moving mass of people coming out of the cars. What a sight! There a bridal couple making a marriage tour, with countenances radiant with pleasure; here a pale face, with sunken eyes, and emaciated form, finding her way to the grave, chased by Consumption; there the riches of Dives, here the poverty of Lazarus; there the revelry of Belshazzar the king, here the mourning of the widow of Nain. As Merton reflected on these different phases of human life, he thought how frequently they are all experienced by the one human soul. As the gamut contains all the notes of the scale, so some men seem to experience every varied phase of human life, from the highest point of power to the lowest depths of degradation and woe.

Merton spent some time in the city, and while there saw such marks of poverty as he never before had seen, and never afterwards forgot. The sight of poverty and want was always most painful to him; and no greater pain could he ever experience than that which he sometimes felt, when obliged to be dead to an appeal for aid.

At the beginning of the school year, Merton had also taken a trip by boat from Boston to New York; and when coming up the Sound, he was so struck with the solemn grandeur of the scenery, that he could not help soliloquizing: "How many, happy as we, have gazed on this immortal current, who now have ceased to be remembered forever! How many hands, once clasped in love or prayer, are now folded, in the stillness of death, across the silent breasts lying along the shore of this unmindful stream! It reveals no secrets, tells no tales, represents no parting scenes, pictures no bosoms trembling with pleasure, nor paints a soul engulfed in woe; but heedless and unmindful, it keeps on its course amid all the changing scenes of life. Neither smiles nor tears; neither nuptial songs nor funeral dirge; neither the cry of joy that a child is born, nor the wail of despair that a loved one is dead, can move the heart of this mighty monarch, this conqueror of time. Where are the many tribes of men that, one after another, in the ages gone by, have wandered up and down these shores? Where are the many friends, once so dear to us, who have disappeared in the darkness that enshrouds so impenetrably the whole world? Some small memento, worthless in itself perhaps, but priceless to us, is all that now remains to remind us of their love, or that they once did live. We strain our sight with gazing, we pain the ear with listening, we break our hearts at waiting, yet they come not; 'till the heavens be no more, they shall not awake, nor be raised out of their sleep.' Loudly as we may pray, and confidently as we may believe, the question, where are they, still remains unanswered and unanswerable; and the only solution of the mysterious problem of immortality, seems necessarily postponed till our death. This, indeed, soon comes. As all streams hasten to the sea, there to be swallowed up in its all-engulfing waters; thus the ever flowing flood of time carries us onward, till we too are lost in the unfathomable ocean of oblivion. But how few have reason to hope for life beyond the grave, according to the principles of our own faith! How few, even in Christian lands, have saving faith in Christ! and what an insignificant part of humanity are marching under the banner of the Nazarene! Can it be possible that those who believe not in Christ's divinity, are forever lost! If this be true, how much better had humanity never been born! What an awful mistake must the Creator have made!"

Thus did this earnest soul converse with himself. However ardently he prayed, labored, and studied, there yet remained with Merton an ever conscious sense of deep uncertainty. The vacancy for something higher and nobler than he yet possessed, was not filled; rather was his hunger for a deeper and more reasonable faith day by day intensified. True, he had finished a course in arts, and was now fast completing his work in divinity, by which he had hoped to attain to a satisfactory knowledge concerning the matters he was to teach; but, sad to say, at this time he felt no realization of former expectations. The question may be asked, why at this time he did not turn aside from the work of the ministry. We answer, it was because of the fear that by so doing he might be opposing the will of God, as well as because of the unsettled character of his own doubts. He thought, having done what he had, that he should go on, until he felt more certain of the truth or falsity of the things he then doubted. He could not hear a missionary sermon, without feeling deep offence at what was said; he could not listen to a sermon on the atonement, without feeling shocked at the character attributed to God; he could not listen to the preacher who assigned the heathen to everlasting perdition, and the Christian to everlasting blessedness, without being shocked at his blasphemy. He protested in his soul against the doctrine that God ever had a chosen people; or that eternal blessedness awaits a man, because he happens to be born in a peculiar faith. Let us ask ourselves, was he not right in doing this. Little power has any man over the place where he shall be born, and but little more has he over the choice of his earliest associations. But it is these two factors that enter so largely into the product of his life's forces; and, therefore, according to orthodoxy, that determine the soul's eternal state. I ask myself, why am I a Christian? Is it my fault? Why is the Turk a Mohammedan? Is it his fault? Why is the Indian a Buddhist? Is he to blame? If the Buddhist be consigned to hell, because of that for which he can not be blamed, why should not I, in like manner, be consigned to hell, because of that for which I am not to be blamed? Why was I brought up in the Church of England? I certainly did not make the choice. Why was the Chinee brought up to believe in Confucius? He certainly did not choose the faith he should be raised in. Merton could not help thinking, if the Buddhist should be damned for accepting a faith his father and mother taught him, and believed in by his race, that he should be damned for doing likewise. He could not help believing in Christianity, as best for him, and his race; but he was inclined to believe that, as God had given him a religion, so had He given others, or else to conclude that God acts with partiality and injustice. He clearly saw that much of his faith was based on mere opinion; that he was what he was, largely because of custom, habit, training, associations, and other such accidents; and that for these accidents, no man can be justly blamed or praised. He was the more confirmed in this belief from the knowledge that the most intelligent of every age had not received, and would not receive, Christianity as commonly taught; that the philosopher's interpretation of Christianity is one thing, and the theologian's another,—the former looking deeper into the nature of things, the latter skimming along on their surfaces. In other words, while the philosopher seeks real knowledge, the theologian seeks to establish opinion, or "what saith the church?" Thus the end of the philosopher's work is truth; but of the theologian's, dogma; and since Merton saw that truth and truth alone could save, he was inclined to side with those who sought it, as with those who acted from knowledge, rather than with those who acted from custom or habit. In other words, he saw the meaning of Aristotle's statement, and was forced to acknowledge its truth:

"Διὸ καὶ τοὺς ἀρχιτέκτονας περὶ ἕκαστον τιμιωτέρους καὶ μᾶλλον εἰδέναι νομίζομεν τῶν χειροτεχνῶν καὶ σοφωτέρους, ὅτι τὰς αἰτίας τῶν ποιουμένων ἴσασιν, τοὺς δ' 'ὥσπερ καὶ τῶν ἀψύχων ἔνια, ποιεῖν μέν οὐκ εἰδότα δὲ ποιεῖν ἅ ποιεῖ, οἷον καίει τὸ πῦρ . . . . ἀλλ' οὐ λέγουσι τὸ διὰ τί περὶ οὐδενός, οἷον διὰ τί θερμὸν τὸ πῦρ, ἀλλὰ μόνον ὅτι θερμόν—Therefore, we consider the architect, in every case, to be more honorable, to know more, and to be wiser than the manual laborer, because he knows the causes of the things done; while the mere manual laborer, as one of the soulless creatures, works without really understanding what he does. He works as the fire burns. He never gives a real reason for anything, such as, why is fire hot; he simply says it is hot." (*Meta. I.* 1. 11—14). Thus in truth is it with the theologian: he never gives a satisfactory reason or cause for anything, and, as a rule, never seeks it; he simply says, it is so.

It would be, perhaps, too much to say that Merton, at this time, positively disbelieved any of the fundamental principles of Christianity; but it is certain that he had many doubts concerning the inspiration of the Scriptures, the genuineness of miracles, the story of the fall of man, vicarious atonement, eternal damnation, and salvation by faith.

With all his skepticism, he did not feel any more uncertain about the groundwork of his faith, than other young ministers with whom he was associated. As far as he could understand, the difference between himself and them was that they hushed up their fears, while he gave vent to them. Yet, knowing that the morals of Christianity do not depend on its dogmas, he thought it proper, and believed he was in duty bound, to be a minister of Christ. He did not as yet know, what he afterwards learned, that it is dogmas rather than truth or reason, which the churches seek to enforce. For it is not by one's own holiness, we are told, that he may hope to be saved, but only by that of another; not by a harvest of righteousness, the product of one's own heart, but by the imputed righteousness of Christ. Surely the time is fast approaching, when doctrine so pregnant with injustice, and so destructive of morality, will be heard no more.

Merton had now completed a three-years course of study in divinity; his only duties remaining yet unperformed being the delivering of his sermon before the faculty, and the preparation of his graduating thesis. He chose as his text for the former, "And his rest shall be glorious;" and as his subject for the latter, "Science and Religion." In the preparation and delivery of the sermon, he experienced but little difficulty; for it is surely not a work of great labor to show that as a result of a noble and pure life, a sense of satisfaction and security possesses the soul, such as nothing external to the soul can give or take away; for it is inbred. Virtue, the highest good of all, is its own reward. And since God is the very fountain of all that is good, he is truly the fountain of virtue. We may therefore rightly say, that the rest which follows a life of virtue, is God's rest; and, in this sense, that "his rest shall be glorious."

But Merton did not find the same ease in the preparation of his thesis, for reading at his graduation. Every scientific work brought him proof enough of the antagonism between science and religion. Open war was declared on every page; no quarter was to be granted. The battle was raging fiercely; and, he was told, it would never cease, till superstition, which was everywhere preached in the name of religion, should fall to rise no more. He could not fail to see that ministers were using every artifice, every trick of logic, to escape the questions at issue. Nor was it the less important matters that were attacked: the very foundations of dogmatic Christianity were being stormed, on all sides, by the heavy artillery of science. Nor was the fire proceeding from one or a few fortresses of science; but from all along the line the guns belched forth their destructive missiles, tearing the ranks of dogmatism to pieces. But this overpowering charge of science, clad in impenetrable armor, and equipped with all the means of warfare that truth has at its command, did not appear to Merton so fraught with dire destruction, as the fact that the very ranks of dogmatism were full of disorder, confusion, and disloyalty. Face to face with its ancient and most dread enemy, Science, and weakened by dissensions and fears within, dogmatic Christianity, it appeared to Merton, would do well, if ere long it had enough of loyal soldiers to bury its dead. It was no raw recruits that dogmatism had brought into the field, but the old veterans who had borne their banners victorious in many a battle against freedom and truth. Every company carried its own banner, as well to make each soldier the more readily responsible to his own commander for his bravery, as to make its command more easy and efficient. On the different banners, all blood-stained, and many now lying on the ground, befouled with dust, Merton read the names of their divisions: "Special Creation," "The Immaculate Conception," "The Divinity of Christ," "Special Inspiration," "Special Revelation," "Blood Atonement," "Vicarious Sacrifice," "Imputed Righteousness," "Salvation by Faith," "Election to Grace," "Reprobation," "Eternal Damnation," and "No Other Name." While some of these companies were stubbornly resisting the attacks of science, and yielding their ground only inch by inch; others were fleeing in all directions, heedless of their commanders' orders, or of the dangers of their brethren.

In his thesis Merton labored hard to repair the breaks he observed in the ranks of dogmatism, and to raise out of the dust the banners of the various defeated legions; but he experienced but little success. In his heart, however, he was not sure whether the precipitous rout of the allied forces of dogmatism was owing to bad generalship, or to lack of power and virtue in the legions themselves. He hoped the cause would be found to be in the former, and not in the latter; and that under better generalship, and spurred by the memories of past victories, the allied forces of dogmatism might yet regain their lost ground, and wave once more their flag victorious and triumphant. So, for the present, he tried to quiet his fears, and hope for the best. But how fleeting is such a quiet! how vain is such a hope! Merton had beheld a glimpse of the truth. He was passing out of the house of bondage; and, however slow, in due time such souls are sure to come into the Promised Land.

To Merton the sweetest of all names was the name of Jesus; and surely no sweeter name can be pronounced by the lover of righteousness. But the truth was not yet fully grasped by him, that it was this sweet Jesus who found in the organized church his most inveterate enemy: it was the church that condemned and crucified him. And as often as the mind of Jesus has been manifested in the church, so often has the human being who bore it, been subjected to persecution and frequently put to death. The full knowledge of this truth was to come to Merton afterwards. For

the present he thought it right, not only to offer himself
to God a living sacrifice, as was his most bounden duty;
but also to the orthodox church, as the only authoritative
expression of the voice of God. The thought of his heart
was most truly expressed in the following little poem,
which he found, at the time, in a periodical:

    Any little corner, Lord, within thy vineyard wide,
    Where Thou bidst me work for Thee, there would I abide;
    Miracle of saving grace, that Thou givest me a place
           Anywhere.

    Where we pitch our nightly tent, surely matters not,
    If the day for Thee is spent, blessed is the spot.
    Quickly we the tent may fold, cheerful march through storm
                                [and cold,
        With thy care, anywhere.

    All along the wilderness let us keep our sight
    On the moving pillar fixed, constant day and night,
    Willing led by Thee to roam
           Anywhere.

CHAPTER VI.

SELF-DECEPTION.

And ye shall know that the Lord of hosts hath sent me.
(*Zechariah.*)

Just before taking his degree in divinity, Merton, like all other young men similarly situated, was earnestly considering the question where best to begin his chosen work; and in seeking the solution of this problem, he was greatly perplexed. In this state of mind he fell into conversation one day with Mr. Carter.

"Where will you begin your labors, Mr. Carter?" asked Merton.

"I have long felt a drawing toward Indiana," he replied. "I wrote a presiding elder there, who urges me to come. He says young men are wanted there full of power and the Holy Ghost. He also mentions a very desirable vacancy, in a nice town of several thousand people, having a salary to begin with of not less than ten hundred. I have made the matter a subject of long and earnest prayer; and I feel quite sure that the Holy Ghost draws me that way. It is a great blessing, Bro. Merton, that we are not left to ourselves to decide such matters. He that is with us, has promised to lead us into all truth, and into the way we should go. Yes, I am going to Indiana. It is a good opening. Besides, I can not disobey the voice of the Holy Ghost. Where, Bro. Merton, do you feel the voice of God calling you?"

"I have always felt it my duty, Mr. Carter, long and earnestly to consider such important matters before making any decision. Even then I know mistakes are likely to happen; for we are very fallible creatures. But I am sure God has given us our reason with which we should weigh all things for and against, and determine the results as best we can. The farmer may sow wheat or plant corn, and he will choose to do this or that, as being, in his judgment, the most beneficial to him. He may be a very good man; but if also a wise one, he will not expect an answer from God to the question, whether to choose this or that is the better. The miner seeking to strike a vein of ore, may cross-cut here or there, and according to his skill in mining, will be, in general, the correctness of his determination. I have never heard of a company who would choose, as the superintendent of their mine, a man of prayer in preference to a man experienced in mining. In our classes, Mr. Carter, I have often heard the professors advising you more thoroughly to study the lessons assigned you; but I have never heard them advising you to pray over them."

"I do not understand you, Bro. Merton," he replied. "Do you intend to say, you do not believe in the call of the Holy Ghost?"

"I will first ask you, Mr. Carter, to define the word, 'call'. What do you mean by it? Does God write you a letter? send a personal message to you? talk face to face? or is it a conclusion you arrive at from certain mental impressions?"

"I mean by a call from the Holy Ghost, a feeling in my heart that such and such is the truth."

"How do you come to such conclusions, Mr. Carter? Do you recognize the truth you speak of through your heart, or through your intelligence?"

"I recognize its truth through my heart bearing witness to it."

"Very strange, Mr. Carter. I have heard that man's heart is the great centre of the arterial system, that it supplies the whole body with fresh blood to the end of life; but I never knew before that it pumped brains as well as blood, or that it was supposed to be the seat of intelligence."

"I did not say it was the seat of intelligence."

"Did you not say, Mr. Carter, that you recognize certain truths through your heart?"

"Yes, I did; but that is different."

"Is not recognition the work of intelligence? Is it not an intelligent act?"

"Yes."

"If recognition is the work of intelligence, and intelligence is not a work of the heart; how, then, can recognition be a work of the heart?"

"I hardly understand what you are trying to get at. One thing I know: I believe in a call."

"Believe on, Mr. Carter. I presume our little talk will do us no harm. May your call be a good one. For myself I can only say, I hope I may choose wisely. I am sure I would go wherever I thought I could do the most good."

"Very good, Bro. Merton; but I am very sorry to know that you do not believe in the call of the Holy Ghost."

"I thought we had done, Mr. Carter; but permit me to ask, how you distinguish an impression made by the Holy Ghost from that made by any other power? You see a piece of land having good surroundings, and believe it will soon advance in price. You then have an impression that it will be wise to invest. If a clerk hears of a good clerkship, in a thriving town, he has an impression that it would be good to accept it. Now, I wish to know in what sense do these impressions differ from that of which you speak?"

"I suppose an impression is an impression. I do not suppose they differ at all."

"Then, if they are the same, how can you be sure that the impression of your call has not been produced by other powers than the Holy Ghost?"

"Good-day, Bro. Merton. You go your way, and I'll go mine. Let us see who will get there."

Thus these two young men parted, the one full of love for the truth, the other full of fanaticism and ignorance. The little education Mr. Carter had received, was had in the theological school—a poor place to obtain information. Nor must it be supposed that Mr. Carter was peculiarly faithful or devout. Indeed, in the judgment of many of the students, he was morally unfit for the work of the ministry.

Merton firmly believed in a living God; and in the Holy Ghost, as the same Person acting on the minds of intelligent beings, and raising them into a higher life. He believed that prayer serves to strengthen and sanctify the soul, in the same manner as food serves to strengthen and fortify the body. But as he did not believe that God ever directly accomplishes for man, what food is known to accomplish; so had he grave doubts that God ever interferes with the natural order of things, notwithstanding prayer and supplication. But by "natural order" it must not be supposed that Merton understood anything low or common. In his heart he was inclined to believe that nature is the grand totality in which God is ever manifesting himself; and that the laws of nature are only the constant manner in which the universally present, and immutable, Divine Being operates in it. As man is nothing apart from his body, so God is nothing apart from nature. Mind and body make man; so the material universe, and the soul which operates it, make God. He could not help coming to this conclusion. For if God is infinite, He can not be absent from any point of space, nor atom of matter, and if God can not be absent from any atom of matter, He can not be essentially different from nature. Let us take the least possible portion of nature, a mere atom of so-called matter. What have we? We answer, a mere point of force, an infinitely small particle of nature. It is evident that two infinitely small points can not occupy the same space, at the same time; and that since God can not be apart from any portion of nature, the infinitely small portion of nature we are now considering, must be of the Divine Essence. With Merton, therefore, nature was a living thing, a divine organism, the garment, covering, dwelling-place, or tabernacle of God.

Thus if Merton doubted that God ever acts outside of the order of nature, it was because he could not believe that God is a changeable Being. And since it is the natural order, that for whatever man possesses, be it money, power, or wisdom, he must labor in some way or other, until he obtains it; Merton could not understand, how it would be reasonable to expect from God such interference with the natural order, as Mr. Carter claimed. Merton had firm faith in prayer. It was a soul-food without which he had never lived. But he thought of prayer, not as a means of compelling, or coercing God; but as a means of compelling, coercing, or educating himself, better to interpret the mind or will of God. Thus by prayer he might be enabled to form a better judgment, where and how to begin his work; but he doubted that God would grant the minister information on terms easier than those on which He grants skill to the mechanic, wisdom to the philosopher, or right management to the farmer. He knew well it is a peculiar favor the minister frequently claims; but he was also convinced there was no reason for such claim. Like many similar superstitions that are beyond the pale of proof or absolute disproof, it is acquiesced in by the ignorant;

but the intelligent reject it, as wholly without warrant, and contrary to all known facts. Nor are the ignorant ever consistent in their belief. When seemingly to their interests, they avowedly believe in such miraculous interposition; but when not to their interests, they in reality reject it. This was true of Mr. Carter. It was only a few days after the conversation given above, when Merton again met Mr. Carter, who said:

"How is your thesis, Bro. Merton? I suppose you feel satisfied that you are prepared to deliver it all right?"

"I have put much time on it," Merton replied. "A day or two more, and you will know more about it than I can now tell you. I suppose you are all right with yours?"

"Yes, I'm all right; but I chose a very difficult subject—'The Workings and Witness-bearing Power of the Holy Ghost.' However, it is something that young men, going out into the active field, would do well to contemplate; and I thought it a good opportunity to say something on the subject. The house, you know, is sure to be crowded on Commencement Day. There will be no lack of hearers; and the good that may be accomplished, can not be overestimated."

"It is indeed a fine subject, especially when elucidated by a person acquainted with the matter. With your gesticulating power, oratorical ability, and splendid erudition, we may all look for something unusual; and I do not think any of us will be disappointed. A man of your talents, Mr. Carter, should find a fine opening in the field somewhere. It is a pity that you should be buried in some obscure country village, or with people that can never appreciate the richness and depth of your thought. It may be that God will bring things to pass so that you will find a field worthy of your piety and ability. Let us hope it may be so."

"Thank you, Bro. Merton, thank you; I have good news on that subject. Only yesterday I accepted a call to W., in Kansas. It is a flourishing town; the church has a very nice stone parsonage; the people are united, and full of the spirit; and they offer me twelve hundred a year. I am about to be married; and the call is very acceptable to the young lady I am to make my wife. She is quite refined, has been well brought up; and I would not like to take her into some little out-of-the-way place. I am sure that I feel quite thankful to the Holy Spirit for so acting, on me and others, as to bring about this very desirable opening. I suppose you have settled on your future field?"

"No, sir, I am sorry to say. I have been waiting, however, and longing to receive such aid as you profess to have at hand. It may be that the Spirit does not come my way. Of one thing, however, I am sure: I should be glad if He would do for me what, you say, He has done for you. I wonder how is it, that some feel so certain of things, while others do not? You remember how uncertain the great and holy Socrates was. And even Christ said: 'Father, if it be possible, let this cup pass from me.' It would seem that Christ did not know, what the future was to bring him. I do wonder how these things are so. Surely, God does not make fish of one, and flesh of another! Surely, He is the Father of all, and treats all with the same tender care."

"O yes, undoubtedly, Bro. Merton. But it may be that some have missed their calling. Every man is made for a special work. If a man is outside of his proper work, God will not help him in the way that I mean; only the Holy Ghost assures us that we have chosen the work God wills us to do."

"So you have settled on your future field, Mr. Carter. You have a call of twelve hundred, with a nice stone parsonage, and a fine people, in a nice town,—the very place for your future wife. What salary were you offered in Indiana? You remember you spoke of it to me a few days ago."

"I was offered ten hundred there."

"Was there no nice parsonage in connection with the place?"

"No; that place had no parsonage. The minister who went there, would have to pay his own rent."

"Was not the town a flourishing one? were the people not well united?"

"Yes, it was a good town. The people are not, however, so well united there, as where I am now going."

"So, then, as I understand you, Mr. Carter, you prefer going to the place you have just accepted, because the church is better united, offers a better salary, has a nice parsonage, and is more agreeable to your future wife. These are very material reasons indeed. Your choice, I suppose, was determined by the will of the Holy Ghost, who reveals himself within you."

"I think so, Bro. Merton. I feel that God is leading me to W."

"Mr. Carter, do you imagine that God can will one thing to-day, and another to-morrow! Do you suppose He has forgotten that He advised you, a few days ago, to go to Indiana!"

"No, sir, I do not; but God acts according to the needs of things. The last few days the conditions of things have changed. What was good for me then, is not good for me now."

"Thank you, Mr. Carter. How very useful it must be for one to have a god so accomodating, so readily adjustable to circumstances! Let us hope, if your call is what you want, that he will not forget to-morrow, that you are making arrangements to-day to go to W."

The young men parted never to meet again. Merton was greatly offended at the thought that a man calling himself a minister of the majestic Christ, could thus make God a tool, or bring the Divine Majesty down to the level of low and changeable man. And yet the logic of Mr. Carter is the logic of most pulpits of the land. The great weakness of Mr. Carter, lay in his inability to hide more effectually the erroneous nature of his views:

>"The world is still deceived with ornament.
>In law, what plea so tainted and corrupt,
>But, being seasoned with a gracious voice,
>Obscures the show of evil? In religion,
>What damned error, but some sober brow
>Will bless it, and approve it with a text,
>Hiding the grossness with fair ornament?
>There is no vice so simple, but assumes
>Some mark of virtue on its outward parts."
>
>*(The Merchant of Venice.)*

CHAPTER VII.

THE GREATEST IS CHARITY.

Nate dea, quo fata trahunt retrahuntque, sequamur;
Quidquid erit, superanda omnis fortuna ferendo est—
Goddess-born, wherever the fates may lead, forward or backward, let us follow. Whatever may happen, every fortune is sure to be overcome by him who endures it.   (*Vergil: Aen. V. 709.*)

WHILE in the seminary, Merton's attention had been called to the wants of the church in the state of Kansas; and shortly after finishing his divinity course, he corresponded with a bishop concerning the propriety of going there. The bishop answered his letter very fully, and spoke of a church, in a certain city of that state, needing a pastor; and advised Merton, at the same time, to write the presiding elder of the district, where the church was situated. Having addressed the latter concerning the matter, Merton received an answer to the effect, that the vacancy had been for some time filled. While unable to give him that appointment, the elder urged Merton to come to Kansas, filling his letter with the most glowing accounts of the country. The advantages to be had in coming there, he said, were very many: the climate was unequalled; the people were reaching out their hands; and the possibilities for the minister could not be surpassed. A few days afterwards, Merton received a letter from another presiding elder, of the same state, offering him the choice of two, as he said, very desirable appointments.

At first Mrs. Merton was very unwilling to go so far west; but after a little persuasion, she consented, hoping with Merton that the voice that called him, was the voice of God. But to her the parting with her parents was painful in the extreme. It was far away she was to go; and the wife of a minister had no money to waste on pleasure trips or excursions. It was not, therefore, probable that she would again see them for a long time. However, preparations were soon made. They were rushing towards their destination, and, in the course of two or three days, found themselves in the city of Atchison. Here they were met by the minister of the town, who gave Merton every possible assistance, manifesting great kindness, and showing much interest in his welfare. Leaving the residence of this hospitable minister, in a few hours Merton arrived at the end of his journey, late in the evening. The next morning was very beautiful; and it was indeed a magnificent sight that met his gaze. Vast plains stretched away, as far as the eye could see; standing fields of tall corn indicated the richness of the soil; and a beautiful stream of water bespoke other possible industries. The sun rose in most glorious splendor; the sky was cloudless; a cool and gentle breeze came from the south-east: indeed, both heaven and earth seemed to have done their best to give to Merton a royal welcome.

While at the residence of the elder, however, Merton discovered that that gentleman had broken his promise— that the appointment which in his letter he had promised to keep for Merton, had been given to another. When asked for an explanation of this, the elder's excuse was that he knew which was the better of the two appointments, and had according to his promise, reserved it for Merton. The judgment of the minister, and of many others who knew the both appointments, did not, however, agree with that of the elder; for they insisted that the elder had acted with bad faith, in filling the better appointment a little before Merton's arrival. But being a stranger in a strange land, Merton thought it best to make no remonstrance; but in his heart he wondered why an elder could act so dishonorably. Nevertheless, he was greatly troubled; for he knew too well that the remaining appointment was one full of difficulties; and he doubted that it could supply Mrs. Merton and himself with even the necessaries of life. But he was not to be easily discouraged. Crowns of glory follow as the reward of wearing crowns of thorns.

Previous to departing for his field of labor, Merton and his wife had been invited to spend a few days at the residence of Mrs. Wright. This lady was extremely corpulent. When she laughed, she laughed all over. She was about five feet three inches tall, and weighed not less than four hundred pounds. Her neck, short by nature, was made to appear still shorter by the very fleshy condition of the shoulders and bust. Indeed, the head upon her shoulders appeared not unlike a hen sitting in her nest—almost covered up by the surroundings. But she was a noble-hearted and generous lady. Never had Merton or his wife been more hospitably entertained than by Mrs. Wright; and it was with many forebodings of evil, that he left the house of this genuine Christian, to face the difficulties of his unknown appointment. But he was full of work, and full of hope; and neither he nor his wife could doubt that all things would be well. Besides, the presiding elder had assured them over and over that a very hearty welcome was awaiting them, where they were going. "When you arrive at Micropolis," he said, "you will find Bro. Truthful waiting at the depot for you. He has made all arrangements, and everything will be satisfactory."

Merton was not long in going to Micropolis, the principal town of his charge. He found the depot in its place; but the "good brother" who was to receive him, was not there. After making some inquiries, however, he found Mr. Truthful without much difficulty. He was greatly surprised to hear that he was expected to meet Merton at the depot. "I assure you," he said, "this is the first I have known of your coming. The elder has sent me neither letter nor word about the matter; and I do not know what right he had to make such statements to you. It is, however, a pleasure for me to know you, and I give you a hearty welcome."

Merton had stated in his letters to the presiding elder, that wherever he went, it would be necessary that room and board should be provided for himself and wife; and the elder assured him that this matter would be provided for. Mr. Truthful, however, had heard nothing of this; nor could he think of any place in the town, where acceptable board and room could be had. "The town, Mr. Merton," he said, "is new; and the people, being without much money, build themselves very small homes, in order to save expenses. There are but few families who have rooms for the accommodation of strangers or guests. All that I can do for you, you may rely upon it, I shall do. I will go with you now, and see what can be done."

At first they went to the residence of a good member, a Mrs. Brady, who said: "I would be so glad to have you with us, Bro. Merton; nothing could be more pleasing than the company of yourself and wife. My house, however, is already full and running over; I couldn't find room even for my mother." They then went to the house of a Mrs. Webb, who was not a member of any church, but had enough humanity in her to invite them to stay, and take dinner. "Although I have no spare room in my house," she said, "and am unable to have the pleasure of taking you to board with us, I must insist on your taking dinner with me, especially as it is so near dinner hour; and I am sure Mrs. Merton will be glad to rest a little while."

After dinner they continued their search for room and board; but no acceptable place could be found, except at the small hotel. There the charges were so high, that Merton feared his expected income would not enable him to assume the responsibility of paying the bills; nor was such a place, for other reasons, agreeable to a man of Merton's character.

Having failed in their search, Mr. Truthful pressed Merton to come and stay with him for a few days, until some other arrangement could be made. Merton felt the invitation had been sincerely made, and he therefore gladly accepted it. Mr. Truthful was a prosperous farmer, and resided about a mile from the town. His wife was found to be a most kind-hearted woman, ready to submit, for the sake of her guests, to great discomfort. But such a nature was the last in the world Merton could impose upon.

The evening was spent in earnest conversation as to the needs and conditions of the appointments. Merton discovered that several ministers, some with very fair ability, had been laboring there, but with little success. The stations, four or five in number, and separated from four to ten miles one from another, had but very few members, most of whom were extremely poor, scarcely able to support themselves, and not at all inclined to give of their penury toward the support of the preacher in charge. The ministers who had been stationed there had been literally starved out; and most of them had left, leaving many debts behind them. The evening's conversation brought no encouragement to Merton; the information he obtained was not suitable for a sedative, after a day's fruitless labor.

On retiring, Merton was greatly pained to find that the room assigned himself and wife, was that of Mr. and Mrs. Truthful; and he determined that come what would, he could not allow himself to be the recipient of favors that brought such discomfort on his host. In the morning he found that the family of Mr. Truthful was a very large one, and that there were not sufficient rooms for their comfort, even when all were given up to the exclusive use of the family. This knowledge settled Merton in his determination not to stay there another night.

In order to make some excuse for leaving, without giving offence to the kind-hearted people who had so hospitably received them, Merton, after breakfast, told them it was absolutely necessary that he should find some permanent boarding-place,—a place where he could set up his books, and have the same for use. He assured them that he could never forget their kindness; but that even apart from the necessity of seeking some permanent place to board and room, he felt sure that their remaining there must inconvenience the family; and that this, he would not consent to do.

"I am sorry," said Mr. Truthful, "that we are no better prepared to accommodate you than we are. To such as we have, you are entirely welcome, no matter what discomfort or inconvenience it brings us. If you can stand what we have, we will get along somehow. Mrs. Truthful and I are used to these little things."

"Mr. Truthful," said Merton, "I am sure your goodness would lead you to do anything for us; but comfort at such sacrifice we could not allow ourselves to receive."

"It is a shame," replied Mr. Truthful, "that the elder did not acquaint me with the fact of your coming. I feel sure that had I known of it in time, something might have been done. It is not very encouraging to you, Mr. Merton; and I feel greatly pained at the condition of things. I will see, however, what can be done to-day; but I have no great expectations from this people. In the past I have frequently entertained hopes, only to have them every one blasted. I have had many bitter disappointments since I have been living here. The people are quite willing to have a minister among them, provided some one else keep and support him; but they are scarcely willing to assume any responsibility themselves."

"Never mind, Mr. Truthful," replied Merton, "I am not discouraged. I can not believe but that all will be right in time. A few souls like you in the work, and it will soon be moving. If we can not find accommodations here, we will proceed to Littleville. It is only four or five miles distant, I believe; and if we are obliged to do so, I think we can walk that far."

After a search of two or three hours, very good rooms were found at the residence of Mrs. Taylor; and Merton began to make preparations to go there. Just as soon as he thought the difficulty for the present settled, some two or three of the good church members came hastening, and said: "Do not go there for the world. It will ruin you, and disgrace the church. You are a stranger here, and do not know her character. We therefore feel it our duty to put you on your guard. We are sure if you go there, you will give unpardonable offence to the people of the church. No decent person, in the town, would stay over night at her house. We are sorry to have to say anything about this business; but, as members of the church, we feel it our duty."

Thus ended Merton's last attempt to find board or accommodations in the town of Micropolis. Among all the members of the church, there had not been found one who could accommodate them with rooms and board; and none of the members, with the exception of good Mr. Truthful, had offered them a night's shelter. Strangers they were in a strange land, homeless among their own; and no man said to them, "come, tarry thou with me." Merton was heart-sick; but the thought of his duty gave him courage to persevere.

Having resolved to proceed to Littleville, Merton hastened to a livery-stable, in search of a conveyance; but none could be found. Nothing was now left but to walk to Littleville, a distance of four or five miles. It was late in the afternoon, and the day was exceedingly hot. Under the circumstances Merton wished to go alone to Littleville, find accommodations, obtain a carriage, and return for his wife; but Mrs. Merton insisted on going with him. "If you go," she said, "I go; I am not afraid but that I can walk four miles. It would be almost impossible for you to go there and return again for me to-day; so I shall not stay behind you."

"But," said Merton, "there may be difficulties on the way. Rivers have been greatly swollen lately; bridges have been carried away. Besides, the way is altogether strange to me. It is much safer for you to remain at Mr. Truthful's residence, until I return for you, either to-day or to-morrow."

"Please, do not ask me to remain behind. However long the journey, and great the difficulties, in company with you I gladly undertake them all, in preference to remaining behind. To be with you, will be a pleasure; to stay behind, unbearable pain."

No man can withstand the pleadings of a beautiful woman. It was therefore decided that they should set out together for the hoped-for resting-place; although Merton had many misgivings as to the wisdom of such a course.

Soon they were walking along the banks of a murmuring stream. They had never before heard its gurgling waters, nor seen the feathered tribe moisten their vocal organs to sing their songs of joy. As Merton heard their hymns of praise, he recalled the words of him who said:

"The foxes have their holes, and the birds of the air their nests; but the Son of Man hath not where to lay his head."

They had succeeded in walking two or three miles over the burning sand, after having crossed the little brook, when Mrs. Merton said: "See, Harry! here are two roads. Which do we take? One goes through the corn-fields, and the other across the prairie."

"Since neither of us knows anything about the way," replied Merton, "I presume we are each equally certain; but let us take this one leading over the prairie. It is at least easier to travel."

Walking along for a short distance, they met an old woman and a boy riding on a wagon. "Madam," said Merton, "are we on the right way to Littleville?"

"Lord! no sir; you must go back, and take the road leading through that yer corn-field. It is a mighty hot day for sich folks as you to walk to Littleville. If I hadn't a heap of work to do to-day, I would drive you right over there; but ain't got no time now."

"Thank you, Madam," replied Merton. "We'll manage to get along. We are much obliged to you."

Retracing their steps, they soon found themselves passing through the most luxuriant corn, from ten to twelve feet high. Being very hungry, Merton appeased his appetite by eating some ears, as he travelled on.

"I wonder are we ever going to get to Littleville?" said Mrs. Merton. "This is the longest four miles I have ever travelled. When we started, they told us that it was about four miles; after travelling an hour, that woman tells us it is still three miles distant. It seems to me that the miles in this country are like men's consciences. Hark! What is that?"

"I do not know," replied Merton; "but I know you are tired. I presume the distance from Micropolis to Littleville is more than four miles; but it is always thus with tired feet. You have never known the day when you could walk far; much less are you able to do so on this burning sand. Listen! I guess that must be what you heard just now. Is not that the sound of a river? It seems to me so. Surely, a Jordan does not roll between us and the Promised Land!"

"If so, Harry," she answered, "it would be hard to say which to do, go into the overwhelming waters, or surrender to Pharaoh and his hosts. But there is your Jordan, and a big one it is. I thought I heard it. I fear in our case the fiat is gone forth: 'Ye shall not go over thither.' We may have a time watching the stars to-night. Wouldn't it be fun! We should never forget it."

There rolled the river in its peaceful bed, shaded by tall, over-hanging trees. No bridge was visible; it had been carried away by the late floods. What was to be done? The river was wide, but apparently not very deep; so Merton determined to lose no time in trying its depth. Drawing off his shoes and stockings, he began to wade across the stream, carefully selecting the shallowest parts. He found the stream from eighty to ninety feet wide, and from one to three feet deep. Having thus found the depth of the stream, he returned for Mrs. Merton. Taking her in his arms, he waded across as before, though progress was much slower, and to his feet most painful, walking over a pebbly bottom, with a hundred and twenty-five pounds in his arms. Once having gained the other side, it was but a short time before they were in the little village of Littleville, knocking at the door of the residence of the person whom Merton sought.

"Does Mr. Blossom live here?" asked Merton of the lady who opened the door.

"Yes, sir; Mr. Blossom lives here. Do you wish to see

him? I am Mrs. Blossom."

"I am very glad to have the pleasure of knowing you, Mrs. Blossom," replied Merton. "I am Mr. Merton, your preacher newly appointed to this charge. It may be you have heard of my coming, through the presiding elder. This is my wife. We have been told that we might have board and accommodation at your house. If so, we shall be glad to stay with you, paying whatever you think is right. We had hoped to live in Micropolis; but could not find acceptable accommodations there."

"Accomodations at Micropolis! Nobody who knows the people of that town, would go there for anything. If you had been acquainted with them as I am, you would have looked elsewhere for favors. Of course, like most other western people, the folks there aren't any too well fixed; but the trouble with them is, they aren't willing to do what they might. My home is not a big one, and it isn't fixed up like I want it to be; but if I don't know what it is now to live in a nice house, I did once. I was brought up in Indiana, in as nice a home as the best of them ever had; and, besides, I was taught by my parents to be kind and obliging to folks in need, as long as they did what was right."

"Almost any place, Mrs. Blossom, provided it is clean, is acceptable to us just now; especially to Mrs. Merton, who is exceedingly weary from the long walk."

"Long walk! Do you mean to say, Mrs. Merton, that you have walked all the way from Micropolis?"

"Yes, Mrs. Blossom; I have accompanied my husband."

"Come right in, sir. We are just at tea, and should be glad for you to join us."

At the table Job's comforter came: "The preacher who preceded you," said Mr. Blossom, "was an unmarried man He was just the kind of a man for this place, for he was able to rough it. Still he didn't take very well. They called him 'Wild Bill.' He used to preach with his coat off, and his sleeves rolled up, and a sash around his waist. When he left, the poor fellow didn't give us a farewell sermon. In fact, nobody knew that he was going, he left·in such a hurry. This haste in leaving was the cause, I suppose, of his forgetting to pay his board-bill; and I reckon he is too busy heralding the Gospel to remember such little trifles now. Previous to the coming of 'Wild Bill,' a married preacher had charge here. This fellow's father was well fixed, lived near here, and was his main support. At the commencement of his work, the father gave him a nice pair of ponies, and a buggy to get around in. This preacher used to hold forth pretty good; but somehow he didn't take, although he had a nice little woman. One of the members, knowing that the minister's wife didn't like squash, carried him a whole load as quarterage. After he drove away, the preacher and his wife, looking at the wagon-load of squash, burst into tears. At the end of the year, notwithstanding his father's help, he was forced to leave for want of support, and to sell his ponies and buggy, to have money to get away with. I believe he left a few debts, but that's to be expected; it's about the only marks a preacher leaves behind him, in this country, to prove he's ever been here. Preaching out here doesn't appear to be a very flourishing business. A good many take to it, and for a time carry around their goods; but, take my word for it, the people won't invest. I don't know how this thing is; may be they found it didn't pay in the east. I assure you, Merton, I am not saying this to discourage you; I'd be the last to do that. You know, I'm a member of the church myself; but, then, I don't go to church, for the reason that I let the good brethren fight it out among themselves; and it's just as good as a circus sometimes to see them at it. On the whole Mr. Merton, you are come to a pretty tough place."

These remarks were poor sauce for Merton's dinner; but he had to use it, although it made his meal of herbs almost indigestible. In his heart he wished he had never seen Kansas. He felt greatly hurt at Mr. Blossom's insinuation, implied in what had been said about ministers going away, forgetting to pay their board-bills, and leaving debts behind them. Nevertheless, he appeared not to regard it, except to remark that whether successful or not, he certainly would not go away, forgetting to pay his board-bill, or leaving debts behind him; that as he was then free from all such incumbrances, so he intended to remain free from them. Mr. Blossom replied that he did not, of course, suppose that Merton would cheat any one out of board-money or anything else; he only wished to show what kind of preachers had been stationed there. The explanation, however, did not remove from Merton the consciousness, that Blossom suspected that he might be once more cheated out of his board-bill.

On the morning of the following Sunday, Merton preached, at Micropolis, from the words, "Strive to enter in at the strait gate;" and in the evening, at Littleville, from the words, "If I wash thee not, thou hast no part with me." At each point the audience was good, and composed of representatives of numerous Christian bodies, the Winibrennarians being in the majority.

At the close of the day he was very tired, not less from walking more than ten miles, than from the labor attending the services; yet the hope of doing good and of better times strengthened him to bear with his disagreeable circumstances; but he felt greatly disappointed with his charge.

The Sunday following he preached, in the morning at

Littleville, in the afternoon at Centre, and in the evening at Micropolis. This involved a journey of thirty miles on horseback. The close of the day found Merton excessively weary, and not a little suspicious of his adaptation to the people and place. Tired as he was when the work of the day had been finished, he had to travel to Littleville, a distance of more than four miles, in as dark a night as he had ever known. Through the thick darkness he groped his way over the railroad ties, cheered by the consciousness of having done his duty. One bridge had been crossed; but yet another was to come much more dangerous than that. The ties of the former were spanned by boards, but the ties of this were not spanned; and underneath them ran a roaring torrent of water swollen to such a degree from the late rains, that it threatened to carry away the whole structure. The intense darkness, and the roar of the torrent below, made him hesitate, tremble; and the frequent flashes of the vivid lightning made the scene still more appalling. He could not see where to step, and one false step would hurl him into the flood beneath. What then would Mrs. Merton do! The thought made his head swim; and to prevent himself from falling, he crossed the most dangerous part of the bridge on his hands and knees. Again and again in his heart did he rebel against the work he had to do; and as often did he say: "It is my Father's hand that leadeth me, and he doth all things well. Through the dense darkness, He will bring me to the light."

When he arrived at Littleville, he found his beloved wife wild with fear, standing at the chamber window, gazing in the direction he was to come, and trying to pierce the gloom to discover his approach. Her joy at his arrival can be better imagined than described. "O Harry! Harry!" she cried, "I felt sure you had fallen through the bridge; it was so pitch-dark. I fancied I could see your form carried down the stream; and all I could do, was to wring my hands in despair. Oh, how I thank God you are come!"

The next Sunday, Merton preached in the morning at Smith's, from St. James III. 13. The little house was more than full. After service he set out on horseback for Hibernia; but on the way a drenching rain came on, wetting him through and through. The thunder was so loud, and the lightning so fierce, that his horse became unmanageable. In addition to this, he lost his way, going about three miles beyond the preaching-point. When he arrived, the people had gone, supposing from the lateness of the hour, that he was not coming. From this point he rode on to Micropolis; but it continued to rain so violently, that no services could be held there.

That night Merton was unable to return to Littleville. The long ride of from twenty-five to thirty miles, most of it through drenching rain, made him so tired that any resting-place was acceptable.

The wife of the gentleman at whose house Merton passed the night, held some very peculiar, religious views. The next day the husband said to him: "I guess you found my wife a rum one, elder; didn't you?"

"Your wife, sir," replied Merton, "has some strange ideas; but in such matters, it is better to be liberal. It may be, in the near future, she will modify her belief somewhat."

"Not a bit of it, elder," he replied, "not a bit of it. Come what will, she'll stick to her trumps, though every player leaves the table; and, for my part, I think she's about right. Since there are so many denominations, I see no reason why she can't have one; so I say to her, 'go right on; set up your church, and make me a bishop.' I tell you, elder, she's a good one. You'll do a heap of good by talking to her. I guess you'd better use your powder and shot on more paying game."

In a few days, Merton and his wife left the residence of Mr. Blossom, having been pressed to spend a month at the home of Mr. Soulless, who was a wealthy farmer, living about ten miles from the city of Micropolis.

CHAPTER VIII.

THE CURSE OF AVARICE.

οὐδὲ γάρ οὐδέ κεν αὐτὸς ὑπέκφυγε κῆρα μέλαιναν
ἀλλ᾽ Ἥφαιστος ἔρυτο, σάωσε δὲ—

Nor could I have escaped black destruction,
Had not Hephaestus snatched and saved me.
(*Homer: Iliad V. 22.*)

WHILE journeying across the prairie to the residence of Mr. Soulless, the following conversation occurred between Mr. Buttolph and Merton:

"So you are going to the residence of Mr. Soulless. Well, I hope you will enjoy your visit; but you will find him a crabbed old fellow. He is rich enough, sure. If you happen to strike him right, you can make use of him; but if you don't, it's all over. Soulless is pretty well known around here. Those that get into his hands, never get out again. I have had not a little experience that way myself. And, by the way, Brother Merton, I've had experience in this country in more than one way. I left the city of William Penn, some years ago; and came out west, hoping to improve my health. I used to preach often in the east, and had not been here long before they induced me to take charge of this circuit. The first year I labored almost night and day, and tried in every way to build up the work. Constantly exposed to all kinds of weather, my health broke entirely down; and at the end of the year, I was forced to resign the work. All I received of this people for my whole year's labor, was sixty dollars. I tell you, Brother Merton, you may expect what you will; but I'm sure you'll not receive from this circuit the one-half of what you expect. This may dishearten you; but it's God's truth."

"But," replied Merton, "the elder has guaranteed me support."

"As to guarantees, Brother Merton," said Mr. Buttolph, "they are worth as much as the elder who made them. Of one thing I'm sure: they don't count for much in this country."

"It may be so," replied Merton; "yet I can but hope that matters will not be so bad as you predict."

"Faith is a good thing, Brother Merton, especially when you have the loaves and fishes. But I've never seen the man who could remove a mountain by it, even though it were no bigger than a grain of mustard seed."

On the following Sunday Mr. Smith, a kind and good man, took Merton across the rolling prairie to his different appointments, Mrs. Merton, for the first time, accompanying him. The intense pleasure Merton felt at having his wife with him, can be fully understood by that man only who is blessed with a woman beautiful, accomplished, and lovable for his wife. The husband's love for such a woman is well expressed by Tennyson:

> She is coming, my own, my sweet;
> Were it ever so airy a tread,
> My heart would hear her and beat,
> Were it earth in an earthy bed;
> My dust would hear her and beat,
> Had I lain for a century dead;
> Would start and tremble under her feet,
> And blossom in purple and red.

At eight o'clock in the morning, they sprang into the little carriage drawn by two fleet and pretty ponies, and started for the fields of labor; the first of which, after a few miles of round-about driving, they reached about the time for morning service. After delivering a sermon, at this place, based on the words, "I will not leave you comfortless," Merton started for the next appointment, Hibernia, seven miles distant. On their way they took dinner at the house of one of the principal members—a dinner composed largely of vegetables and a wonderful preserve made, as the good lady informed Merton, by boiling tomatoes in molasses. As Merton ate it, he hoped that the recipe for its preparation would be forgotten by the next generation. It was nearly black, and had to Merton a very disagreeable taste. With the color of this rare preserve, the table-cloth and the walls of the dining-room seemed to perfectly correspond. So this good church-member was not only religious, but she had, as we see, an eye to unity and conformity.

Leaving the house of this good Samaritan, they hurried on to Hibernia. On their way they came upon some wild plums, which they ate with a relish. They were glad at having such delicious dessert to banish from their palates the taste of the pitchy composite they had just been compelled to swallow.

The meeting at Hibernia was a great success. The services opened with the singing of the well-known hymn, "A charge to keep I have;" and, surely, such a discordant, rasping clamor was never before heard. Mrs. Merton afterwards said it was like the sharpening of ten-thousand saws all at once. At the close of the sermon, which was based upon the words, "Escape thee to the mountain, escape for thy life, lest thou perish," the principal members thanked Merton for the discourse; and promised to raise a large portion of his salary, if he preached to them every alternate Sunday. Merton could not help regarding such a people favorably, uncouth and ignorant as they evidently were.

From Hibernia they drove on to Micropolis, the last appointment for the day. Here Merton preached from the words, "Behold I have spoken to you from heaven."

After the discourse, Merton spoke plainly of the condition of things—of what he thought had to be done, if he remained with them. "You know, my dear friends," he said, "that I have no conveyance to take me from one point to another. I hardly think that any of you can expect me, myself, to invest in a horse and buggy to do the work, when I am not certain of receiving enough for the bare necessities of life. I put the question to you as business men. Who of you would be willing to make such an investment on similar hopes of return? Briefly, the case is thus: If you will provide me with board and proper accommodations for myself and wife, and with means to travel from one point to another, I will remain with you, without any further promised salary; if you can not do this, I must leave you. I shall expect a definite answer to this proposition in a few days. You must, gentlemen, do what you think best in the premises."

After the service they begged him not to think of leaving. One man who hitherto had given scarcely anything toward church-work, offered thirty dollars a year toward his support. Mr. Truthful said: "We've got you here now, and you must not leave us. The people never came to preaching before, as they do now; and our hopes were never so bright as at present. Last night I scarcely slept, thinking of you, and how best to manage this work. I knew we had a man with us now, who was capable of building us up, and that he was talking of leaving. The more I thought over the matter, the more it seemed to me, your leaving would be a terrible blow to all our expectations. I do hope something may be done to hold you here; I'm sure I'm ready to do my part."

Merton replied: "I am sure of that, Mr. Truthful, from what you have already done for me. But I think you cannot but see the justice and wisdom of what I have said. Should I stay, I know well that such as you would make my burden a part of your own; but I can not see you crushed with such a disproportionate care for my welfare. If the people want me, they must do their part; for whether for weal or woe, I will not stay otherwise. In this matter, Mr. Truthful, I must and will be independent. I'm glad I said what I said. Let the people decide. It will be better for both you and me. You must cheer up. If I go away, you will have no bitter regrets. You have done nobly; for which I thank you. And, don't forget, if you have no preacher here, such a man as you may worship God in your own home; for you carry Him about with you in your heart, the real temple where God delights to dwell."

The day's work was ended. It was quite late; and there yet lay before Merton a long ride over the prairie, before he would come to his resting-place.

"You must be very tired," said Merton to his wife. "I fear this long ride has been too much for you."

"O no! It has been one of the happiest days of my life. And what a pleasure it has been to me, to know that I have been by your side! Besides, Harry, it helps one to be somewhat reconciled to living in such a place as this, when he sees how eager the people are to hear the truth. I think the congregation at Hibernia did nobly. If only your other people would do as well as they, there would be no trouble about our getting along in this place. It is true, I shall never forget their horrid singing; but when I think of that, I shall also remember their earnestness and generosity. If I could have a circuit composed wholly of such folks, I would not care if it were in the wilderness, I would like to be a preacher myself; but if I'm not a preacher, I'm a preacher's wife, and that's the next thing to it; isn't it, Harry?"

"By no means," answered Merton. "You are not the next thing to a preacher, but a thousand times ahead of him. I would rather have you than all the preachers in the state; and if you add to these all those in the Holy Land, I still prefer you.

'Was ist mir alles Leben gegen dich und meine Liebe.'

If you want them, you can take the preachers. I would rather hear one of your sermons than all the preachers' harangues ever delivered. I say with Deucalion:

'Namque ego, crede mihi, si te quoque pontus haberet,
Te sequerer, conjunx, et me quoque pontus haberet.' "

"Harry, you are always full of your naughty talk. I am afraid you will never lose your mischievous spirit."

About this time the grasshoppers filled the country. They looked, when flying under a bright sun, like falling snow-flakes. They devoured everything green in their way; filled the houses, and made the water almost undrinkable. They would, strange to say, devour even what tobacco-chewers call, "an old quid."

On the following Sunday, Merton preached, in the morning, at Smith's; in the afternoon, at Centre; and, in the evening, at Micropolis. At the last place his subject was based on Heb. IX. 13; Rev. XIX. 6.

The room at Micropolis was very full, the air overheated, and charged with the odor of tobacco. Being sickened himself, and seeing very many ladies in, perhaps, a worse condition, Merton rebuked the practice of wholesale and indiscriminate tobacco-spitting, in language as mild as possible; but not without creating some ill-feeling. Said Mr. Truthful, after the service was over: "I do wish, Mr. Merton, you had not spoken of tobacco-spitting. It is a dirty practice, but one which every one, almost, is guilty of here, I've heard nothing but good this week about our preacher; but now I shall hear many say, 'Your preacher had better mind his own business.' It's hard for people to break off such habits."

"But, Mr. Truthful, had that nuisance not been stopped, I should have been unable to proceed with the services. I was already sick at the stomach. I protested in very mild language; and the favor I asked, I'm sure, should have been willingly granted. I would not gladly offend any one. I have never used tobacco in any form, and although I like well enough a little of its odor, I could not possibly endure the foul filth expectorated before my eyes from the mouths of a whole congregation. If the people are so wedded to this practice that they cannot give it up, while the services are proceeding, I have another reason for leaving."

That night, while returning on horseback from his work, as tired as ever man could be, about five miles from Micropolis, and several from any house, Merton saw, as he thought, sitting on their haunches, three large, stray dogs. When riding along he had been thinking of his circumstances; and considering all things, he felt greatly disheartened. Every Sunday he was forced to travel about thirty miles to reach his different appointments, always depending on some one's good will for a horse to ride on. As yet he had no house, no place to call home, not even an acceptable lodging-place; and he felt in his heart no bright prospects for the future. For himself, his heart was sore enough; but as he thought of his wife, he felt more impatient, and concluded something should be done. While thus reflecting, he was brought within about fifteen feet to the animals, when he realized, to his horror, that they were three large, grey wolves. The stars were shining most beautifully, and the moon was moving through the heavens in all her unveiled glory. As he passed the animals he clapped his hands, and shouted at the glaring-eyed monsters. No sooner had he done this than, with a frightful howl, they sprang at the horse. The latter gave a snort, and dashed away so suddenly, that Merton almost lost his balance, and came very near falling off. It was a young horse, and as yet had hardly been worked. Over the prairie went the beautiful, intelligent, and frightened creature, like the very lightning, pursued by the maddened, hungry wolves, which were all the time trying to get at Merton's feet. He scarcely hoped, knowing what a poor rider he was, to escape their distended jaws. In a short time they had succeeded in pulling out from under the saddle, a blanket which Mr. Smith had spread there, and which, at this time, must have been hanging low down at the horse's side. As soon as this was done, they stopped pursuing Merton; and the whole prairie seemed resonant with the howls of the ferocious beasts. But even though no longer pursued, the horse would not be checked. On it rushed like a meteor, until it dashed into the yard of its owner. There stood Mr Smith wondering what could have happened, and there stood the horse shaking and trembling like a leaf.

While pursued by the wolves, Merton's thoughts would often revert to his wife; and he earnestly prayed that he might not be taken from her, and she be left a stranger in a strange land, without money or friends.

Eight o'clock the following Saturday night, Merton left the residence of Mr. Soulless, and in the darkness made his way across the prairie to the residence of Mr. Smith. It had come to Merton's knowledge that the former had loaned the latter quite a sum of money, and that he was exacting fifteen per cent interest. Mr. Smith was a very poor man who had known better days, but who now was living in abject poverty. His wife, surrounded by wretchedness and want, was fast falling a prey to anxiety and care. Merton could not help feeling deeply for them in their miserable state; and he hoped, by speaking to Mr. Soulless, that he might persuade him to exact less interest; but he had misjudged him. He was hard-hearted, unfeeling, unscrupulous, caring little for the wail of the orphan, the cry of the widow, or the bloody sweat of the unfortunate borrower that might be in his hands, provided only he got his fifteen per cent; and yet this man was a prominent member of the church; indeed! he was the very pillar of it.

"O, what a goodly outside falsehood hath!"

When Merton spoke to him of the unfortunate circumstances of Mr. Smith, and of the wretched condition of his wife and family; how he was heavily in debt, and had to pay fifteen per cent, an interest, Merton said, ruinous to any borrower, he got very angry, and, as it were, cried out in the words of Shylock:

"The pound of flesh which I demand of him,
Is dearly bought, 'tis mine, and I will have it."

Merton was very sorry to have offended him, but wished, if it were possible, to make him deal mercifully with Mr. Smith, who was a member of the same church, and certainly in most deplorable circumstances.

"If you do not approve of my business conduct, Mr. Merton," said Mr. Soulless, "you can leave my house, sir, and leave it to-night."

"I do not approve of your business conduct with Mr. Smith, sir," said Merton; "nor do I think that either law or Gospel will justify any man in charging another fifteen per cent for the loan of money, at the same time demanding first-class security."

"I have loaned Mr. Smith, sir, money on several occasions; and what I have loaned him, I shall expect him to return according to agreement."

"I understand, Mr. Soulless," replied Merton, "that you have done as you say; and, without much doubt, as you have already taken from him, little by little, much that he once possessed, so will you in due time take from him the balance; for I insist, no farmer can possibly pay fifteen per cent, and save his farm."

"My business, sir, is my own, and something with which you have nothing to do. As you have presumed to meddle with it, I have already said what you can do."

"Mr. Soulless, I have heard you express your desire, and it will immediately be complied with, though we were to use the prairie for a bed, and a stone for a pillow. We shall not again meddle with your business, nor with you. It may be, however, that some day God may meddle with it. Let us hope that He may, that justice may be done both to you and Mr. Smith. I am sure, as a member of the church, you ought to be satisfied with God's judgment."

"A moment ago, sir, you said you were going to comply with my desire; let me ask you to do so immediately."

Thereupon Merton collected the few things he had there, and by the aid of a lantern, went out into the darkness, leaving Mrs. Soulless and her daughter in floods of tears. These ladies besought Merton to look over Mr. Soulless' actions, and remain with them; but he felt the insult was too great, honorably any longer to continue as their guest. The mother and daughter were greatly pained at parting with Mrs. Merton; but thanking them for all they had done for her, with an affectionate kiss she bade them good night, never to see them again.

Mr. Smith lived about three-quarters of a mile distant, and in the darkness Merton found it very difficult to find his residence. After some wandering about, he was glad to find a light in the window; and from the character of the man, he knew well that it was for him, or any others in like circumstances.

On opening the door, Mr. Smith was amazed to find Mr. and Mrs. Merton there, seeking shelter for the night. They were willingly admitted, and given the best the house afforded.

Next morning, at the breakfast table, Mr. Smith said: "It is a wonder to me, Brother Merton, that you could stay there as long as you have. Mr. Soulless is a very passionate man, ready to bite any one who may by chance come in his way. His soul is as hard as his money, and that's hard enough to grind out the life of any man. It is my fault, of course, that I ever got into his power; but I fear I have now as little chance of escape, as the fly in the claws of the spider."

"I am sorry, Mr. Smith, that the unpleasantness occurred between me and Mr. Soulless," replied Merton; "but I thought, and think, it was my duty to do as I did Since it has occurred, it has determined me to leave this place, and leave it immediately. I have no home, no conveyance to take me from point to point, no proper boarding-place, nothing, indeed, that can make life bearable for me and my wife. To stand this any longer, would be degrading to myself, and insulting to her. I shall bid this place farewell this week."

"Under the circumstances, Brother Merton, I could not blame you; especially since this trouble has occurred between you and Mr. Soulless, who would now make your stay here as unpleasant as he possibly could. Being the pillar of the church, it is in his power to do you not a little harm. No, sir, I could not blame you for your decision. Personally I am very sorry to see you go; but as things are going, I do not think I can long remain here. I fear I shall soon lose the little I have, being completely in his power, and especially since I am not as strong as I was. From my very heart I pray that, wherever you may go, God may bless you."

Merton no more doubted that Mr. Smith was sincere in his prayer, than that he himself had labored in vain with a christless Christian for justice to his fellow-man. While Mr. Soulless could make an affecting prayer, and give an ideal experience, he could smile at the misfortune of the widow, and laugh at the calamity of the fatherless.

Illum et labentem Teucri et risere natantem,
Et salsos rident revomentem pectore fluctus. (*Vergil: Aen. v. 181.*)

CHAPTER IX.

LAMPS WITHOUT OIL.

> *Extemplo Libyae magnas it Fama per urbes—*
> *Fama, mallum qua non aliud velocius ullum,*
> *Mobilitate viget, virisque adquirit eundo:*
> *Parva metu primo, mox sese attollit in auras,*
> *Ingrediturque solo, et caput inter nubila condit.—*
>
> Instantly Rumor rushes through the great cities of Libya—
> Rumor, a monster than which no other is more swift.
> She thrives on her mobility, and acquires force by going:
> At first small through fear, soon she lifts herself into the skies,
> And though treading on the ground, buries her head among the clouds. (*Vergil: Aen. iv. 173.*)

MERTON now sought and obtained an appointment in another conference. Having learned that the bishop presiding over the assembly was one of his old teachers, Merton called on him, in the morning, before the conference was opened.

"From what I know of you, Bro. Merton," said the bishop, "I judge you have acted unwisely in coming out west. You are not the kind of man, nor is your wife the kind of woman, that is wanted here. You would have done much better, had you remained in a more civilized community. This conference is quite full, as it is; no good appointment is vacant, that I know of; and for the few good places to be had, there are already twice too many applicants. I know of only one place not already provided for, Moth and Mazar. If you choose to go there, I will see that you have the opportunity. It is a very undesirable appointment. Something better would be done for you next year, undoubtedly; and I will have a small missionary appropriation made, to help you out this year.

But I doubt very much that you and Mrs. Merton can live on the income you will receive there. Still, if you wish to try it, you can."

Merton replied that as things were, he thought it better to accept such work as the conference had at its command, and to trust to the future for something better. The appointment was given him; and soon he was on the cars rushing toward his destination. While thus travelling, he met a bishop and a minister of the Protestant Episcopal Church:

"You are returning from the conference, I presume," said the bishop.

"Hardly returning, sir," answered Merton, "but rather coming. I am a total stranger to this part of the world, having just received my first appointment. I am but a short time out of the schools; and I am really longing to be at my post of duty."

Having inquired concerning Merton's education, nationality, and early faith, and being informed, the bishop replied:

"It seems to me very strange, Mr. Merton, why such a man as you could be contented in your church home. The Episcopal Church is really the same as the English; it is also in great need of men who are, like yourself, educated, and energetic. I hope, Mr. Merton, that you may think of the claims of your mother church; and, if possible, come over to us. We will give you a hearty welcome, and send you to preach the faith once delivered to the saints. I am sure you would be much happier in your mother's house. The prayer-book would be very becoming in your hands; although it has been a stranger to you so long. We would kill the fatted calf, and make merry at your return. I ask you, Mrs. Merton, to use your influence with your husband, and seek to bring him back to his old allegiance."

"Bishop," replied Mrs. Merton, "you can depend on me doing my best. I greatly prefer the Episcopal Church to any other, because of her forms as well as her history."

"Mr. Merton," said the bishop, "I will take the pleasure, at my earliest opportunity, of mailing you a prayer-book, and a copy of the canons; and if you wish, you can take orders with us in one year from now. Your duty is clear, and the path is easy."

The bishop was quite a gentlemanly-looking man, and made a good impression on Mr. and Mrs. Merton.

Having finished his conversation with the bishop, who, in the meantime, had left the cars, Merton was approached by the minister who had had charge of his appointment the preceding year. After introducing himself, he said:

"Bro. Merton, I feel it my duty to warn you of Bro. Squareman. He is a very peculiar man indeed, always ready to make mischief in the church, and to speak evil of his neighbors. Be very careful how you treat him. If you show much regard for him, your chief members will be offended; if you show little, he is likely to lose his soul. He thinks he has not been well treated; blames the minister, blames the brethren, blames everybody. Nor is his wife much different. She is one of those evil-tongued women ready to explode at any moment, and as full of danger as a powder-magazine. The relations of this brother and sister with the church are at present very much strained; and the least friction will break the last remaining link that binds them to you. In your congregation you will find another man, Bro. Headstrong, a man full of zeal, but fuller still of ignorance and perversity. He wants a good deal to say; but you can stand that, since he pays well. Between Bros. Headstrong and Squareman there is a very bitter feeling arising from an old sore. We had a church trial about it; but no good ever resulted. Indeed, I think it made the matter worse. This feeling does lots of mischief in the circuit. You are going to an extremely difficult charge, one poor in money, but rich in quarrels. God give you grace to conquer."

Merton thanked the gentleman for his advice; at the same time, he could not help feeling that he should have felt happier, had he never received it. He had but a moment to wait, however, before another good brother approached him, and said:

"I think the bishop must have lost his head, to send you where you are going, Bro. Merton. It does appear to me sometimes that if our appointments were all put into a bag, and shaken up, and drawn by the preachers blindfolded, they would be more appropriately filled than they are to-day. I am truly sorry that you are going to Moth and Mazar."

"Why so, sir?" asked Merton.

"I have preached there, Bro. Merton, and know the people well. You will not remain six months, and should not. They never have had a minister whom they did not abuse, and I guess never will. You will find no roses in your path there, I assure you; but thorns grow there everywhere, and plenty of them, too. I don't wish to dishearten you, God knows; but I speak the truth. You are not going to the people who need you, you are going where you will spend your energies in vain; and take my word for it."

The minister having returned to his own seat, Mrs. Merton said: "It seems to me that all the powers of darkness combine, on this train, to dishearten you, before you even know the people to whom you are sent. They speak of members abusing one another! If this is not abuse that

I have heard from them, then I do not know what abuse is; I must not only be in a strange land, but I must also hear a strange language. I wonder if they are a fair sample of the whole! Surely they are spiritually dead. Yet, how fair the corpse looks at a distance!"

"Never mind, darling," replied Merton. "You are not yet confederate against me; and, until that happens, I shall not lose courage. Ministers are but flesh and blood. It may be they mean well; and, perhaps, what they have said, may really be of great use to me. Let us hope such may be the case, anyhow."

"Flesh and blood you say, Harry! I hardly know. By looking at them, we can see they have flesh enough; but that they have any blood in them, I am not certain; they certainly appear to act altogether as bloodless creatures. Such evil words and such discouragement! I feel I shall, ere long, greatly modify my childish ideas about the profession to which you belong. I very much doubt that they are either as harmless as doves, or wise as serpents. I don't believe that what they have told you, is worth remembering. If I were you, I would go to my appointment as if I had never heard anything about the people, and not with prejudice in my heart against them. I wish those preachers would mind their own business, and let us alone."

"Say no more about it, darling," replied Merton. "We are come now; and I expect we shall find some one here waiting for us."

CHAPTER X.

FAITH WITHOUT WORKS.

αἰὲν ἔχων ἀλάλημα οἰζύν—
Wherever I roam, suffering unceasingly attends me.
(*Homer*: *Od. xi. 167.*)

IT was a strange place to which Merton had come. The town was composed chiefly of one short street, formed of detached, low-built houses, and dilapidated stores. The side-walks were as irregular as waves on the ocean's beach; and in front of the stores, sat men puffing volumes of smoke from their cherished pipes, and talking of politics and religion. Among them was Mr. Smalleyes, who had come for the purpose of taking Merton, in his carriage, to his new appointment, a place ten miles distant from the railroad depot.

Merton was to preach at three points, namely, Mazar, Moth, and Budds. At Mazar, his place of residence, there was neither church nor meeting-house, but the rudiments of a village; at Moth there was a nice little church, but no village; and at Budds there was neither church nor village, the preaching being done in a school-house.

In making his pastoral visits, Merton first called on Mrs. Rattlebones. Here poverty reigned, her prime-ministers being laziness and intemperance. Merton was not invited to a seat, for there was no such thing in the house. Filthy as this dwelling was, they knelt together in prayer; and the heart of the wretched woman seemed comforted. The chief cause of the filth and squalor surrounding this poor creature, who had seen better days, was her good-for-nothing husband, who roamed at large as a philosopher, when he was not drunk in the nearest village.

A short time after making this visit, Merton was playing a game of croquet with the Misses Smalleyes, when Mr. Rattlebones chanced to pass by. Seeing Merton, he entered the yard, approached him, and said:

"Wa-a-l now! I have played at almost every kind of game in Christendom, and with almost all the ladies in this yer country; but that game beats me. What do you call it?"

Merton answered it was croquet, at the same time inviting him to join them.

"I reckon not," he replied. "Whenever I indulge in such low games, I allers find myself unfit afterwards for higher pursuits. Different men have different constertutions. It may be that I was made a leetle too fine for the common things of this yer world; but we all, you know, must do the best we know how with the stuff the Man above has given us. At least them's my sentiments. I don't say this to disturb the elder. Perhaps he's one of those tough ones; if so, I say go right on, and enjoy yourselves. If I could so demean myself, I would jine you in a minute."

What reply could be given such a man? Merton looked at him for a moment, and saw what might be called the very incarnation of drunkenness. His limbs were trembling, his eyes blood-shot, his visage pale and shriveled, his whole frame fleshless, and his general appearance revolting in the extreme. After a moment's hesitation, Merton replied:

"You do right, sir, in not abusing your finely constituted organism, or impairing your very delicate, mental powers; but I sincerely hope that you'll never use any other means more likely to accomplish these results, than the playing at croquet."

"You can bet on that, elder," he said, "I allers take

care of myself. The Man above commands us to do that; and my mother brought me up that way. Train a child up, elder, in the way he should go; and when he comes old, he'll not depart from it. That's Gospel, elder, isn't it?"

Mr. Smalleyes then made his appearance. After shaking hands with Merton, he said:

"That was a fine sermon you gave us yesterday, elder; everybody was much delighted. To-day they are all talking of our good luck in getting you here. Our last preacher was one of the best we've ever had in Moth; and he was as lazy as he could be. Mr. Beereyed said that he should have been sent to chop wood, the only thing Nature had fitted him to do. Before this fellow, we had a preacher who was enough to disgust anybody. Even while preaching his sermon, he would chew and spit tobacco; and when visiting us, he not unfrequently would lift the rug, and spit under it. I have seen him spit right across the parlor. It is because of such men, Brother Merton, that our church here has been disgraced, and made a nest of discord.

"I am glad," replied Merton, "that the people are pleased at my efforts; but I am truly sorry to know that there is such a thing as a nest of discord here. Yesterday I saw very many intelligent people in the congregation; I must say that I was surprised at their general appearance. With such intelligence, how can you permit a nest of discord to be found in your social tree? There was one lady who sat in front, near the aisle. She was a fine-looking person, and seemingly well educated. Do you know to whom I refer?"

"The name of that woman, Brother Merton, is Mrs. Woundedheart. She is, indeed, an educated woman, and therefore the more to be feared. She is the most dangerous person in your charge. My advice to you is, keep away from her. Although a woman, she has the serpent's sting. Charm you she may at first; but as truly as you visit her, so truly will you curse the day."

In a few days Merton found himself knocking at the door of Mrs. Woundedheart's residence. He felt a longing desire to know something more of this woman with the "adder's sting." The door was opened by a very pretty young girl, of about eighteen years. She recognized Merton, and invited him in, saying her mother would be there in a moment.

"How do you do, Brother Merton?" said the lady. "This is indeed an unexpected pleasure. I little supposed that our new pastor would dare show such kindness to me, while he was staying at our near neighbor's. I am sorry to tell you, Brother Merton, that I am not very regular in my attendance at service; indeed, I scarcely ever go to church at all. Our church here is all in disorder. I suppose you've already discovered that; if not, I assure you, you soon will. People have no confidence in the leaders, none at all. My husband will never go again. He says he can worship much better under the poplar, than with a band of hypocrites. Mr. Smalleyes, your leading man, is as mean a man as this world has ever known. The truth is, he makes it his chief business to lie about me and mine. He tried for years to ruin us. We've had several law suits with him, and there are more to come. He has tried even to blast the character of my daughter here, and he has nearly ruined my son. He is a very wicked man, and his chief assistant is Mr. Beereyed, who is drunk on whiskey one day, and full of the Holy Ghost the next. My son says that Smalleyes makes the bullets, and that Beereyed shoots them. Mr. Smalleyes, you know, is a coward, and gets

Mr. Beereyed to do openly what he contrives in secret.''

"My dear Mrs. Woundedheart, I do not see how you can suppose I should know that Mr. Smalleyes is a coward. We came to see you, and know you. We wish you to come to our services, and help us build up the work. Never mind Mr. Smalleyes. Perhaps if you should return kindness for the injury you suppose he has done you, it might be the best medicine you could give the disease as it exists. But do not tell me any more about Mr. Smalleyes. You are a lady of superior education, of refinement, and must know the evil effects of such bitter feeling among the scattered parishioners that generally compose these country congregations. Under present conditions, no successful church work, I fear, is possible. Your minister's spirit must be broken, and the church pews remain empty, unless this bitterness be put away. How much happier were your own heart, how much brighter your own home, if you would only consent to let that spirit govern you, which ever manifested itself in the life of him whose followers we profess to be. I do not say the blame lies with you; but I do say that a woman so superior to her neighbors as you are known to be, should seek to use the gifts with which God has blessed her, to soothe rather than irritate, to comfort rather than trouble, and to win by words of kindness rather than repel by provocation. I do believe, Mrs. Woundedheart, that no investment brings the human soul such wonderful returns as that of kindness or forgiveness. And as we invest it, our stock is more and more increased, while all the parties interested are equally benefited.''

"Excuse me, Mr. Merton, but I feel I must unburden my griefs to you; it will greatly help me to do so. I have no desire to speak evil of any one; but I mention who are the chief officers in our church here. I gave you but two of the names. Another one is Mr. Longshanks. He is not so bad as the other two. His wickedness is chiefly against himself, in filling himself up with whiskey, with which he keeps his cellar well supplied. He is a trustee; but nobody puts any confidence in his word. If he sells, he gets as much as possible; if he buys, he gives as little as possible. As far as that goes, his hand is against everybody, and everybody is against him; but, still, I think he is about the best member you have in your church here, and he doesn't profess to have any religion; indeed! he laughs at it. The best men we have here, never go to church; they have had too much of it already. Mr. Hardtocrack, for instance, is as good as a man can be; but he never goes to church. He had a very pretty daughter to whom Mr. Smalleyes' son was engaged. While in this relation, this young blackguard betrayed her. What did his father do? Why he sent him out of the country, and left the poor girl to live in open shame. Mr. Backslider is another good man. He had made a note promising to pay the church authorities the sum of two hundred dollars toward building the church here. Things went against him. His note became due; he couldn't pay it. Mr. Smalleyes thereupon sued him, and forced him to sell what little stock he had to meet it. He now spends all his spare time in cursing the Methodists. Mr. Blackbird was treated in like manner, and to-day is a bitter enemy to the church. The minister went around with a subscription-paper; Mr. Blackbird signed it; his promise became due; he was unable to meet it; he was sued, and forced to pay it at the expense of selling his stock. Even the church building was built in a very strange way. They went around with a subscription-paper, with the understanding that the church should be built, where the majority of the subscribers should vote it to be built. When the money was all pledged, an official meeting was held, at which it was decided to build it where it now stands, Mr. Smalleyes influencing the meeting by promising the church sufficient land to keep a cow, and make a garden for the minister. But in the deed he gave, he took care to have inserted a clause, whereby the land all reverts to him in ten years, unless certain conditions are fulfilled. These ten years are almost expired; and if you folks are not careful, he will soon possess the land again. He has been raising corn on it for years, without paying one cent rent. He should be made to pay rent in full with interest. With that money they would soon have a round sum toward building a parsonage."

Merton left Mrs. Woundedheart's with a sore heart. She was a woman of education, and had been well raised; but her heart was so full of bitterness, that there was scarcely room in it for the good thoughts it once contained, nor for that charity which all should feel for their fellow-men.

Merton had hoped to escape horseback riding by leaving his old appointment; but in this respect his hopes were not realized. To reach one of his stations, he had now to travel on horseback twenty-eight miles. Yet, for many reasons, his present appointment was better than the former. His salary was larger and more certain, and he had a parsonage to live in. Often, however, his soul would rebel against filling his scattered appointments: especially when he found such animosity existing in the hearts of the members of his charge. The words of the bishop, at the conference, were ringing in his ears: "You would have done much better, had you remained in a more civilized community." And, then, the knowledge that so many inferior men filled the most important positions, made his lot still harder to bear. At such times the words of Marcus Aurelius:

"If a thing is good to be said or done,
Do not think it unworthy of thee."

would give him courage to persevere; for, surely, the work he was doing was a noble one.

Merton found the people at Budds far superior to any other on his charge, more educated, more united, and more generous. It was a pleasure to preach to such. On his return he was glad to reveal this fact to Sunshine. She was comforted with his report, and said: "I do hope you will not hear so much abuse there. Do you not fear a person who has so much evil to tell about his neighbor? I myself believe that he who acts thus in regard to another, will do so in regard to us, when any occasion arises, real or imaginary. She who carries a secret in her open hand, hides a dagger in her sleeve. Do you not fear its point?"

"Sunshine, I confess I do; but I will try to wear an impenetrable armor. There is plenty of poisonous miasma on my circuit. Its poison, I think, can best be guarded against by keeping within the influence of the rays of your sun. I do believe a woman like you has a very subduing power over the naughty tongues of still more naughty people. When we come to open war, I think I will push you to the front. Wouldn't that be the right way to do?"

"It would certainly be the way for you to escape, if you would like to do that at the cost of my life; but I have no fear of going to the front. I know you will take care of me, Harry; but how to take care of you, is the problem."

"Sunshine, we will walk a straight course; and let us hope and pray that God will take care of us both."

"Harry, how do you really like your work? I'm afraid that your endeavor to bring harmony out of the existing discord, and order out of the present chaos, will make you ill, or break you completely down. Day and night you think of nothing else than how best to heal old sores, unite divided parts, and get a little bread to eat. The work you are doing, is noble, no doubt; but I'm certain you might do a similar work in a more agreeable place. The seed you sow is more than the harvest you can expect to reap."

"Sunshine, do not forget the lines:
>'We have no right to bliss,
>No title from the gods to welfare and repose.'"

"Repose is one thing, Harry, and agreeable activity another. I do not ask repose or bliss, but such activity as may be conducive to the real good of all concerned."

"Here is Mr. Smalleyes, Sunshine. Let us hear what he has to say about my prospects in Mazar."

"Mr. Smalleyes," said Merton, "there is a good deal of apparent, spiritual life in the church people at Mazar. Mr. Fraudulent especially appears to be an unusually active man."

"Have you ever been at his house, Mr. Merton?"

"No, sir; I have not been there as yet. I hope, however, to go very soon."

"Don't be in a hurry, Mr. Merton; I think you'll be satisfied with one visit. They have a large farm, and are considered very well-to-do; but they are extremely dirty people. There is a sickening odor in their house; and the old woman and the young wife have faces as black as a man's hat. His family, however, are cleanliness itself when compared to his cousin's. In the home of the latter, you might plow up the dirt. But, then, it is useless, and perhaps wrong in me telling you who will know it soon enough. Besides, I am not a man to talk about my neighbors. I say, let every man find out for himself. It is more satisfactory all around."

"Has Mr. Fraudulent been a member very long? He

seems to be a man of genuine piety."

"That's a man, Mr. Merton, who, like myself, is a trustee of the church; but I wouldn't trust him for a cent, unless I wished to lose it. I believe he would cheat his own mother, if he could. He is the tightest man about here to drive a bargain; he'll stand bantering an hour for a cent. You'll know Bro. Fraudulent soon enough, unless I'm greatly mistaken. As an officer of the church, I have often had occasion to come into intercourse with him. He is a hard case, I assure you."

Shortly after this, Mr. and Mrs. Merton accepted an invitation to spend two weeks at the residence of Mr. Longshanks, who was a very wealthy farmer, and had a charming woman for a wife. He was the owner of about two square miles of as valuable land as could be found in the state, and had it stocked with a great number of fine cattle. Both he and his wife were also well educated. Under the circumstances, a very pleasant visit was anticipated.

CHAPTER XI.

IMPUTED RIGHTEOUSNESS.

σοὶ δ' αἰεὶ κραδίη στερεωτέρη ἐστὶ λίθοιο—
Always is that heart of thine harder than stone.
(*Homer: Od. xiii. 103*).

As Mr. and Mrs. Merton drove up to the house, Mr. Longshanks came out and welcomed them.

"Ha! ha! ha!" he said. "This is just what I and the old woman have been looking for. We're going to feed you on red-legged chickens, if they don't run under the barn. I want to feed you up, so that you may give us another discourse like that you gave us last Sunday. It makes me feel happy, when I think of the God-send we have this year. Ha! ha! ha! Well, we'll do our best. Come in; come in. I want to have a good time to-day."

In a short time it was arranged for Mrs. Longshanks and Mrs. Merton to visit the city together, thus leaving Mr. Longshanks and Merton alone. They were seated in the parlor, when Mr. Longshanks began:

"Well, Brother Merton, tell us how you like this great and glorious country; and tell us how you like your charge. Don't you think that the American Eagle should flap its wings a little more proudly, when hovering over such a country as this?"

"I think it is a beautiful country, sir," replied Merton; "and I hope to see prosperity in it. That, however, must depend not a little on such as yourself. A good many make light work of doing what one could never accomplish."

"I presume I shall do my part, anyhow, Brother Merton; but I don't go in much, and never did, on religion. I may as well say the truth about the matter. I know I'm a a church member and a steward; that I'll readily confess;

and I believe I'm what they call a trustee ; but that ends it. I don't profess to be a saint like some of your brethren."

"It seems to me, Mr. Longshanks, that a thing that's worth doing, is worth doing well. If religion is worth having, it is worth having in its purity. It is good for a man to live every day, as if it were his last day."

"That I don't believe is possible, Bro. Merton. I consider such sentimentality good enough for poetry, but it doesn't make good prose."

"I think it does, Mr. Longshanks. Such a life consists simply of doing one's duty. Surely, that is not impossible. Nelson expected every man to do that."

"Many beautiful sayings have come from the lips of men in great distress, or great peril ; but take life as we find it, and I deny that it is possible at all times, and under all circumstances, to do exactly one's duty."

"I should hardly think a Christian would have a lower idea of life's possibilities than a heathen, Mr. Longshanks ; yet we hear Marcus Aurelius saying :

"'Since it is possible that thou mayest depart from life this moment, regulate every act and thought accordingly.'"

"I hope, Bro. Merton, to make some progress in religion this winter ; but the truth is, we've had such a pack of howling fools sent us to preach, that I'm almost sick of the name of religion. The last fellow we had sent us, would stand upon the platform, Sabbath after Sabbath, and deliver what he called sermons, something that showed neither brains nor religion, a kind of hotel hash ; but he would faithfully visit us, whenever he wanted a five-dollar bill. He was accused of lying, stealing, laziness and tale-bearing. The greatest fault I had to find in him, was that he hadn't brains enough to last him over night   He, however, was about the best we've had.   At one time we had a great revivalist here, who took with the people immensely, as he was considered by the brethren a man full of the Holy Ghost and of power. It was not long before it was discovered that he was an agent for a disreputable house in San Francisco, and he came very near getting several young girls in his hands. Indeed! it was through his relations with them, that his whole nefarious scheme was brought to light. I tell you! when this became known the brethren were struck with consternation, as if by the fall of the tower of Babel. My! what a noise there was in the camp! The holy brethren lost the power to say 'amen' for a long time. I say, Bro. Merton, what do you think of revival methods?"

"I have never been, Mr. Longshanks, a friend of them. I have always seen that as the pendulum swings back again on attaining its maximum height, so the people after the spasmodic efforts of revival meetings, fall back to their normal state, having spent their energies in vain. In addition to this, I have witnessed so many evils at such exciting meetings, as have made me an enemy to them."

"Well, Merton, you ought to have been present at one we had last year. Brother Headstrong, your leading man in Mazar, was there. He is the most ignorant man we have around; but he has much to say at the meetings. At the one in question, after the preacher had tried to warm up the people all in vain, brother Headstrong arose in his seat and said:

"'Dear friends, the sarpents are among you, the fiery sarpents. You're in the wilderness of sin. When old Moses was leading the children of Israel, the sarpents was sent. Did they bite the good folks? No, they bit the wicked folks. Just so in like manner is it to-night. You can't see them with your material eyes, for the things of this world discerneth not the things of God; but with my spiritual eyes I see them all around you, switching their fiery tails. Soon they will dart their fiery forks into your poor souls;

then what will you do? Now is the accepted time. Now is the day of salvation. One look at the cross, and you are saved. And now is the time for Christians to tell these poor sinners here what the Lord has done for them. If your sins is forgiven, brethren, you know it, and you'll tell it; you'll proclaim it on the house-top; the people in Gath will hear what God hath done for the children of men. No man can set in his seat, and have the power; and if you haven't the power, you're none of His. No man with the Sperit in his heart, can set still; for where the Sperit is, there is freedom. Why, bless you, brethren and sistern! I donnaw what to do to set still a moment. The power fills my whole soul, pushing me onward and upward to the city of the New Jerusalem. I fancy I can see them now, with all their harps, and flutes; yes, flutes! I am one of those who loves flutes; they're so much like the human voice. Rise, brethren! Tell these sinners how to escape the fiery sarpents, before the poison from their fiery tails shall curdle through their blood, and they be with the damned cast out forever. Rise, my brethren! or Gabriel may come and scourge you.'

"In this way, he went on until I could stand it no longer, Merton. I had to burst out into one of my genuine laughs. Ha! ha! ha! my laugh was loud and long, and attracted the attention of all in the house. For this thing Mr. Headstrong never forgave me; but I couldn't help it for the life of me. It was such a farce. I am glad you don't approve of such methods in religion. As for me, as I have already said, I don't profess to have any; but I guess you'll find me, in the long run, about as good as the best of them. In money matters I'm generally on hand, Bro. Merton; and this year you can depend on me doubling my former yearly subscription. I am willing to pay for a good thing, when I have it. As for helping you in the meetings, you'll find enough help and to spare of that sort in brother Headstrong. He can talk a whole regiment to death, and even shut up an average half-dozen women. He's a camp-meeting in himself alone. But let me advise you to give him plenty of rope. Do not cross him. Give him his way; indulge him in his conceit. He pays well, even if he does talk more than all the rest put together. Brother Fraudulent is another on whom you can depend for a good ghostly experience ; but he doesn't come up to brother Headstrong. I say again, give the latter his way. The crazy old loon will do nobody any harm, and he can do you lots of good : he can fill your pockets.

"Let me ask you what is to be done about our church debt. I wish to say to you in confidence that I have given my last dime to that cause; not to save the whole concern from going to David Jones' locker, would I give another cent. We owe nearly a thousand dollars to the Church Extension Society. If this is not soon paid, the church building may be sold. For my part, I shouldn't care if it was; and I believe hundreds around here would rejoice. There have been far more wranglings and quarrels, since the building of that thing, than there ever were before; and many think a bon-fire is the very best use it could serve. Besides, everybody believes that somebody's pocket-book was pretty deep at the building of that church, or that money was dropped into a big hole somewhere. Without doubt the good brethren who had charge of that matter, are believed, in this part of the country, to have fattened up considerably on account of it. But, be that as it may, I will not pay any more toward the removal of the debt. I have paid my share, and Longshanks pays no more.

"Say, Bro. Merton, tell us how you enjoyed yourselves at the residence of our very polite neighbors, the well known and far-famed Smalleyes."

"We enjoyed ourselves, while visiting them, very much. They seemed to do everything possible for our comfort. Indeed, I sometimes felt a little uncomfortable at their constant exertions to make things agreeable for us."

"Dear me, Merton! how happy I should be, were I such a father! But how could Longshanks expect to father a child smart enough to set the River Thames on fire! or beautiful enough to resemble a cask of lager beer, as Miss Columbine does! How charming she looks in her short dress! Cleopatria is nothing beside her. What a beautiful figure! I wonder that boys should persist in going to the city in search for a base-ball, when we have such a charming one at home. What a charming bride she'd make! I fancy I can see her now. With what grace she moves! Majesty decks her brow, and virtue adorns her person. I can see her enter the church, swinging on the arm of her beloved. There she is — a perfect square, four feet ten by four feet ten! Just think of it, almost a hundred and twenty-five solid feet! The very thought of it makes my blood, not cold, as they say, but almost boil. What a prize for a Hercules! I don't wonder that it is said that the sons of God came down, and took to themselves as wives the daughters of men; but I do wonder that no god sees his chance in fair Columbine. I wonder who will be the first to enter into the Promised Land? who will be the first to take possession of this symmetrically developed, and robust young goddess? who will lay the beds of roses which her fair form may give fragrance to? By my soul, if only I were free! but I'm bound hand and feet, as if to a column-stone; and I fear the stone will hold me. In whatever direction you look, you see the marks of beauty spreading out from her, as limbs from a tree. Happy the man whose fruitful vine is she! In the mother we behold the moon, in the father the sun. Or I sometimes compare Mr. Smalleyes to Newton, and his charming and erudite wife to Sappho. O, yes! I understand why you should so appreciate your entertainment there; they are a remarkable family. You'll find that out, more and more, as they have the opportunity of displaying to you their wonderful talents. Have a little patience, Brother Merton, and your delight will rise to ecstasy."

They were now interrupted by the entrance of Mrs. Longshanks and Sunshine, who had just returned from their visit to the city. Merton felt their coming a great relief to him; for he hardly knew what reply he could have made to such an ironical harangue. Indeed, he was longing once more to receive the mild rays which he always felt in the presence of his wife.

"Harry," said Sunshine, "you can't imagine how kind and attentive Mrs. Longshanks has been to me. She seemed forgetful of herself, looking to my little wants. When returning I was one time a little afraid; for we were pursued by some run-away horses, which almost put the spirit of flight into ours. But Mrs. Longshanks is so strong! I soon found out there was not much cause for fear with her. When speaking of you, she seemed unable to use praise enough. She said she never knew a minister she liked, as she likes you. She doesn't profess to have any religion; but I really believe that no better heart can be found on your charge, than that which beats in the breast of Mrs. Longshanks. I am so glad, darling, that she is such a friend to you. It does your Sunshine good to hear you praised. Who is that, Harry, gone into the other room with Mr. Longshanks?"

"I think it is Mr. Fraudulent, Sunshine. I remember hearing Mr. Longshanks say that he was expecting him. He wishes to purchase a piece of land from Mr. Longshanks."

"Yes, Mr. Merton," said Mrs. Longshanks, coming

into the room, "but I do not know how successful Mr. Longshanks will be. The truth is, Mr. Fraudulent wishes to purchase it at his own price, and then give his note for it."

"I should think timber-land the most valuable you could possess, Mrs. Longshanks," replied Sunshine, "in a country where so little timber is found growing."

"Yes," said Mrs. Longshanks, "it is; but the piece in question is almost valueless to us, since Mr. Fraudulent lives so near it. He has already taken most of the best timber, and the balance will soon go the same way."

"Do you mean to say," said Merton, "that Mr. Fraudulent, a steward in the church, would fell your trees, and steal your timber?"

"Do I mean to say so?" replied Mrs. Longshanks. "You had better ask Mr. Popelover, Mr. Merton; he can give you all the information necessary on that subject."

"Mrs. Longshanks," Merton continued, "you can not think that I would ask for such information concerning any of my people; but I say to you, as to one of my own flock, is it possible that you can believe Mr. Fraudulent guilty of theft?"

"Well, then, Mr. Merton, I answer emphatically, yes."

"I can't fix him," said Mr. Longshanks, coming into the room. "I have a plan though, and I mean to bring him to terms. The farm of Mr. Popelover joins that of Fraudulent. They hate one another, and have for years. I told Fraudulent that Popelover wanted the land. The moment I said that, I saw him wince, as under the smart of a whip. He knows well that, if Popelover purchases it, the road to his farm, from that quarter, will be cut off; while at the same time the Popelover farm will be greatly increased in value. Because of this fact, I think I can make a lever of the old Popelover to lift Fraudulent with;

and if I don't raise his hair, then my name isn't what my mother gave me."

"Mr. Longshanks," asked Merton, "do you think that Mr. Fraudulent offered you a fair price for the land?"

"That's not the question, Bro. Merton," replied Mr. Longshanks. "I have the advantage of Fraudulent now, for the first time for many years, and I should be a fool not to use it. Business is business all the world over. Besides, I have no reason for kindness to Fraudulent. If I had justice from him, I should receive not only a fair price for the land, but also the full interest on the value of the timber he has stolen during the last ten years."

"It is terrible, Mr. Longshanks," said Merton, "to hear such an accusation made against a steward in the church. How do you suppose I should regard it, were I in another house, and should hear the host thus make charges against you?"

"I don't know how you would regard it," answered Mr. Longshanks; "but one thing I do know, and that is, you will not have the opportunity of hearing any host, or anybody else, make such charges. Longshanks is well known around here; and where he's known, his word is as good as his note."

"I say nothing for the purpose of disturbing your feelings, Mr. Longshanks," replied Merton; "but I am so sorry that one of my children should be obliged to think so much evil of another. I think children of the same family, in God's house, should try to look over one another's faults; and, as much as possible, to aid one another in overcoming the difficulties of life. Oh, Mr. Longshanks! I sometimes fear the gospel affects the outside more than the heart within. Christians appear no more merciful or honorable than others in their business transactions. I would to God that there were less of dead, and more of living, gospels among us."

"Gospel or no Gospel, Brother Merton," replied Mr. Longshanks, "my experience is, 'each one for himself and God for us all.' You can take that for your text anywhere in this great state, and it will be received as the only sound business principle a man can act upon. As for Mr. Fraudulent, any sympathy you may have for him, is unnecessary, and uncalled for; nor would he thank you for it, should he know you gave it to him. Skin for skin is his text; and I know well that, if he could, he would eat me skin and all. He wouldn't hesitate to rob his brother, which very thing he is believed to have done. I am sorry this thing should have occurred in your presence, as you seem to have a surplus of what my favorite poet calls the milk of human kindness. I think, however, that a few years experience in this great state may dry up somewhat the fountain which at present yields so plentifully with you. Let us hear no more about this subject now. I wish to enjoy your company while with us, and for you and your wife to have a pleasant visit. You are welcome to anything we have in our house; but, please let Mr. Fraudulent fight his own battles; and as he is a much larger man than you are, he surely is able to do it."

It was about a month after this conversation that Merton, sitting one evening in the parsonage, said to his wife:

"I now know all the stewards and trustees; and I do not remember ever hearing one speak well of another. I had hoped that the officers of the church would be exemplary men. Instead of that, all I hear is one accusing another of lying, stealing, drunkenness, or fraud. My life-giving Sunshine! were it not for you, I should sink away under the thoughts of my wounded spirit. What a farce is the profession of most men! What a superficial effect has the preaching of the Gospel on their lives! It is enough verily to shake the faith of any man in Christianity, as the only divine religion, when he knows and sees the conduct of its adherents! Do the members of our churches live any better lives than those who make no profession whatever? I have my doubts that they do. The ethics of Aristotle or Plato, who certainly were not Christians, would damn to the very depths of hell the average church-goer. It was but yesterday that a sincere Christian woman said: 'The churches are full of infidels'. There is more truth than fiction in her saying. So-called Christian civilization differs from heathenism more because of its power to wear an outside garb, than because of any superior inner qualities."

Merton was coming to see more and more that the true value of any religious faith, should be measured by its power to make men better in this world, the only world we know anything about. But such evidence as he had, went to prove that professors were no kinder, no more charitable, no more merciful, no more forgiving, no more honorable in their dealings—in short, no better than those who made no profession; indeed, he sometimes thought that the latter were the nobler men. Who was he who first called on them in their new home, and inquired if they were comfortable or not? He was one of the so-called children of this world. Who was he who generously supplied them with fuel for the winter? Was he a Church member? Verily he was not. He was but one of those who are said to compose the family of Satan. Truthfully could they say: "We were sick, and the world visited us; naked, and it clothed us; in prison, and the world gave us our freedom; hungry, and the world fed us." Yet, though Merton was heart-broken, he could not disbelieve that true religion is both natural and valuable to man. He felt in his soul convinced that the faith which he professed, could not be a true one, could not be a reasonable one; and, therefore, not such as might naturally be expected to make its adherents better. Nor was he long in discovering, according to his judgment, the vitiating principle in the faith of those to whom he preached; and that principle he believed to be faith in the doctrines of vicarious atonement, imputed righteousness, and salvation by faith. He could not but see that belief in such doctrines, must tend to weaken man's perception of the relation necessarily existing between cause and effect, and make him less fearful of doing wrong from the dread of the penalty necessarily resulting. If a man believes he must suffer the consequences of his own actions, he is likely, from fear of suffering, to avoid doing wrong; but if he believe he can lay his sins on Jesus, or on any other mediator, he is not likely to be so careful of his actions, especially when by erring a little, he can, as he thinks, give himself some kind of enjoyment or gratification. Being fully persuaded of the truth of these conclusions, in all his sermons, he laid but little, if any, stress on the doctrines above mentioned, as, in his judgment, vitiating; but all stress on character, as being the only true test of worthiness in this world or that to come. That which would best prepare man to live in this world, he held would best prepare him to live in any world. His sermons, therefore, would naturally become more and more distasteful to the ignorant members of his charge, who believed more in the loudness of the shout, and the depth of the groan, as the test of righteousness and true worth in God's sight than in the life and action. His doctrine they could not well stand; for well they knew that if they were to be judged by their works rather than their faith, a very large percentage of them would be shut completely out of the kingdom of heaven, as being unworthy to dwell with those who have washed their robes, and made them white, in well doing.

CHAPTER XII.

BROTHERLY LOVE.

Χρειώ με κατήγαγεν εἰς Ἀΐδαο—
Necessity compels me to go down to Hades.
(*Homer: Od. xi. 164.*)

Merton had not been long established in his new charge, when he was pressed to pass a day or two at the residence of Mr. Squareman. This gentleman was a very prosperous farmer, living very near the village, and owning a large house having fine orchards and gardens surrounding it. Meeting Merton at the door, Mr. Squareman greeted him very heartily; and soon they were seated in the comfortable parlor.

"We are right glad to have you visit us, Bro. Merton," said Mr. Squareman; "we have been expecting you for some time, but until now expecting in vain. But I suppose it has been with you as with other preachers,—slanderous tongues have kept you away."

"Mr. Squareman," said Merton, "your supposition, I assure you, has no foundation whatever. Besides, nothing but direct refusal to see me ever prevents my calling on my people. They are all alike dear to me,—all the objects of my solicitude. When they rejoice, I rejoice; when they weep, I weep. I have no favorites."

"Yes, Bro. Merton, that's very good, very beautiful," replied Mr. Squareman; "but you don't know our neighbors. Where we came from, people felt kindly towards one another; but here all are one's enemies. The chief officers of the church in Mazar delight in slandering and lying. Positively, of all things on earth, of all the sins a man can be guilty of, I do think slandering is the worst. It is something you will never hear in this house; we shut our doors against it. Of course, we sometimes speak the truth about matters; but slander is something that both my wife and I consider beneath a square man. If ever we speak about our neighbors, we do so with righteous judgment, knowing that as we judge, so shall we be judged. When we are offended, we sometimes let the world know it; and no man that ever lived, can stand what the officers of the church in this place do, without being offended and showing it. We say, it would be a sin for a man not to be offended, when truth is trodden under foot, and sin walks in high places. Look at that Meekface, for instance. What a man to be a steward in a church! He has done all he could against me in a law-suit, and has been the means of my losing hundreds of dollars. From the very beginning, he has been an enemy to me, although a brother-member. To tell the truth, Bro. Merton, that man can't possibly repeat what he hears, without changing it so that no man would know it. His whole family are natural liars. It's a disease that's hereditary in the whole Meekface family. What I'm saying is no news to you; it's impossible that it should be. No man could live around here two months, without knowing the reputation of that family."

"My dear Mr. Squareman! excuse me, I beg you, but what you say, is certainly news to me; and since I hate to be made the keeper of secrets, let me beg of you to say no more about the Meekface family. Let us talk about each other. We know ourselves so much better than we know Mr. Meekface."

"That's all right, Merton, and, so far as that goes, very well said; but as I was saying, I wouldn't trust that fellow the length of my nose. Indeed, I have a dog here that's better at heart than he is. If things arn't altered here pretty soon, the church will go to the ground. We've had preachers here that wouldn't even call upon us, because of the lies of that man and some of his imps. Such preachers I consider unworthy of notice. You're welcome, sir, welcome, and I hope at all times that you'll find me a square man.

"The last minister here wasn't as good a man as his wife, by a long shot. The fellow here before him,—well, he was a fool born and bred. You could see it in his face, and know it by his speech. But that isn't the worst of it—Just think of a minister living with another man's wife, as he did. Why I've heard his own children swear that he wasn't their father. What an example for a community! And, then, of all liars, he'd beat all; why! he was worse than Tom Pepper; and you know what the folks say of him. After he'd been going around here for a long time lying about me, I met him one day, coming up the hill here by the house. I stopped him as a square man would; indeed! I stopped him as I'd stop my dog, and gave him a piece of my mind. You ought to have seen him. Why! he was ashamed to be seen; he couldn't look me in the face for a moment, but stammered and stuttered, and hung down his head like a whipped cur. I don't care who the man is, Bro. Merton; but I speak my mind, and that's the way some say that I'm peculiar, that I'm not converted, that I haven't the power. I'll tell you, I don't want conversion, if such hypocrites as we have around here, are converted. Thank God! I was converted many years ago; but I don't want the prayers of those who are almost past repentance, and who are hardly fit to pray for themselves. 'Physician, heal thyself,' is what I say to such. No kiss of a Judas for me! Squareman akes no part in such mean, dirty business. I tell you what it is: If I could sell my farm, I'd soon make short work of it,—I'd soon pull up my stakes, and quit this country.

'Tisn't fit for a decent man to live in. The very face of that Meekface condemns him. I tell you, Bro. Merton, I speak the truth when I say I wouldn't believe him on his oath. I don't believe he knows how to tell the truth.

"Another of your principal men is Bro. Fraudulent. Not long ago I needed a hundred dollars for a year. When I asked him for the loan, he told me money was scarce, and wanted twelve per cent and good security. I said to him: 'Look here, Bro. Fraudulent, I'll give you twelve per cent, and good security. That security is my word. If my promise, as a member of the same church, isn't good enough, I won't give you any better security.' Well, I couldn't get the money; but I afterwards went to a sinner, and got it on my own terms. At another time I asked him for a small loan. He said he had no money; at the same time I was certain that he had not less than two hundred dollars in the house. The whole community will join me in saying, there isn't a bigger rascal outside the state's prison."

"Mr. Squareman," asked Merton, "how far does Mr. Headstrong live from here?"

"Haven't you been there yet, Bro. Merton?"

"No, sir," said Merton.

"Well, Bro. Merton, you'll be there soon enough. Don't be in too much of a hurry. We know something of that man. When we first came here we stayed some time with him; but we paid full price for everything we received. What did that fellow do but blab all around that he had kept us there for nothing! I tell you, Bro. Merton, that fellow is not a square man. He has a fine farm and some money; how he got it, God knows. In the early days, he went to California. I expect it was there he fell accidentally upon his money; for it does not seem to me that he ever could have gotten it in a community where one has to work for what he gets. Bro. Headstrong is not a square man, and he has no more sense than my old boot; nobody has any faith in his words. He has a boy that he thinks very smart; but I regard him as a soft-head. The boy has made some signs and scratches, and he and some other fellow correspond with them on postal-cards. Because he does this, they think him very smart. I'd like to know how a boy could be considered smart for corresponding in a language that nobody knows anything about, except himself and some other fellow just as foolish. I am sure that the people around here will join me in saying that all the Headstrong family haven't brains enough to last them over night. Of course, you couldn't make him believe it; he thinks he is the greatest man around here. He tells everybody that without him the church in Mazar couldn't possibly stand. On the contrary, nobody of common-sense believes it can stand with him. It beats all to see what church officers you have in Mazar. What a trio, Headstrong, Meekface, and Fraudulent! I tell you what it is, the church that stands on such a foundation, stands on the sand, and must fall, when the winds blow and the rains descend. And I say, let it fall.

"Brother Headstrong has a near neighbor who used to be in the church, and he's one of the very best fellows in the whole community. In the church, he used to be quite active, doing whatever his hand found to do, working like a member of the Lord's kingdom should work. How did Headstrong treat him? He had a favorite dog, a very rare kind, and one which a man would be proud to own anywhere; and out of mere envy, the old Headstrong, because he didn't possess such a one himself, shot him, pretending he was worrying some of his sheep. In this way, by one act after another, Headstrong drove him out of the church; for how could any man remain in a church, where he received such treatment from the hands of the very pillar of it! From that time to this, he regards Headstrong as the very image of sin; which, I think, is a merciful judgment, for I sometimes imagine he is sin itself."

"But, Mr. Squareman, would it not be best for you to go to these men of whom you are speaking, make your complaint known to them, and endeavor to come to an understanding?"

"I have tried that. often enough, Bro. Merton. I wouldn't say what I have, if I didn't hope that you might be able to get them to see their wickedness, and get their heart changed."

"Thank you, Mr. Squareman; I shall always do the little I can to bring about harmony among my people. But in speaking of others, I know of only one just rule: never speak evil of others, except before their face. There may be exceptions to this rule, Mr. Squareman; but I am sure, if you and I should act according to it, it would be very much better. I have no doubt you have grievances against the men you speak of; but did you ever think that, in their heart, they believe they have equal grievances against you? I visit their homes, and without a doubt they speak of your ill-treatment of them. In such case, what can I do? I do believe that if you brethren were to meet one another in a conciliatory spirit, you would find most of your reasons for ill-feeling would disappear, as snow before the sun. If you yourself would only go half way, I think your apparent enemies would come to meet you."

"Yes, Bro. Merton, that may be. But the truth is, I have all I can do to attend to my own affairs. I wouldn't go the length of my nose to meet a man like Meekface, whom I consider as surly as my dog."

"But, Mr. Squareman, I ask you not to do this for your own sake, but for the sake of Christ and his church. Surely, if we are not willing to forgive, we can not expect to be forgiven. We pray to be forgiven, as we forgive others."

"Yes, Bro. Merton, but you don't catch me kneeling to such men as those; nor have I any desire to open my mouth, simply to fill the mouths of others. Besides, you don't know a half of it, and I haven't time to tell you."

"No, Bro. Merton," said Mrs. Squareman, "you don't know a half of our trouble. Only a few days ago Mrs. Meekface said she would never forgive me for all the lies I had told about her. God knows I haven't told any lies. For all the evil that woman has said of me, I am willing and do now freely forgive her. She can curse, but God will bless; she can pray for evil to overtake me, but it will only bring down fire upon her own head. God knows those that are his, and he knows me. I have given my case to Him."

"But, Mrs. Squareman," said Sunshine, "is it not possible that Mrs. Meekface feels just as you do about it? that she is the injured party, and you the transgressor? It may be that if you should go to Mrs. Meekface, and deny that you had ever intentionally injured her, she would say the same of herself in regard to you. Then each of you seeing that there was no real ground for offence, would forget the past, and be friendly with each other."

"It is possible, Sister Merton, but I couldn't possibly believe it, after doing all I have done. I won't give up trying though; I pray for her every day that God may give her a better heart, and open her eyes that she may see her evil ways."

On leaving the residence of Mr. Squareman, Sunshine and Merton thought, that though they had lost hospitable hosts, they had found relief from spirits full of fault-finding and bitter complaint. They felt greatly discouraged; but they were not without that which Thales said was the greatest of all possessions—hope.

A few days after their visit at the house of Mr. Squareman, they called on the Meekface family. During their visit, Mr. Meekface said:

"You have been lately calling on Bro. Squareman; so I heard one of the neighbors say."

"Yes, sir," replied Merton, "we were there about a week ago."

"You must have found them delightful company," continued Mr. Meekface. "We're not able to live in such a fine house as they; I don't know how it is, unless they are blessed for their liberality."

"A fine house is nothing to me, Mr. Meekface. I would greatly prefer to have my soul well clothed than my body. Do not trouble yourself too much about the inferior character of your house. Make the best of what you have. You know that the silver and the gold are the Lord's."

"Yes, Bro. Merton; but if all were to sing that tune, the preacher wouldn't get very fat. He would be one of the lean kind."

"If a minister labors faithfully, Mr. Meekface, I should say he was worthy of his hire."

"Yes, Bro. Merton; but some men don't see it in that light. Everybody uses his own eyes, and some folks around here, may be, are color-blind."

"Everybody," Merton replied, "should make the best use of his own eyes; but if they be defective, he should be led by the eyes of others, or he will fall into the ditch."

"Then some folks, Bro. Merton, must soon be in the ditch. The truth is, it is next to impossible to get one cent out of the Squareman family for the support of the minister. He owes five dollars now; but he'll never pay it. He never has anything for church-work, but a plenty to fix his house up with. If he paid as we, he wouldn't have a better house than other folks. I know it's hard to speak evil of others; but I speak for his good. I do hope you'll succeed in getting some spiritual life into that man ; but if you do, you'll do something that nobody else has been able to do.

"No doubt you've heard many things about us, but he can't say any evil ; and, besides, nobody has any faith in his word. If you could hear Mrs. Squareman pray, you would think she was a saint ; but nothing but a miracle can ever save that woman. They have oily tongues, and keep them running all the day long ; and I guess they'll never stop running, until they're worn out. It's a great pity they're in the church. To have such people in the church, is like a drowning man having a lump of lead tied around his neck. Some folks think that Mrs. Squareman is out of her head, and I'm inclined to think that she is. A saint to-day, she has seven devils to-morrow. If you cast them out, you'll do well. If the devil isn't their governor, then I don't know for the life of me, who can be. He brags all the time of being a square man ; but a more one-sided genius never lived anywhere. I have been here a good many years, have labored in every way to build up our little church, have given money that should have been kept for my own family, have labored in the Sunday-school, and gone night after night to the protracted meetings, trying in every way to bring the folks into the church ; but as far as I can see, there's no use in trying to do anything, where such folks are all the time hard at work pulling down."

"Mr. Meekface, believe me, you have no need to suppose that my judgment is formed of one of my people, from what I hear another say of him. I assure you, my respect for you has not been lessened, by what I may have heard from the lips of others about you. I have found it is a very untrustworthy foundation to base a judgment upon. In reference to Mr. Squareman, it may be, he is a weak brother, and you a strong one. In such case, perhaps, you could help him by reaching out a kind hand to save. A kind word, an affectionate greeting, a brotherly grasp of the hand,—these can restore, when nothing else can save. I so much wish you could help Mr. Squareman to a better view of things, and that you could work together. My own hands are weak, and my heart sometimes seems to fail within me. If only we could get rid of some of our fault-finding spirit!"

"I'm not fault-finding, Bro. Merton; but as far as Squareman goes, I've done my last for him."

Weary, wounded, and worn, they left the house, and sought the shelter of their humble little parsonage. Just before coming to the door, they were met by Mr. Popelover. Merton remained to talk with him, but Sunshine entered the house to prepare the tea.

"How do you do, elder? I am very glad to see you. You're come to a pretty tough place here. It doesn't concern me, I'll admit; but I can't very well help sympathizing with a minister who comes here. Some years ago the people here had a very good kind of a man to preach to them; but they rewarded him by starving him out. He had to carry material to build his own stable. He had a young wife, who was treated barbarously. The poor fellow appeared heart-broken. He stood it a short time, when, utterly disgusted with the whole business, he left the ministry, and went on a farm. I think he showed good sense. The last preacher they had here, appeared to me to be a woman; the one before, I regarded as a very dishonest man. When I know a man to be dishonest, I know it. You have plenty of such characters in your church. I know some of them who go over yonder to pray, after they've turned their stock into my corn-field. I suppose the consciousness that their cattle are doing well, enables them to pray fervently. I haven't much faith in such prayers. I met Bro. Fraudulent the other day, and said: 'Bro. Fraudulent, suppose a man should steal a span of my horses, can he get forgiveness without returning them?' 'Most certainly,' he said. 'A man is forgiven not for what he does, but because he believes in Christ. We are saved by faith.' I told him if that was Methodism, I wanted nothing to do with it; and that if it were Christianity, the sooner it were put down the better."

"Mr. Popelover, you are a Roman Catholic. You must know yourself the conditions of divine forgiveness. Either you misunderstood Mr. Fraudulent, or he has misinformed you as to the doctrines of Methodism. If you will promise me to come to services next Sunday, I will undertake to tell you at that time what my own ideas on the subject are."

"With that understanding, elder, I will promise you to be at the church next Sunday."

On the following Sunday, Mr. Popelover, true to his promise, was present at services, and proved a most attentive listener to the sermon, which was based on Matt. v. 23-24. In this sermon Merton spoke so plainly on the doctrine of divine forgiveness, that some of the members were not a little hurt, as afterwards became known.

CHAPTER XIII.

FALSE SPIRITS.

Thou therefore which teachest another, teachest thou not thyself?
(*Romans.*)

AFTER preaching the sermon mentioned in our last chapter, Merton perceived that Mr. Headstrong, a very prominent and influential member of the congregation, began to be less and less regular at services, and, finally, ceased coming altogether. When Merton discovered Mr. Headstrong's protracted absence, he resolved to call on him, and find out the reason of his non-attendance.

A little after entering his house, Merton said:

"Mr. Headstrong, I have missed you for some time. What is the matter with you? I hope you have not been ill."

"No, Brother Merton, not exactly; I have had the rheumatics. If you had them a little while, you would know all about my staying away from prayer-meetings."

"I am truly sorry, Mr. Headstrong, to know that you are such a sufferer. I sincerely hope that in a few days you may be yourself again. I need your presence and help so much."

"I love the meetings, Brother Merton. There is not a man in this place, that's worked for them as I have. I've often gone, and left my wife in floods of tears, and exposed to dangers also. But, then, a woman's crying is nothing to me, when the meeting is concerned. Women are weak things, anyhow."

"I could hardly approve of such conduct, Mr. Headstrong," replied Merton. "The first duty we have, is to take care of those who depend on us."

"Angels can keep us from dashing our feet against a

stone, Bro. Merton; God can protect his own. I don't believe in pleasing the whims of a woman, when the well-being of heaven calls me away. I believe in trusting Providence; he who doesn't, lacks true, saving faith. Such a one should get converted, before he goes out into God's vineyard to convert others. We must first have the power ourselves."

"But, Mr. Headstrong, would it not be as reasonable to say that he who trusts Providence to do for him what he might do for himself, lacks common-sense? And what is the use of faith without common-sense?"

"I've old notions, Bro. Merton, and they have come to me through experience; I got some of them out in California, after I had crossed the plains. I don't want any of your untried opinions. Some young fellows think they are right smart; but men of experience don't want no time to take the conceit out of them. In business matters I do as well as the best of them, and in speritual things I can beat them any time. There's lots of book-larning in the world, but 'tisn't worth nothing; such folks quarrel with Providence every day. They are very smart in their way: they insure their lives and their houses. You don't catch me insuring my life. What is insurance, if it isn't quarreling with God! No, indeed! Headstrong isn't found wasting his money in insurance. God insures me and mine; that's good enough for me. I don't believe that a man who insures his life, has the sperit of God in him. How can we expect to enter the kingdom, if we fight like that against the ways of Providence! Again, some folks keep organs and dolls for their cheldern. This is the sin of Israel, worshipping idols. No organ in Headstrong's house; no dolls for my cheldern. Them's my opinions all the time, and they're come to me through hard experience. I've been a class-leader for many years, and have come to this knowledge through powerful, internal reasoning. The devil and all his sooty hosts couldn't never change me a particle. When I say a thing, I say it; when I know a thing, I know it; and Headstrong knows two or three things. Tell you what, Bro. Merton; you might get Bro. Squareman, or somebody of his kind, to accept your doctrine; but nobody with the Sperit won't. A man strong in spiritual things, strong in the faith, and led by the Sperit, isn't going to be moved an inch by your views. I wish you hadn't preached that sermon on the 'Conditions of Divine Forgiveness.' You greatly offended some who are led by the Sperit. Bro. Fraudulent was mighty displeased. You stepped on many a toe by saying what you said. But the one most offended is Bro. Fraudulent; for everybody knows you meant him."

"Mr. Headstrong, you are making serious charges against Mr. Fraudulent. What right have you, or anybody else, to say that I referred to him in my sermon?"

"Because everybody knows right well that Bro. Fraudulent done to Mr. Popelover, just what you said; and that's the way that Fraudulent was so angry."

"Mr. Headstrong, simply because I happened to speak of a sin which you say Mr. Fraudulent had been guilty of, no one could therefore rightly infer that I alluded to him. Such a conclusion would be very unjust, whether made by you or any other. But suppose I did know it. Should I because of that knowledge, cease to rebuke such sins? If so, it would follow that I should cease to speak of any sin whatever, since it is quite possible there is no sin that has not been committed by somebody."

"Bro. Fraudulent don't believe in preachers meddling with the business of the members. And I might as well tell you, Bro. Merton, that Bro. Meekface supports him in his views. They both say that the preacher is a thing that is here to-day and gone to-morrow, but that the members are fixed. They say they have never heered your equal as a preacher, when you stick to the Gospel, and tell those sinners, those folks outside the church, the great danger they're in; but that you know nothing about trading in horses, nor selling corn and wheat. Fraudulent is ashamed to go around, since you preached that sermon. As things are, I can't never hope for a glorious revival."

"Mr. Headstrong, when the hub is rotten, the wheel carries but little; he who has a beam in his own eye, should not counsel others to take a mote out of theirs; a man with a legion of devils, should not seek to exorcise him possessed only of one. The first duty is for the chief members of the church to get within themseles a revival of honesty and truth; then we should have reason to expect others would begin."

"I find you are fixed in the error of your ways, Brother Merton. I prophesy, though, that you would do better in this circuit, if you had a leetle more of the Sperit in the inner man; and a leetle less of book-larning in the outer. I can't come to church, where I hear the cheldern of Zion held up for the cheldern of this wicked world to laugh at. I like the preacher to tell sinners what they must do to be saved. This makes the old warrior's heart rejoice; but I can't stand it, to see the cheldern of Zion hang down their heads. Tell me, Brother Merton, were you ever converted?"

"I certainly supposed I was, Mr. Headstrong, when I was quite a boy; but I do not claim to be a child of God so much because of this belief, as from the fact that I have always tried to love and worship God my Father, and to be kind and forbearing in all my dealings with my fellow-men. In other words, as I have never, to my knowledge, been far away from my Father's house, I firmly believe that I am now at home, living in his presence. I trustingly place my hand in his, believing that though the way may be dark, I shall in good time be brought into the light."

That's very good, Brother Merton; but that's just where your weakness is. You, my dear brother, have never experienced the blessed power. It is not your fault altogether. It is more the sin of theological schools, and so-called larned professors. I tell you, one poor, ignorant man led by the Spirit, knows more of divine things than all the schools put together. It is the Sperit that teaches us, not book-larning."

"I thank you for your advice, Mr. Headstrong, but would it not be well for you who are so full of the Spirit, to learn to judge less harshly, to seek more of the spirit of forgiveness, and to show by your works that you have learned those divine things which, you say, you are so competent to teach. I cannot but believe, Mr. Headstrong, that the only sufficient evidence we have, or should seek, of a genuine conversion, is that the convert live an honest, upright, and consistent life. I want no faith which is not followed by right works."

"Such language, Brother Merton, shows that you are yet in the gall of bitterness, dead in trespasses and sin. Woe be to the man who seeks to draw others into the light, when he is in gross darkness himself. Not by works, Brother Merton, not by works, which are as filthy rags, but by the blood of Jesus. According to thy faith so shall it be. I do not know what will become of the church. It seems to me that unless God awakes, and puts on his glorious strength, that Zion must soon totter and fall; and great will be the fall thereof. Good day, Brother Merton; think prayerfully of what I said. It may be the Sperit will find you out."

As Merton left this man, he could but feel contempt as well as pity for him. While boasting of dwelling in the fullness of light, he was shockingly irreverent with God, and most abusive to others, if they dared to differ with him. Nor could Merton fail to recall the lines:

> "To make the lips
> Of truth speak falsehood; to their own liking
> Turn the meaning of the text,
> And prove their reasoning best,
> Though propped on fancies wild as madmen's dreams."

As he walked along pondering on the ignorance and superstition of the people he ministered to, he was met by Mr. Truthseeker:

"How do you do, elder. Your sermon has created quite a sensation in Mazar. Everybody has something to say about it. It was enough to make any man think, and I for one didn't escape. Two or three of your members, however, are greatly offended. They have their old notions, and would as soon part with their lives, as part with them. I have heard some men say that they would give their last dollar rather than see you leave Mazar. So I guess you have no need to feel discouraged. Those who are offended, are of very little account here, even though they are the centre of your praying-band. If you could only succeed in getting them converted, there would be some hopes for Methodism in this place; as it is, it is a laughing-stock. Since you have been here, there's a class of men coming to church, that never came before. It is something novel, you know, to hear it taught that it is the character, the moral uprightness of the man, which determines his acceptability with God. I am not a member of any church, and never shall be, until it assents to doctrine like I hear you preach. You may take my word for it,—the community here approves your course. Here comes a man unlike myself. He is a member of the Baptist Church. Let us hear what he has to say about it. He heard your sermon last Sunday; and as he is a good judge, I would like to know what he thinks about it."

"Good morning, elder," said Mr. Workandpray. "That was a powerful discourse you gave us on the 'Conditions of Divine Forgiveness.' It went to the point. Whether or not it may be considered as exactly like what is generally preached, I declare it seems to me the only sensible sermon on the subject I ever heard. But I tell you, elder, it made some fellows kick mighty hard. Speaking of your principal members, elder, makes me think of the time I first came here. Having attended the services one evening, I happened to hear Mrs. Squareman pray, who was then a stranger to me. I was mighty struck with her prayer, and on going home with Mr. Meekface, asked him who was that woman that made that fine prayer. 'She must be a fine character' I said."

"'I thought so myself once,' he said; 'but as you are a stranger here, my advice to you is, have nothing to do with that woman. She's a whited sepulchre.'

'Not long after this, elder, Mr. Outspoken went to the residence of Mr. and Mrs. Squareman to board, until he could get his own place a little fixed up. Well, he said that back-biting commenced at supper-table, and continued till bed-time, when they would take down the big Bible and have evening prayers. Mr. Outspoken protested against this. He said he didn't see no use in back-biting one moment, and going to prayers the next. He thought the two didn't work well together. But what he said, had but little effect on their tongues. They told him that they held up the people whom they were speaking about, as a warning to others.

"I tell you, elder, you must not care what such characters say or do. They are well known here; and they are regarded as spotted sheep. The worst they can do to you, is to refuse to pay their subscriptions. If you offend them, they will likely do this; but something should be done to stir them up. You have a good and honest name now. Don't lose it for fear of them. If you lose their support, you gain that of other men, men like Loveright and Godsaveall; and they are better able to support you than any of your members."

As Merton passed into the little parsonage, Sunshine met him at the door, and said:

"Harry, Mrs. Fencestridler has been visiting me. She made many apologies for not calling before, and left all these things you see here, to fill up our cupboard with. She said it was a treat to hear you preach; and that the people out at Woodland, were longing for you to come out there. I do think, Harry, that a good many people here are so kind, especially those outside the church. I do believe that such people are kinder to you and me than those who call themselves members of God's kingdom."

"Such is not strange, my darling. It was in a measure true with Christ. He came to his own, and they received him not. I certainly could not stand the actions I have seen in many of the people of my charge, were it not for your presence. I sometimes feel almost in despair; but as soon as I come under your beams, I feel hopeful. The life I receive from you, gives me energy to battle under difficulties, however great, for the sake of the beautiful being called by my name. When I want to feast on you, I stand and gaze, lost in wonder at the beauty and loveliness of your form, and unable to express my thoughts in words. My love for you is too deep, my admiration for you too high, to express in any language. I seem to have a richer feast by silently watching you; and I feel, as it were, afraid to let my thoughts loose, lest the air carry them to others, and they share with me the feast I enjoy. I suppose it is selfish with me. But I am not sorry that I find my heaven in your presence; nor are you, I hope, that I want you all to myself:

"O, Maedchen, Maedchen,
Wie lieb' ich dich.
Wie blickt dein Auge.
Wie liebst du mich.

So liebt die Lerche,
Gesang und Luft,
Und Morgenblumen
Den Himmelsduft.

Wie ich d'ch liebe
Mit warmem Blut,
Die du mir Jugend
Und Freud' und Muth

In neuern Liedern
Und Taenzen gibst.
Sei ewig gluecklich,
Wie du mich liebst."
    (*Goethe.*)

CHAPTER XIV.

DEBASEMENT OF RELIGION.

What meaneth the noise of this tumult?
(*I Samuel.*)

THE disaffection among the stewards of the church, resulting from the preaching of the sermon on "Divine Forgiveness," caused them to seek every means of impeding Merton in his work, and embittering his life. They finally contrived a plot whereby he would be unable to have the further use of the church building. The building was the property of another people; and they, having no minister that year, had permitted Merton's people to have the use of it. Although the one denomination hated the doctrines of the other, in order to have their revenge, the stewards of Merton's church persuaded the rival church people to initiate revival services, that by so doing there might be an apparent reason for denying Merton the use of the church pulpit. The rival people readily consented, being already very jealous of the large congregations attending Merton's services.

It was Sunday morning. Merton had finished his discourse, and had just announced his services for the following Sunday, when Mr. Worthington, a leading member of the rival church, rose in his seat, and said:

"I beg to announce that in the future, or at least for the next two or three months, we shall want the exclusive use of this house. We are going to hold revival services."

At this Mr. Remington arose, and replied:

"Mr. Worthington, did you not promise me that Mr. Merton should have the use of this pulpit for next Sunday?"

"No, sir, I promised no such thing," answered Mr. Worthington; "and it's a falsehood to say that I did."

"I am surprised at you," said Mr. Remington; "and I want nothing more to do with you, or any one else who would use such words, after having promised me faithfully, as you certainly did, that Mr. Merton should have the use of this house next Sunday."

"Never mind, gentlemen," said Merton; "it is not worth quarreling about. It may be we can hold services elsewhere. In the meantime, we will hold services next Sunday at the parsonage."

On his way to the parsonage, Merton was accompanied by Mr. Loveright, who said: "Don't you mind them, Mr. Merton. I heard even one of their own members say, a day or two ago, that if they closed the door against you, he would break it in. Those revival services are a disgrace to any community. I remember one that was held where I lived, some years ago. The services were a grand success, many people having been converted; for the leaders were said to speak with great unction. Everything went on most promisingly. One night the leaders failed to put in their appearance. People wondered what had become of the mighty workers who had wrought such wonders among the people of the church. The next morning, however, their wondering ceased; for a great many went to the stables to find their best horses missing. The leaders of the revivalists were nothing but a band of horse-thieves. I and my wife knew a very successful revivalist who generally ended his work by seducing one or two young girls. I often wonder why people can put confidence in such men. Who knows them? Nobody. They pass through the country like meteors, and disappear the same way. A minister living among us, is a person we know. We can hold him accountable for his actions; but with revivalists, unless in special cases, we can absolutely do nothing. How can we tell the character of a man who comes from a distance, and known by nobody in the community? I have learned that a man can weep, and pray, and shout, and still be a devil. I am one of those who have no faith whatever in revivalists, and I hope you will have nothing to do with revivals."

"I hardly know what to do, Mr. Loveright. I shall calmly think the matter over, and what I think is best, that will I do, cost what it may."

"I tell you, elder, a revival meeting would never have been thought of in this place, this winter, were it not for Mr. Headstrong. He is very angry with you, because you have not permitted him to blow his horn, as much as he wished to. Although a very ignorant man, he is a mischievous one, and delights in doing all he can to injure those who cross him in the least. One year, he is a Methodist; next he's a Baptist; God knows what he'll be in the end."

It being fully known that Merton had refused to take any part in revival services, the disaffected members worked for a short time in union with the rival people, having invited Mr. Wheat, a preacher stationed at Stanton, to come and work for them in union with the evangelist. He came, and for a few days the two denominations appeared to labor in harmony. Soon, however, they began to quarrel over the division of the spoils. It was then that Mr. Wheat, becoming disgusted, ceased all further efforts. Before leaving the village, he called at the parsonage. On entering the house, he said: "I am sorry, Brother Merton, that I was ever fooled into coming here, especially without your invitation. I see I have done wrong. I ought to have known that they were a nest of hornets. I hope you will forgive me; I will do no more of it."

"My dear sir," replied Merton, "I certainly shall forgive you; but I can not understand why so-called ministers of the Gospel can be guilty of doing what you have done, unless the power which calls them to preach, is the pocket-book rather than the Holy Ghost. In my simplicity I refused a lucrative position for the sake of preaching; but what do I see among my so-called brethren, but a race after a few dollars."

"I don't know, Brother Merton," replied Mr. Wheat, "how you feel about it; but if I could get more money in any other honest calling than by preaching, I certainly should feel it my duty to get it. The preacher of the Gospel must first of all look out for the wants of his family; and those things are best supplied, when we get most money."

This saying surprised Mr. and Mrs. Merton, the latter having heard Mr. Wheat say, only the night before, that the Holy Ghost had called him to preach the Gospel to all mankind. She had as yet scarcely learned that the holy ghost of many ministers is the pocket-book and nothing else; but it was not very long before she became, as all others who fully study the question, completely convinced that, if ministers were to get less money, and acquire less prominence than men in other callings, the churches would nearly all be closed, and Christianity, as it is preached to-day, be a thing of the past in less than twenty years.

One evening, about half-past eight, Merton visited the revival meeting. The house was like a pandemonium: it was full of giggling and groaning; and over all the maddening scene were cast the eyes of the lustful evangelist raving with the insanity of religious excitement.

Approaching Mr. Truthseeker, the evangelist said:

"Young man, do you love God?"

"I do," was the reply; "do you?"

"Do I!" said the evangelist; "I am perfect in love. I love God with all my soul, with all my strength, with all my mind, and with all my heart, and my neighbor as myself. I fear, young man, you are in the enemy's territory. Come and learn of me, and I will show you wondrous things."

"I am not certain," replied Mr. Truthseeker, "how much you know about holy things, if you mean shotes and horses; but I am certain you have never learned good manners, nor how to behave as a gentleman. If you had, you would never have filled the pulpit, at a time when it was promised another."

"I am an evangelist, young man, and never allow my pulpit to be filled by another who might interfere with my methods, and deny my doctrines."

"You may be sure he would," was the reply, "for no man, professing to be a gentleman, could see your methods, and hear your insane utterances, without branding you what you are,—an ignorant scoundrel."

"I reckon, young man, you're a leetle off; I will call on you again, when your right reason returns, if the day of grace isn't passed."

"I am open to an interview," retorted Mr. Truthseeker, "if you come looking like a decent man; but with your present appearance, I can't promise you one."

Leaving Mr. Truthseeker, the evangelist approached the young Mr. Loveright:

"Young man," he said, "I've saw you here a right good number of evenings. Are you seeking? can't I persuade you to come forward."

"Don't bring your mouth so near mine," replied Mr. Loveright; "you smell too much of the weed."

"Young man! don't you think that you're a leetle saucy?"

"Not so much as you are impertinent," answered the young man. "I profess to be a temperate man, and don't wish to be intoxicated by your drunken spirit and tobacco-soaked soul. The room is big enough for both; keep your distance."

At another time the evangelist approached Mr. Freund, and said :

"Say, young man, I want to see you become converted, and happy like me."

"That's all good enough," said Mr. Freund, "but I really consider myself so much better than you, that I should deem it an unpardonable sin in me, to become as you are."

The evangelist then took the platform, and made an address in which he set forth all the imaginary terrors of the dying-bed, the woes of the damned, and the wrath of God against the unrepentent. Of these he painted such an awful picture that none could look on it, without feeling a thrill of horror pass through himself.

During the evening Miss Meekface approached Miss Godsaveall, and was persuading her to go forward, when, it being seen by Mr. Godsaveall, he said :

"Miss Meekface ! you dare approach my daughter again with any more of your lying inventions, and corruptions of the truth, and I will teach you a lesson, you will not be apt to forget. How dare you make such a farce of religion ! We are not come here to receive help from you or your kind, but to witness to what depths of ignorance and superstition such as you may be reduced."

Mr. Godsaveall spoke so loudly that he attracted the attention of the house, at which the evangelist arose and said : "Brethren, to your knees ! The devil is in the house; he is hardening the hearts of the wicked ; he is hindering the work of the Holy Ghost ; he must be cast out by the way he came in."

Mr. Godsaveall was a conspicuous man in Mazar, noted for his integrity and gentlemanly conduct. That such a man should be classed with devils, was more than the people could stand. Quite a tumult arose ; and such a feeling of discord was engendered in the hearts of the praying band, that any future success was made impossible.

The result of these revival-meetings was what had been prophesied: jealousy, ill-feeling, and bitterness received a new lease of life; and even those who had been the most friendly with the evangelist, could now be heard saying, he was a "fool," a "horse-trader," and a "liar."

Merton's services were never better attended than during the Baptist revival-meeting: it had no power to draw away the better class of people.

During those days it was gratifying to Merton to receive constant proofs of the people's good-will in the form of gifts of wood, coal, flour, etc. We give an example of the manner in which these presents were brought:

"Harry," said Sunshine, "there is some one at the door." On opening the door, Merton saw the hired man of Mr. Godspeed, who said: "Elder, excuse me; but Mr. Godspeed has sent me up with this bag of flour, and this five-dollar bill, as part payment for the sermon you gave last night, the best, he says, he ever heard in his life. He also wishes me to say that there's more where this comes from."

Shortly afterwards another knock was heard. This time it was Mr. Loveright, who had come to see them:

"Well, elder," he began, "I thought I would come down to inquire if you wanted anything like coal or wood, or anything I might be able to get for you. I have never, in all my life, taken such interest in religious matters; and the reason is, because of the wholesome sense you give us in your sermons. I can accept your doctrine, and so can any man of common-sense. What have you lost, elder, by doing as you have done? You have lost three howling, ignorant hypocrites, while you have gained almost every thinking man in Mazar, and you have received two dollars for every one you would have received, had you done other-

DEBASEMENT OF RELIGION.   153

wise. The leading men in this church, elder, are certainly unworthy of conspicuous places, except in gangs of notorious characters. Have you ever heard that Mr. Smalleyes is believed to be guilty of murder?"

"Yes, sir, I heard it a little after coming here; but I know nothing of the truth of such report. It is a very serious charge to make."

"There are a great many here who believe the charge is true, elder. Mr. Allimmersion and Hardtocrack who were among the very earliest settlers here, affirm the truth of the report. They say he has put two men out of the way, one being a laborer to whom he was in debt more than a hundred dollars, the other, a cattle-dealer."

"It is a terrible accusation," said Merton. "One of our members wished to have the charges investigated; but I know of no sufficient grounds for bringing charges against Mr. Smalleyes."

"One thing is sure, elder : you have a class of men for church officers, whom nobody will trust, and who will not trust one another ; a class of men known to be among the most dishonest in the whole community. Ever since I've been here, I've seen nothing but dishonesty among the chief members; and the preachers whom they have sent here, have been but a little better. Only a few days ago, Mr. Godspeed sent out his man to purchase wheat. He bought a fine lot of Mr. Fraudulent, and paid the cash down. On delivery, the first load was found to be as purchased, the second load proved to be mixed. Hastening to the residence of Mr. Fraudulent, the miller obtained conclusive proof that Fraudulent had brought a pile of poor wheat from an adjoining room, and mixed it with the good. The hired man was as angry as he could be, and wished Mr. Godspeed to go to law about the matter; but Godspeed said : 'No; but as long as I live, I will never buy a grain of wheat from that wicked knave again;' and every one knows that Godspeed means what he says. Now, this is just done by one of your principal men. Why! I'm sure, if such things were done among the Blackfeet Indians, he doing it would be hung, as they would hang a horse-thief.

"The other night there was a prayer-meeting held across the road from us. During the evening, Headstrong made a long and seemingly earnest prayer in behalf of Squareman who was present. The latter was boiling with rage, while on his knees, at the thought that such a man should pray for him. After the close of the meeting, Squareman said : 'I took no part in the meeting, nor did I blab about my conversion ; but, if I thought I wasn't a hundred times better man than you are, Headstrong, I wouldn't only leave the church, but I'd leave the world. You are, what you've always been—a snake in the grass; but your bite can't harm me.'

"Nor do the chief members at Moth do any better. A few days ago Smalleyes accused Woundedheart of stealing his whipple-tree, who replied to the accusation : 'You're a liar ; and if you don't leave my premises, I'll boot you.' 'You'll be booted in a few days,' replied Smalleyes ; 'for I am going to have you up again ; and if this time I don't fix you, then my name isn't Smalleyes.'

"'Once more I tell you, get off my premises,' said Woundedheart, 'or I'll make mince-meat of you.'

"Smalleyes seemed disinclined to go, whereupon Woundedheart struck him. They fought like tigers until Smalleyes was a sickening sight. After almost killing Smalleyes, Woundedheart went to the residence of Beereyed, the most familiar friend of Smalleyes. He found him and punished him most fearfully. Finally the youngest Beereyed attacked Woundedheart with an axe, and in this way rescued his father. This trouble will bring on more law-suits. My own belief is that no church can hope to prosper, while it has such characters for its leaders,—characters who are a disgrace to any community."

"Elder, you are going to have a quarterly meeting, in a few days. Where is it to be held?"

"It matters not to me, sir," said Merton; "I have done with this people. I have not been pleased with my field of labor. Nevertheless, had I received anything like fair treatment, I would not have left them just yet; although I have for some time purposed in my heart to leave the church with which I am now connected. You know the people of this charge; and you know the treatment I have received from them. I regard the work of a man as much the fruit of his faith, as the fruit of the tree is the product of the soil. If the works are bad, the faith is bad, the heart is bad. I fear that my principles are not such as will receive a general and ready acceptation from the people of this church. I have determined to seek other affiliation. To this end I have prepared a written request, asking permission of the quarterly conference, to withdraw from all connection with this people. Inasmuch as I have never been ordained, and am only a preacher on trial, the quarterly conference has full power to grant my request. But wherever we may go, both Mrs. Merton and myself shall always remember the great kindness you have shown us. You have, indeed, been a true friend to us."

"I have only done my duty, Mr. Merton. I have been more than repaid by your manly opposition to the abominable farce that we have had here, under the name of a revival."

CHAPTER XV.

UNREASONABLE DOGMAS.

Reason must be our last judge and guide in everything.
(*Locke.*)

IT must not be supposed that Merton's decision to leave the denomination with which he had been connected, was reached without much thought and anxiety. He had spent many years with that body, had thoroughly studied the dogmas of that church, and sought in every way to find some reasonable defence for them; but he had sought in vain. So notwithstanding the great anxiety that must have filled his breast, while contemplating such a change, Merton resolved to yield to the demands of his heart and soul for a more liberal faith. This faith he hoped to find in the Episcopal Church.

There were also other reasons that might have deterred Merton from executing his purpose: all his old acquaintances, the members of his own family, and his most intimate friends were in the church he was leaving. He knew well that parting from that body meant, to no small extent, leaving his friends. He should not again join them in social gatherings, nor unite with them in singing their songs of praise. No good blood ran in the veins of these he was forsaking for those he was seeking; for the ministers of the latter body looked on those of the former as, at most, only laymen without any power to administer the sacraments, or perform any priestly function, in the church of God. Merton knew all this; but yet he could not bring his soul any longer to accept those narrow dogmas whose bitter results he had seen so clearly manifested.

It was hard to sever ministerial relations; but Merton was comforted at the thought that what had been done, had been so well done.

Merton's first ministry was now ended, and he felt glad at heart. Having had for some time many doubts concerning not a few of the fundamental doctrines of so-called evangelical theology, he felt great abhorrence toward the doctrine of salvation by faith, as generally taught and believed by its leaders. In his opinion such a doctrine was no less morally dangerous than philosophically absurd: morally dangerous, because it confers on the unjust unmerited benefits, but fails to reward the really good and meritorious, therefore removing the only sufficient sanction for a virtuous life; and philosophically absurd, because it separates the shadow from the substance, and bases itself upon the magic of miracles. Says Aristotle:

"Μία χελιδων ἔαρ οὐ ποιεῖ, οὐδὲ μία ἡμέρα. οὕτω δε οὐδε μαχάριον καὶ εὐδαίμονα μία ἡμέρα οὐδ' ὀλίγος χρόνος. Εὖ λέγεται ὅτι ἐκ τοῦ δίκαια πράττειν ὁ δίκαιος γίνεται. Οὐκ εἴη δ'ἀν οὐδε τιμῆς ἄξιος φαῦλος ὤν, τῆς ἀρετῆς γὰρ ἆθλον ἡ τιμή, καὶ ἀπονέμεται τοῖς ἀγαθοῖς—One swallow does not make a spring, nor one day; nor does one day, nor a little time, make a man happy and blessed. It is well said that man becomes just from the practice of justice. Nor should a man who is base, be considered worthy of honor; for honor is the reward of virtue, and is assigned to the good." (Nico. Eth. I. 7, 16; II. 4, 5; IV. 3, 15.) But, unlike this rational teaching of Aristotle, the doctrine of salvation by faith, so prominent in preaching, teaches that the dying thief or murderer may by one act of faith be as worthy of entering into the heaven of heavens, as the most virtuous soul who has labored all his days to do good, and refrain from evil. More than this: it says that such thief or murderer may, by trusting in another's righteousness, receive the reward of eternal life; whereas the morally pure and noble-minded, by trusting in his own righteousness and not in another's, will be adjudged worthy of eternal damnation. The murderer or the vicious-minded cries to God, as such naturally would, for forgiveness; and looking to Christ's merit, he no sooner cries than, washed in the blood of the Lamb, he is made as white as snow, and fit for his heavenly home. But the murdered, cut off without warning, falls into outer darkness, where there shall be weeping and wailing and gnashing of teeth, to rise no more forever out of his deep, dark dungeon of pain and woe. Reason tells us that character should be the only test of moral worth, this doctrine denies it; reason tells us that purity of soul can only be attained to by long and persistent effort after the good; this doctrine holds it can be attained, without money and without price, in a moment, in the twinkling of an eye, even by one faithful look at the cross of Christ. Reason assures us that every man should be rewarded according to his own deeds; this doctrine teaches that man will receive the highest reward the Infinite One can bestow, not because of his own good deeds, but for the sake of those of another. Cicero teaches that *eudaimonia* or *beata vita* (true happiness) is the direct result of one's own virtuous actions; but this doctrine teaches that the *beata vita* of Christ, which naturally resulted to him from his own beautiful and virtuous life, may be miraculously mine by imputation, no matter how degrading my life may have been; that is, it teaches that the shadow may exist apart from the substance. As well might we teach the existence of a child without a parent, or of a product without its factors. Merton could not accept such a ruinous doctrine. He believed, as he should, that no man can be saved in this world, and, therefore, in no other, by any righteousness excepting his own. This righteousness, Merton felt certain, is produced by doing well from noble motives. He could not help accepting the teachings of Aristotle, which is simply the teaching of common-sense; on the other hand, he could not believe in the doctrine of salvation by faith, being, as it is, contradictory to all our ideas of justice, and to natural law. He was glad, therefore, to have done with that popular form of faith which makes this doctrine so prominent in its theology, whether considered in its theoretical or practical sense.

Again, Merton could not see any justice in the doctrine of a fixed state after death. Rather was he conscious that every inference he got from life in this world, went to disprove it. There are countless hosts of men who, though they put forth strenuous efforts to lift themselves above and out of their surroundings, yet die in despair, engulfed in the immoral filth in which they were born and raised; likewise are there multitudes who, though they put forth scarcely any efforts of their own, yet because of their inherited tendencies, family relations, early associations, and education, live fairly good, moral lives, and die what are called good church-members. According to the doctrine of a fixed state after death, the former are eternally damned, while the latter are eternally blest. Now, if any man can see a particle of justice in such judgment, he must certainly look through other eyes than those of reason. Certainly there would be no justice in such decrees. If it were possible for the God of the universe thus to judge, it is certain that He, being of such character, must remain unknown to us. But such conclusion, if accepted, would make every priest in the world without means of support, and homeless. In the nature of the case, therefore, it is one which theologians will not be likely to accept; although they could not reasonably do otherwise than accept it, if the dogma of a fixed state after death be true. Because reason assures us, that such a doctrine is most unjust; and, if reason in this consideration be self-deceived, then it certainly may be in any other consideration, and, therefore, in that of God's will concerning us.

I am descended from devotional parents. Being moral and law-abiding themselves, they naturally sought to have their descendants so. It is certain, therefore, that I inherited a moral and religious nature, or tendency. I have never found it necessary to make any special efforts in order to live, what is called, a moral, or even religious life ; rather have I found that my hereditary tendencies and early teachings and example, have made it hard for me to "kick against the pricks," or not to worship the God of my fathers. I know others who, descending from notoriously immoral progenitors, and brought up in the surroundings of their birth, have lived and died, only to repeat the life and death of their progenitors. It is true, in many cases, they have longed for something better,—better food, better clothing, better associations, better thoughts ; but as the leopard can not change his spots, so they have failed to better very much their condition, and in their death have simply showed how their fore-fathers died. Now, I have no doubt whatever that many of those have made more exertion after a higher life, than some who have shone in church and society as suns ; yet, while the latter are eternally blessed for their little effort, the former are eternally damned for their strenuous but fruitless endeavor after a better life. In other words, while the one is blessed for doing what he never did; the other is damned for not doing what he could not possibly do. That the God whom I adore, could so judge, I can not, I will not, believe ; for thus believing, I should be guilty of blaspheming his most holy name.

Again, it is certain that while some are born with highly developed devotional powers, others are born with scarcely any at all. In the former case, the child is almost sure to be religious; in the latter case, almost sure not to be so. As some are born with good eyes, and become sharp-shooters, so some are born with highly developed, spiritual sight, and become leaders in the moral and spiritual world. But is it possible that a just God can blame me, because I am not a sharp-shooter, when my eyes were such from my birth, as to make it impossible for me to see well? In like manner, is it possible that a just God can damn me for not being religious, when in my very nature I lack the devotional elements? Let those who will, believe such calumny against the wise God and Father of all; I will not. Here will I stand, God helping me: though every created being in the universe be guilty of injustice, I will never believe that the Fountain of truth and life can be. Therefore I do not believe in the doctrine of a fixed state after death, because of the injustice necessarily attending it. Nor could I believe in such doctrine for the following reason: God is necessarily everywhere present, pervading and upholding all things. He is therefore present in this world. But there are no evidences of a fixed state in this life; on the contrary, all is constant change. Every sun-rise brings with it new opportunities, every sun-set carries with it lost ones. The possibilities of improvement remain throughout our life,—hope never dies. There being but one God, or one universal Mind ruling and pervading all things, it would seem most reasonable to believe that as He governs here, so He governs elsewhere; and that, therefore, since during our present life the possibilities of improvement remain with us, so throughout the life which is to come, such possibilities must continue.

The Judgment-day is not a far off event, but is ever with us, and the character of that judgment, is well and certainly known. It is far better expressed in the Theosophic doctrine of *karma* than in so-called Evangelical theology. The words of the Vedas are certainly true and just: "According as a man act, and according as he believes, so will he be: a man of good acts will become good; a man of bad acts, bad." Inasmuch as Methodism is most uncompromising in asserting the fixed nature of the future state, Merton was glad for this reason also that he had left its fold.

Having ceased to act in union with his old people, Merton's congregation invited him to preach to them independently until he should be called away, or while his duties permitted. This he did, at the same time giving especial attention to the performance of such duties as might hasten his admission, as a minister, into the Protestant Episcopal Church. The several kindly written letters, received from the bishop of that church assured him of a most hearty welcome; but he would have to receive the rites of confirmation, and ordination, before he could assume any ministerial work; for as yet he had never been ordained, not even by the church he had left; and even if he had been, such ordination is not accepted as valid by Episcopalians. It was therefore to such preparation as was required for the reception of these rites, that he gave his particular attention. It must not be supposed from what we have said, that there was any severe labor connected with Merton's entering the Protestant Episcopal Church. As far as the rite of confirmation was concerned, there was nothing for him to do but merely to receive it; and the same might almost be said with regard to his ordination, the learning required for ordination to the priesthood being but little in amount, and common in quality. Even this little is frequently greatly lessened by the bishop, who has power by canon to dispense with the examinations in Hebrew, Greek, and Latin, the only parts of the examination that could be considered at all difficult. The examinations in the ancient languages mentioned, even when fully borne, may be passed by an applicant who has but little more than an elementary knowledge of them.

Merton was not a little pained to leave some of the people of his charge; especially may this be said of the people at Budds, who had always been most attentive to all his wants, and faithful in their attendance on the services. Not one unpleasant thing ever occurred to mar his happiness; but their kindness seemed to increase the longer he preached to them. Such friends as these, it was painful to leave; but the pain was as that which precedes the joy that a child is born into the world. Although not yet fully born into the light, Merton's soul was struggling to get entirely free; and the sense of comparative freedom, with the prospect of still wider liberty, made him pour forth his soul in thanksgiving to God. As angels rolled away the stone that stopped the upward flight of Jesus, so had God removed one at least that had kept the soul of Merton shut up in sepulchral gloom. It was indeed his first resurrection.

THE SONG OF CREATION.
BY HENRY TRURO BRAY.

Shining seraphim who are watching by the tomb-imprisoned Lord,
Waiting the prophetic moment, serving the Eternal Word;
Decked with majesty and power from Jehovah's awful throne,—
Tell me, ye celestial legates, if ye've rolled away the stone.
List the glad chorus which floats on the wave:
Light is now streaming through the gloom of the grave.

Hark! the peals of jubilant heaven fill the universal deep,
Rising from th' angelic choir, surging 'neath the Eternal's feet;
Breaking all the awful stillness which pervades the dark abyss,
Filling every heart with rapture, deluging the world in bliss.
List the glad chorus which floats on the wave:
Death is made captive in his kingdom, the grave.

Hark! the tremulous, resonant harmony pulsates through cre-
 [ation's space,
Vivifying nature's being, quickening it with streams of grace.
Rushing on, the seraph-chanters thrill the globes with cadent tread,
And the sympathetic atoms vibrate deep among the dead.
List the glad chorus which floats on the wave:
Life is now throbbing in the death of the grave.

See these flashes of lightning so vivid! How the deafening thun-
 [ders roar!
Look! the hosts of heaven, prostrate, vail their faces, and adore!
Nature's soul is all attendant, conscious of these portents dread—
From the throne the voice proceedeth: Christ is risen from the dead.
Fly ye bright choristers down from on high;
Jesus is risen, and man shall not die.

CHAPTER XVI.

LOYALTY TO TRUTH.

Die Unschuld hat im Himmel einen Freund--
Innocency has in Heaven a friend.
(*Schiller: Wilhelm Tell.*)

Lines on the birth of Merton's first little daughter;

Beautiful, beautiful sky,
Decked with pearls so bright;
Palace of angels on high,
Flooded with roseate light!
Thy worlds forever in harmony roll
To the music of God who is harmony's soul.

Beautiful, beautiful earth,
Beating with life-giving love,
Bursting with laughter and mirth,
Radiant with light from above!
Thy lawns and thy bowers, entrancingly sweet,
Are a temple of God where we kneel at His feet.

Beautiful, beautiful child,
Light that scatters our gloom;
Cheerful and trustful and mild,
Emblem of life from the tomb!
May angels to thee as guardians be given,
Directing and guiding thy footsteps to heaven.

(H. T. B.)

It was only five months after having left his old associations, when Merton was ordained to the ministry of the Protestant Episcopal Church. He loved the pulpit as the place where reason, as a flower, should scatter its perfume, and display its beauty.

Merton was probably never entirely free from doubt. But fully believing that there is a substratum of truth in all religious teaching, and not as yet being fully convinced as to what that substratum is, or is not, and fearing lest by yielding to his doubts, he might lose the truth itself, Merton decided to keep on, ready and determined, at all times, to cast to the winds any belief that he held, as soon as he should become convinced of its falsity. While in doubt, he might hesitate to speak; but when convinced that something taught as a vital, religious principle, was only a base superstition, nothing could prevent him from asserting his convictions.

Merton believed that man is first of all, and more than all, accountable to God for the privileges of life, and that the highest privilege of life is the enjoyment of reason. It is the reason that elevates man above the brute creation; and it is by the use of reason that man determines the ways of nature and of nature's God. Through the reason, therefore, does God reveal himself; and by the use of reason does man make himself most like God. The man, therefore, who stifles his convictions, and silences the thoughts of his soul, interrupts the divine revelation, prevents the Divine Being from manifesting himself, and thus most clearly sins against God, the Holy Ghost. True it is that man, not being God, must frequently err in the use of his reason; but so is it equally true that man, being man, without the free and untramelled use of his reason, must fall to the position of a slave, lower himself to the plane of the brute, and make it impossible that he should be the subject of a virtuous thought or act.

Merton was always led by a love for the truth, conscious that by a knowledge of the truth alone could man hope to get salvation. Loyal to Truth, he could not be forced to betray her, whether by threat of ecclesiastical censure, or by conscious fear of the loss of position. Should the reader have asked, what is the truth; Merton would have answered: It is the agreement of the idea with the facts and conditions of the thing under cognition; but that man can not be held accountable for not having, at all times, correct ideas about the objects of his cognition, but only for acting according to the truth, as far as he is able to determine it. The man who does wrong, while striving to do right, is moved by a noble motive, though accomplishing no virtuous act, and such a man can not reasonably be condemned of sin against God; but the man who happens to do right, without putting forth a conscious effort to accomplish it, can not be said to have performed a virtuous act, nor to have been the subject of a noble motive. Such an act is no more virtuous or noble than the act of a dog in following its master, or of the cow in coming to her milking-place. One may, therefore, do right, and yet be a great sinner; because he may not have used his reason to determine whether the act he was about to perform, should or should not be done. Thus he hid in a napkin the greatest gift of God to man. God as God is free to act; and his action, since He is infinite, must at all times be agreeable to the truth; but man as man, being the child of God, and therefore godlike, while he also may be at all times free to act, can not act at all times agreeably to the truth, but only to his convictions, or to the truth as far as he is able to determine it. The man who is loyal to his own convictions, while in his heart at all times on the side of truth, will sometimes be found supporting an error. This follows from the fact that he is not God; it does not show a lack of goodness or virtue. On the other hand, the man who is not loyal to his own convictions, can never be called a good or virtuous man; nor can he ever really know the truth: for in the heart thus false to God and itself, nothing truly good or beautiful can take up its abode, much less truth, the supreme good of all. Nothing could make Merton false to his own convictions. This was clearly shown at the time of his ordination. While passing his examination in Systematic Theology, he boldly said that he could not accept the examiner's view of a question, and insisted on his own. The examiner thereupon appealed to the work of Pearson on the Creed. Merton replied that he was sorry for the church that Pearson had held such views, as it most clearly proved to his mind the author's ignorance of almost the first principles of science; that however high Pearson might stand in the estimation of churchmen, he himself could not accept his conclusions on the subject in question. The examiner then replied that Merton's view was heretical. To this charge Merton answered, that if his views were heretical, so much the worse for the church; that if they ordained him, they would be obliged to ordain a heretic, since he would not change his view of the matter for Pearson or any number of Pearsons, unless they were able to prove, to his satisfaction, that he was in error.

"Allow me to call the bishop, Mr. Merton, that we may have his opinion on the question," said the examiner.

The bishop having been asked the question, answered precisely as Merton had.

"But, bishop," said the examiner, "you are certainly wrong; for Pearson holds that such a view is heretical."

"What does Pearson say?" asked the bishop.

The examiner then took Pearson, and slowly read his views, whereupon the bishop said:

"All right; I stand corrected. I presume neither Mr. Merton nor myself wishes to be at war with good old Pearson, who has weathered so many storms. I take him to be a very good navigator in these perilous times."

"Well, bishop," replied Merton, "I do not know whether I am really right or not; but I do know that a man should think too much of his own opinion to change it, simply because Pearson, who was but a man like other men, teaches the contrary. He gives me no sufficient reason, in what he says, for abjuring my view and adopting his. If I am heretical, it is better that it should be known, and that I should now know it, that I may stop before it is too late. I can not change my view of the question simply to conform to those of Pearson, nor for anything less than sufficient reasons; and these have not been adduced."

"It is not a matter of such great importance," said the bishop; "I presume differences do no harm in the long run. They only serve to stir us up a little."

"I can't think it right, bishop," said the examiner, "to give it up in this way. Mr. Merton should certainly know that Pearson is with us a standard work; and that men who come to us, are expected to conform to the standards in use among us. I myself feel like protesting against such freedom."

"Tisn't a very vital matter," replied the bishop. "It may be Mr. Merton will come over to Pearson's side yet; I think he will at least."

"It may not be a very vital matter," answered the examiner; "and I presume it is not. Yet I insist that no one should be ordained in our church who cannot heartily assent to the teachings of such standard writers as Pearson."

"Did you yourself never have a doubt in your heart about many matters that by some would be called essentials of the faith?" asked the bishop. "I do not know that I am called upon to answer such questions," replied the examiner. "One thing sure, if I have had such doubt, nobody has ever heard me express it; and what isn't expressed, can't do much mischief. There's an old saying that a sin unrevealed is half forgiven; and there's much of truth in this. A heresy unexpressed will not have the effect of drawing honest souls away from the truth." "I differ with you totally, sir," replied Merton. "If one thing be more detestable than another, that which is the most detestable of all, is a man who believes in his heart one thing, and teaches another. Nor is the man much better whose heart is eaten with doubt, when he declares that it is the temple of certainty. If I had, as you say you have had, doubt about the truth of what I preached, I would either state that doubt, or I would refuse to preach on that subject. Not to do this, would be to deceive my hearers, and debase my own consciousness. Let me be ten-thousand heretics rather than one deceiver. But I fear the pulpits are full of men who do just as, we infer from what you say, you have done."

"I don't think," said the examiner, "that I have given you any right to make any inferences whatever. If you choose to make such inference, you have the liberty of doing so."

"I must say," replied the bishop, "one would naturally make such inference from what you have said. But let us hear no more about this matter. If it were a vital question, I should hesitate to proceed any further, before getting Mr. Merton's assent to it; but it is not. It is impossible to get all men to be of the same mind. If Mr. Merton determines to adhere to his opinion of the matter, I shall not make it a reason for refusing ordination. I do not think his view can justly be considered heretical."

"All right, bishop," replied the examiner; "I am willing to be governed by you in the case; but it does appear to me that according to Pearson, it is an heretical view."

CHAPTER XVII.

THE CALL OF DUTY.

This above all,—To thine own self be true;
And it must follow, as the night the day,
Thou canst not then be false to any man.

(*Shakspere.*)

Merton had now been settled for some time as the minister of a very nice congregation, in one of the southern states. The parish had been in a declining state for several years; and at the time of Merton's coming into it, it was thought to be almost beyond recovery. But Merton's zeal became everywhere manifest, in the Sunday school, in the pulpit, and in his pastoral visits.

In the pulpit he seemed on fire with the intense earnestness of his soul. No one could doubt his sincerity: he preached most to himself; and when thus preaching, he appeared to convince himself of the truth of the cause he was so earnestly pleading; and in convincing himself, he convinced his hearers. His congregation grew, his people loved, trusted, almost worshiped him. But as the "gods do not give man all things at once," such peace and prosperity were too much for one man to enjoy. The cup for man's bliss, in this world, though shallow, is scarcely ever filled; but his cup for misery, though deep, is frequently running over. But Merton's people were apparently trying to fill his cup with bliss. They were working in harmony; they attended faithfully on the services of the church; they rejoiced at his presence in the pulpit, and in their homes; and they ministered gladly to all his wants. While day by day they thus increased the contents of his cup of bliss, they added nothing to his cup of misery, but sought to take from it the little it contained. They were a generous, whole-souled, noble people; and Merton loved them as if his own.

It was a hot, sultry climate; the atmosphere acted on one like a steam-bath; and Merton had been accustomed to a northern temperature. The fact that he was not as yet fully acclimated, exposed him to various prevailing diseases; and his extraordinary labors weakened his system, making him still less capable of resisting disease.

Finally all the premonitory symptoms of yellow fever came upon him; pains in the back and limbs, yellowness of the skin and eyes, and supraorbital headache; yet he would not desist from his labors until compelled for the lack of strength to stand. After a sickness of about ten days, he again was able to move around; but so great was his weakness that the people pressed him to take a vacation, and go north for two months to recuperate.

On the day of his leaving, it was everywhere known that yellow fever was in the city; and the physician who attended Merton after coming north, insisted that he had had the disease; and of the truth of this physician's diagnosis, neither Merton, nor those who saw him, had any doubt whatever.

From a loving mother, faithful brother, and a most devoted wife, Merton received every possible care; and he himself made use of every means calculated to aid in the restoration of his health. But with all the care and attention he received, it was nevertheless at least two months before any degree of health and strength returned. Even then he was pale, weak and emaciated; but he felt more cheerful, a little stronger, and on a fair road to recovery.

At this time he wrote to his vestry, telling them of his condition, and offering to return immediately, if they were in need of his presence. To this letter the wardens replied, begging him not to return. "It would be madness in you," they wrote, "to return to this place, at the present time. Your presence would only add fuel to the flame, as you have not yet been fully acclimated. Don't come back under any circumstances. All your people that could get away, have left the town."

Weak and broken as he was, Merton would have returned to the town in a moment, when the yellow scourge was at its height, had the wardens or his people expressed the least wish for his presence; but they earnestly advised him not to return. They being on the ground, and being well acquainted with all the attending circumstances, should know better than Merton what was needed, and what he should do; and Merton therefore properly enough determined to act according to their judgment. Now there happened to be a clergyman in the South, free from danger himself, who for certain reasons was an inveterate enemy to Merton. This man took it upon himself to force Merton to return. Merton informed him that he held himself, weak as he was, subject to the call of the people. Such information was not enough for this clergyman, who, it would appear, would not have gone into mourning, in case of Merton's death. Finally he plotted against Merton with the bishop; and being an old acquaintance of this clergyman, the bishop was led to side with him, and thus became an enemy to Merton, even taking away the small appropriation that had been given him to assist in building the parish up, thus making it impossible for Merton to go back, even when sufficient strength returned. Dear as this people and minister were to each other, they were driven asunder by the machinations of an evil-hearted clergyman. Merton was always ready to go where duty called him; but he was not such as could be forced by an enemy into doing anything against his will. Had the members of his congregation expressed any desire for his presence, he undoubtedly would have gone back immediately, on the very wings of love, although it would, in all probability, have cost him his life. But we do not mean by this that he would have thought it wise to return. We mean that he would have laid down his life rather than that his people should ask for his presence in vain, or think of him as being afraid of the disease. But as he did not think it, as no one should, a sign of bravery to sacrifice one's life, where duty does not call; he obeyed the advice of his people, rather than the dictation of his enemies. If the belief were true, that the prayers of a minister at the dying bed, or the reception of a sacrament by the dying, could materially affect the future of the soul, then there would be no question but that, weak as he was, Merton should have gone back, even against the expressed wish of his people; but such belief he did not and could not accept; nor did he believe that any enlightened and unprejudiced mind can. He never had any faith in death-bed repentance; and he fully believed that one good nurse was worth any number of praying priests, at the bedside of a sick man. That the mercy of God is conditioned on the prayers of a minister, or heaven opened by the power of the church, he considered not only an absurd but a blasphemous claim. Thus believing, the only use, in his judgment, he could be to the sick, would be to act as a nurse; and knowing that his weakness and inexperience rendered him unfit to act in that capacity, he concluded it wise to accept the advice of competent men who warned him not to return; and to stay where his life, in all probability, would be spared as a blessing to those most dear to him, and dependent on his exertions. And although, as he afterwards learned, the bishop of the diocese was not pleased at his decision, he doubted not that any sane and unprejudiced man would have approved his course. The bishop was by nature kind-hearted and most affable; but he was now very old, and so weak-minded that, influenced as we have said, he was easily led to act detrimentally to Merton's interests.

Where duty calls one, there should he always be found, serving God and humanity. Thus performing our part, danger may surround, and threaten us on every side; but greater is the danger that must ever threaten him who shuns the performance of his duty. In the former case, while the death of the body is at most only contingent, the life of the soul is certain, because discharging one's duty ennobles the nature, and tends to the elevation of the whole race; but in the latter case, while the life of the body is probable, the death of the soul is inevitable, because the wilful avoidance of one's duty, debases the higher nature, and tends to the degradation of humanity. The preservation of the body at such a cost, is vastly too expensive. Here it is certainly true: He that would lose his life, shall save it; and he that would save his life, shall lose it. Nevertheless, the body is no less the work of God than is the soul, though the office of the former is considered less noble than that of the latter. It is, therefore, a very grave sin to wilfully destroy the body, or injure any of its members. And even where one's actions unintentionally result in the death of the body, great sin must be incurred, if such result should have been prevented by the proper use of reason. Many a man has been given, especially by the press, the death of a hero; when wisdom assures us, it was the death of a fool. The noble nature shuns no danger that ought to be encountered, and runs into no danger that ought not to be faced. Where duty had called Merton, there he never knew what it was to be afraid; but he always thought it most unwise, if not sinful, to rush unreasonably into danger. Says Aristotle, than whom probably no nobler person ever lived, and whose wisdom has, perhaps, never been equalled:

"Ὥστ᾽ ἐπεὶ ἡ ἀνδρεία ἐστὶν ἡ βελτίστη ἕξις περὶ φόβους καὶ θάρρη, δεῖ δὲ μήθ᾽ οὕτως ὡς οἱ θρασεῖς μήθ᾽ οὕτως ὡς οἱ δειλοί δῆλον ὡς ἡ μέση διάθεσις θρασύτητος καὶ δειλίας ἐστὶν ἀνδρεία . . . .
Ἡ γὰρ ἀνδρεία ἀκολούθησις τῷ λόγῳ ἐστίν, ὁ δὲ λόγος τὸ καλὸν

αἱρεῖσθαι κελεύει. Διὸ καὶ 'ὁ μὴ διὰ τοῦτον ὑπομένων αὐτά, οὗτος ἤτοι ἐξέστηκεν ἢ θρασύς. Ὁ μὲν οὖν δειλὸς καὶ ἃ μὴ δεῖ φοβεῖται, ὁ δὲ θρασὺς καὶ ἃ μὴ δεῖ θαρρεῖ· ὁ δ' ἀνδρεῖος ἀμφω ἃ δεῖ, καὶ ταύτῃ μέσος ἐστίν. Ἃ γὰρ ἂν ὁ λόγος κελεύῃ, ταῦτα καὶ θαρρεῖ καὶ φοβεῖται — Since true manliness is the best state in relation to fear and rashness, and since it is necessary that the truly brave should be neither such as the rash man is nor such as is the coward, it is evident that the middle state between rashness and cowardice, is true manliness. True bravery is obedience to the reason, and reason bids us strive for that which is noble. Therefore, he who, when surrounded by danger, is not guided by reason, is either cowardly or rash. The coward fears where he should not, and the rash man is fearless where he should not be. But the truly brave acts in both instances as he should, and, therefore, fills the middle position; for he is both fearless and fearful as reason directs him." (Eud. Eth. III, 1, [3-4, 10-12.])

As far as the fear of death has affected me, I have often longed to die, to escape, as it were, from a prison, and to see if perchance there be something better in store for me; no less than to be forever free from a world, where the insincere and the pretentious are received with the plaudits of the crowd, while the candid and truly learned seek in vain for recognition. It can not be doubted that humanity is as greatly deceived, as it is given to deception. Mankind likes flattery, and to be made the heir of great expectations. It is this in man that offers such great opportunities to the hypocritical, the insincere and the pretentious, whether in the pulpit or elsewhere; it is this that gives the holy knave and the rascally politician such open fields to reap their golden harvests. But longed as I have to die, reason bids me wait my time; to be brave, sincere and true, no less for my own sake than as an example to others. I wonder not, however, at people committing suicide; for it takes a brave man to withstand the many evils to which more especially the good are frequently subjected; the less brave, becoming disheartened, seek rest in death. As Agathon says:

"Φαῦλοι βροτῶν γὰρ τοῦ πονεῖν ἡσσώμενοι

θανεῖν ἐρῶσιν—Base mortals, being worsted in the conflict of life, prefer to die."

But the truly brave will abide his time, doing as best he can, whatever his hands may find to do; showing a noble example of patience and suffering to his own and to others, hoping thereby to ennoble his own character, and to elevate the race. He will not sacrifice his life nor jeopardize it, except for noble and worthy ends; but where the voice of reason calls him, there, if it be proper, he is willing to yield his life into the hands of Him who gave it. It was in this spirit that Merton acted with reference to his work in the South. The act of the bishop, however, in withdrawing from the parish its appropriation, was designed to make it impossible for Merton to be supported. After waiting several months to see if the bishop would not relent, Merton sent the secretary of the vestry his resignation, to take immediate effect, thus severing all relations with the parish he could not fail to like, and with a people he could not fail to love. If ten thousand lives were given him, and the use of ten thousand tongues, yet he would not forget their kindness, nor cease to speak of them with gratitude and love.

It was a short time after his resignation, that Merton received the following letter from one of the principal communicants:

"My dear Friend;—I must write you to express my distress at the news of your resignation of the charge of our Church. I have seen nearly all the people, and they express the greatest regret and distress; and all are resolved to accept nobody else. We need you so much,—indeed I can not reconcile myself to the idea of your never coming back. Will you not come back to us? All are so much distressed at your not returning. Can you not be induced to come back? Why should you care for what any one else might do or say, when all of us want you. Do say you will come back. I can not express to you the disappointment of your people."

"Your friend, M. C."

To answer in the affirmative was impossible. The barriers an unkind bishop had set up, were too high for Merton to surmount. At this uncalled-for act of the bishop, Merton could not help deeply grieving; but in those periods of deep despondency, his wife would buoy him up; and no man could have long despaired, with such a source of life and strength so near at hand.

Ich sprach zur Sonne: "Sprich, was ist die Liebe?"
Sie gab nicht Antwort, gab nur goldnes Licht.
Ich sprach zur Blume: "Sprich, was ist die Liebe?"
Sie gab mir Duefte, doch die Antwort nicht.

Ich sprach zum Ew'gen: "Sprich, was ist die Liebe?"
Ist's heil'ger Ernst? ist's suesse Taendelei?"
Da gab mir Gott ein Weib, ein treues, liebes,
Und nimmer fracht' ich was die Liebe sei.
(*Ritterhaus.*)

CHAPTER XVIII.

CLERICAL SKEPTICISM.

Wisdom from above is pure and without hypocrisy.
(*St. James.*)

MERTON now obtained a parish in another state. He had met the bishop, who pressed him to take work in his diocese. "Stay with me, Mr. Merton," he said: "I believe you are the very man I have been looking for. It seems to me God has sent you to me. I will make everything for you as pleasant as I possibly can. I treat my clergy well. I try to act to them as a father, and wish them to treat me as such. Their happiness is mine, and I make it a rule never to betray their confidence. If you stay with me, I think you will not regret it. We have a flourishing state, and the church work of the diocese is in a flourishing condition. Men and money are all that's wanted. Help me build up this great work."

The bishop appeared so affable, and spoke so kindly, that Merton resolved to accept his invitation; and immediately took work under him.

He had not been long in the diocese, before he met a clergyman who was rector of a neighboring parish, when the following conversation took place:

"Well, Mr. Merton, how do you like your present position?"

"I am very well pleased with it," replied Merton. "You, I believe, have been in this diocese a great many years. From what diocese did you come?"

"I came from Pennsylvania here; but I heartily wish I had never left that state."

"Why?" asked Merton. "You have a good parish, and a loyal people. On the whole, it seems to me, you should be quite a happy man."

"Happiness, Mr. Merton, is a word. As an existing state, it is rarely, and perhaps never, found. For my part, I no longer hope to attain to such a state of mind."

"I do not know, sir," answered Merton; "but it seems to me that a man filling the position you fill, should not only have the hope of being happy, but even the present experience of happiness."

"I know, Mr. Merton," replied the clergyman, "that it is much to say I have lost hope; but I have had great discouragement. When I came here, the bishop made me great promises. I was at first the chief minister in this diocese, and the bishop's right-hand man. I was made the head of all the educational institutions; and the bishop sought to advance my interests. Things were soon changed. The large institution over which I presided, burned to the ground; and there are not wanting those who believe that the bishop burned it. One thing is certain: at the time of the destruction of the institution, there had been in it, for several days, an emissary of the bishop. This fact made out a strong case against the bishop, inasmuch as he was known to be opposed to the site of the institution; and the further fact that he afterwards used all his powers to remove the centre of educational work, and finally succeeded in doing it, almost made the case complete against him. I do not say much about it myself; but I am sure that the people of my parish believe the bishop was a party to the burning up of my institution."

"It is a very grave charge even to suspect one of doing," replied Merton. "The bishop has been very gracious to me; and I hope we shall be good friends. I am sorry that you have been disappointed in your hopes; but all of us are more or less."

"Disappointed, Mr. Merton, is hardly a name for it. I have

been grieved, hurt, deeply wounded, at my treatment. I have a thousand times wished I had never seen the diocese. It has so discouraged me that I am almost unfit for any work. I tell you, between the worry and duties of a parish minister, and the mischief-working power of a jealous and unfriendly bishop, there is little chance of rest or peace; as for happiness, it is simply out of the question."

"Even with all your trouble," replied Merton, "you have the satisfaction that you are doing God's work, and of having upon you his promised blessing. After all, that is more than all else."

"You are but young as yet in the work, Mr. Merton. Things will not look as green to you sometime in the future, as now. Experience brings great changes over man's heart and mind."

"I presume you are right as to that. Even in my own case, I am conscious of very great changes that have passed over me, within the last few years. Only a dead man is not subject to change. But granting that, yet it still is true, that no work is so noble, as that of trying to lift up fallen humanity."

"Fallen humanity! Mr. Merton, what do you mean by such language? Do you mean to say that you believe in what is called the fall of man?"

"No, sir; not as generally understood. I could not think of believing that by one man's sin, all mankind fell; that Adam is the trunk, and we the branches. The doctrine of evolution, now universally received in some form or other, has shown that such a belief is absurd. But I do believe that we all have come short of the glory of God; and that humanity, as a whole, is in great need of holy examples, and fearless and scholarly instructors who may lift them up, by pointing them out the way to a holier and better life."

"That is acceptable doctrine, Mr. Merton. I feared you

believed that humanity had fallen into some big ditch or other, dug by the theologians of days gone by. I am glad you have graduated out of such crudity. It is a noble work, I confess, to be engaged in raising mankind up into a higher life; but much of the pleasure derived from such activity, is embittered by the sense of having all around us scheming priests and plotting bishops. Indeed, I have often wished I had never seen the ministry, nor put on a surplice."

"I can not exactly understand you;" said Merton. "I am glad I am a minister. I think no work gives such blessed fruits, and that no life can be so well spent, as that of a faithful minister of God."

"I think you are exaggerating, Mr. Merton, the value of ministerial labors; but that is quite natural. For myself I doubt not that I could have done more good in the world, had I chosen exclusively educational work; nor do I think the rewards of such labor are second to any."

"The works of the mind and its education are truly excellent," replied Merton; "but surely the work and education of the soul are vastly superior. The minister has to do with educating the soul, while the teacher has to do with the intellect only."

"You forget, Mr. Merton, that the minister, nine times out of ten, deals with, and speaks of, only unknown quantities; while the teacher has to do only with known realities. The foundations of priestly labors are based on faith: knowledge is beyond his sphere. You remember the words of Tennyson:

> 'We have but faith: we can not know;
> For knowledge is of things we see;
> And yet we trust it comes from thee,
> A beam in darkness: let it grow.'

On the other hand, the work of the teacher is based upon experimental facts. The work of the former is of some other world, heavenly, but of which nothing whatever is certainly known; while the work of the latter is of this world, earthly, and therefore fully comprehended. I think on the whole, Mr. Merton, putting the value of the work with the certainty of the instruction, that the teacher's position is the more desirable. I certainly wish that I had given my life to the work of teaching. No work can be more divine than that of training youthful minds; no building more divine than that which is given to such noble work. I always feel more of the Holy Ghost when inculcating the truths of science, than when reading many of those nice-sounding, unsubstantiated, and incredible platitudes of the prayerbook."

"The prayerbook," replied Merton, "may contain many things hard to believe, and harder still to understand; but there is surely a vast difference between a place where mental instruction is given and a church where God Almighty is worshiped and glorified. The school is built by man; the church is built by God."

"You are now giving us a little more of unsubstantiated doctrine, Mr. Merton. A building is nothing of itself,—neither holy nor unholy. It is the work done within the building that gives character to it; and, as I said before, there can be no higher work than that of training youthful minds. Therefore the school-building is as much a temple built by God, as is the cathedral. The church is an institution founded and continued in the world by good-minded men, for the purpose of doing good. This is the most that can be said for it. It is divine so far as its work is divine, and no farther. I am sure that very much of church work is anything else than divine. I must reassert what I have already said: there is no nobler or diviner work than that of the teacher. I hope, however, you may always be as zealous and hopeful, as at present. Nevertheless, I fear that a few more years of active service, in church work, will have a tendency to change your views.

You will find that there is something more than a naughty world to deal with; you will find some naughty brethren; and perhaps you may find the latter worse foes than the former."

"I hope," said Merton, "that your fears may never be realized by me; and that you may yet rejoice that you never chose teaching as a profession. Your life has, in some things, been a disappointment; so your rejoicing may, in God's own time, be unexpectedly great."

"Thank you, Mr. Merton. Before we part, allow me to say that what I have said to you, I have said in confidence. I would not speak to every one as I have spoken to you. Please, do not mention my name in connection with the substance of our conversation. It would do no good; it might do much harm."

Having promised not to mention his name in connection with the matter of conversation, Merton bade him good-night; but he could not help thinking, how greatly disagree the heart and countenance of the average pulpit orator. Hypocrisy is always and ever bad; but its evil is proportionate to the greatness of the subject in the treatment of which man professes to be what he is not. It is difficult to conceal the truth in any case; most of all, in religious matters. In the words of Emerson: "Who is the better for the philosopher who conceals his accomplishments, and hides his thoughts from the waiting world? Hides his thoughts! Hide the sun and moon. Thought is all light, and publishes itself to the universe. It will speak, though you were dumb, by its own miraculous organ. It will flow out of your actions, your manners, and your face."

Many as the beauties are that may, as the result of persistent efforts, adorn the soul of man; no accomplishments or mental possessions can ever outrank sincerity and truthfulness.

CHAPTER XIX.

WORDS AND WORKS.

Justitiae partes sunt non violare homines, verecundiae non offendere—
Not to wrong man, nor offend modesty are principles of justice.
(*Cicero.*)

IT was at the diocesan convention. All the clergy, with the bishop at their head, were met together to consider the matters pertaining to the welfare of the church.

After a good deal of clerical electioneering, and maneuvering, which might well have excited the admiration of the most astute politician, so skilfully is the slate prepared, and with such tactics are the favorites elected, all the dirty and rusty machinery being at the same time carefully oiled with spiritual unction, that as little friction as possible may be created, the various committees were appointed, and the officers and delegates elected, and things shaped in accordance with the determination of the ruling majority, with the exception, perhaps, of those matters over which the bishop himself had exclusive regulation. It was then that the committee of which Merton was a member, was asked to meet, in the evening, in a room, at the residence of the bishop of the diocese. There was at the time a friend visiting Merton, who was most refined in manners, most gentlemanly in appearance, very scholarly, and one of the most skilful physicians and surgeons in the land. This gentleman had been brought up a Quaker; but was then what is generally called an unbeliever. Merton was very desirous of bringing his friend into the church; and thought it would be wise to introduce him to the bishop. To this end he invited the gentleman to accompany him, on the evening in question, to the bishop's residence, knowing that the bishop would be there, and that there would be a good opportunity for introduction and conversation. The gentleman readily consented; for he expected a pleasant time with the bishop, who was fat enough for a jolly, good-natured prelate.

The members of the committee being hard at work preparing the reports, Merton was obliged to leave his friend in the care of the bishop; and he hoped that by such intercourse with the head of the diocese, his friend might be influenced to come into the church.

The bishop sat in a large, easy chair, smoking a cigar, and having his feet elevated high upon the back of another chair. While in this position, the bishop was guilty of conduct which is everywhere regarded as indicative of the lowest vulgarity. Every one was astonished; and Merton felt as if he should cry for the rocks and hills to fall on him, that he might be hidden from the gaze of his friend, who appeared filled with righteous indignation.

The work of the committee having been finished, Merton leaving the residence of the bishop, passed into the open air, in company with his friend. No sooner had they gained the street, than his friend exclaimed: "Great God! Is that your bishop! By Jove! he beats a cow-boy. That beats all I have ever heard, or conceived of, in my life. Solomon says there is nothing new under the sun, and he is supposed to have been a wise man; but he little knew of the many inventions of this wonderful age; he never was introduced to the head of this diocese. Your bishop should have been sent to the World's Fair; even now he would make a fine addition to Barnum's museum, if the monkeys didn't expel him. After this my faith in evolution will be greatly increased; for I swear no monkey living in the days of Solomon, could be guilty of such conduct, and yet remain in simian society; and if to-day it should be, its fellows would beat its brains out with a cocoanut shell."

"My dear doctor," said Merton, "I am no less shocked than you. While I never thought the bishop a very refined or very polite gentleman, I have had no cause for supposing he was insulting. It may be we should consider the act wholly unpremeditated."

"Nonsense, Mr. Merton; you know better."

"Well, doctor," said Merton, "let that pass; and in order to restore your usual equanimity, I will tell you something ridiculous indeed."

"If you have anything of that kind, Mr. Merton, let us have it. Perhaps I can laugh myself out of the rage I am in."

"One morning," continued Merton, "when I was rector of St. Peters, Lowton, I heard a knock at the door. On opening it, I saw a clerically dressed gentleman holding a valise in his hands. He appeared a stranger to me, and to have a wild, almost insane look about his eyes."

" 'Good morning, sir,' he said. 'This is the Rev. Mr. Merton, I believe. I am just coming from the mountains. Please excuse the absence of my clerical tie. I really had no time to make my toilet.'

" 'Are you a minister of an Episcopal church there?' I asked.

" 'Yes, sir. Don't you remember me, Mr. Merton? I am surprised. Some people are that way. They don't remember names nor faces. I may forget a name, but I never forget a face. I think the faculty of remembering names and faces one of the most useful to man; but, of course, I readily excuse you, as we were never very well acquainted. Still, I think it a duty devolving on the profession, to study how best to remember names. Don't you think so, Mr. Merton?'

" 'Yes, sir,' I replied. 'I certainly would like to remember names better than I do; however, I recognize your countenance. I have seen you somewhere; where I know not.'

" 'O, Mr. Merton,' he said, 'how very forgetful! I am

the Rev. Mr. Insanitas who was present at your ordination to the priesthood.'

" 'Excuse me, Mr. Insanitas,' I replied, ' I had forgotten your appearance ; however, I remember you now. Come in, sir, and take dinner with us. It is almost dinner hour.'

" 'Now I am in your study, Merton', he said, ' perhaps you would like to know, why I am here. I will tell you. A few days ago I left the little cabin where I live by myself, and went out calling. About half-past three or four o'clock, I called on Mrs. So-and-so, who, as usual, received me very politely. Almost unconsciously the time passed away ; and the hour for tea having arrived, I was invited to take tea with her. As Mr. So-and-so was absent in the mountains, and would not return for some days, I thought it would be a favor to the lady, should I prolong my visit a little. So after tea we sat down, and talked about the affairs of the church until eight o'clock. I then felt a chill coming over me, and expressed my fears to the lady, saying I wished I could lie down a few minutes. She invited me to rest on the lounge, and gave me a shawl to cover myself with. I did so, and the rest and warmth seemed to help me. While thus resting, she told me it was nine o'clock, but that I had no need to hurry, unless I felt able to go. I told her I would leave in a few minutes. Before I knew it, I was fast asleep, and did not awake again before half-past ten, when, to my surprise, I discovered the lady had left the house. The next day it was rumored abroad in the village, that the Rev. Insanitas had gone to the house of Mrs. So-and-so, in the absence of her husband, and taken tea with her, and stayed until very late at night ; that when she desired him to leave, he didn't take the hint ; that finally she went across the road, and asked a neighbor to come over, and put him out of the house ; and that the gentleman replied, that Mr. Insanitas might go to the devil for all he cared ; that he would have nothing to do with such a crazy lunatic. The next morning every kind of disgraceful thing was said; and in two or three days, reports of tarring and feathering me were current all over the place. Knowing the state of things, I packed my valise, and left. Now, really, if a woman should have come into my cabin, I would have gone through the window, if not through the door, in a minute. I really despise the sex; and I swear I'll do the work no more, which brings me in constant intercourse with them. Preaching I like well enough; but pastoral work I do despise, and I'll do it no more.'

"What do you think of that, doctor? I told Mr. Insanitas, I was very sorry to know that he was so much persecuted; that my experience with the female sex was just opposite to his; that I had always found the women my trustworthy friends; that I had great pleasure in visiting them; and that the pastoral work of the ministry was very delightful to me."

"Well, Merton," replied the doctor, "I think Mr. Insanitas as you call him, is a fit subject for the lunatic asylum, as your bishop is for the menagerie."

"My dear doctor, if one thing more than another tempts me to quit the work of the ministry, it is the knowledge of the inferior manhood which enters it."

"It is rather late for you to know that, Merton; I supposed it was a fact known to all. It has been known to me all my life. Of course a man will find exceptions; but the rule is that a man who possesses brains, will go where he can use it, and not where, in the very nature of things, it must become as stagnant water."

"But, doctor, I think the pulpit should be the very field of labor where the profoundest and highest mind could accomplish the most for himself and others."

"I'll admit, Merton, that it should be; but I deny that

it is. In proof of this, I think we have seen and heard enough to-night in the person of your bishop."

To this reply Merton could make no answer; and he feared greatly that the example of his bishop had no tendency to hasten the time when his friend should enter into the active service of the church.

Some time after this, at another diocesan convention, Merton was invited to preach for one of the clerical delegates. It was communion-day, and Merton was assisting in the celebration. When the time had come for the consecration of the elements, all the congregation left the building, with the exception of six or eight. Notwithstanding this fact, Merton saw that the clergyman poured out wine enough for at least twenty communicants. In a few minutes all had communed; but as yet much of the so-called element, representing the blood of Christ, remained unspent, and a little of the element representing the body. Some were therefore invited forward again, and once more they partook of the bread; but no wine was offered them. Merton also received a second time of the bread, but not of the wine. Merton was on his knees, reverently worshipping God, when the celebrant, taking the chalice in his hand, gulped down the wine, as a drunken Dutchman drinks his lager. Merton really thought that the clergyman would choke himself; but he was too well accustomed to strong drink, as was afterwards discovered.

A person might charitably think that it was simply a mistake with the celebrant, to consecrate so much wine; but not so. Before consecration he had counted the number of communicants remaining; and besides he did not make the same mistake in consecrating the bread: for of this but little remained after all had partaken the first time. To make it still worse, the celebrant had no sooner entered the vestry, than he deliberately took the vessel in which the communion wine was kept, and drank more, at the same time offering it to Merton, who refused. On the way to the clergyman's residence, where Merton had been invited to dine, they passed a beer-saloon, into which the clergyman invited Merton to enter to drink a glass of ale. Two or three days before the celebration mentioned above, while at the convention, at a reception given at the bishop's residence, this same clergyman, being alone with Merton, drew from an inside pocket a bottle, saying: "Take a little, Merton. It is some fine old Irish whiskey."

Merton thanked the gentleman, but declined to partake.

When speaking of these occurrences, in his own home, Merton said, "Oh, my wife, I was shocked at such irreverence, and disgusted at such indecency. That such men can call themselves messengers of the Most High, is enough to make the blood of a noble man run cold."

"I sometimes think, Harry," she replied, "that it is a good thing people do not see the hearts of men who stand in the pulpits. I fear, if they did, the cry, 'exeant sacerdotes,' would soon go forth."

Similar instances of such clerical deportment and irreverence, as have been given in this chapter, might be indefinitely multiplied. But let it suffice to say that we have only given what we thought necessary, to place before the thoughtful reader another factor in the development of the soul-life of Henry Merton; another proof that much dogma may be believed, while little reason is exhibited.

CHAPTER XX.

DISHONORABLE CONDUCT.

Fundamentum justitiae est fides, id est dictorum conventorumque constantia et veritas.

The fundamental principle of justice is faith, which means constancy and truth with reference to our words and engagements.

(*Cicero.*)

THERE is certainly nothing in man so worthy of praise, or so much to be desired, as a proper sense of honor, or the possession of what is rightly called high-mindedness. Honor first of all has reference to the keeping of one's word. "*Turpe est fidem violare,*" is an old proverb; and it is undoubtedly true that in the keeping of his word, the honorable man is most distinguishable from the dishonorable. Another characteristic of honor or high-mindedness, is the desire to confer benefits and not to receive them. The noble soul will suffer much rather than humiliate himself by asking favors; while at the same time, his great desire is to scatter blessings as he goes. In the conferring of benefits, there results a feeling of pleasure; while in the receiving of benefits, although good may sometimes thus be accomplished, there results, in the noble heart, a sense of shame. The noble nature, therefore, is especially distinguishable from the ignoble by the possession of these two virtues—the keeping of his word, and the conferring of benefits. There are no virtues so useful to man as these two. In all our business relations, in all our social intercourse, these virtues leave their blessings; while their absence leaves its curse.

Now, as no position in life should be thought more elevated than that of the priest, it follows that no man should possess these virtues to a higher degree than he. But Merton discovered to his sorrow that either from a lack of these virtues, or through wickedness in wilfully transgressing the obligations arising from their possession, for the sake of gain or pleasure, priests are frequently found who give but little evidence of possessing any such virtue as high-mindedness or honor.

It was a beautiful morning, and Merton was at his studies, trying to reconcile, however vainly, dogma and reason, when a gentleman came unexpectedly into his room, having opened the door without knocking, or giving any warning of his approach.

"Hello! This is the Rev. Merton, I believe. I am Dean Megalauchus. I am on a fishing excursion, and thought it a good time to make your acquaintance. Those delivering the faith once given to the saints, and living so near one another, can benefit sometimes by interchanging ideas."

"My own experience, Mr. Megalauchus," replied Merton, "has convinced me that there is little interchange of ideas between clergymen. Each one is wedded to his view, and determined never to be divorced from it. The average clergyman is a hydrozoa: he never lets go of what he attaches himself to. This seeming faithfulness is not, as one might think, the result of manliness, in holding on to the truth; but of cowardice, in fearing to acknowledge conscious error. History gives us many names of great and noble men who have consecrated themselves at the altar of Science, and thereby brought us the richest blessings; but few are they who have possessed that noble manliness which enables one to abjure some life-long and cherished belief. I am glad to know you dean, and hope you can preach for me next Sunday."

"Well, as to that, Mr. Merton, if I can't preach for you, I can give your people a lecture. What would you like for a subject? You know the wants of your people better than I do; and should be better able therefore to judge what subject they would prefer to hear me lecture on."

"I should say, Mr. Megalauchus, that you would prefer to choose your own subject. Most men have some subject on which they feel themselves able to lecture; and it must be admitted that the highest proof of one's incompetency, is his claim of being able to speak on all subjects. Choose that, sir, on which you are best prepared."

"You know, Mr. Merton, I've been all around the world. Just say what you would like me to speak on. I would as soon speak on one subject as another."

"Very strange, Mr. Megalauchus," said Merton. "The sun goes all around the world every twenty-four hours, yet I would never think of inviting it to deliver a lecture. I do not think mere going around the world, can prepare any man to deliver a lecture worthy to be heard. Among those who have been around the world most frequently, are found many most coarse, and most void of intellectual ability. I hardly think that you would have approved my act, should I have invited the martyred Cook to preach for me on St. Paul's Epistles to the Romans."

"Well, it is not likely we can agree on all things, Mr. Merton, and, may be, we must disagree on this. Everybody has his own ideas about such things, and it is useless to try to change them. All I have to say is, name your subject, and let the rest go to me. It will be time enough to find fault, after I shall have failed to give you satisfaction."

"Suppose, then, Mr. Megalauchus, that you deliver a lecture on science and religion. It is a subject in which I myself am very much interested, and on which I should be glad to receive any information that you may possess."

"Splendid, Mr Merton! You have hit the nail on the head. Nothing could be more suitable to me, and the times are ripe for it. You mean for me to speak on the so-called disagreements between science and religion, do you not?"

"Yes, sir. Infidelity is rampant in this city. Most of the influential men are unbelievers in the dogmas of Christianity. Few of them go to church at all, and those who go, go more for the sake of social relations than for any belief in the four Evangelists. If you can do anything toward healing this sore, I am sure you will assist greatly in spreading the faith of which you have just now spoken."

"All right, Mr. Merton. You will see that the lecture is well advertised. If there is one thing I hate in this world, it is speaking to a half-empty house. I would like for you to get it in the papers of the city, as well as speak to your congregation about it. On what day of the week shall I deliver the lecture?"

"Thursday evening would be a good time, Mr. Megalauchus. I believe no other evening is as good."

"All right, all right. I'll be on hand Thursday evening; and I promise you a good time. I think I can show your people that the word of God remains true, though every man be a liar. Remember Thursday evening."

Agreeable to their understanding, Merton had an item inserted in the newspapers, that the Rev. Mr. Megalauchus, of Churchton, would deliver a lecture at the Episcopal church, the following Thursday evening, on Science and Religion. He also spoke of the matter in his visits.

It was about six o'clock on Thursday evening. All preparations had been made, and Merton was momentarily expecting the Rev. Mr. Megalauchus. An hour passed, and yet the gentleman had not come. Merton then began to feel apprehensive lest Mr. Megalauchus should prove to be like some of the many other clergymen he had known, who thought so lightly of their word. When the hour had arrived for Merton to go to the church, he went, taking with him one of his old lectures, determined to deliver it, should Mr. Megalauchus fail to be on hand. The lecture was entitled, "The Earth Past and Future." The Rev. gentleman did not make his appearance; and Merton entertained the audience as best he could with his own lecture. He felt, however, greatly ashamed that the people of the city should be thus treated by a clergyman of the church.

In a day or two Merton addressed Mr. Megalauchus a letter asking an explanation of his conduct. It was answered in due time. "I was so busy," he said, "with the dear little fishes that I could not bring myself to forsake them. They came to me in such numbers that I might have fed the multitude in the wilderness. So attentive to me were they, in all my wants, that I felt it would be disrespectful in me to leave them. Under such circumstances I am sure any one would excuse me. Give my excuse to the people, and tell them I will come again some time, and redeem my promise."

Merton replied: "Although too much pride is an evil, yet I believe every one should think more of himself than of 'the little fishes.' I do not think it an honor to you, sir, that you think more of fishing than of keeping your word inviolate. In the future, believe me, I will endeavor not to disappoint my people with the promise of a man able to lecture on anything, and who has been all around the world simply to learn that his word is of less value than a few little fishes."

To this letter Merton received no reply; nor did he ever see Mr. Megalauchus again; and certainly he had no desire to.

At another time, Merton was visited by a minister who said he was in great need of money, and begged Merton to lend him ten dollars for two or three days. Merton had but little money; and the little he had, he more than needed for home use. But so pitiable were the minister's pleadings, especially to a nature so ill adapted to withstanding the pleadings of misery as Merton's was, that even against the advice of his wife, Merton loaned him the money, on his promise to return it within five days. "Here sir", said Merton, "are the ten dollars. I can ill afford to part with the money at this time; but on your promise to return it within five days, I let you have it."

"As sure as there is a God in heaven, Mr. Merton," he said, "I will return you the money by that time."

"I will give you ten days, sir," replied Merton, "and, mind you, if the money is not in my hands by that time, I will remember you as a base man."

"I am quite willing for you to do so, Mr. Merton;" he said; "but there will be no danger about your money. The minister who would receive such kindness from another, and fail to return it, is not worthy to stand in the pulpit. Believe me, you have no cause to fear."

From that day Merton never saw the minister, nor did he ever receive the money. Some persons might charitably imagine that his mind was afterwards too much engrossed with the pursuits after holiness, and with the preaching of the faith once given to the saints, to remember such little trifles; but we hold that charity is greatly misused when given to license dishonorable conduct. There is no place for charity here.

On a beautiful Sunday morning, Merton invited Mr. Robins to preach for him, having learned that he greatly desired to do so. The gentleman preached an old-fashioned sermon: there is no salvation outside the church; life only through the blood of Christ; faith and not works brings salvation; the Episcopal minister is the only authoritative minister of Christ; and the Scriptures, as a whole and in every part, are divinely inspired and infallible writings. His sermon was a fair enlargement of what is given us by Schiller, in his great play of Mary Stuart, as the words of that famous but ill-fated woman:

> Denn der allein ist es welcher selig macht—
> For that alone is the faith which gives salvation

Much of the discourse was very offensive to Merton, who thought the action of Mr. Robins very discourteous at least, since he, being a guest, should have respected the well-known feelings of Merton.

As soon as the services were over, and Mr. Robins and Merton had come into the vestry, Merton made the statement that the sermon had greatly offended him; and asked why he had chosen such an offensive subject for his pulpit. Mr. Robins thereupon acknowledged his own doubt about the truth of the statements he had made, by admitting he could not say in his heart he believed them. However, he had made them, he said, from the force of custom and habit, and because they were in general believed by church people. He was sorry, he said, that he had offended Merton, and wished he had preached on some less debatable subject. On questioning him, Merton discovered that he knew scarcely anything of modern thought, or of the more prominent modern authors. So radically lacking was he in the information of the present day, that he confessed he was ashamed, and said: "I wish Dr. Merton, that I could be near you, to make myself better acquainted with the results of modern scholarship; for even the little education I had, I have never improved, being not naturally given to study. I am conscious that there is a great conflict in the world between what is called revealed religion and advanced thought; but I have had scarcely any scientific education,—just enough to trouble me with doubts and fears, not enough to point me out the path clearly one way or the other. So in my doubts I go on keeping on the safe side. If I didn't do this, nothing could result but trouble with my bishop, and ruin to myself and family."

Now this man who could thus admit his doubts, was but

a short time afterward made a bishop of the church. On this occasion he took good care to hide whatever doubts or fears his bosom possessed; yes, indeed, and the reason may be readily inferred: the power, and prestige, and salary of a bishop, were more than weighty enough to balance any little conscientious scruples of belief he had hidden in his bosom.

In the parish of Woodville, where Merton was rector, there died an old negress. Having been baptized by a neighboring clergyman, the poor woman, at her death, requested Merton to permit this minister to make a few remarks at her funeral. The minister was very aged, being somewhat more than four-score years old; and the people of the parish generally considered it a kind of amusement to hear him preach, so incoherently and irrelevantly did he speak. But Merton determinined that the wishes of the poor colored woman should be respected; and therefore invited the Rev. Mr. Gordon to speak at the funeral, at the same time informing him that he would see to the liquidation of whatever expenses might be incurred by his coming. The expense of coming, however, would be very light, as his parish was very near to Merton's, and free entertainment would be given him. Mr. Gordon delivered his remarks in the room beside the coffin, in the presence of a great many negroes. Being a very poor preacher, it was natural that but few whites would wish to hear him. After the preliminary services, they departed for the cemetery. On their way to the burial-ground Mr. Gordon was merry and jocose, and even given to levity. On arrival at the cemetery, he asked if Merton would permit him to bury the dead. Merton replied: "No, sir; among my own people I always bury the dead. While they are living, I do my best for them; when they are dead, I perform the last offices."

The rites were finished, and they had moved back a

short distance from the grave, when Mr. Gordon was handed a folded bill. Merton saw a wave of pleasure pass over Mr. Gordon's countenance as he took the money, and placed it in his pocket. They proceeded towards the gate, where the carriage awaited them; but before they reached it, Mr. Gordon was forced to put his hands into his pocket, and draw forth the note, that he might know its worth. As he drew it forth, and saw it was a ten-dollar bill, he grunted out, "Ha! ha! bless the Lord! very good, very good!" and without further comment, put the bill back into his pocket. Now, every one should know that the money belonged to Merton, as well because he was the rector of the parish, as because he had performed most of the labor. It was Mr. Gordon's duty to give the money to Merton, and Merton's to see that Mr. Gordon was paid for such assistance as he had rendered. As Mr. Gordon was an old man, and almost eaten up with the love of money, Merton had fully made up his mind to present him with the bill, had Mr. Gordon handed it over to him; but as he did not, from that time Merton lost all respect for him. As this minister was without a sense of what was becoming, so was he selfish to the very heart. All the way to the cemetery, he talked of everything except of death or the grave; and all the way to the rectory, of everything except of handing Merton the money, or any portion of it. Merton never spoke of this dishonorable act; but he could never again invite so base a man into his parish.

It was the like of this action that made Merton frequently resolve, sometime afterwards, that when he died, he would be buried without priestly rites. There are, however, some good and true men in the ministry. Such are a comfort to the dying, and render desirable services at the burial of the dead. Nevertheless, the hypocrisy that Merton had witnessed at so many funerals, made the thought very painful to him, that such might be acted over the burial of his own remains.

At another time the bishop of the diocese visited Merton's parish, to administer the rite of confirmation. By chance their conversation turned on the question of denominational ministerial authority. Said the bishop:

"It can not be doubted that you are the only authorized minister in this city. It is possible that you may consider the different denominational ministers here as your lieutenants, or assistants, or as laymen; but you can not think of them as authorized ministers of Christ, and remain loyal to the church. Even the Roman Catholic priest is here without any right or authority; since their very first coming into this country was an intrusion, and an offence to the church of Christ. The Episcopal Church was the first Catholic Church in this country; and therefore she is the only one that to-day is here by divine right. You must not surrender your birthright for a mess of pottage."

And yet this very bishop, on the next day, in his sermon before the congregation, among which there were many of the ministers of the city, lauded the achievements of the various denominations; and called their ministers, "dear brethren," and the chosen vessels of Christ to bear his gospel to the ends of the world. And all this was done for the purpose of winning the hearts of the congregation, and getting from them a large offertory. Merton was greatly offended at such dishonorable conduct; at the man who behind the backs of those ministers, could deny their orders, or their ministerial authority, and yet before their faces, for the sake of base gain, call them his brethren, and chosen ministers of Christ.

The Rev. Mr. Ruckles, who had invited Merton to call on him, was the minister of one of the wealthiest congregations in the metropolis. During their conversation he said:

"Your faith, Mr. Merton, is my faith; but I dare not speak just as I believe. Should I do so, it would only increase the existing trouble of my people, who are already sufficiently burdened with their own religious doubts and fears."

On another occasion, Merton was invited to dine with the Rev. Mr. Frink, who had a very conspicuous position in the same city to which we have just made reference. While at dinner Mrs. Frink took an active part in the conversation; and Merton was not a little surprised at the skeptical nature of her views.

"Merton," said the Rev. Mr. Frink, "I want you to know that my wife is a first-class infidel."

"Who could be other," she replied, "after becoming acquainted with the history of the church, and the real nature of things. Is it not all for money, anyhow?"

During Merton's visit Mr. Frink clearly stated his disbelief in the deity of Christ, in a fixed state after death, in the inspiration of the Scriptures, and in the resurrection of the dead; although he was supposed to be an orthodox preacher, and received his salary as such. Alas, that such deception could be found in the hearts of ministers! Truly, as Goethe says:

Nach Golde drängt,
Am Golde hängt
Doch Alles.—(*Faust*, 2802).

We will not multiply the instances of dishonorable conduct that Merton witnessed in his brethren; we have only given such as we thought would suffice to show another phase in the development of the new heart and mind which, in due time, were created in the being of Henry Merton, —a heart and mind consonant with reason, however much at variance with dogma.

CHAPTER XXI.

THE DOGMA OF CREATION.

For in six days the Lord made heaven and earth, the sea and all that in them is. (*Ex. xx. 11*).

Nihil autem nec maius nec melius mundo, necesse est ergo cum deorum consilio et providentia administrari.

But since nothing is greater nor better than the world, it follows that it is governed by the counsel and providence of God.

(*Cicero: De Nat. Deo. II. 31.*)

NOTWITHSTANDING the painful life of Merton, owing to the mental tempests through which his soul was passing, his relations with his people and the citizens of the town were most pleasant. By all he was regarded as a man of purity of life, and of the highest educational attainments. It was because of his recognized scholarship that he was asked to prepare and deliver the following lecture based on Exodus xx. 11: "For in six days the Lord made heaven and earth, the sea, and all that in them is."

The literal sense of these words can not be misunderstood; nor would there seem any more reason for questioning the meaning of this sentence than of that in which it is asserted that a carpenter built a house in three weeks. But within the last few years, comparatively speaking, it has become the custom, with the more scholarly theologians and ministers, to insist, under the pressure of scientific facts, that the word 'days,' in this sentence, does not mean days in reality, but periods of indefinite duration. Now, should a common architect, after having made the assertion, that a certain piece of work had been done in a certain number of days, declare, after his assertion had been found to be false, that he meant any certain period of time that might have been found requisite for the completion of the work, and not days in reality, honest men would regard him as a humbug rather than as a competent architect. But if an architect should be refused such an easy escape from the results of his own gross ignorance, surely God could not, on any reasonable ground, ask humanity to credit Him with meaning any time required to suit the occasion, after having distinctly stated, that the required time was six days. Indeed, whatever leniency one might be supposed to show an architect, who after all his supposed skill, is but fallible man, and therefore subject by nature to mistake in thought and expression, there could be no ground whatever for allowing God any such excuse, who can not plead imperfection in thought, nor fallibility in judgment; and who must know better than to use, in his statements, any words that would necessarily lead men to make false conclusions. To the fair-minded man, it seems like begging the question, to assume that God means any indefinite periods of time, when He plainly says six days; and such an assumption does appear, on every ground of reason, to be most unwarrantable.

This daring spirit that reads into certain words of the Bible a meaning totally different from their literal import, is of very modern birth; and in a person who confessedly admits the divine origin of such words, it is a spirit most unworthy, irreverent, and condemnable. It is most dishonorable to charge God with the use of words that He did not intend using, that convey a false meaning, or that are necessarily subject to false construction, or to ambiguity. God can not be deceived in the understanding of his own works, nor desire to deceive his own creatures in investigating them; nor can He ever fail to choose the right word needed to convey the information He intends to impart. We therefore insist on the grounds of the majesty, greatness, and goodness of God, that if the world was not created in six days, the words at the head of our lecture can not have come from God, can not have had a divine origin; and since no passage can be found in the whole Bible whose origin has been more universally acknowledged to be divine, it follows that the disproof of the literal truth of these words must cast great discredit on the divine origin of the Bible as a whole.

We notice that the words of the Bible are, 'heaven and earth.' Commenting on the meaning of these words, Bishop Kidder says, 'they are used to express what is otherwise called the world or universe;' and Bishop Pearson tells us that the Hebrews used them to denote 'the grand extremities within which all things are contained.' In simple English, therefore, the biblical statement is that God created the universe in six days.

The time that has elapsed since the work of creation was completed, or since God entered upon his Sabbath, was, until very lately, believed by theologians to be quite definitely known. In the generally received version of the Bible, Archbishop Ussher's chronology is used. This gives us 4004 years B. C. for the time since the work of creation was completed. Hales considers the event occurred 5411 years B. C.; Jackson, 5426 years B. C.; Petavius, 3983 years B. C.; and Bunsen gives the time 20000 years B. C., as about the date of Adam's creation. This last date is declared by Reginald Stuart Poole to be one 'not only independent of, but repugnant to the Bible.' Mr. Poole gives us, as the date of Adam's creation, some time B C. between 5361 and 5421.

In the discussion of these words of Scripture, we shall in general confine ourselves to established or universally recognized geological and astronomical facts.

Nothing can be more certain than this, that all scientists regard the universe (we do not mean the matter of which the universe is composed) as having had a beginning, as having developed under law and order, and as being subject to decay and death. Between science and miraculous occurrences there is an unending strife: the admission of miracle is the exclusion of science. Science, therefore, has no place for miracle in its consideration; and the man who teaches miracle, or uses it, or depends on it, in the explanation of any phenomenon does by that very act itself exclude himself from the company of scientists, and conclusively show that he has not had a scientific education worthy of the name. Whatever object of scientific thought one may proceed to investigate to-day, there he will find that evolution, under some form or other, is universally received as the great law by which such object has been developed from the starting-point of its existence.

When we speak of the earth, we know with absolute certainty that it is a planet related to the other planets of the solar system as brother to brother; and that the solar system itself is a stellar system similarly related to the other stellar systems that form our universe—the universe which the Bible says God created in six days. Now, although no competent scientist would be so rash as to set a limit before which none of the systems of this universe could have existed; any and all competent scientists are ready to stake all their reputation by asserting, without the least hesitation, that these stellar systems had their origin under ordinary development, and in the abysmal depths of past time. Says Newcomb, one of the foremost living astronomers: 'The widest induction of modern science agrees with the speculations of thinking minds in past ages, in presenting the creation of the material universe as a process rather than an act. This process began when the present material universe was a mass of fiery vapor, filling the stellar spaces; it is still going on in its inevitable course, and it will end when sun and stars are reduced to cold masses of dead matter. The nebular hypothesis is indicated by the general tendency of the laws of nature. It has not been proved to be inconsistent with any fact; and it is almost a necessary consequence of the only theory by which we can account for the origin and conservation of the sun's heat.'

We have said that the solar system is but one of a family of stellar systems. Now, as children can not be without parents, so these various stellar systems that look out upon us from the awful depths of unfathomable space, could not be without once having had a parent body from which they originated. But to speak of the time that has elapsed since that parent body existed, would be but to use numbers so great as to be beyond all our powers of comprehension, and therefore a waste of time. We will therefore not speak of any time limit before which the parent body or bodies of this our universe must have existed; but will confine ourselves to the attempt at arriving at something like a definite age for its offspring,—for instance our own sun, a body which the Bible says God created on the fourth day

This central body of our system is a most wonderful orb. Helmholtz tells us that our forefathers were right in regarding the sun as the giver of all life, as the ultimate source of almost all that has happened on the earth. Says Tyndall: 'He rears the whole vegetable world and through it the animal; the lilies of the field are his workmanship; the verdure of the meadows, and the cattle upon a thousand hills. He forms the muscles, he urges the blood, he builds the brain. His fleetness is the lion's foot; he springs in the panther, he soars in the eagle, he glides in the snake. He builds the forest and hews it down, the power which raised the tree and wields the axe being one and the same. The sun digs the ore from our mine, he rolls the iron, he rivets the plates, he boils the water, he draws the train. He not not only grows the cotton, but he spins the fibres, and weaves the web. There is not a hammer raised, a wheel turned, or a shuttle thrown, that is not raised and turned and thrown by the sun.' And our own popular scientific teacher, Edward L. Youmans, says. 'In the fall of the avalanche, the roar of the cataract, and the flow of the river; in the crash of the thunder, the glare of the lightning, and the sweep of the tornado; in the blaze of conflagration and the shock of battle; in the beauty of flowers, of the rainbow, and the ever-shifting clouds; in days and seasons; in the silent growth of plants, and the elastic spring of animals; in the sail-impelled or steam-driven ship, and the flying train; in the heavy respiration of the laboring engine, and the rapid click of the telegraph;—in all the myriad manifestations of earthly power, we behold the transmuted strength of the all-energizing sun.'

It is not at all doubted by astronomers that each and all of the countless members of our universe have had their origin from one common fiery mist or nebulous ball. This is called the nebular hypothesis. In its modern form the hypothesis is generally credited to Herschel; but since his days it has been variously modified by different astronomers, although its main principle has not in any respect been altered.

According to astronomer Norton the great disruption of the nebulous mass by which the primary systems of the heavens were generated, may have occurred in any one of four possible modes:

By a simultaneous disruption of the whole of the nebulous mass;

By a simultaneous disruption of the nebulous body along a limited number of meridians;

By an irregular disruption;

By a disruption beginning at the equator, and extending gradually towards the poles.

Mr. Norton regards the last form of disruption as a deviation from the normal type, but at the same time as that by which the stellar systems were most likely originated. The irresolvable nebulæ he regards as vast nebulous masses that became detached from the polar regions, and from which 'clusters have been derived that are now at an earlier stage of development, and at a greater distance than the telescopic stars and clusters.' Annular nebulæ he thinks may have resulted from the polar matter being mostly drawn to surrounding points of condensation, or not having yet condensed into true stars, or into stars comparatively minute. Planetary nebulæ he refers to this same kind of development.

" If we assume,' says Mr. Norton, 'all systems of stars to have been derived by separation from rotating nebulous bodies of vast extent according to one or the other of a certain small number of types of evolution, the forms and internal conditions that would be inevitably passed through, in the progress of ages, would be the counterpart of the various forms and apparent structural conditions of the clusters and nebulæ actually observed.'

In speaking of the origin of the systems of the heavens, Young says that any one who considers the way in which other perfect works of Nature usually come to their perfection, must conclude that it is far more likely the systems grew than that they were built This eminent author thinks it not probable that the original nebulous mass had nearly as high temperature as that of the sun at present. He regards it likely that the original nebula was in the form of dust rather than fire-mist, that it consisted of fine particles of solid or liquid matter, each particle enveloped in a mantle of permanent gas. Still he does not deny that Laplace may have been right in ascribing a very high temperature to the original nebula; he only insists that a high temperature was not necessary for the evolution of such as our incandescent sun.

Laplace is supposed to have held that the bodies farthest from the centre must have originated first; but Lockyer, Norton, and many others think it probable that many bodies may have originated contemporaneously, more than one having been liberated at the same time, or several bodies having been formed from different zones of the same ring.

In speaking of the subject of the origin of the celestial systems, Newcomb and Holden say: 'The nebular hypothesis is a philosophical conclusion founded on the widest study of nature, and pointed to by many otherwise disconnected facts. We learn from it that the universe is not self-sustaining, but is a kind of organism which, like all other organisms, must come to an end.'

Loomis regards the nebular hypothesis as probably true; Olmstead and Snell think it more in accordance with the Creator's plan that the systems grew than that they were created, and set in motion as we now see them.

I might continue indefinitely this list of authorities; but it were a useless labor, as it is impossible to name a single competent authority who does not hold that the celestial systems are all, as we have said, the results of evolution, or who does not deny that any of them was ever brought into existence by any such creative act as is plainly taught in the first chapter of Genesis.

Having shown that in the mind of the scientific world there is no doubt that all the stellar systems have had one common origin, and have acquired their present form and order under the operations of law working through vast ages of time, we may now seek some solid scientific grounds for estimating the age of our system.

Our sun is one of the vast number of stars which, as

we have stated, were thrown off, or in some manner or other derived, from one common universal nebula. How long this nebula existed before such segregation commenced, it were vain to imagine; nor are we able to state whether our sun is the oldest or youngest star; whether the stars farthest from the centre of our universe were first formed, and those nearest the centre, last; or whether they came into existence by the formation of nuclei throughout the nebulous mass, as happens in the churning of butter. What we can definitely state is that the parent of the stars, the nebulous mass, must have been in existence ages before its offspring, the stars themselves; and that if we can show the stars, the mere offspring, existed untold ages before the time at which the Bible says the world was created, we shall thereby know the account in Genesis must be still more incorrect, since it asserts that God created the universe in six days; for the word universe, necessarily includes the parent of the stars, the nebulous mass.

In arriving at an adequate conception of the age of the solar system, we shall base our investigations upon the conclusions already deduced,—namely, that all the various members of the solar system once existed in the form of a nebulous mass which had been previously thrown off, or in some manner or other derived, from that universal fiery mist or nebulous matter out of which the various stars or primary bodies were in like manner all formed.

Most people know that heat is a mode of motion. If you rub your hands together, you experience warmth; and by repeatedly hammering a small piece of iron, you can make it too hot to hold. As heat is only a mode of motion, heat and motion are interchangeable. A person uses a ton of coal in getting up steam, to raise to a certain height a certain amount of mineral. After it has been thus raised, should it be allowed freely to fall to the place from which it had been taken, the heat generated by the fall, allowing for the loss by friction, would exactly equal the heat expended in raising it.

Such men as Hirn, Joule, Maxwell, Tyndall, and others have conclusively shown that the amount of work done by an engine, is exactly equal to the quantity of heat lost. This fact is a well known principle of physics.

That the heat of the sun does not arise, as many suppose, from its combustion, is a statement easily capable of demonstration. 'If the sun were solid carbon, and if a constant and adequate supply of oxygen were present, it has been shown that, at the present rate of radiation, the heat arising from the combustion of the mass would not last more than 5000 years.' (Newcomb and Holden.)

Few persons have anything like an adequate conception of the amount of heat radiated by the sun into space. By experiment it has been found that 83.4 foot-pounds of heat per second fall upon every square foot of the earth's surface exposed to the perpendicular rays of the sun; and since the surfaces of spheres are to one another as the squares of their radii, we know the amount of heat radiated from the sun's surface is to that received by the earth, as the square of the sun's distance from us is to the square of his radius, or as 46000 to 1. This gives us 3,869,000 foot-pounds of heat radiated from the sun's surface every second,—an amount equal to 7000 horse-power.

Sir John Herschel's actinometer and Pouillet's pyrheliometer are said by Deschanel to have given the best results in determining the amount of heat radiated by the sun. Pouillet finds the heat sent yearly by the sun to the earth to be sufficient to melt a layer of ice 30 metres thick all over the earth. Sir John Herschel's estimate is about the same.

Since the sun's radiation is about 2100 million times

the amount received by the earth, it is said by Deschanel that his total radiation is sufficient to melt a thickness of two-fifths of a mile of ice per hour over his whole surface.

Such an enormous supply of heat could not be maintained, for any length of time, by combustion. 'It would require the combustion of about 1500 lbs. of coal per hour, on every square foot of the sun's surface. The opinion that the sun's heat is maintained by combustion, can not be entertained for a single moment. A pound of coal falling into the sun from an infinite distance, would produce by its concussion more than 6000 times the amount of heat that would be generated by its combustion.' (Croll: Climate and Time). Should a pound of matter fall into the sun from an infinite distance, its energy would be 65,000,000,000 foot-pounds,—sufficient to raise 1000 tons five and half miles high.

Helmholtz says that if the sun were of uniform density throughout, 'the heat developed by a contraction amounting to only one ten-thousandth of the solar diameter, would be as much as is emitted by the sun in 21000 years.' (Deschanel). It is largely through the investigations made by this most eminent scientist, that an explanation of the sun's heat, in every way satisfactory to the scientific world, has been found. This explanation is known as the cantraction theory; and it is adopted by the leading philosophers of all nations. It is, moreover, the simplest and most reasonable, since its main principle necessarily results from the law of gravitation.

Having shown that the celestial bodies were never created, in the usual acceptation of the term, but grew into their present form and condition under natural laws, operating through vast ages; that the sun's first existence was not, as the Bible says, subsequent to that of the earth, but vast ages before it; that the sun's radiation is not by combustion, nor from the mere giving out of his own natural heat, but from the contraction of his own substance under the laws of gravity,—we may next ask, how long has this contraction been in progress.

First, we should say that a body such as the centre of our system was and perhaps is, might go on for vast ages radiating its heat, and contracting, not only without a fall, but actually with a rise, in temperature. The fact on which this assertion is based, is said to have been discovered by Mr. Lane, of Washington. It would seem strange, but it is admittedly no less true, that a gaseous body losing heat by radiation, and contracting under gravity, must, instead of falling in temperature, actually grow hotter and hotter, until it ceases to be a perfect gas. The energy acquired by the contraction, is more than that lost by radiation. In the case of a solid or liquid this is not so. Contraction may supply heat for radiation; but it can not raise the temperature of the contracting solid or liquid body, nor keep it from gradually falling. Little by little the temperature of such a body must be reduced to that of surrounding space.

The condition of our sun to-day is known to be one that is neither a true gas, nor a liquid, nor a solid. In parts it is a true gas, as is proved by the spectroscope; in other parts, as in the photospheric clouds, there is much liquid; while in yet other parts, it is possibly solid. The present relative proportions of true gases and liquids in our sun are such as to keep his temperature about stationary. (Young.) These proportions can not, of course, last indefinitely long. The increase of the liquid part must, at a comparatively early date, destroy the present stability; then the temperature will surely begin to fall. This fall may have already begun.

According to the theory of contraction now about

universally accepted, a shortening of the sun's radius of only about 125 feet a year, will suffice for the whole annual radiation. Such a small amount of contraction could not be noticed by us with any known instruments. Indeed, it would take 9000 times the amount of such annual contraction to enable us to verify by observations the fact of the sun's shrinkage. Should the annual contraction of the sun's radius be greater than 125 feet, his mean temperature must be rising; but if there be such rise, it can continue, comparatively speaking, for only a very short time.

The present temperature of the sun is very high; but nothing like definite information can be had on this point. Secchi thinks the the temperature of the solar surface is about 6,100,000 degrees C.; Rosetti gives what is known as the effective temperature of the sun, at from 10,000 to 18,000 degrees C.; and Siemens sets it down at 3000 degrees C. Where such wide divergencies of opinions exist, we must admit that our information concerning the sun's temperature is very limited. We may say, however, that if the sun were as near to the earth as the moon is, our earth would melt and vaporize. The most powerful burning-lenses conclusively show this. For a body placed at the focus of one of these, is virtually within 240,000 miles of the sun's surface; and it is known that at such a focus all substances known to us are melted and vaporized.

In answering the question, how long has the sun been in existence, Newcomb says: 'If we take the doctrine of the sun's contraction as furnishing the complete explanation of the solar heat during the whole period of the sun's existence, we can readily compute the total amount of heat which can be generated by his contraction from any assigned volume. This amount has a limit, however great we may suppose the sun to have been in the beginning: a body falling from an infinite distance would generate only a limited quantity of heat, just as it would acquire a limited velocity. It is thus found that if the sun had, in the beginning, filled all space, the amount of heat generated by his contraction to his present volume would have been sufficient to last 18,000,000 years at his present rate of radiation. The heat evolved by contraction from an infinite size, or by the falling of all the parts of the sun from an infinite distance, shows the extreme limit of the heat the sun could acquire from internal change, and this quantity, as just stated, would last only 18,000,000 years.

Speaking on this same subject, Young tells us: 'No conclusion of geometry is more certain than this,—that the contraction of the sun to its present size, from a diameter even many times greater than Neptune's orbit, would have furnished about 18,000,000 times as much heat as the sun now supplies in a year, and therefore that the sun can not have been emitting heat at the present rate for more than 18,000,000 years, if its heat has really been generated in this manner; but it is not unlikely that the sun may have received energy from other sources than its own contraction. Altogether it would seem that we must consider the 18,000,000 years to be the least possible value of a duration which may have been many times more extended. If the nebular hypothesis and the theory of the solar contraction be true, the sun must be as old as that,—how much older no one can tell.'

In our estimation of the sun's age, based on the contraction theory, no allowance has been made for any original heat; but the computed age is simply the time required for the dissipation of the heat that would be acquired by the solar contraction, or the contraction of the nebulous mass, on the supposition that the nebulous matter itself possessed no original heat.

Now apart from the demands of geology, it is in every way reasonable to hold that the original nebulous matter had a very high temperature. Where did this nebulous matter come from? It could not have been always existent; for on such supposition, contraction could not have had a beginning. The very supposition of contraction is founded on the fact of physical change in the nebula. The tendency to contract is a necessary result of gravitation. If the nebula had always been, contraction would have always been; but this latter is a supposition contrary to the theory itself. The nebula, therefore, must have had a beginning; and it is certain enough that this beginning was in a cause or causes exactly opposite to those which are now hastening a general equilibrium of temperature throughout the solar system. The original nebula, in other words, must have resulted from the collision of two large globes, or an indefinite number of small ones. This would give the nebula out of which the solar system has been formed, an original temperature, and force us to add to the past life of the sun very many millions of years.

That the original nebula had a very high temperature, all astronomers regard as very possible; and geologists assert that it is absolutely certain, since nature itself testifies to the truth of the fact in the strata of the earth.

An original nebula with a very high temperature is easily accounted for on the supposition of collision. If two globes each one-half of the sun's dimensions should collide, each moving with a velocity of 563 miles per second, they would generate in a single moment no less than 70,000,000 times as much heat as is now annually radiated by the sun. (Croll: Climate and Time). This would give us in all for the past life of the sun about 90,000,000 years.

Prof. Helmholtz holds that the earth, a child of the sun, must have been 350,000,000 years in passing from a temperature of 2,000 degrees C. to 200 degrees C.; and Dana says that at the end of the archaean age, the temperature of the earth was not probably over 38 degrees C.; and gives us 50,000,000 years as about the time since the commencement of the Silurian age, Of the time that had elapsed before the Silurian age, this author says it was 'very long.' Le Conte says the Azoic age was longer than all the remaining history of the earth, and calls it 'an infinite abyss of past time.' (Geology, 378). Winchell tells us that the time required for the changes we find in the earth, must have been vast; and the noted physicist, Sir William Thompson, on grounds other than geologicol, estimates the age of the earth's crust at 100,000,000 years; and the earth, as before stated, is a mere offspring of the sun.

The early earth was not unlike our present sun. It was at first nebulous, and after many millions of years became a globe of molten rock. While it was in a gaseous state, the result of contraction, as we have said, would be a rise in temperature; but as soon as it became largely liquid and solid, the loss by radiation would more than equal the heat evolved by contraction. Its temperature would therefore begin to fall; and this decrease will never cease. Farther and farther from the surface will the earth's molten state recede, until the earth shall have lost all her internal fires. This decrease of the earth's natural heat would be much more rapid, were it not for the thick crust superimposed on the molten matter, which protects the earth as the polar bear's coat preserves the animal's heat. Humboldt and Elie de Beaumont give 21 miles as the thickness of the earth's crust; Bischot, 24; Osmand Fisher, 25 to 30; and Newcomb says: 'The whole earth is red-hot at a distance of from ten to fifteen miles below its surface. We have every reason to believe that the increase of 100 degrees a mile continues many miles into the interior of the earth.

The earth is really a sphere of molten matter surrounded by a comparatively thin solid crust on which we live.' Indeed, it seems the ancients must have been fully acquainted with the internal heat of the earth. Tertullian, one of the great fathers of the church, says: 'By ourselves the lower regions of hell are believed to be a vast cavern in the interior of the earth.' This good father determined, you see, to locate the orthodox hell in a place hot enough.

Sir William Thompson estimates the yearly loss of heat by the earth, as sufficient to melt 777 cubic miles of ice.

It is quite generally held that the earth was hundreds of millions of years old before it was cold enough for the abode of life, such as we now know. We have already given Helmholtz' estimate, 350,000,000 years, as the time the earth required to pass from a temperature of 2,000 to 200 degrees C.; and Dana holds that the earth was many millions of years after this, before it became the abode of life.

It is universally held that the Azoic age of the earth was of greater duration than all her subsequent ages; yet we know little or nothing of the life of the Azoic age. Some of the lowest orders of life were undoubtedly represented at the close of this age; but the true life-history of our globe is generally held to have commenced at the beginning of the Paleozoic times, which age Dana estimates as having lasted 36,000,000 years. Then came the Mesozoic and Cenozoic ages, for the duration of which Dana gives us 9,000,000 and 3,000,000 years respectively.

We have coral reefs more than 2,000 feet thick, for the building of which geologists insist not less than 384,000 years were required.

Since the days of Sir Charles Lyell, to whom the science owes its thanks for its establishment upon its present sound and philosophical basis, geology has been making rapid strides. Its voice to-day is attentively listened to in the councils of the wise, and its conclusions are received with the approval of the scientific world.

Geologists may demand more millions of years than physicists are willing to give them, and physicists may differ among themselves many millions of years; but where the birth of the universe is acknowledged by all to have been an event which must have occurred at such a remote period in the eternity of the past, a few millions of years are of little importance in the consideration of our question.

Abundant remains of man are found in the Quaternary age; and it is held by very many that he first appeared in the Tertiary. 'Fossil remains of men have hitherto been found in late Tertiary deposits.' (Huxley). 'That man,' says Winchell, 'existed in remote preglacial times, is not improbable;' and computing it on astronomical grounds, Croll and Wallace say that the glacial epoch began 240,000 years ago, and lasted 160,000 years. This conclusion is accepted by Geike and many other English geologists. The astronomical consideration of the age is based on the precession of the equinoxes and secular changes in the eccentricity of the earth's orbit.

It would seem, therefore, that 240,000 years is the least time we can consider man as having been an inhabitant of the earth; and we are sure that the leading ethnologists and anthropologists of the world, would not much demur to this statement. Says Huxley, than whom none is better qualified to speak,: 'There can be no doubt that the existing fauna and flora is but the last term of a long series of equally numerous contemporary species, which have succeeded one another, by the slow and gradual substitution of species for species, in the vast interval of time which has elapsed between the deposition of the earliest fossiliferous strata and the present day.'

We have given sufficient proof that the Biblical word.

at the head of our lecture, do not convey the truth; that God neither created the universe in six days, nor any member thereof; nor even the earth, one of the least of the members of the solar system, nor any of its fauna or flora; that creation has been a gradual process from the least to the most differentiated,—from the nebulous ball down to the fiery earth, from the lowest living organism to the highest human genius.

We should learn from the evident inaccuracy of these biblical words, to regard the so-called revelation of God in the past, as subordinate to that ever-present and increasing manifestation of the Divine Being, witnessed in the myriad investigations carried forward by the inquiring mind of man, who in himself, though but an erring child, is the highest revelation of the Infinite Father.

CHAPTER XXII.

THOUGHTS OF AN HONEST PRIEST.

He would not flatter Neptune for his trident,
Or Jove for his power to thunder. His heart's his mouth:
What his breast forges, that his tongue must vent.
(Shakspere)

AFTER having delivered, one Sunday morning, a sermon on the Person of Christ, Merton was visited by his senior warden, who soon began the following conversation:

"Mr. Merton, I notice that in your sermons you frequently use such expressions as, If Christ be God; If eternal punishment be true; If Christ was immaculately born; If we live after death; etc. I supposed these matters were not open to question; therefore I can not see that you have any right to the use of 'ifs'. Have you really any doubt about these things? Do you really doubt the dogmas of the church?"

"Though I can not say, Mr. Howard, that I really disbelieve any of the great dogmas of the church, I nevertheless candidly admit that I have my doubts and fears. If you ask me, for instance, 'Do you believe in the divinity of Jesus Christ?' I would answer, 'yes'; but should you ask, 'Do you believe without a doubt that Jesus Christ is God?' I could not truthfully answer affirmatively. One may say, as thousands do, that he believes in the divinity of Jesus Christ, and yet not believe that he is the infinite Deity, the life, fullness, and potency of the whole universe. So also may one say, 'I believe,' his heart at the same time being torn with a tempest of doubt and fear. If ministers were asked, 'Do you believe in the divinity of Jesus Christ?', for the most part, and for many reasons, they would answer, 'yes;' but if they were asked the far more searching question, 'Is there no doubt at all in your heart that Jesus Christ is God Almighty?' I know from my relations with them for the last fifteen years that they could not truthfully answer the question affirmatively. I have been acquainted with many ministers, I have talked seriously with many; but never with one who, when closely questioned in confidence, would not admit the existence of the uncertainty which dwells, to a greater or less extent, according to the degree of education, in the breast, as I believe, of all I have ever known. This could not be otherwise; for who of all the learned critics, philosophers, scientists and historians, having examined the evidence contained in Scripture and elsewhere, upon which are founded the dogmas of orthodoxy, is satisfied, beyond doubt, of the truth of these dogmas? I answer, not one. This also could not be otherwise; for in the words of a contemporary writer: ' There is hardly one fact known to be the undoubted result of modern science, which does not shatter to pieces the whole fabric of orthodoxy.' Among those who have made a thorough investigation of this subject, the opinion of Mill may in general be said to be held in common: 'In the Christianity of the Gospels, at least in its ordinary interpretation, there are moral difficulties and perversions of so flagrant a character as almost to outweigh all the beauty and benignity and moral greatness which so eminently distinguish the sayings and character of Christ. . . . The divine message, assuming it to be such, has been authenticated by credentials so insufficient that they fail to convince a large proportion of the strongest and most cultivated minds; and the tendency to disbelieve them appears to grow with the growth of scientific knowledge and critical discrimination.' (Utility of Religion.)

"Ministers are men, and some of them are educated. Of

the educated portion all have their doubts and fears in common with the rest of mankind. But why, it may be asked, do they then not acknowledge these doubts more plainly than they do? Such a question may readily be answered: Why does not the lawyer expose to judge and jury the weakness of his case? Why does not the physician acknowledge his ignorance of the disease which, like a hawk, eats the life of his patient away? He who can answer these questions, and every sensible person can, is equally prepared, if he only will, to give a satisfactory reason why the minister exposes not the weakness of his creed; and he who can not give such a satisfactory reason, would likely receive no help from me, however fully I might explain it; for being credulous and superstitious, it is very improbable that he would be capable of appreciating such an explanation, or that his opinion would be changed by argument.

"For my part, I have never sought to hide the doubts and fears which more and more have found a lodging-place in my heart. I can not deceive you; nor will I contend for what I believe is contrary to fact or reason. This I can not do.

"'Fingunt simul creduntque,' is an old proverb, and means that when one makes an hypothesis in explanation of any phenomena, he will at once contend for its truth. An ignorant preacher declaring vehemently the thoughts of his heart, is wont to say he speaks by the inspiration of the Holy Ghost. If a man contends wilfully for the truth of error, he paralyzes his mind, and renders himself incapable of searching for further truth; even if he only unintentionally does this, he is liable to be confirmed in the belief of his error. These results are seen with fearful effects in religion. We find Augustine, for instance, a rational-minded Christian, before his contention with Pelagius; but after this he becomes as much of an extremist on the one side, as Pelagius was on the other. Indeed I can not think that the teachings of the latter are near as baneful as those of the former. Augustine lays down premises, and through his blinding passion to conquer, strives, according to the proverb, to make himself and others believe that his conclusions are true. Adam, he tells us, was created with a nature 'posse non peccare et non mori,' that is, with such a nature that he might have lived free from sin and free from death; but having transgressed, Adam, he says, became 'non posse non peccare et non mori,' that is, became such that he could not live without sin nor without death. Now, since man is declared in Scripture incapable of self-redemption, Augustine holds that it is evident that as many as are saved, are saved by grace; and since all are not saved, although they would be, that it is not because of their lack of desire, but because of the eternal and unconditional decree of God. Thus we find Augustine denying the freedom of the mind, offering us an absurd gospel, and presenting us with a god the most unjust and base. All this he does in contention for what he has assumed. This is the predestination theory which has its advocates in the Christian church of to-day, and which, if true, would induce me to be very charitable of the devil's sin, and conclude God not only the author and builder of hell, but also of all the sin in the universe. Such false doctrine kills the soul of the teacher, and certainly unfits it for noble living or noble dying, by philosophically destroying the highest incentives to virtue, and reducing man to a mere tool.

"Belief saves nobody; the truth only saves. If we would be saved, we must know the truth, for truth only has the power of giving life. But if a man would preach the truth and the truth only, he must dig carefully and deep, as if for hidden treasures. To do this there is need of a mind well furnished not only with theological knowledge, but also with that of science in general; for every science is subsidiary to theological knowledge. The minister, therefore, should be a man of the broadest culture, tenacious of the truth, and fearful of nothing but error. He should be satisfied with the substance only, and not with the shadow; with the reality, and not with the appearance.

"It must be admitted that such teaching as you receive from me, must make men think for themselves, and, therefore, cast off to a great extent the shackles of dogmas and superstition. It enforces the fact that it is not belief nor a name which saves the soul, but truth and truth only; and since man can be saved by truth only, such teaching leads him to inquire carefully into the character of his religious belief. The natural result of such teaching is to make men rationalistic, and therefore ready to discover any error in their religious belief. Such men soon find that there is much of Christian dogma which can not stand the investigation of a critical mind.

"I am glad indeed, in a certain sense, that you are so well satisfied; but I am equally glad that the declaration of the church, being such an interested party, is not sufficient to prevent my mind from thinking, or force on me the belief that there is no longer any room for further inquiry. Concerning the deity of Christ, it is not sufficient that the apostles asserted it, or that even Christ himself declared it. Have I not the right to demand proof as to the ability of the apostles, to determine the grave questions at issue? Have I not the right to demand the production of the evidence upon which they base their judgment? May I not demand that the evidence produced shall be such as would force from me to-day the acknowledgment of the deity of a person who, living amongst us, might be said to perform similar miracles?"

The gentleman answered, "I suppose such demands would be just and fair."

"Not only, my friend, would they be, as you say, just and fair; but it would be my duty to make such demands. If we examine, in a critical spirit, the statements made in the Gospels, the halo of glory which is now superstitiously shed about them, soon disappears. In the first place, there are the authors of the synoptic gospels, Matthew, Mark and Luke. To the author or words of the fourth gospel, it is useless to refer, since both the author and his words are subjects of too much uncertainty and speculation. What shall we say of the three who remain to testify to the life and words of Christ? I answer, we can say nothing; for of their persons and lives we have no really satisfactory and authentic information. From tradition and the little we find in the New Testament itself concerning them, it is generally inferred that they were ignorant men, and, therefore, we say, totally unfit to discriminate between the miraculous and the natural. When I ask for proof of it, I can not find that the apostles had sufficient ability to determine the questions at issue. Indeed, in the early ages it was a much disputed question, whether the apostles could even write; and to-day the question is far from settled. In the second place, if I ask for the production of the evidence upon which the apostles base their opinions, what do we find? Why, I am presented with a few documents disagreeing in many material points, and whose authors are either wholly unknown, or subjects of contradictory judgments. Let us examine more closely. Even if we admit that the author of our present Gospel of St. Matthew, was the same person as the Matthew who is said to have been the apostle of Christ, still it does not help us much; for Papias distinctly says that this Matthew 'put together the oracles of the Lord in the Hebrew language, and each one interpreted it as best he could.' Of this original work of St. Matthew we know absolutely nothing; and it does not increase our confidence in the copy we possess, to be told by Papias that each one translated the original as best he could. The greatest writers of the world acknowledge that our Matthew is not the original Matthew. If, then, I demand the genuine work of St. Matthew, I am offered instead, according to some, only a translation whose accuracy I must question, because of the suspicion cast, by the words of Papias, upon the author's ability; and, according to others, only a compilation made from other writings, the chief of which was probably the original Gospel of St. Mark. Stating it more briefly: of the writer of the original St. Matthew we have no definite and satisfactory information; we do not possess the original, nor know of any one that ever did; the Gospel of St. Matthew which we possess, is not the original St. Matthew, but at best only a translation made by some unknown person whose ability to perform such labor must be questioned, since he did it only 'as best he could'; or, lastly and probably, it may be the compilation of an unknown author, based chiefly upon the original Gospel of St. Mark. I ask any candid and unprejudiced mind, is there no room for doubt about the statements made in such a gospel. Such a question admits of but one answer. When we come to the Gospel of St. Mark, we find no better satisfaction. Of the person and life of St. Mark we know nothing, or worse than nothing, except the little we gather from the New Testament; on the latter we can place, in our judgment, but little reliance, as well because it is a witness testifying in its own behalf, as of the unsatisfactory character of what is there said. If I ask, therefore, for proof of the ability of St. Mark to determine the questions at issue, it is impossible for me to get it. It is generally conceded by the most impartial and prominent critics, that our Gospel of St. Mark is not the original Gospel of St. Mark; but, first, an emended copy made either by an unknown person or the author of the original; or, secondly, that it is the result of not less than two, and probably many, revisions, the first of which may, or may not, have been made by the original author, and the second, or subsequent ones, by some person or persons unknown, who, at the time of their revision, made many additions to the original work. And, now, if we ask did St. Mark witness the occurrences he describes, we have to answer, he did not ; for we are told by Papias, who of all was most likely to know, that St. Mark never saw the Lord, nor heard him speak ; but that, becoming a disciple and interpreter of St. Peter, he wrote his gospel from what he remembered of St. Peter's teaching :

'Ὅτε γαρ ηκουσε του κυριου ουτε παρηκολουθησε αυτω. Μαρκος μεν ἑρμηνευτης Πετρου γενομενος ὁσα εμνημονευσε ακριβως εγραψεν'.

"In St Mark, therefore, we have no eye-witness to the occurrences he relates. The original gospel of St. Mark was simply a memorabilia of the teachings of St. Peter, penned by Mark, his disciple and interpreter, after St. Peter's death. If then I demand written proof of the occurrences which St. Mark relates, I am offered at best the written testimony of one who never witnessed the occurrences he describes; while in all probability I am offered not even this much, but, according to some, a document supposed to be an emended copy made by the original author; or, according to others, a document which has passed through several revisions, and received many alterations. I ask, can any candid and unprejudiced mind receive without question the statements made in such documents ? Is there no room for doubt about the assertions made in such a gospel ? Such a question admits of but one answer—and that answer I would give, though all the earth should give a contrary one—truth and reason demand it.

"And now we come to the consideration of the last of the synoptic gospels, the Gospel according to St. Luke. The author of this gospel is supposed to have been a companion of St. Paul. By some he is said to have been a physician, by some a painter, by others both. He was probably a native of Antioch and a Gentile Christian. But what we know of St. Luke, may be sufficiently inferred from the words of Prof. Reuss: 'Such a work was undertaken by a man who was strongly drawn to it by his interest in the matter, and who, by his connection with the apostlês, or at least their immediate pupils, was probably placed in a condition to accomplish his task as well as it could be done in his time. This was the unknown author of our Third Gospel.' Here we find St. Luke called by this learned critic the 'unknown author'; and this title, as far as we know, justly describes him. So then, if I ask for definite and satisfactory proof that St. Luke had the ability to determine the questions at issue, I am unable to get it; yet he was probably the most scholarly of all the apostles.

"Further, it is admitted by all that St. Luke was not an apostle, that he was not an eye-witness to the occurrences he relates; and it is quite generally admitted that his gospel is a critical work based upon various written documents, the chief of which was probably the original Gospel of St. Mark. I ask any candid and unprejudiced mind, is there no room for doubt about the statements made in such a gospel? Such a question admits of but one answer. There is one thing, however, that can not be answered without casting obloquy on the ministerial profession, — that is, why can ministers who profess to lead the world into truth, dare refer to these documents as infallible and inspired writings? In conclusion, let me ask you to read this from the great and truth-loving Mill, which I think a lucid and just statement of the whole subject; and, while you read, think:

"'To all these considerations ought to be added the extremely imperfect nature of the testimony itself. Take it at best, it is the uncross-examined testimony of extremely ignorant people; credulous as such usually are; unaccustomed to draw the line between the perceptions of sense, and what is superinduced upon them by the suggestions of a lively imagination; unversed in the difficult art of deciding between appearances and reality, and between the natural and the supernatural; in times, moreover, when no one thought it worth while to contradict any alleged miracle because it was the belief of the age that miracles in themselves proved nothing, since they could be worked by a lying spirit as well as by the spirit of God. Such were the witnesses; and even of them we do not possess the direct testimony; the documents, of date long subsequent, even on the orthodox theory, which contains the only history of these events, very often do not even name the supposed eye-witnesses. . . (The evidence is) not of a character to warrant belief in any facts in the smallest degree unusual or improbable; the eye-witnesses in most cases unknown, in none competent by character or education to scrutinize the real nature of the appearances which they may have seen, and moved moreover by a union of the strongest motives which can inspire human beings to persuade, first themselves, and then others, that what they had seen was a miracle. The facts, too, even if faithfully reported, are never incompatible with the supposition that they were either mere coincidences, or were produced by natural means; even when no specific conjecture can be made as to those means, which in general it can. . . I can not attach any evidentiary value to the testimony even of Christ on such a subject, since he is never said to have declared any evidence of his mission, except internal conviction; and everybody knows that in prescientific times men always supposed that any unusual faculties which came to them they knew not how, were an inspiration from God; the best men always being the readiest to ascribe any honorable peculiarity in themselves to that higher source, rather than to their own merits.' (Essays on Religion.)

"Conscious of the uncertainty in meaning of so many passages of Scripture, recognizing the great disagreement among the most eminent scholars as to the divine origin of the book we call the Bible, and knowing the truth of Goethe's words:

> 'Der Goetter Worte sind nicht doppelsinnig—
> The words of the gods are not ambiguous.'
>
> (*Iph. auf Tauris*),

don't you thing I have good grounds for the use of 'ifs' in my sermons?"

"Well, I should say you had. But it is a great surprise to me. If the people were to know the truth about things, the churches would soon be emptier than they now are; but I am sure it is better to know the truth than to found one's hopes upon matters that can not stand investigation."

Thus saying the gentleman departed, and Merton was alone with his thoughts. Silently as his heart was beating, his soul was in a tempest; and he was powerless to say, "peace, be still". He was afraid he had done his friend more evil than good by disturbing his sense of security, however much deceived his friend may have been; yet he could not be false to his own convictions of duty, nor give false ideas concerning his own belief.

Merton's faith in the Scriptures as a sacred revelation from God, was fast leaving him. He had read the Old Testament through nearly three times, in the original language; and the more perfectly he became acquainted with it, the less he thought of it. He could not be blind to the immorality contained in its pages, to its many contradictions, to the wicked and most infamous conduct of not a few of those who are said to have been men after God's own heart, to the fact that it ascribes to God motives such as no good man could have, and actions such as no good man would or could be guilty of doing, nor to its childish and false notions concerning the origin and working of the great cosmos of God.

The New Testament is, of course, a higher development. It is the fruit of many trees, only one of which, the Old Testament, is Jewish. The Grecian and Eastern philosophies and religions are manifest factors of the New Testament. Taking the Bible as a whole, it seemed to Merton that it could not possibly be the work of men whose minds and pens were guided by God. If so, then we must not only be made after God's own image, but God must be in our image: mutable, irritable, malevolent, envious, jealous, given to having favorites, imperfect in wisdom, subject to improvement and repentance,—in short, the God of the Bible is but an enlarged man. Harnack says Augustine was the first great theologian to anthropomorphize God, or give Him a personality similar to our own. He may have been the first *eminent* theologian to do this; but all theologians whether before or after Augustine, and all biblical writers, have been guilty of the same dangerous error. Knowing these things, Merton could not believe in literal inspiration: yet he could see no reason for doubting, that not a little of the Bible is true for all people and time, and therefore to be believed. This is the truth he sought to find; and having found it, to set it forth in all his preaching, earnestly and without fear. But in thus subjecting every doctrine to the discrimination of the reason, Merton could not save himself from violating the received dogmas of the church, nor from falling under the ban of the ecclesiastical authorities.

CHAPTER XXIII.

DIVINE CONCEPTIONS.

Λαοδαμείῃ μὲν παρελέξατο μητίετα Ζεύς,
ἡ δ' ἔτεκ' ἀντίθεον Σαρπηδόνα—

The all-wise god Zeus embraced Laodamia, and she conceived, and brought forth the divine Sarpedon.

(*Homer: Iliad, vi, 198.*)

Le dieu Bel lui-meme m'a cree, le dien Marduk qui m'a engendre, a depose lui-meme le germe de ma vie dans le sein de ma mere—

The god Bel himself created me; the god Marduk who begot me, deposited the germ of my life in the bosom of my mother.

(*Babylonian Inscription*)

THE Hon. Mr. Gray was very ill, and not expected to recover. He was a member of Congress, a man of some means, and was much respected by those acquainted with him. He was a Scotchman, and possessed that candor and open-heartedness characteristic of his race. His wife was a communicant of Merton's parish; and she wished Merton to visit her husband as frequently as possible. Mr. Gray himself, however, was not a member of the church; and did not believe even in the immortality of the soul.

It was a beautiful day. Merton had knelt at the bedside of the sick man, in earnest prayer; and was then sitting on a chair, engaged in conversation with Mr. Gray.

"Merton," said the sick man, "I want to tell you, that Em., my wife, thinks the world of you, and that I like you very much. I like your sincerity, admire your scholarship, and greatly esteem your candor. Now, you must not feel offended at what I am about to say. I like you to visit me; but I want to ask you not to offer prayer when you make your visits—I do not believe in prayer; nor do I believe that after death a man continues to be. I know you are extremely liberal; but you have not arrived at my standpoint. Visit me whenever you are able; but visit me like the rest: do not offer prayer. Man's character is made by work, not by prayer; and to pray for my welfare after death, is to pray for that which will have ceased to be. As for the divinity of Christ, and the Christian dogmas in general, I do not believe they are worth a consideration."

"My dear friend, you believe in God as much as I do, and therefore have a right to pray. God is not the God of the Christian only, but also of all those, like yourself, who look to Him for help and strength. And as a friend and counsellor, I have the right to pray that God, our common Father, may give you strength to stand the evils you now have to bear. The divinity of Christ is nothing to me. I know it is a dogma of the church, that never has been established. But the existence of God does not depend upon the divinity of Christ, nor any other dogma; but it is the acknowledgment of universal humanity. Man as man reaches out his hands after the hidden, yet everywhere present and felt, Deity. God is the object not only of the Christian heart, but of the heart of humanity. It is as natural for the human soul to turn to its God, as for the flower to turn to the sun. You, therefore, as man, not as a Christian, have the right to act as man, and lean on Him who alone can give you strength to bear your present evils; and I as man, not as a Christian, have the privilege to call on our common Father for the brother that I have upon this bed, in so great distress. As a believer in humanity, I pray to God for you, and not as a believer in the dogmas to which you refer. But if you do not believe in human nature, if you believe that its convictions are false, then, of course, it is useless for me to point you to it, as my warrant for prayer."

"Thank you, Merton," he said; "I like you, like to hear you talk. But, still, when you come to see me, do not pray. I prefer that you should come as any other friend. A great many come to see me, and I want you to come among them, as they come."

But, my dear friend, to do what you say, would be to

disgrace my calling. It would be to acknowledge that my life is that of a humbug, and that I am but an impostor. Now, I consider myself a true man, earnestly believing what I preach. Therefore I could not become a party to a scheme which actively or passively acknowledges that I am acting the part of a mountebank. Unless you permit me to visit you as a minister of God, I can not come to see you; for I could not thus deny Him who, I believe, hath sent me."

Merton went to the rectory, and wrote him a long letter in which he set forth more fully the reasons why he could not again visit him, unless he could be received as a minister. This letter, as Merton was afterwards told by Mrs. Gray, was at the sick man's request frequently read to him, during the last few days of his painful life, and she thought it had a great influence over him for good; for at his death, which occurred in Washington, D. C., a short time after Merton wrote him the letter, he expressed some belief in the immortality of the soul, and the hope that he would see his family again.

While Merton considered the deity of Christ to be an unprovable dogma, the truth of the fatherhood of God he believed attested by the whole of nature. That the disciples of Christ declared, and believed in, his divinity, Merton saw no reasonable grounds to doubt; but he also knew that many other individuals had been declared divine by men far superior in ability and judgement to the apostles of Christ, and, yet, that no one to-day thinks for a moment of accepting their testimony as proving the divine nature of such individuals. Homer, Hesiod, Plato, Socrates, and many others, assert that certain men were divinely begotten; but great as these writers were, we can but smile at their words. They assert that certain individuals were sons of God:

"Οἶσθ' οὖν τίνες τούτων ἀγαθοὶ βασιλεῖς ἦδαν Μίνως τε καὶ
'Ραδάμανθυς οἱ Διὸς καὶ Εὐρώπης παῖδες, ὧν οἶδ' εἰσὶν οἱ νόμοι.
. . . οὐ γὰρ ἔσθ' ὅ τι τούτου ἀσεβέστερόν ἐστιν οὐδ' ὅ

τι χρή μᾶλλον εὐλαβεῖσθαι, πλὴν εἰς τοὺς θεοὺς καὶ λόγῳ καὶ
ἔργῳ ἐξαμαρτάνειν, δεύτερον δ᾿εἰς τοὺς θείους ἀνθρώπους."

That as divinely begotten beings, some of them were specially instructed by God himself:

"Λέγει γὰρ τὸν Μίνων συγγίγνεσθαι ἐνάτῳ ἔτει τῷ Διὶ ἐν λόγοις
καὶ φοιτᾶν παιδευθησόμενον ὡς ὑπὸ σοφιστοῦ ὄντος τοῦ Διός . . .
Τὸ γὰρ Διὸς ὄντα παῖδα μόνον ὑπὸ Διὸς πεπαιδεῦσθαι οὐκ ἔχει
ὑπερβολὴν ἐπαίνου."

That as divinely begotten beings, they are made judges after they depart this life:

"Καὶ τοὺς μὲν ἐκ τῆς Ἀσίας Ῥαδάμανθυς κρινεῖ, τοὺς δ᾿ ἐκ τῆς
Εὐρώπης Αἰακός· Μίνῳ δὲ πρεσβεῖα δώσω ἐπιδιακρίνειν, ἐὰν
ἀπορῆτόν τι τῶ ἑτέρῳ, ἵν᾿ ὡς δικαιοτάτη ἡ κρίσις ᾖ περὶ τῆς
πορείας τοῖς ἀνθρώποις."

That as divinely begotten beings, sacrifices are due them:

"Ὦ Κρίτων, ἔφη, τῷ Ἀσκληπιῷ ὀφείλομεν ἀλεκτρυόνα. ἀλλ᾿
ἀπόδοτε καὶ μὴ ἀμελήσητε."

(Plato: Minos xii, xiii; Georgias lxxix; Phaedo lxvi.)

"Thou shouldst therefore know that some of these men were good kings, as, for instance, Minos and Rhadamanthus who were sons of God, begotten by Europa, and who were the authors of the laws; for, except it be to sin against God, nothing is more base, or more to be guarded against, than this,—to sin in word or deed against divinely begotten men."

"He affirms that Minos passed nine years in discourse with God; that he was accustomed to visit God for the purpose of receiving instructions from him as if God were a wise philosopher."

"The fact that he was the only son of God to receive personal instructions from God himself, confers the highest honors on Minos."

"Those coming from Asia, Rhadamanthus judges; those

from Europe, Aeacus. To Minos, because of his dignity, I will assign the position of counsellor, whenever the other two are at a loss what to do, in order that the judgment concerning the destiny of man, may be as righteous as possible."

"Crito," he said, "we owe a cock to Asclepias. Sacrifice it, and forget it not."

Reading these lines, Merton could not fail to see that other persons besides Jesus Christ, have been called sons of God, and said to have been instructed by God himself; that as Christ is, so they have been, held to have the power of judgment in the other world, and to be proper objects of prayer and sacrifice. So fully did the great and pure-minded Socrates seem to believe in the divine nature of such beings, that, as his dying injunction, he commanded Crito to offer in sacrifice to Asclepias the cock he had vowed. But notwithstanding the greatness and wisdom of such writers, the reading of these words evokes only a laugh to-day, and rightly so. It seemed to Merton that a supernatural act could be proved only by supernatural evidence; and as all indirect or written evidence must, in the very nature of things, be natural, and the deity of a being could not be established except by supernatural acts, it seemed to him that the deity of Christ could not be proved by any such evidence as we possess; that, therefore, the only way to prove his deity, is that each person have such direct and positive evidence, as no man could refuse to accept. For his own part, Merton was obliged to confess that he had never received such evidence. He had never witnessed a miracle; therefore he could not possibly say that he was satisfied with the evidence he had of Christ's divinity; but he wished, as his disciple, to make himself and others, more worthy of being called the children of God.

To teach the deity of a person, is to teach a most stupendous miracle; even that a virgin should bring forth a son, is something at variance with all the known laws of nature. Now, the two grounds of probability are conformability with known laws, and the testimony of others. Where the event in question is contrary to human experience, in the words of Locke, "the most untainted credit of a witness will scarcely be able to find belief." But in the case of the New Testament miracles, it is much worse than this: for as we have seen from Mill, in our last chapter, the witnesses to these reported miracles are not considered worthy of untainted credit.

Only those who by nature are sincere, and fill a position which they fear may be false, can imagine what Merton used to suffer in those days. He was uncertain what he should do. He loved the blessed name of Jesus, and would not knowingly fail to give him all the honor due his most beautiful life; but, on the other hand, to believe in a person in human shape as being the infinite God, when you are satisfied that the person's deity has never been established, seemed to Merton a most dangerous thing, and to border on idolatry and blasphemy.

In such grave doubts, Merton was never forgetful to ask God for help, who is conscious of all his children's troubles, and ready and willing to help them. Indeed, Merton's very breath was but a prayer that his steps might be ordered aright. Again and again would he, in the dead of night, reach out his hands to God, that He should take them, as it were, saying: "Lead me, O my Father, in the way I should go. Let me not stray from Thee. Oh, my God, be Thou my friend and savior. Give me wisdom to understand, and courage to do, the right. Thou wert the God of my father. He trusted in Thee, and Thou didst not forsake him. So let me see thy face, and live. Take not thy Spirit from me, lest seeing not thy face, I die. Thou knowest my mental troubles and deep anxieties. Come near me, I pray Thee. Inspire my soul with a sense and love of the truth. Heal my wounded heart; bind up my broken spirit; encourage my desponding soul. Hear me, my Father, for I am in great distress. The road I tread is dark. Let the light of thy countenance fall on it as a lantern to my uncertain feet. Guide me, Lord, for I am thine; oh, guide me for thy dear name's sake."

Thus did Merton live, tossed about on the seas of doubt and distress, but at all times ready to lay his life down for the truth, if only satisfactory proof were given him that he possessed it.

> "God sends his teachers unto every age,
> To every clime, and every race of men,
> With revelations fitted to their growth
> And shape of mind, nor gives the realm of Truth
> Into the selfish rule of one sole race.
> Therefore each form of worship that has swayed
> The life of man, and given it to grasp
> The master-key of knowledge—reverence—
> Infolds some gem of goodness and of right;
> Else never had the eager soul, which loathes
> The slothful down of pampered ignorance,
> Found in it even a moment's fitful rest."
>
> *(Lowell.)*

CHAPTER XXIV.

THE JUDGE'S STATEMENT OF THE CASE.

οὓς τέκεν Ἀστυόχη μαρθένος αἰδοίη Ἄρηι κρατερῷ—

Whom the adorable virgin Astyoche brought forth to the mighty god Ares. (*Homer: Iliad ii. 513.*)

MR. JUDEX was a scholarly man, honest in his convictions, and of a most inquiring mind. He had come to spend the evening with Merton. It was a very cold night, and they were all seated around the big heater, which seemed to laugh with pleasure at every new supply of maple or oak. Mr. Judex had been brought up in the Roman Catholic Church; but was, at the time of making this visit, an unbeliever.

"My father," he said, "intended me for the priesthood; but after acquiring a more intimate knowledge of the lives of the priests, and a somewhat superficial knowledge of the basis of the dogmas of the church, I refused to proceed with my studies for the priesthood, fell first into doubt, then into so-called infidelity. There is no body of men who are more full of unbelief than the educated clergy of the Roman Catholic Church; but like other ministers of the so-called gospel, they perform their functions, simply as a genteel way of making their living. Seeing that their followers delight in humbug, they think it no evil to supply them with this means of pleasure, especially since by doing so they always manage to keep themselves fat and in good liking.

"Previous to my entrance upon a course of study for the priesthood, I had acted for a long time as priest's boy; and it was while acting in this capacity, that I first began to doubt the sincerity of the men who served at the altar. I was not long at my studies before this doubt so increased that I regarded every priest I met, as at heart a knave. I found it impossible to believe that any man of average intelligence could attempt to maintain, upon so shadowy evidence, such a stupendous cause. This may have been an extreme view; but as I look back upon it now, I do not think it far astray.

"After coming to the United States, I took up the study of the law. It was after I had become settled in my profession that I went over some of my old studies, as a lawyer goes over his case ; and I was not long in coming to the conclusion, that we have no evidence whatever for accepting one-tenth of the dogmas of the church, and none whatever for believing in the reported miracles of the New Testament. I saw plainly enough that even if the writers believed what they reported, it is no satisfactory evidence of the truth of their reports; for in like manner have thousands reported seeing fairies and ghosts, yet such reports find no acceptance with us to-day. Again, we all say the sun goes around the earth instead of the earth going around the sun; and there is more in this saying than we are apt to think. It shows for a certainty that there was a time when people believed it. But the fact that such a belief was undoubtedly held, is no reason that we should hold it to-day. All the reported miracles of the New Testament are susceptible of ready explanation,—first, on the ground that belief in miracles was general, during the age in which the reporters lived ; and, second, on the ground that those who wrote the accounts of the life of Christ, invented the stories about the miracles, as in their judgment being necessary to the credibility of the rest, since every great hero was expected to perform such. The story about the divine conception is really laughable, and would cause a sensible man to question the character of the Virgin Mary, did he not know that such divine conceptions have happened in the world a great number of times. Any man who had become great in the eyes of the vulgar, whether a warrior, magician, legislator, or teacher, would surely be calendared as having been the result of a divine conception. It was therefore but natural that the ignorant followers of Christ should imagine that he had been divinely conceived, and declare it to their disciples. But it is preposterous to ask any man of common-sense to believe in such divine conceptions to-day. It is a good thing to be a true follower of Christ; but it is an insult to ask me as a pre-requisite to such discipleship, to accept the absurd and wicked stories about his divine descent. I am not certain, indeed, that such a character as Christ ever lived, and you know well that this opinion has been, and is, shared by no small number of eminent scholars; yet I am willing enough to assume that he did live, that he had an honest mother called Mary, and an honest father called Joseph, that he grew up and became a great reformer— Socrates as it were arising from the dead. I am willing enough to suppose that such a person as Jesus lived; that he was born as others are born, and died as many others have died—a martyr for the truth. But more than this no man should be asked to believe, who knows anything of the present and past history of the world; and more than this I for my part do not believe. I insist that it is no less absurd to believe the miraculous stories about the person of Christ, than the similar ones about the persons of other men—Buddha, for instance. Indeed, you know well that some of the most eminent thinkers of this age believe that Jesus is no more nor less than Buddha somewhat transformed to suit Jewish tastes and notions; that all the gospels are no more nor less than the stories about the birth, life, and death of Buddha, somewhat modified by time and place, to suit the reformed Jewish mind. I do not know that this supposition is true; but I am sure there must be some ground upon which to base such supposition, or it would not be made by men who stand second to none in the world; for an eminently good and wise man can find no pleasure in asserting his belief in a conscious falsehood. I must admit that the analogy between the birth, life, and death of Buddha, and the birth, life, and death of Jesus, seems almost exact; and it is by no means impossible that the Buddhistic traditions floated around among the Jewish people, clad as it were in Jewish clothing, and that, in due time, they assumed the form they have in our present gospels; for it would be an easy matter to change the name of the hero, making it a Jew called Jesus, instead of an Indian called Buddha. Look at the analogy: Buddha was born of a royal and virgin mother, so was Jesus; Buddha's advent was announced to the virgin mother by a mighty angel, so was that of Jesus; at the birth of Buddha a new star appeared in the east, so it was at the birth of Jesus; wise men brought costly offerings from afar to the shrine of the infant Buddha, so was it with the infant Jesus; at seeing the infant Buddha we have a learned priest singing a nunc dimittis, and at the sight of the infant Jesus we have Simeon doing likewise, and both declare they had seen the promised Messiah; when it was known that Buddha was born, a wicked king, fearing him as a future rival, sends spies after the boy, so was it during the infancy of Jesus; Buddha is one day missed by his parents who found him some time aftewards in an assembly of learned Rishis, surprising them with his questions and answers; so likewise was Jesus missed by his parents, and afterwards discovered, in a similar manner, amazing the Jewish doctors. Buddha had a fore-runner, a herald; so had Jesus. Buddha fasts in the desert, is tempted by the prince of evil spirits, and chooses his disciples; so Jesus fasts, is tempted by the devil, and chooses disciples.

Buddha had a beloved, a doubting, and a traitorous disciple, so had Jesus. Buddha compares the preacher to a sower, his gospel to a mustard-seed, false preachers to blindmen leading the blind, a repentant sinner to a returning prodigal; so did Jesus. At Buddha's death the earth trembles, the rocks are rent asunder, and the sainted dead leave their graves; so is it at the death of Jesus. The Buddhistic church has convents, several orders of celibate monks, ecumenical councils, and an infallible pope supported especially by the priests who contribute toward his support from the money they receive for reading masses for the repose of departed souls; so is it with the Christian church. If this is not a sufficiently perfect parallel, I know not what would make one.

"You say that no man of common-sense believes these absurd stories about Buddha. I suppose you mean, no man of common-sense in European countries. For we know that there are hundreds of millions, many of whom are very learned men, who do believe these stories, and are most earnest followers of Buddha to-day. I am sure that no man with common-sense who lives blest with the scientific knowledge of this nineteenth century, believes in these Buddhistic stories; but for the same reason he denies these, does he also deny those concerning Jesus. Still, a person would think that a Buddhistic priest would have the advantage over the Christian, since the faith of the former was well established, and very widely recognized, before Christianity was known, or thought of. I find no reason for accepting the teachings of the Buddhistic church concerning their great founder, except that he may have been, and probably was, a wise and great man; I find no reason for accepting the teachings of the Christian church concerning their great founder, except that he may have been, and probably was, a wise and good man. The Christian church denies the claims of the Buddhistic, and I think rightly so; the Buddhistic church denies the claims of the Christian, and I think with equal right. As no evidence has ever been adduced upon which the scientific mind can found his faith in the miraculous accounts concerning Buddha, so has there no sufficient evidence ever been adduced upon which he may found his faith in the miraculous accounts concerning Jesus. The weakness of the one, is the weakness of the other; both stand upon superstition, both fall in the presence of science. Of the two accounts there is but little preference to be given to the one over the other. It seems, however, that the Buddhistic is the more acceptable, absurd and impossible as it is; because it is easier to accept, and believe in, one stupendous miracle, than in a multiplication of miracles. But each account is absurd, rejected by science, and unsustained by any evidence that would be held sufficient, in a court of law, to prove I had sold my horse to my next-door neighbor. Taking away the superstitious element, every part of which is the laughing-stock of the reasonable man, I am willing to admit the superiority of the Christian system. But I am not willing to admit that the Christian system is superior because of the supposed superiority of its reputed founder, of which I do not feel certain; but rather because it is the religion of the more enlightened nations of the world, who in their advancing stages, have cast off from their religious faith not a little of the superstitious element, and, no doubt, will yet cast off the balance. Religion is a central fact of man's nature; and the fact that it is so, has enabled the priests of every religion to play upon the hopes and fears of their fellowmen, as a cat plays with a mouse; and certainly to dupe their followers more than any lawyer ever attempted to dupe his client, or mislead the jury. When I say priests, I do not mean exclusively Christian priests; but

I mean those of every faith and cult. There surely must be a truth in religion; and it is the feeling after this truth on the part of the human mind and heart, that has enabled the priests to foist, for their own benefit, upon their respective followers, the mass of miracles and other superstitions which so mar the beauty of the central truth, as to make it almost invisible. For my own part, I have long since given up attending church services. As a rule, I never go at all. If I go, I go more for the sake of the man, whom I may wish to oblige or assist, than for any faith I have in the divine character or even usefulness of the church. I believe in a Supreme Power who is made visible by his works; and that seeing his works, men have ever been, and probably will ever be, formulating theories about his nature, attributes, how He created the world, and how He leads the human race to a higher and better life. It seems to me that there must be a God who is the Creator, Savior, Redeemer, Sanctifier, and Father, of mankind; and I believe that man should endeavor, according to the best of his ability, to live a pure and righteous life. As to the question of immortality, I am not, and never expect to be, decided. I can say I have hope in it; I can not say I really believe in it. It has never been proved, I am certain, that man exists after death; it may never be proved. Still I can not see that it is irrational to hope for a future life; and I therefore hope in a life to come. I am called by many, foolish for indulging in such a hope; but for my part, I shall continue to remain in this hope, until some one proves to my satisfaction that I am in error. It costs me nothing, and does no harm to anybody else, so far as I can see. This is the sum total of my religion, Merton. I have no less; and I assure you, I want no more."

CHAPTER XXV.

THE JUDGE'S CONCLUSION.

τῷ Ἀσκληπιῷ ὀφείλομεν ἀλεκτρυόνα—
We owe in sacrifice a cock to Asclepias
(*Plato: Phaedo, l xvi, 118, 13.*)

THE night was extremely cold; the heavens clear; the stars shining brightly; and the frost seeking to penetrate every crevice in the parsonage. Merton determined to retire early; and to that end knelt, with his little family, in prayer.

"O merciful Father," he said, "direct our uncertain feet. Strengthen our minds to know thy will, and our hearts to do it. Fill us, O God, with thyself that, our souls being purified by thy most glorious presence, our thoughts may rise clean and pure, as water from the living, limpid spring. Take not thy holy presence from us, O merciful Father. Dark is the way and chilly the night. Lighten our paths, and warm our hearts, O God of our fathers. Look in pity on the dear little babes Thou hast given us, and on the mother whom Thou hast so greatly honored, in permitting her to give them life. Oh, let our lives be precious in thy sight. From Thee nothing is hidden, to Thee all is apparent; and on Thee we hang as a babe on its mother's breast. Hungry, Lord, we cry to Thee for food; thirsty, we come to Thee for drink; weary, we come to Thee for rest. Feed us, merciful Father, with the bread of heaven; assuage our thirst with the waters of life; lift up the light of thy countenance upon us, and give us peace, for thy name's sake."

It was at this instant that Mr. Judex knocked at the door:

"I am come up," he said, "to renew our religious discussion." "With your religion, Judge," replied Merton, "I have no complaint; but surely, in judging every priest you meet as a knave, or as false at heart, you do some of them a great injustice?"

"Perhaps I do, Merton; but I think, as a whole, my judgment is correct. I am fully satisfied that ten out of any average eleven priests I may chance to meet, would receive a righteous judgment."

"But, Mr. Judex, do you not as a lawyer frequently say, that it is better to let ten guilty men escape than punish one innocent man?"

"Yes, Merton; and that is the spirit of the law. Besides, I think it a wise and safe principle to act upon."

"So do I, Mr. Judex; but in conformity with this principle, would it not be better to judge the next eleven priests you may chance to meet, as innocent men, thereby letting ten guilty ones escape, than judge them all as knaves, thereby accusing one innocent man?"

"I do not consider the cases exactly parallel, Merton. In the law we have to do with a world perfectly known to us all, and with courts of justice, and juries, before which we ourselves may at any time be brought. I hold there is nothing like this in the church: nothing there is positively known; all has to be taken on faith; and the whole faith, when accepted, goes to the fattening of the priests who are wolves in sheep's clothing. In the law there is perfect impartiality. If we would rather let ten guilty men escape than punish one innocent man, it is because we ourselves to-morrow might need the benefit we offer another to-day. In the one case the principle is acted upon for the safety and well-being of the citizens as a whole, living in a well known world; in the other case it would be acted upon for the safety and well-being of the priests who, in return for such privileges, can offer their dubious teachings about a world that no living being knows anything about, except the priests, and many of them are honest enough to admit their utter ignorance. I insist the cases are not parallel. In the law the principle acts with regard to all alike; in the church it would act especially, if not exclusively, for the benefit of the ecclesiastics. Again, I am not certain that the priests as a class do really add to the elevation of the world. That they do, I think is fairly to be questioned. Indeed, I have sometimes thought that their work ought to be abated as a nuisance. Because of this I do not think that they are worthy of the benefit of a doubt. You may say that you are certain they do accomplish good in many ways. All right; no one denies it. But are you certain they do not accomplish more harm in other ways? This is the question. I hold that the work of the priest produces as much harm as good; and I believe it produces more."

"Mr. Judex, did you not say some time ago, that religion is a central part of man's nature?"

"Yes, Merton, I did."

"Can anything be more vital to one's interest than the well-being of a central part of his nature?"

"I presume not."

"Is it not necessary to the well-being of a central part of man's nature, that such central part be guided aright, as it is developing?"

"Certainly."

"Who is it that guides this central part except the priests?"

"The priests are the reputed guides; but I hold they are blind-guides leading the blind."

"That is not the question, Mr. Judex. The question is, whose duty is it, to whom is the work regarded as belonging, to guide this central part of man's nature?"

"Well, of course, it is regarded as belonging to the priests; but I think it might be better developed without them. It couldn't be much worse than it is."

"If anything be essential to man's happiness, would you not admit that that something should be taken cognizance of by the state?"

"I suppose that whatever is essential to one's happiness, should be regarded as an object of the watchful care of the state."

"Well, then, Mr. Judex, if you admit that religion is an essential part of man's nature; that its proper guidance is essential to man's happiness; that whatever is essential to man's happiness, is a proper object of the watchful care of the state; and that the guidance of this central part of man's nature, is generally regarded in the state as belonging to the priestly order,— do you not thereby admit that priests are proper objects of the watchful care of the state?"

"Well, as you put it, I guess I do."

"If then, Mr. Judex, priests are proper objects of the watchful care of the state, by what can they be guarded except by the law of the state?"

"I presume if the state doesn't protect them, nothing else will: for St. Joseph and the Virgin Mary won't do it."

"But, Mr. Judex, if the priests, as you say, are to be guarded by the laws of the state, would it not be according to law, to treat them as you treat the rest of the citizens, and give them the benefit of a doubt."

"Supposing I admit that, what then?"

"It seems to me, Mr. Judex, it would follow that you should regard the next eleven priests you may chance to meet, as you would regard any other eleven citizens of the state, and suppose them all innocent men, even if by so doing you let ten guilty knaves escape, rather than suppose them all guilty, and thereby possibly accuse one innocent priest."

"You are good at splitting hairs, Merton. You may have made your point, but you have not changed my mind a particle in regard to priests as a whole."

"Mr. Judex, you must not suppose that I have any too high regard for priests. I assure you my experience has led me to think of them as anything else but gods. But they are a class of men we find existing in the world, and in the state, as far back as our knowledge extends; and even when real knowledge of their existence fades away, there are still traces left of the presence of priests, or medicine-men."

"Then you class priests with medicine-men, do you, Mr. Merton?"

"Their work is certainly similar, Mr. Judex, although as classes the two have become differentiated. You might say that medicine-men are infant priests, or that the both bodies are sub-orders of the same order."

"Well, Merton, with your definition of a priest, I think I can afford to give the poor brute the benefit of a doubt. I will have in mind your definition, when I see the next priest entering on his incantations."

"All right, sir; that is all I ask. I can now talk with you, and believe that you regard me as a sincere man, and that you will continue so to regard me, until you have positive knowledge that I am not. You have sometimes come to the services, since I have been here; and as you come in the future, I should certainly feel very uncomfortable to look into your face, did I think in my heart that you thought me insincere. It is for this reason that I have spoken as I have, that I might lead you to admit what you have admitted."

"I do not think that anybody, in this town, could regard you as insincere. You are too out-spoken for that. If one thing more than another has brought me to hear you preach, it is my belief that you in heart and soul are sincere. But you must not forget, that you do not preach as others do; your doctrine is radically different. If it were not so, I would not come to hear you, however sincere you might be;

for I should then regard you as a sincere dupe; and with such I have lost too much time already."

"Do not forget, Mr. Judex, that the next eleven priests you meet, are to be treated, as you treat other men."

"I have already promised you, Merton, I will give the poor wretches the benefit of a doubt."

"What you have said of Buddha, Mr. Judex, is highly interesting. I have not much to say with regard to it, except that I have no faith whatever in the divine nature of the great teacher. I do not say, however, that he may not have come into the world with a mission to perform, nor do I deny that he may have performed it rightly and wisely, under the guidance of God. I think this is possible. And I am also willing to admit, that I can not see on what ground the Christian priest expects to preach the divinity of Christ to the Buddhists, if he refuses the proof the Buddhist priest adduces for the divinity of Buddha. It does appear to me that in character and value the evidence adduced to prove the divinity of the one, is similar to that adduced to prove the divinity of the other. I candidly believe that, were I a Buddhist, the Christian priests would find it impossible, to make me believe in the divinity of Christ, on the evidence they adduce in support of it."

"Then you do not believe in the divinity of Christ, as I understand, Mr. Merton."

"I can not say, Mr. Judex, that I really disbelieve in Christ's divinity; but I must say that I feel quite uncertain, quite unsatisfied, concerning it. And I believe with my whole soul, from my knowledge of priests, that the pulpits are full of men who feel unsatisfied as to Christ's divinity; and I am certain that there always have been very earnest and learned followers of Christ, who have refused to accept his divinity, or regard him in any other light than as a man with a divine commission. I can not but admit with you that the miracles of the New Testament are unsubstantiated. Indeed, I do not believe it possible to substantiate a miracle with any less than direct and miraculous evidence. As to the internal evidence of the New Testament for Christ's divinity, I can not see how it can be satisfactory. How do we know that a mere man could not have produced the precepts of the New Testament? If the mind of a mere man is capable of understanding these precepts, it would seem to follow that the mind of a mere man might have been their author. But more than this, I can not find any principle in the New Testament, radically different from those found elsewhere. It is true, that certain principles are more enlarged upon, brought more to the light; but nothing can be found in the New Testament radically new. In other words, all the principles of the New Testament have certainly been produced by human authors, because they are known to have been current long before Christianity was established. The fatherhood of God, rewards and punishments, immortality, heaven and hell, prayer and sacrifice, priest and temple, penitence and divine forgiveness, the sanctifying power of the Holy Spirit, the duty of man to man and to God,— all these principles were taught long before the advent of Christ, and by people other than the so-called elect. I do not believe, therefore, it is possible to prove conclusively the divinity of Christ from the contents of the New Testament, nor by miracles except by direct and miraculous evidence. But although I do not believe that the divinity of Christ has ever been established, I am unwilling to say that Christ is not divine; I simply say his divine nature has never been proved."

"When you speak, Merton, of the fact that the divine nature of Christ has never been established, I can not help thinking how false the position of the minister is, and how greatly he misrepresents the truth of things. If a man says he has never seen any proof of Christ's divinity, the average minister's reply is, 'That, sir, was given to the apostles long ago, and we have their testimony for it.' I reply that the people who lived contemporaneously with Christ, did not believe in his divinity. This fact is proved to a certainty from the fact that they put him to death. What man that ever lived, or ever may live, would attempt to put a being to death, believing him at the same time to be God? Jesus Christ was accused of blasphemy. This accusation, however unjustly founded, proves the case that his accusers did not believe in his divinity. The minister says, 'His divinity was proved through certain select men.' I answer, what a shame to use such beggarly language! Was the God of the universe so weak that He could not satisfy his children's rational demands? Does God desire that his children should worship every being declaring himself to be God? Now a man must either worship or not worship every such being; and since to worship a being in human form, or any other form, who is not really God, would be a most grievous sin, I hold it would be an offence against the majesty of God, to worship any being declaring himself to be God, unless the man asked to worship him, be given such proof of his divine nature, as he can not doubt. This is all the people asked who lived contemporaneously with Christ. Did they receive such proof of Christ's divinity? It is wicked to say they did, when it is admitted that Christ was put to death; and that even his own disciples, through fear, fled from his side, and with oaths denied him. It seems to me Celsus, even from the garbled account we have of his work, would make shorter work of the ministers of to-day, than he made of the ministers who lived at the time of his writing. I am sure that neither Jew nor Gentile would have crucified Christ, if he had been satisfied of Christ's divine nature. Who would dare lay his hands upon whom he believed to be the infinite God? Says Celsus, the Jew, writing in the second century, and admitted by Origen to have been a learned man: 'How should we deem him to be God, who not only in other respects, as was currently reported, performed none of his promises, but who also, after we had convicted him, and condemned him as deserving of punishment, was found guilty of attempting to conceal himself, and endeavoring to escape in a most disgraceful manner, and who was betrayed by those whom he called disciples. He who was God could neither flee nor be led away prisoner. He who was a partaker at a man's table, would not conspire against him; and if he would not conspire against a man, much less would he plot against a God, after banqueting with him. And, which is still more absurd, God himself conspired against those who sat at his table, by converting them into traitors and impious men. What great deeds did Jesus perform as being God, having gained no one over during his life, not even his own disciples, underwent those punishments and suffering? By what train of argument were you led to regard him as the Son of God? If Jesus desired to show that his power was really divine, he ought to have appeared to those who illtreated him, and to him who had condemned him, and to all men universally. While alive he was of no assistance to himself, but when dead he arose again, and showed the marks of his punishment, and how his hands were pierced with nails. Who beheld this? A half-frantic woman, as you state, and some other one, perhaps, of those who were engaged in the same system of delusion, who had either dreamed so, owing to a peculiar state of the mind, or under the influence of a wandering imagination, had formed to himself an appearance according to his own wishes, which has been the case with numberless individuals; or, which is most probable, one who desired to impress others with this portent, and by such falsehood to furnish an occasion to impostors like himself. From such signs and misrepresentations, and from proofs so mean, no one could prove him to be God, and the Son of God. The disciples of Jesus, having no undoubted fact upon which to rely, devised the fiction that he foreknew everything before it happened. And certain Christians have corrupted the Gospel from its original purity to a threefold, and fourfold, and many-fold degree, and have remodelled it, so that they might be able to answer objections. Even although guilty of falsehood, ye have not been able to give a color of credibility to your inventions.' Don't misjudge me, Mr. Merton: I love the name of Jesus, and believe he was a blessed man, a loving brother, a faithful teacher, and one worthy to be a leader of men; but I do not believe that he was God, or that he ever claimed to be, however much he may have been understood as making such claim. It also seems that most of the objections of Celsus, the learned Jew, are valid ones. They are just such as a learned man, in my opinion, would make to-day. I say nothing derogatory of the character of Christ; but I say what Celsus said, and which I think Christ would say: if a man wishes to show that he is God, he must prove his divine nature universally, and by such miraculous works, as can not leave room for doubt. I may be called a heretic, but that is nothing to me; so was Christ, so was Socrates. Even Origen, the very man who undertook to answer Celsus, and who was undoubtedly the most learned of all the early Christians, was called a heretic, and, in the year 231, degraded from the priesthood, and excommunicated by the bishop of Alexandria, and never afterwards restored. So if I am called a heretic, I shall find myself in the best of company. But speaking with regard to yourself, Merton, does not your church hold the divinity of Christ as one of its fundamental dogmas?"

"I believe it does, Mr. Judex. In my teaching I do not deny the divinity of Christ; but I am inclined to make little of such a dogma, by magnifying others far more important."

"The teaching of the church, Merton, about the divinity of Christ, is insulting to the mind of man. What man, do you suppose, would refuse to believe what God declares, if he were sure that God declares it? And if God declares his will in a way which makes it uncertain to man, man certainly can not be blamed for not believing it. But since I can not believe that anything faulty ever came from God, I do not believe that God ever gave such unsatisfactory proof as we have for the divinity of Christ; nor do I believe that a thing having so unsatisfactory credentials, as the New Testament has, could ever come directly from God."

"If the doubts I now have, Mr. Judex, ever grow into a positive conviction that Christ is not God, I will give up the work I am now engaged in; but until then I can not see but that I should go on, and do as Christ did,—not talk of his divinity, but lead men to a better and purer life, and to God, as the fountain of all goodness and truth. I am like you, much dissatisfied with the proof we have of Christ's divine conception, unsatisfied with the proof of the so-called virginity of his mother; and it seems to me the probability against these things, can never be overcome by such evidence as we have in our possession. Still, I think it is right enough to call his mother a virgin, since every pure mother may be so called; and as the mother of our great leader, I see no impropriety in styling her, the Virgin Mary. In the New Testament, even pure men are called virgins. So I can say, 'Born of the Virgin Mary,' since I undoubtedly believe that Christ had, at least, a pure mother called Mary, the lawful wife of an honest father. But while I believe this much of Christ, of anything more I am in doubt. You will understand me therefore: I do not deny Christ's divine nature; I do declare I feel uncertain of it. When you see me in the services, and hear me preach, I only ask that you believe you see and hear an honest, earnest soul who would lay his life down for what he was sure was God's truth. While I am with you, I hope you will help me build up men in a wise and rational faith, one that shall lead to a better and higher life."

"I shall certainly do what I can to help you, Mr. Merton; I am only sorry I can't do more."

"Strength comes to us, my dear Mr. Judex, as we put into action the strength we have:

'Hat man Viel, so wird man bald
Noch viel Mehr dazu bekommen.
Wer nur Wenig hat, Dem wird
Auch das Wenige genommen.'".
(*Heine.*)

CHAPTER XXVI.

HUSK AND KERNEL.

What is the chaff to the wheat? saith the Lord.
(*Jeremiah xxiii. 28.*)

"MR. MERTON, I greatly appreciated your sermon," said banker Pomposity, "on the Miraculous in Christianity. It was a treat to me, and to all who were present, last Sunday evening. It is a rare thing, if not a startling one, to find a minister who admits the truths of science. I myself have long since stood where you now stand. Every one that has any knowledge of the matter at all, knows well enough that whatever occurs, whether now or in times past, is the result of law and established order. In order to believe in the immaculate conception of Christ, I must conclude that man is not man, that woman is not woman, and that God is not immutable but self-contradictory; and all this must I believe on the authority of a few pages of writing not much less uncertain or untrustworthy than the Arabian Nights. It offends me greatly that any minister, through ignorance or fear, should dare preach such stuff in the presence of the average congregation. I am sure that if Jesus Christ wasn't the son of his mother's husband, he must have been illegitimate born; and this latter I do not believe. That the ignorant followers of Jesus might possibly have believed in his divine conception, is no reason whatever that I should believe in it; for in like manner were the founders of many other religions supposed to have been divinely conceived. Indeed, in early days immaculate conceptions were common; for it was nothing unusual for gods to have union with women. The world has been full of incarnations of deity. It is, therefore, nothing strange that the founder of Christianity should have been regarded as an incarnate god, or that foolish people should so regard him to-day. Such belief I have long ago given to the wind, with the whale that swallowed Jonah, and the sun that stood still at the command of Joshua. In the name of common-sense, I hope to hear you speak of something far different; and judging from what I heard last Sunday, I should say my hopes are well founded. There is enough to talk about, when the fables are left out."

"The great majority of Christian people, Mr. Pomposity, do not agree with you; and it is hard to cast to the wind, though they are but chaff, the dogmas which the average member of the church regards as the very foundation of all his hopes. I have but little, if any, faith in miracles, no matter by whom they may be said to have been performed; but in this matter I am clearly in advance of the great majority of ministers; and this fact makes my position a trying one. It is true I find sufficient in Christianity to speak about, after I leave out the legions of devils, its fall of man, its divine conceptions, its story of creation, the golden streets of its heavenly Jerusalem, and the smoke of the torment of its hell; but only the better educated of the ministry agree with me in this matter, and most of them prefer not to disturb existing belief. To do so they know is to expose themselves to the murmurings of the ignorant portions of their congregations, and to the vengeance of their bishops whose power and prestige depend largely on the faithful reception of the monstrous fables of Christianity. You are not saved by belief in the immaculate conception; but rather by living as he lived, who is said to have been immaculately conceived. I am not able to accept the doctrine that I am saved by believing that Jesus is the Most High; rather do I firmly believe that I am saved by doing as Jesus did. He who lives as Jesus lived, will surely receive of that Strength which made Jesus so strong. It is not by faith in Kreeshna, Jahve, Christ, or Allah that a man is saved, for surely devils believe and tremble; but it is by doing the will of Him who sent us, that you and I are called the children of God ; and the will of him who sent us, is to do with our might what we believe in our heart we should do. Thus living, we may make a mistake ; but no other rule is near so sure to gauge correctly the measure of our moral responsibility. He who lives up to it, whatever he thinks of the peculiar dogmas of Christianity, is surely on his way to a better life."

" Merton, you mentioned the name of Kreeshna. What is taught concerning this mythical personage?"

"Kreeshna, Mr. Pomposity, is one of the Brahminical names for the incarnate Deity. He is said in their sacred books to have dwelt on earth in mortal form, and thus to have delivered from his own lips to his chosen disciples the will of the infinite God. This name for the incarnate Deity more especially appears in the sacred book called the Bhagavadgita, a work which Sir Warren Hastings pronounced of the greatest originality, sublime conception, reason and diction; as containing a theology corresponding with that of the Christian dispensation, and most powerfully illustrating its fundamental principles. It is the real bible of the Brahmins, and is believed by them to contain all the sacred mysteries of their religion, delivered by the mouth of God himself. It stands largely in the form of a dialogue wherein the chief speaker is Kreeshna, the incarnate God. It everywhere teaches the unity of God who is represented as the Universal Soul immanent in all things. Concerning immortality it says: 'As a man throweth away old garments, and putteth on new, even so the soul, having quitted its mortal frames, entereth into others which are new. The weapon divideth it not, the fire burneth it not, the water corrupteth it not, the wind drieth it not away: it is eternal, universal, permanent, indivisible, inconsumable, incorruptible, and is not to be dried away.' Concerning our duty it says: 'Be free from duplicity, and stand firm in the path of truth, and turn thy mind to things which are spiritual. Be not one whose motives for action is the hope of reward. Let not thy life be spent in inaction. Depend upon application, perform thy duty, and abandon all thoughts of the consequence.' Whatever we may think of the origin of the Bhagavadgita, much of its teachings are certainly sublime."

"Did this Kreeshna, Merton, call himself God?"

"He is certainly represented as doing so, Mr. Pomposity. In speaking of himself he says: 'Although in my nature I am not subject to birth or decay, and am the Lord of all creation, yet, having command over my own nature, I am made evident by my own power. Thus I appear from age to age, for the preservation of the just, the destruction of the wicked, and the establishment of virtue. Mankind was created by me. Know me then to be the creator of mankind, uncreated and without decay. He who beholdeth me in all things, and beholdeth all things in me, I forsake not him, and he forsaketh not me. The man who believeth in unity, and worshippeth me present in all things, dwelleth in me in all respects, even whilst he liveth. All things hang on me even as precious stones hang upon a string. I am dear to the wise man, and he is dear to me. I am the holy one worthy to be known. I am the comforter and the creator. I am the same to all mankind. They who serve me with adoration, I am in them, and they in me. I am the creator of all things, and from me all things proceed.' These words spoke Kreeshna of himself, Mr. Pomposity, and thus speaks Arjoon of him, his favorite disciple: 'I behold, O God!

within thy breast, the Dews assembled, and every specific tribe of beings. O universal Lord, form of the universe! Thou art the Supreme Being, incorruptible, and worthy to be known. Have mercy then, O God of Gods! thou mansion of the universe! Reverence be unto thee, O thou who art all in all! Infinite is thy power and thy glory.'

"Concerning what the good man may expect after death, the Bhagavadgita says: 'No man who hath done good, goeth to an evil place.' The Bhagavadgita is truly a wonderful work, and one which had been in existence many hundreds of years, when Christianity was first introduced; and its contents are conclusive proof that God is no respecter of persons, and that He is not far from any of us."

"Do you believe, then, Merton, that the book you refer to, is a revelation from God?"

"In one sense, yes, sir; in another sense, no. I believe in the words of Zoroaster:

"' Τον δε νοει πας νους θεον, ου γαρ ανευ

Νους εστι νοητου, και το νοητον ου νου χωρις υπαρχει.

Ονοματα βαρβαρα μηποτ' αλλαξης,

Εισι γαρ ονοματα παρ' 'εκαστοις θεοσδοτα.—

"'But every mind knoweth God; for the mind is not without the Intelligible, neither is the Intelligible without the mind. Never change barbarous names, for there are names given from God in every nation.'

"While I believe no book is a direct revelation from God, I yet believe that the fundamental and universal principles of religions are true, and that they are the natural result of the Universal Spirit dwelling in man as a part of creation. In this sense does every sacred book contain some eternal truth, some revelation. In other words, they are revelations, as any other part of nature is a revelation, no more, and no less."

"I have noticed, Merton, that there are many things in

nature hurtful rather than beneficial. In every flower-garden there are weeds, in every field of wheat there are frequently many destructive insects. So if those religious principles are simply a result of nature, they may be false."

"The weeds, sir, to which you refer, would not have received your notice, were there not flowers to be injured by their presence; and you would never seek to kill the insects, were there no precious wheat to be destroyed. So in religious principles: if the destructive is there, so is the useful; if the weeds are there, so are the flowers. The wheat and the flowers are those universal and eternal principles of religions, which the various faiths of the world embody, and set forth; the weeds and the insects are those differentiating principles of religious faiths, concerning which the judgments of their respective adherents are so contradictory. Or the flowers and the wheat are those principles of religions that bind the different peoples of the world together in theological unity, while the weeds and the insects are those religious principles that set the different peoples of the world at theological variance. I would say, root up the weeds that the flowers may emit still greater fragrance; destroy the insects that the poor may have more bread to eat."

"Might we not regard the various phases of religion, and even their contradictory tenets, as the outcome of different civilizations? If so, would it be wise to destroy what you have said?"

"I would not say, destroy such, Mr. Pomposity; but I would say, never regard those peculiarities of the various human natures and civilizations as essential to true religion, or to true and saving faith in God. Even the same plant will vary, when planted in various climates; and less we can not expect of human nature, as it everywhere strives to perfect its character. We may permit the modifications as useful variations, but we must deny that the variation of one faith must be assumed by the others. When I say, destroy the variations of the religious idea, I only mean that we should destroy the spirit which regards the idea as dependent on the variation, and that we should cease to think of the religion of one people, as necessary to the well-being and happiness of another. The true God of one people, is the true God of all ; and the many gods of the various peoples, is the true God of none."

"I am glad to hear such liberal sentiments, Merton, and I hope you will be brave enough to declare them. I am sick of hearing long-winded sermons on ancient myths, when there is such valuable matter all around us to base what we have to say on."

"I am not much given to hide the thoughts of my heart, Mr. Pomposity; but this same open-mindedness may bring on me the ire of my bishop. Already he has written, praying me to be true to the faith. Our bishop is a good man, and I like him; but he has less cause for listening to the voice of reason, and more for remaining in the house of bondage, than I have."

"I have no place for the bishop, Merton. It is ridiculous to see his nonsense in the chancel. His bowings and genuflections are more than I can stand. He believes in the middle-ages. I doubt he knows the world moves. Such actions in the chancel may be pleasing to some ; but, for my part, they appear obscene. I have never been confirmed, but I am not sorry; for it seems to me, the further one is from the chancel, the better it is for his stomach's sake."

"I have always loved the chancel, Mr. Pomposity, and I love the holy communion. In that holy sacrament, the idea of blood atonement has wholly passed from my mind. If it be true that Christ instituted it, I doubt not that it was symbolic of the offering up of himself as a sacrifice for the truth, as he understood it. And if he commanded that we should do likewise, it was that we, his followers, should denote by that act our consecration to a noble life, and our willingness to die for what we believe to be the truth. It is not the offering up of Christ, that the holy communion shows forth ; but rather the offering up of ourselves, our souls and bodies, unto God. So the value of the sacrament is not the offering up of Christ, but the offering up of the body and soul of the communicant. You and I can do this act at any time ; and, surely, it is but our bounden duty. While I live, I wish to hold myself ever ready to die for the truth. Such a life is a living sacrifice, and one well-pleasing to God. The sacrament, therefore, is not representative of a myth ; but it shows forth a real fact, that I then and there offer myself unto God, a living sacrifice. Such an act is a noble one, and well calculated to strengthen the soul to live a pure and righteous life."

"That is all very beautiful, Merton; but the worst is that the church doesn't agree with you in this matter. The church says : 'Almighty God, our heavenly Father, who of thy tender mercies didst give thine only Son Jesus Christ to suffer death upon the cross for our redemption ; who made there a full, perfect, and sufficient sacrifice, oblation, and satisfaction, for the sins of the whole world ; and did institute, and in his holy Gospel command us to continue, a perpetual memory of that his precious death, until his coming again ; Hear us, O merciful Father, we most humbly beseech thee ; and grant that we receiving these thy creatures of bread and wine, according to thy Son our Savior Jesus Christ's holy institution, in remembrance of his death and passion, may be partakers of his most blessed body and blood.' Besides when the communicant receives the elements from the hands of the priest, he is distinctly reminded, in the most solemn words, that it is the body and blood of

Christ which he takes. It is not ourselves that is offered in the holy communion, Mr. Merton, according to the church; but that sacrament is representative of the oblation of Jesus Christ, who we are told, offered himself up once for the sins of the whole world. This doctrine I do not believe, nor can any sensible man. It is an unreasonable, unjust, and bloody doctrine. It might be acceptable to anthropophagists, but it cannot be to thinking men. No, I will have nothing to do with such an absurd and nature-contradicting rite. If your idea were that of the church, I could accept it, and would try to be worthy of participating in such a sacrament; but I shall have to wait some time before your interpretation will prevail. May the time hasten when such a rational doctrine will be accepted. I see you're impatient to go, and my business demands my presence. Our conversation must cease for the present. In parting, let me say to you, take good care of Mrs. Merton. She looks like a flower blooming for another world, and we want her here. The gods, you know, never gather unripe fruit:

> '*Aber eure Hand bricht unreif nie*
> *die goldnen Himmelsfrucchte.*'"
> (*Goethe: Iph. auf Tauris.*)

CHAPTER XXVII.

DISCUSSION OF A PRIEST AND A WARDEN.

καὶ καλόν γε τὸ κλέος υἱεῖ τε Διὸς μάλα πρέπον—
Such honor is both beautiful and proper for a son of God.
(*Plato: Leges 1.625.*)

IN every parish there are men who, in common, priestly language, are called dead branches. They have been baptized and confirmed, or by some form or other admitted to full membership; but little by little falling off from church attendance, they finally fail to attend at all. Again, there are multitudes of men who, although they have long since lost all faith in the church, and desire to remain away from attendance, nevertheless keep up their church-going, not having sufficient courage to sever their relations, fearing a loss of social prestige. Some, however, have the courage to act according to their convictions; and ministers find it much more difficult to bring such back to their allegiance, than to add new members to the fold.

Mr. Morse was a college graduate, had been a warden of the parish, had lost faith in church dogmas, and had the courage to act accordingly. Said he, one Sunday evening after services:

"I have but little faith, Mr. Merton, in the doctrines of Christianity. I have scarcely attended services for years. Since you have been here, I have come pretty regularly; but just as soon as you are gone, I shall fall back again into my old place of indifference. I have a contempt for the average minister. It is shocking to hear their contradictions; insulting to hear their maledictions against those who refuse to believe in their nature-subverting assertions. Who can believe, for instance, that a being in human shape is the infinite God of the universe! I declare that it is absolutely impossible for a reasonable man to believe such absurdity, as the dogma about the deity of Christ."

"I do not believe, myself, Mr. Morse, that Jesus Christ was God. There have been, and are, men who are relatively very pure. Like a mirror, they seem to reflect the image of what the good man might suppose God to be. Such were Zoroaster, Buddha, Confucius, Mencius, Marcus Aurelius, Socrates, Plato, Aristotle, Jesus Christ, and many others; and it is possible, though by no means certain, that Jesus Christ remains the greatest of all the great. In this sense, and in this sense only, can I believe that Jesus Christ was divine. In one sense all things are divine; for nature in its entirety flows out from God, as light from the sun. Nature itself is an emanation from Deity. Reason can conceive a being in human shape permeated as it were with the Universal Spirit, as a sponge in the ocean is permeated with water; but it can not conceive the ocean as contained in the sponge, nor a man as containing God. If the Universal and Infinite Spirit was not contained in the human body of Christ, then, as the sponge would not contain the sea, so was Christ not God. As permeated with God, he might have been divine; as a sponge permeated with water, would be watery. But as the sponge contained in the ocean, can not be the ocean which contains it; so the finite, limited, human body of Christ, contained in the universe, could not have contained the Universal Being which contained him. As of others, so of Christ; divinity is predicable, but deity is unthinkable, and absurd. It is impossible for an intelligent man to conceive of a place where God is not: it is impossible that God should not fill the whole; impossible that the whole of existence should not be contained in Him; impossible that He should be less than infinite. It is, therefore, impossible that God should be bounded, or outlined, or have any conceivable form; and, therefore, it is absurd to think of the unbounded, formless, infinite Deity as being contained in the bounded, definitely formed body of Christ. And if God was not contained in the body of Christ, then was Christ not God. It is philosophically possible that Christ was full of deity; but that no more makes Christ God, than the fulness of the sponge with water, makes the sponge the ocean. It is possible, therefore, that Christ was in God; but it is impossible that God was in Christ. Or you might say, as the sub-genus vertebrata is manifested in the class mammalia, so may God have been manifested in Christ; but as the sub-genus vertebrata is not wholly contained in the class mammalia, so was it not possible for God to have been contained in Christ."

"Although I have never attempted to give definite shape to my thought on the subject, Merton, I find it impossible to believe that Christ was the infinite God. But have we reason for believing that he was so full of deity as to be absolutely infallible?"

"In answer to your question, Mr. Morse, it is certain that the proof of such infallibility being in Christ, may be looked for in only three directions,— his miraculous person, his miraculous works, and his superhuman teaching. If we examine the evidence for the miraculous personality of Christ, we are unable to escape the logical conclusion, that even though divinity may have been claimed for him, this claim can prove nothing, since similar claims had, and have been, made for the miraculous personality and divine nature of many others. According to eastern theology, the Highest Spirit has manifested himself in human form, at various times; of these forms Vishnu is but one. Says the Svetasvatara-Upanishad: 'That incarnate Self, according to his own qualities, chooses many shapes, coarse or subtile, and having himself caused a union with them, he is seen as another and another, through the qualities of his acts, and through the qualities of his body.' And says Spencer: 'The Dharma Raja is looked upon by the Bhotanese in the same light as the Grand Lama of Thibet is viewed by his subjects,— namely, as a perpetual incarnation of the Deity, or Buddha himself.' And every one knows that the writings of antiquity are full of theophanies. If we compare the accounts of the births of Aesculapius, Hercules, and Jesus Christ, we shall find a striking similarity:

HERCULES.	AESCULAPIUS.	JESUS CHRIST.
'The lay records the labors and the praise, And all the immortal acts of Hercules. First, how the mighty babe when swathed in bands, The serpent strangled with his infant hands: Then as in years and matchless force he grew, The Oechallan walls, and Trojan overthrew. Besides a thousand hazards they relate, Procured by Juno's and Euristheus' hate. Thy hands, unconquered hero, could subdue The cloud-born Centaurs and the monster crew; Nor thy resistless arm the Bull withstood; Nor he, the roaring terror of the wood. The triple porter of the Stygian seat, With lolling tongue lay fawning at thy feet, And, seized with fear, forgot the mangled meat. The infernal waters trembled at thy sight; Thee, God, no face of danger could affright, Nor huge Typheus, nor the unnumbered snake, Increased with hissing heads in Lerna's lake.'	'Once as the sacred Infant she surveyed, The God was kindled in the raving maid; And thus she uttered her prophetic tale: Hail, great physician of the world, all hail! Hail, mighty infant, who in years to come Shall heal the nations, and defraud the tomb! Swift be thy growth, thy triumphs unconfined; Make kingdoms thicker, and increase mankind. Thy daring art shall animate the dead, And draw the thunder on thy guilty head; Then shalt thou die, but from thy dark abode Shalt rise victorious, and be twice a God.'	Ye nymphs of Solyma begin the song! O thou my voice inspire, that touched Isaiah's hallowed lips with fire; Rapt into future times, the bard began: A virgin shall conceive, a virgin bear a son. Swift fly the years, and rise the expected morn, O spring to light! auspicious babe, be born. He from thick films shall purge the visual ray, And on the sightless eyeball pour the day; 'Tis he the obstructed paths of sound shall clear, And bid new music charm the unfolding ear. The dumb shall sing, the lame his crutch forego, And leap exulting like the bounding roe."

"Is it not strange, my friend, that the people should have generally believed in the divinity of such persons?"

"It is very strange, Mr. Morse, that Christians, knowing

the facts as they do, could ever allege such general belief concerning Christ; for nothing is more evident than that Christ's divinity was not generally accepted by his contemporaries. Of this we need no further proof than the facts of his friendlessness, his trial, and his shameful crucifixion; but other proof may be had from the many stories which became current, either during the life of Christ, or shortly after his death. In the Gospel of Nicodemus, the whole multitude are represented as charging Christ with illegitimacy; and Celsus introduces a Jew as accusing Christ of having invented the story of his birth from a virgin. Mary, he says, the mother of Jesus, having been convicted of the crime of adultery with a soldier called Pandera, was driven from the house of her husband, and for some time wandered heedlessly about, until she brought forth her illegitimate son who was afterwards educated in Egypt. I do not like to mention these stories. I believe that Jesus Christ was pure, holy, and noble; that he was in birth, and in life, in every way fitted to be what he was — a leader and savior of men; but I do not believe that he was God. The same reasons which Christians adduce to disprove the divine character of Aesculapius and Hercules, and of other so-called divinely begotten beings, may certainly be adduced to disprove the deity of Jesus Christ.

"Being compelled to believe that we have no sufficient evidence for belief in the reputedly miraculous personality of Christ, can we say we have conclusive proof of his reputedly miraculous works? In considering this question, it will be conceded that the improbability of miracles is very great; and that, therefore, the evidence necessary to substantiate them must be correspondingly great, or most clear and conclusive. If a miracle is not impossible, it is certainly highly improbable for the following reasons:

1: It is contrary to the ordinary operations of nature;

2: Divine partiality and injustice appear inseparably connected with it;

3: It takes a miracle to prove a miracle.

"Since the miracles of the New Testament are held to have been performed for the purpose of proving the character and mission of the miracle-worker, it seems impossible that the Divine Being could have performed such works, without being chargeable with injustice and partiality. For one person has no more right than another to have his doubts removed by supernatural evidence; and if one person more than another be vouchsafed such miraculous evidence, it seems that God would incur the charge of partiality and injustice.

"If a witness declares that he has had miraculous evidence of that which he asserts, there goes with such declaration the implied admission that he would not have believed what he now asserts, had he not received the miraculous proof. But if the declarer acknowledges that he could not have believed what he now asserts, had he not received miraculous proof, he is precluded from expecting a third party to accept what he alleges, unless supported by similar supernatural evidence. In other words, — it takes a miracle to prove a miracle. For belief in miracles, therefore, the evidence must be miraculous and immediate or direct. While it is possible to give a natural explanation of the occurrence of any phenomena, no supernatural one can be admitted or thought of. This is certainly a safe rule; but it is one that makes it impossible for a person professing to have witnessed a miracle, to prove to another party the genuineness of the miracle he declares. For it matters not what the character of the declarer may be, the fact remains — humani est errare, it is human to err; and the possibility of being deceived or mistaken, remains forever greater than the possibility of miraculous occurrences. It is more reasonable, therefore, to believe that the declarer has been deceived or is mistaken, than that he really witnessed what he asserts. To substantiate a miracle the evidence must, therefore, as we have said, be direct and miraculous. That God could give such evidence, can not be questioned; that He does not give such evidence, everybody knows. The fact that He does not, is to us conclusive proof that miracles are unnecessary. The testimony for miracles, given in the New Testament, is highly unsatisfactory, — indeed, as Mill says, insufficient to prove the occurrence even of an ordinary fact; and absolutely worthless when adduced, as it is, to prove the reality of occurrences contrary to the general laws of nature. We do not, therefore, believe that we have any conclusive proof of the divine nature of Christ, from the reputedly miraculous works attributed to him; for such works have not been substantiated, and can not be.

"Shall we next ask if we have conclusive proof of the divine nature of Christ, from the character of his teachings? It has been held by many that the teachings of Christ are superhuman. This belief is sufficiently refuted by the fact that his teachings are agreeable to us, and much more readily comprehended than the teachings of philosophers in general. And when we consider the fact that the teachings of Christ do not contain any essentially new ideas concerning either God or man, the absurdity of declaring Christ's teachings to be superhuman, becomes sufficiently apparent. Whether we consider his person, his alleged works, or his teachings, we have no satisfactory and conclusive evidence that Christ was other than man, conceived and born of woman, and begotten of man; but we have every reason to believe that he came into the world, like many others, impressed with the idea that he had a work to perform; and we believe he did this work nobly, and that he finally gave his life, as Socrates gave his, for the truth he had preached.

"I do not wish, Mr. Morse, to be known as a grumbling child of the Infinite Father. I am satisfied with nature as I find it; satisfied with the certainties of to-day, and the uncertainties of to-morrow; satisfied not only with the knowledge I have of this present state, and the part I perform in it, but also with my uncertainties concerning a future state. On the other hand, I am not satisfied that God should open the heavens to the gaze of one, though it be Peter or Paul, and keep it closed to the gaze of others who strain every nerve to catch a glimpse of it. In other words, all I ask, in this battle for existence, is fair play; and that I expect God to give me."

CHAPTER XXVIII.

QUIETING A MOTHER'S ANXIETY.

Οἱ Διὸς καὶ Εὐρώπης παῖδες. ὧν οἵδ' οἱ νόμοι—
The children of God and Europa, of whom are these laws.
(*Plato: Minos xxii. 31.*)

"MY dear son," said Merton's aged mother, "Mr. Judex, I believe, does not believe in Christ. Am I right in this?"

"Mother," replied Merton, "it will depend on what you mean when you say, 'believe in Christ.' If you mean to ask whether Mr. Judex believes that Christ is God Almighty, I answer, he does not; but if you mean to ask, whether he believes that Christ was a pure and noble man sent into the world to teach you and me how to live a better life, and prepare for a better state, I answer, he does."

"Yes, my son; but are we not told that, unless we believe that Christ is God, we can not enter the kingdom of heaven?"

"We sometimes hear such words, or their equivalent, from the pulpits of the land, mother, without doubt; but when Mr. Gill told us, a little before he left for South America, that he had seen the devil and several of his imps, did you really believe his word?"

"No, my son, but that was the saying of one man, and said only for a short time; whereas the other is said by so very many, and for such a long time."

"Because of the fact that millions of people, for thousands of years, have believed in witches and wizards, do you therefore believe in their existence?"

"No, my son, but then—"

"There is no 'but then' about it mother. That should show you plainly enough that the simple saying of things, does not prove their truth. If the preachers make such assertions, that does not prove that such assertions are founded upon truth."

"But, my dear son, is it not so said in the Scriptures?"

"Different constructions are put on the same passages of Scripture, mother. I do not deny that passages, taken by some to mean just what you say, are found in the New Testament. As for myself, I do not believe that the New Testament anywhere teaches that Christ is God Almighty; and if I thought it did so teach, it would only still more lessen my faith in its authoritative character."

"But, my son, when we pray to Christ, does that not prove that Christ is God?"

"By no means, mother. When the heathen falls down before his stone-image, does that prove that the image is inhabited by God? Our praying to Christ does not prove that Christ is God, for such a prayer may not be warranted. The Episcopal Church has but few prayers addressed to Christ. We pray to God, addressing to Him our petitions, or whatever it may be, through Jesus Christ. This does not make Jesus Christ the object of prayer, but rather the carrier; or, if you prefer it, the person through whom we have access to God. Provided Jesus Christ and God Almighty be one and the same Being, a man who prays to Jesus Christ, would certainly be praying to God; but if they are not one and the same Being, would the man then be praying to God?"

"No, my son, certainly not; but then —"

"Yes, mother, I understand; but let me ask you to cease using such phrases as 'but then.' Very much danger lurks in the use of such sayings. They are blind guides which lead those who follow them into the ditch; they are dark words containing no light. Continuing what I was saying: if a man should pray to God, and Jesus Christ and God Almighty be one and the same Being, would not the man, in that case, be praying also to Jesus Christ?"

"Of course, my son, he would."

"If a man prays to God Almighty, and Jesus Christ and God Almighty are not one and the same Being, would the man not be still praying to God?"

"Certainly, my son: how could it be otherwise. If a man prays to God, he prays to God."

"So I think, mother. I therefore think the only safe rule a man can act upon in prayer is to pray to the Being whom we know to be God, or about whose deity there can be no question. Whether Jesus Christ be God or no, I know not. That he is not God, I know is the belief of the large majority of thinking men, and of all the adherents of the other world-wide religions. Of one thing I am sure, and that is, no satisfactory evidence, to establish his divinity, has ever been presented me. I know, on the other hand, that I am, that the sun rules the day, and the moon the night; and I declare that I firmly believe there must be a Power, conscious, immanent, a Power in, through, and more than, all things; the Power through which, and by which, all things are. To this Power I pray, and, when I pray, my soul is not torn with misgivings as to whether the object of my prayer is God or not. For I am certain there is nothing greater, wider, deeper, mightier, purer, truer, more changeless, or more abiding, than the Power to which I pray. I pray, then, knowing, without one doubt, that if there is a God, which I doubt not, to that God I am praying. Such a prayer is not directed to a person whose deity has ever been the subject of dispute, and is denied by hundreds of millions; but to Him whom the universal voice of adoring humanity declares to be God. Let you and me, mother, pray and hope, strive and conquer; but when we pray, let us be sure that we pray to God. If we wish to pray to Jesus,

I see no reason why we can't, since I think it possible for the saints to hear us. If they could help us when on earth with their prayers, why can they not help us in heaven? But this is a question concerning which I can not speak with any definite knowledge: all is supposition."

"But, my dear son, do you remember when your dear father died, how, with his finger pointing to the wall, he cried, 'See, Lavinia, see the precious blood of Jesus!' Could your dear father die so happy, unless Christ was God?"

"My dear mother, you know how dear my father, while living, was to me, and how sweet his memory is to me to-day. But how many thousands of heathens have hurled themselves into the funeral-fires, rejoicing at the thought that their spirits were about to accompany those of their friends to the skies? How many thousands have thrown themselves under the heavy wheels of the car of their god, expecting through such immolation a more abundant reward! Because they did these things, do you therefore say they acted reasonably, or that their expectations were founded upon truth?"

"No, my son; but —"

"I have already spoken, mother, of the use of 'but,' and said it is a dangerous word to use. The truth is: as a man thinketh in his heart, so is he. No matter what a man believes; if it be a comforting belief, and he have no doubt, he will die with a shout. Thus we find Mohammedans, Buddhists, Brahmins, Christians, and even the American Indian on the eve of entering the Happy Hunting-Ground, all dying with a shout, each alike satisfied that, as Socrates said, he is about to be 'released from a prison as it were.' That a man dies happy in his faith, is no proof whatever that he does not die deceived. When you are at home in Eudoxia, you might be happy to-day, at the thought of setting out to visit me to-morrow, when, at the same time, I might have died yesterday, without your knowing it. But it would be all the same to you, as long as you imagined I was living. My father lived a good life; he was a child of God. As such the Father took him, whether his faith was such as it should have been or not. It is the heart that God looks to — the intention, more than to the form of words. If God should now ask me, 'what art thou?' what could I answer, but 'a poor, wandering, erring child looking for Thee, my Father;' but if He should ask me, 'what wilt thou?' I should say, 'perfect conformity to Thy will, my God.' It is the latter expression, in my judgment, that God delights to hear; for what are we in God's sight, no matter how pure and holy, but weakness and error! Thus with my dear father: the confession he made, when dying, was valuable, not so much for what it showed him to be, as for what it showed he wished to be. No soul, mother, who longs to get nearer to God, can ever be cast out from His presence."

"My dear son, you make things very plain to your aged mother, although I can't reason with you. Many things you say are very strange to me. Your mother loves to hear you talk; you remove the mists that hang before my eyes a great deal."

"I am glad, my dear mother, that you are able to say so much. God grant that you may never have cause to say worse. I wish I could remove the mists from the eyes of thousands who are nearly blinded with superstition and error. But it is hard, mother, to make a man believe that his household gods are not the great powers he supposed them to be; hard to make a man think that the faith of his childhood is not true. But thousands are falling all around us from the faith they once held, as leaves from the tree in autumn. It is impossible that men should continue, in the light of reason and science, to believe much longer the faith of their childhood. It is honey-combed, rotten, crumbling away. It is dying; and I say, let it die, and be gathered to its fathers, the superstitions of the past ages. But it dies hard: preachers and theologians are prescribing new remedies; but the old faiths have an incurable disease: they are unreasonable; they must and will die. They offer us a god unjust and bloody; and this in itself is sufficient to prove their falsity. Says Goethe:

'*Der missversteht die Himmelischen, der sie blutgierig waehnt.*'"
(*Iph. auf Tauris 1. 3.*)

CHAPTER XXIX.

LAW AND ECCLESIASTICISM.

Law serves morality by securing the free development of its power residing in every human will.   (*Savigny.*)

ὡς ἄρα νόμους ἀνθρώποις ἀναγκαῖον τίθεσθαι, καὶ ξῆν κατὰ νόμους—
It is necessary that laws should be established for men, and to live according to law.   (*Plato: Leges* IX. *874.*)

PARTLY arising from Merton's doubts as to the truth of many of the dogmas of the church, and partly to fill the requirements of the university in his course of study for the degree of LL.D., he resolved to leave the active work of the ministry for three years, and devote himself to the study of the law, ancient and modern.

The university was situated in a beautiful village offering a quiet retreat to such as might be mentally disturbed. This in addition to the fact that his new duties would necessarily call off his thoughts from those subjects that had been so greatly troubling Merton, made his sojourn, at the law-school, a physical no less than an intellectual blessing.

In the study of the law, Merton found great delight. In it he discovered something real, not imaginary; something tangible, not a ghost. Having only to do with the world that is, it contains no imaginary factors. Says Aristotle:

"φανερὸν ὅτι τῶν φύσει ἡ πόλις ἐστί καὶ ὅτι ἄνθρωπος φύσει πολιτικὸν ζῷον—It is evident that the city is the natural out-come of these things, and that man by nature is a political animal." (Repub. 1.2,9.) Law is therefore as much the proper product of human development, as the rose is the natural result of the development of the rose-tree. By the study of the law Merton's admiration for ecclesiasticism was diminished, rather than increased; for it is in the relation of the church to the state, that the base cunning and intrigue of ecclesiastics are most brought to light. What the church has not been able to accomplish by what it has been pleased to call, "the power of the Holy Ghost," she has accomplished by the sword and the legislature. By bribes and threats the bishop has generally succeeded in getting from the king such as he sought for the advancement of his own order; which, in ecclesiastical language, is for the advancement of the glory of God.

Since the 17th century, no ecclesiastic has been Lord Chancellor; "and," says Lord Campbell, "I presume the experiment is not likely to be soon repeated."

The sources of law and religion are supposed to be radically different; and certainly they have not the same end in common. Law is founded in utility, and is wholly originated and preserved by the people. Religion, on the other hand, is supposed, by those most interested in it, to have had a superhuman origin; and its prime factors are supposed to be beyond the test of human reason. The end of the law is perfection of known existence; while the end of religion is said to be the proper preparation for an unknown existence. Law is wholly the fruit of human reason; religion is essentially the fruit of superstition and belief. If religion is to be enjoyed at all, all men should be free to follow whatever forms of religion may seem most agreeable to their respective natures, it being understood that no man should be permitted to follow or enjoy any religion opposed to the interests of the state. In judging whether or not any system of religious belief be detrimental to the interest of the state, known facts must be preferred to unknown, the results of experience to the claims of faith. Law should secure the freedom of individual opinion, except where, by the use of such individual freedom, the institutions of state, or the liberties of others, are endangered. That law may fulfill these grand purposes, fanaticism must not be one of its elements; and that it may be a shelter to all, it must not be exponential of the credulity of any. As soon as religion puts its hand to the helm of the ship of state, the security of the nation and its citizens is gone. The end and sphere of law demand that the ark in which the sacred rights and liberties of the people are preserved, be never approached by the hand of him who seeks legislative discrimination in religious matters. Law in its very nature is national; religion in its very nature is exclusive and narrow. We may say with truth that however beautiful the life of Christ may have been, the lives of his followers have been seen to the worst advantage, when they have had power to enforce their views upon others. Christians have been neither charitable, nor merciful, when the laws of the land were determined by the church. Calvin was designed for the priesthood, and held a benefice at the early age of twelve years. Very early he saw the false and dangerous claims of the Pope, and gave up his benefice. He then with great zeal applied himself to the study of the law at Orleans, but afterwards took up theology again. His legal studies sharpened his powers of judgment, and he soon became the most inveterate enemy of Rome, even declaring the Pope to be antichrist. Calvin became the champion of the French Reformation, but as soon as Francis I began to revel in Protestant blood, Calvin was compelled to fly from Paris. He then denounced in fiercest language the tyranny of the Pope, and the unscriptural character of the Roman Catholic Church, and soon convinced his enemies of his ability as a disputant and a leader of men. He swayed the hearts of thousands; his authority and rule rapidly increased, until his victory was complete. The usual result followed. Calvin set up an inexorably rigid church discipline; instituted an ecclesiastical consistory empowered to inflict heavy penalties civil as well ecclesiastical, and through it exercised almost unlimited sway. The citizen was called to answer for every suspicious expression, the incorrigible being banished, and the dangerous put to death. One was imprisoned for speaking slightingly of his doctrine; another was put to death for denying the Trinity. When Calvin was denied by Rome the right of freedom of speech, he denounced the Pope in the most bitter terms; but as soon as he had acquired the authority, he became more oppressive than the Pope himself. The Romish hierarchy is the mother of religious intolerance; but the spirit of intolerance is coextensive with religious superstition, and manifests itself immediately at the excessive dominance of any religious party.

In the year 1534, the English Church severed its connection with Rome by statute xxvi Henry VIII, c. 1; and in 1537 the reformation of the English Church, under Henry VIII, had reached its culminating point. The grounds of this separation were papal tyranny, and political difficulties arising out of the recognition by English citizens of foreign authority. But the English Church having thrown off the yoke of its foreign master, it was not long before the people discovered, that the tyranny of the Pope had only been transferred to English bishops.

From the earlist ages, scepticism has always prevailed among the powerful and the more learned; but the ignorant and the weak have been kept in servile bondage to priestly dictation. Very early in the reformation of the English Church, it began more and more to restrict the liberty of speech, and to enforce conformity to its ritual and dogma. Queries ex officio mero were issued against clergymen, to answer under oath questions which involved their opinions, not only as to matters in which they had, or might have, conformed, but also as to their future intentions concerning conformity. To obtain their ends, the governors of the church resorted to the barbarous cruelty of torture. Acts of Conformity were passed, §§2 and 3 Edward VI, c. 1; §§5 and 6 Edward VI, c. 1, which were afterwards abolished by Mary, sessions ii, c. 2; and on April 29th, 1659, the Acts of Supremacy (I Eliz. c. 1) and Uniformity (I Eliz. c. 2) were passed by parliament. Under these acts, all non-conformists were punished by fines, imprisonment, or banishment. Life became grievous; multitudes left the country. But the great engine of tyranny was the Ecclesiastical Commission. This was established under the eighth clause of the Act of Supremacy, which permitted the queen to delegate her powers to persons appointed to carry out the purposes of the Acts of Supremacy and Conformity. The power thus delegated was indefinite and almost unlimited, all opinions and actions, contrary to the above legislative acts, falling under its cognizance. This unmerciful persecution by the English Church caused a consequent antagonism which sought its revenge in the overthrow of the established church. But here again we find the persecuted soon becoming the persecutors. On January 3rd, 1645, an ordinance was passed by parliament, prohibiting the public use of the prayer-book; and on August 23rd of this year, this prohibition was made general. Thus was the established church overthrown, and humbled almost to death through its own arrogance, and tyranny.

One would think that the Puritans, having thus tasted the bitterness of oppression, would in their days of power be tolerant ; but they were not so. They acted as had their brother ecclesiastics in like position : they proved what may be said to be a universal truth,—oppression always follows the free exercise of the will of an ecclesiastical legislature. The Puritans of the Commonwealth manifested the most bitter spirit of revenge, and set up a government the most intolerant of all. The royalist clergy were deprived of every means of living, and all persons were prohibited from employing them even as tutors. They established a tribunal called the Triers, to which was assigned all authority in matters of church government; and they passed an ordinance against heretical opinions. They even endeavored to deal with private vices by passing several laws against immorality; and they everywhere persecuted the adherents of Episcopalianism. During the eleven years (1649-1660) in which the Puritans had full sway, they set the church above the state, and made gods of their ministers. Said Cartwright, one of their great leaders: 'The magistrates must remember to submit themselves unto the church, to throw down their crowns before the church, yea, as the prophet speaketh, to lick the dust off the feet of the church.' Puritanism was the child of oppression, but it early became the prince of tyrants. So shameful, unmerciful, violent, and tyrannical, had the exercise of their power become that even the Presbyterians hailed with delight its fall, and the restoration of the monarchy. The joy in England at the coming of Charles, was general and genuine, and the bells tolled out the song of gladness.

Ecclesiastics can not be permitted to determined legislation; for so great is their love of power, that they will even destroy themselves to satiate it. They can no more be trusted with government than the tiger with the taste of blood. By permitting ecclesiastics to have the power of determining legislation, the state renders impossible the end of government—the welfare of the citizens as a whole. The welfare of religion should not be considered, when the legislature asks itself, whether or not any particular legislation will be beneficial to the state. It should be determined by the general ideas of the state at large, as enlightened by science and reason. Religion is in its very nature exclusive and arbitrary, and it is as naturally productive of intolerance as the sun is of heat. The seeming liberality which prevails at certain times and places, is not the fruit of religion ; but as a man will give all that he has for his life, so will any ecclesiastical body suffer many grievous things, rather than be pressed to death by the pressure of public opinion. We have no grounds for supposing that different results from those mentioned above would follow to-day the excessive dominance of any ecclesiastical party ; but the spread of scientific knowledge, and the consequent dissipation of superstition and credulity, tending to bring into subjection more and more any and every form of religious faith, gives us good assurance, that the enlightened nations of the world will not again try the experiment of allowing ecclesiastics to shapen legislation to the jeopardy of liberty and truth.

An immoral religion should be proscribed by the state. In considering the fitness of a religion, positive facts showing incontrovertably its evil results, should outweigh all declarations, made by its adherents, that its origin is divine. This rule should be followed for three reasons :

1 : The teachers of all religions are greatly interested parties, and are, therefore, naturally prejudiced in favor of their respective creeds ;

2 : Positive knowledge is superior to mere faith or belief ;

3 : It is not to be believed that God would reveal a religion injurious to society.

The people of the state should, therefore, judge of the fitness of a religion, and their criterion must be present utility. What is right and what is wrong, are questions which always exist in public and in private ; and in answering them, not only the individual, but also the nation will frequently be sorely perplexed. The ecclesiastic holds that many such questions can be answered only by God, and that such have been answered by Him once for all in the Bible. This is natural : it is to the interests of ecclesiastics to say so. But we hold that the correct answer to the question, what is useful ? is also the correct answer to the seemingly mysterious one, what is right ? Right with one nation is right with another nation, only so far as the questions involved affect alike their respective interests. What is really useful to the individual or the nation, is what that same individual or nation believes to be right ; and this is the explanation why good ecclesiastics have been the most infamous persecutors. What they desired, appeared useful to them ; and they, therefore, thought it would be right, and pursued after it with all the power they could command.

As a guide and teacher law is most powerful. Religion has a strong influence over some, law the strongest influence over all. Many of the noblest are not interested in religion, founding their objections on its contradictory character, and the lack of reasonable evidence to support its claims ; but the law is equally binding on all, from the king to the peasant. Its invincible power is recognized by all, because on the enforcement of the law, depends the safety of the individual, as well as the welfare of the nation. The tendency of the law is to exterminate the very impulse to trespass beyond the proper region of free action. Religion interests a few ; law interests all. Law determines our action for a world we know all about ; religion determines our action for a world we know nothing about, all the creeds to the contrary. Law is all-mighty. We see the cowardly and superstitious John, for his disobedience to Rome, licking the dust off the feet of the proud tyrant who arrogates to himself the power of the Almighty ; but in one hundred and sixty-two years from that time, in the year 1365, we see the law asserting itself, in parliament, over kings and popes, by repudiating papal supremacy, and refusing the papal tribute undertaken by John. A king tyrannizes over his subjects, and covers his despotism with the cloak of religion ; but the wrathful nation, recalling its ancient privileges, determines to enforce the law, and they wring from their law-breaking king, on the 15th of June, 1215, at Runnymede, the Great Charter, the bulwark of English liberty. Popes can buy and sell passports to heaven, and give to whom they will their papal indulgences ; but the law brings the proudest usurper down, and humbles him in the dust. From the infancy of humanity to the present time, there never has been wanting forces to impede the free development of the human mind, by suppressing thought, and wrapping the individual in mysticism and darkness. The greatest of these forces has been that of religious teaching, whether Christian or heathen. In the fourteenth century, when English humanity began to groan under oppression, and demand the extension of liberty, the church advised emancipation ; but although she could advise the barons to emancipate their serfs, she had not the virtue to emancipate her own. To secure herself the church could set the king above all earthly power, by preaching divine right and passive obedience. The law, on the other hand, asserting all authority to be in the will of the people, would not thus be deprived of its throne. When James II commanded the young Duke of Somerset to introduce the papal nuncio, the young man replied : 'I am advised that I can not obey your majesty without breaking the law.' 'Do you not know,' replied the king, 'that I am above the law ?' 'Your majesty may be,' answered the young duke, ' but I am not.'

The nation guided by the church, is sure to die ; the nation guided by the will of the people, is sure to live. Spain is an example of the former ; England and the United States, examples of the latter. Italy, while under the rule of the priest, was a carcass; having cast off the ecclesiastical yoke, she was coming to the front among the great nations of the world. The hand of the priest paralyzes everything it touches; the will of the people, when expressed in law, raises the nation up.

The power and saving nature of the law is well expressed by Lord Coke: "By the common law," says he, "every man's house is called his castle. Why? Because it is surrounded by a mote, or defended by a wall? No! It may be a straw-built hut; the wind may whistle through it, the rain may enter it, but the king can not."

Such characters as Hardwicke, Camden, Thurlow, Roslin, Redesdale, Grant, Eldon, and others, permeate the whole nation with the spirit of justice, and move it onward toward the goal of perfection. Whether we consider the pillars of government, the pilots of the ship of state, the makers of commerce, the leaders of society, the originators of peace, or the guides of individual action,—we shall find first and foremost, in power and example, the great lights of the law.

The greater the priestly power in a nation, the less its sympathy. When England was most governed by priests, she could hang up men by the feet, and smoke them as if hams; could exile every Jew, and most barbarously treat thousands of ill-fated people; could shut up within dungeon walls at the behest of a bigot called Clement IV, a Roger Bacon, on the charge of heresy, although he had spent a large fortune for the advancement of science, and was confessedly the most learned man of the age. The nation is in danger, if under the heels of the priesthood; ecclesiastics are not to be trusted, either as judges or legislators; the apparent fraternal feeling which at times exists between different denominations, is not the result of the spirit of kindness, but is manifested for the sake of self-preservation, infidelity and public opinion forcing it; Christians when in power have been neither charitable nor merciful; ecclesiastics can not be permitted to determine legislation; reason is above dogma and the bible; the teachers of all religions are naturally interested parties, and therefore their declarations must be received accordingly; religious teachers have helped to keep the mind of man in darkness; the nation is sure to die, if guided by the priesthood, for the priest paralyzes whatever he touches.

The fact that the truth of these allegations was apparent to Merton, sufficiently attests his doubts as to the revealed nature of Christianity, and his distrust toward church and clergy.

Merton had read very extensively on the history of the Christian church, carefully reading all of the more celebrated works written on the subject in the English language; and his conclusions were such that, in a letter to the bishop, he said: "If a man wishes to arrive at infidelity, the shortest and best road is to make himself thoroughly acquainted with the history of the church." Merton was sure that no persons had shown such unwavering hatred, such maliciousness, such cunning and guile, such baseness and treachery, such revengeful and murderous spirit, as had the priests and bishops of the church. When the Hussite Reformers were at war with the papists, they burnt priests and monks in pitch, and put to the sword whole districts, with the exception of a few women and children; while, on the other hand, the murderous hatred of the papal party carried them to such atrocity, that they even bought their enemies at so much a head, afterwards to put them to a most cruel death. Terrible as this strife was, it is not inaptly characteristic of priestly wars in general. Merton was certain that while theoretically a philanthropic body, practically the church had never hesitated to use, whenever it had deemed its interests at stake, all the power it could command, by fair means or foul, to persecute its enemies, bind mankind with its shackles, and force upon them its decrees, however detrimental to the welfare of humanity in general. He wondered not that Henry II, who initiated the rule of law in England, to whom may be traced the court of King's Bench, the equitable jurisdiction of the chancellor, and trial by jury, who was one of the ablest and most efficient monarchs that ever lived, and whose friendship was sought by the contemporary sovereigns at any price, should die cursing the whole order of ecclesiastics. Merton saw clearly enough that wherever the priest had had the highest political power, there the welfare of the nation had always been at the lowest point. Well and truly does Goethe say:

"*Aber Leib und Gebein ist nicht zum Besten verwahret,*

Wenn die geistliche Hand der weltlichen Zuegel sich anmasst—

Life and limb are never best protected, when the priestly power has the reins of government."

(*Hermann and Dorothea vi. 300.*)

CHAPTER XXX.

ONE GOD ONE HUMANITY.

Nunquam igitur laudari satis digne philosophia poterit—
Never therefore will philosophy be able to be sufficiently worthily
praised. (*Cicero*)

PHILOSOPHY is the love of wisdom, the knowledge of things as they really are, or the search after causes. It is the highest of all studies, it alone using all the others, and unifying them. To prosecute succesfully the study of philosophy, the mind must be eminently free from bias, and thoroughly equipped with knowledge. Not all who have sufficient information, are thereby qualified to teach philoscphy; for they may be unable to cast-off their prejudices, or rid themselves of some obnoxious growths, the results of seeds sown in days gone by. Nor are all who are free from bias, competent to teach philosophy; because they may not have sufficient information. To the disgrace of many of our so-called universities, men are often found on their faculties, teaching philosophy, who have neither the requisite, general information, nor the years which alone bring fully developed and settled minds. None is qualified to teach philosophy, who has not years, experience, an unbiassed mind, and vast imformation.

It is universally admitted that a greater philosopher than Aristotle has never lived; and Plato is as beautiful, poetical, and religious, as Aristotle is great. It was Plato who spoke as but few men ever spoke, and perhaps with wisdom equal to that of any, on the mysterious problems of life and death. Who sets forth in more glowing terms than these philosophers the value of justice and wisdom, or the danger of injustice and ignorance? Who among the world's prophets has given us a higher conception of God?

who, a higher conception of man? He who would answer these questions truthfully, or not at all, will, in my opinion, keep silence, if he wishes not to disturb the belief that truth and righteousness were first made known by Jesus Christ. For who could believe this, after hearing Plato say:

"διὸ καὶ τὰ μεγάλα ἁμαρτήματα κc᾽. ἀδικήματα σμικρότερον εἶναι χρὴ νομίζειν κακὸν πάσχειν, ἢ δρᾶσαι.

"Οὔτ᾽ ἄρ᾽ ἀνταδικεῖν δεῖ οὔτε κακῶς ἀντιποιεῖν οὐδένα ἀνθρώπων, οὐδ᾽ ἂν ὁτιοῦν πάσχῃ ὑπ᾽ αὐτῶν.

"καὶ θεοῖς ἄρα ἐχθρὸς ἔσται ὁ ἄδικος, ὁ δὲ δίκαιος φίλος.

"Οὐκ ἄρα πάντων γε αἴτιον τὸ ἀγαθόν, ἀλλὰ τῶν μὲν εὖ ἐχόντων αἴτιον, τῶν δὲ κακῶν ἀναίτιον.

"Therefore, to suffer the greatest evils and injustice, must be considered a less evil than to do them.

"It is not right to return to man injustice for injustice, nor to do him evil for evil, no matter what one may suffer from their hands.

"And to God the unjust man is hateful, while the just man is dear to Him.

"Nor is the Good (God) the cause of all things, but of the good only, and not of the evil." (Epis. VII; Crito X. 14, 16; Civitas I. 352; II. 379.)

Again, in his Civitas (I. 351), he tells us that no state can continue to exist without justice; and in his Apology (XXI, XXIX), he says that evil is much more to be feared than death, as death can not possibly bring the good man any harm, since it must bring him either an eternal sleep, or introduce him to a better life.

As Merton became more fully acquainted with the works of Plato and Aristotle, he felt more and more offended at the shameful injustice done these great and noble teachers by Christian ministers of all ages. If the very essence of justice consists in the giving to each his own, surely the average Christian minister has none too much of this virtue. Sunday after Sunday is Christ quoted as the author of sayings and teachings which had been said and taught ages before he came into the world. What a discovery is this to the sincere and thoughtful soul who hitherto has imagined that the world was in gross darkness prior to the coming of Christ! Such sayings and teachings quoted in proof of Christ's divinity, lose all their value, for this purpose, when it becomes known that the same, or similar, were taught by teachers who had long preceded him. The more Merton studied the ancient philosophers, the less did he find it necessary to refer the moral principles of the New Testament to Christ as their real author; and the same may be said of all, or nearly all, its more distinctively religious principles. As he listened, he heard older voices than that of John the Baptist, crying "Repent ye, for the kingdom of heaven is at hand;" and older voices than that of Jesus, saying: "Fear not little flock, for it is your Father's good pleasure to give you the kingdom."

The just man can not take from a more ancient author what is really his, and attribute it to Christ; nor could Christ, as a good and just man, be pleased at such robbery. But however much Christ would be offended at the act, the Christian priest still goes on, refusing to grant unto Cæsar, in his poverty, what is evidently his, although it be but to add a denarius to the store of a reputedly infinite being.

While I have here referred exclusively to ancient philosophers, it must not be understood thereby that I lightly regard the great benefits resulting from the spread of contemporary science; on the contrary, I see in very many of these philosophers great saviors of humanity; and in modern scientific discoveries, such blessings as the ancients might have longed to possess, and longed in vain. But I have referred exclusively to ancient thinkers, lest the reader should suppose that those to whom reference has been made, might have been affected by Christian teachings or sentiments.

No candid person can suppose that Aristotle who died three hundred and twenty-two years before Christ was born, could have been influenced by Christian teaching, and his writings are a gospel in themselves. Still further removed from all Christian influences was Plato, Aristotle's teacher, who left the world three-hundred and forty-seven years before Christ came into it ; and many a gospel might be taken from the writings of this noble man, and not a little of the Christian gospels is contained therein. Contemporary philosophers have many advantages over their ancient brethren ; nevertheless, in beauty of diction, sublimity of thought, reverence of mind, and moral worth, the ancients have never been, and are not likely to be, surpassed. What they did, they did well. We are told that the great Lord Burleigh always carried, in his breast-pocket, Aristotle's Rhetoric and Cicero's de Officiis, and that he thought these two works sufficient "to make both a scholar and an honest man." In some respects, however, the ancient philosophers had advantages over their modern brethren. In their days the scholar was more highly respected, and much less embarrassed with the cares of a life whose demands seem to increase, as the years roll on. Nevertheless, he who would find a prophet, or a preacher of righteousness, or "the voice of one crying in the wilderness," can readily do so in the great and noble thinkers of the present age. It is true, the work of some has been in general antagonistic to prevailing thought, and, therefore, so-called destructive ; but it should not be forgotten, that it may be much wiser to tear down a structure, and build anew on its foundation, or on a firmer one, than to repair it. Moreover, the blows these so-called destructionists have struck, have been aimed at images false to the reality, at ideas the product of over-wrought imagination, at doctrines and dogmas not founded in truth. To such destructionists the good and true man can only wish long life and success, in their effort to break down the images "set up in every high hill, and under every green tree." But, besides such writers, the past century has witnessed many a constructive worker giving to the world gospels purified from the filth of superstition, and cleansed from the foul impurities of priestly influence. Let honor be given these voices of God, for the gospel they preach, and the light they shed on our path; but it should not be supposed that the distructionist is less honorable than the constructionist; for the former goes before, and clears the way, to make straight the path of the latter. They are both great powers of God; they are both his servants sent forth with a message to a world boasting of its light, but groping in gross darkness; and they each alike help to bring about the day when all men shall see the glory of God, in the elevation of the race; when all nations shall be recognized as God's chosen people, and not the Jews and Christians only; when the road to heaven shall be as broad as the pulsating heart of humanity, beating after its God; when the possibility of progress shall be declared as continuing as long as God and creation exist. That day is fast approaching; and when it comes, much of the joys of heaven will be experienced on earth, much of the lamentations of hell be hushed forever. The more Merton contemplated the work of the great and good of old, the more was he offended at a doctrine that regards them as outside the pale of God's elect; and the more he regarded the purity of their lives, and their love for truth, the less he felt inclined to preach a doctrine which, while it opens wide the Father's arms to the Christian prodigal, declares even the noblest heathen to be in danger of eternal damnation. In those thoughtful days, the sense of the oneness of humanity was so strong in Merton, that he could not doubt that the love wherewith the Father loved him, was equally extended to all his brother-men. Even the thought that God might elect the one, and pass over the other, would give him pain. He saw on earth one great object of God's care, humanity; he saw in the spirit-world one object of human prayer and praise, God. Whether they call Him Jahve or Jove, Deus or Zeus, El or Allah, Woden or Manito, Brahm or the Spirit, Gott or the Good; whether they worship Him in costly temples, with priests decked with gold and precious stones, or amidst stately trees, useing the blue, arched roof of heaven as their temple's top; whether in deep humility, with ashes upon their head, or with self-inflicted lacerations,—to Merton it was evident that in all cases the intent of the soul is the same—the worship of Him who, under however many names or forms He may be known or conceived, is recognized by all as the Life, Strength, Lord, Saviour, and Father of men. Knowing these things Merton was loath to resume a work, from the doing of which it would be necessarily inferred, that either silently or openly he admitted that outside the Christian church, there is no known hope of salvation. But through the persuasive voice of his wife, and the hope that he might be allowed to preach a wider faith, Merton resumed the work of a Christian priest, after having passed some years in the study of law and philosophy, and eight months regaining his health, on the western prairies. Said he: "Perhaps the Lord is calling me. I will spread my sails, and yield to the wind that drives me; perchance I may carry a precious cargo to feed the hungry, and cloth the naked; and finally, when my voyage is over, find some haven of rest. Thou, Lord, seest me. I will go trusting Thou has sent me, and ready to do thy will." Nevertheless, a thousand doubts and fears filled his breast. He could not help remembering a little book he had read in his boyhood, the "Heavenly Footman." But it seemed that, instead of having two spirits, an evil and a good one, he had a thousand, all striving to make him do their bidding. But as in mechanics a body can move but in one direction, though acted upon by a thousand forces, so with Merton; the resultant of all his spiritual forces sent him back to the pulpit. But anxious as he was to do the will of him who sends every man into the world, Merton yet felt a pain at the thought of resuming pulpit work. Now he was conscious of a freedom for which he had often longed. The broadness of the prairie, the clearness of the sky, the brightness of the sun and stars, the vividness of the lightning, the pealing of the thunder, the roaring of the wind, were all calculated to inspire independence of spirit and freedom of action. As he looked over the vast and rolling plains, he would think of the broadness of God's creation, and the narrowness of his creed, which man had created; and often would determine to rid himself of the shackles which bound him, and escape from the slave-master's coils. The thought that he was free from bishops' dictation, gave him a peculiar satisfaction. Should death there overtake him, it would find him ready; and the earth that would receive him, was dearer than consecrated ground. No funeral dirge would have been said over his body; no hollow, priestly prayers would have been given to the wind. As he would have died in peace, so without sham or pretense would he have been given to the earth to await his lot. Having resumed his work, Merton, one morning after preaching a missionary sermon, was thus addressed by his wife:

"Harry, why are you so much troubled?"

"I am troubled," he answered "at the thought of the disagreement of my mind with the teachings of the church at whose altar I serve. Much found within her walls is very dear to me; and she is the most tolerant of orthodox churches. But when I think of the dogmas to which, as a minister, it is presumed I subscribe, and know that in my soul I can not believe them, I am tossed by the wild conflicts within, as a boat in a tempest. One of the most painful things I ever had to do, was to preach that sermon on missions, and take the offertory for the general missionary society. By such act it is, and ought to be, understood that I believe in missions. The foundation of all missionary work is, that out of Christ all nations are in a lost and hopeless state; or, at least, that without faith in Christ as their Redeemer and God, there is no known salvation for any people. You know I do not believe that the so-called heathen nations are lost, or that they are without a known salvation, any more than we are. I have often told you I have no doubt that the honest and faithful Brahmin, Buddhist, or Mohammedan, is a child of God, and heir to a better life after death, in the same sense, and with the same right, as I am. If there is any use in missionary labor, it consists only in the possibility of giving the uncivilized nations of the world a higher form of life. It is not needed to bring them into a state of salvation; for in that state every child of man is, and always has been. If I believed otherwise, I should have to say, ' Poor God ! What can be done for him ! The happiness of himself and his children is wholly dependent on the good-will and activity of the missionary society.' All nations have, as they believe, their redeemers, their divine mediators, and holy revelations; and this is all we can say for ourselves. We believe certain things which distinguish us as Christians; but of those same things, we can prove absolutely nothing. In such belief I can put no real confidence. On this one thing I wholly rely: the universal fatherhood of God. God dwells in all things, in all men; and He is reflected by each man as man's mind is polished with intelligence, and his heart with purity. All men receive Him in some measure; of this we are sufficiently certain from our knowledge of the religious nature of universal man. The fact that man is a religious being, is proof enough that God is equally mindful of all. But apart from this, I am sure that a just and good God must be equally mindful of all his children. The various nations of the world may dwell in different rooms, but they all dwell in their Father's house, and feel his divine presence; or, we might say, the various children of the one Father may attend different classes in the same school, but all have the same wise Superintendent, and all pass from a lower to a higher grade, having at the same time, no matter what grade they may chance be in, the guidance and smile of the one great Teacher who careth alike for all. I do not believe that the nations without Christ are lost; nor do I believe in wasting money and many lives in forcing on a nation a form of religion not adapted to their peculiar nature; for our religion is no more agreeable to their nature, than our climate is to their vegetation."

"It would be hard for me to differ with you who have been my guide and teacher. With your own hands did you baptize me, and under your instructions and ministry was I confirmed. Most of the information I possess, I have derived from you. But concerning the matters of which you speak, I have thought the same nearly all my life, as you think now. I never could see, why a just and merciful God could let his light shine on one mere corner, and let the rest of the earth remain in outer darkness, only to curse it for not having his light. Nor have I ever understood, why a good and just God could rightfully blame any man for not receiving a new religion, when he is satisfied of the truth of his own; nor why He could rightfully blame a man who, finding no reasons according to his own honest convictions, for the acceptation of Christ as God, refuses to believe in his divinity, but lives a pure and noble life. For my own part, I believe that every one who satisfies his own conscience in such matters, or, in other words, lives as he thinks he should, will go to heaven after death. God gives all his children such teachers as they need, and such light as their eyes are best prepared to receive. To us he has given Christ, and the light of his blessed gospel. As a follower of Christ, I hope I may be worthy of my many privileges; but nothing can make me believe that God has any favorites. I believe the heathens call God 'Father;' and I doubt not that they have the same right to do so, as I have. Harry, if I were you, I would not trouble myself so much about it. Every one knows how good and noble you are. A pure life is worth ever so much theology. Let that comfort you; and let theology alone."

"My darling wife, what you ask is an impossibility. It is as impossible for me to live without thinking, as without eating, and this ceaseless thought it is, which makes my life a martyrdom. Every honest minister must feel that he is necessarily bound by the theology of the church to which he belongs, as a prisoner is bound by his chains. The latter, as he tries hard to break away from his shackles, soon finds the iron cutting through to his flesh; and the former, as he tries to preach a reasonable doctrine, soon finds his church dogmas cutting through to his soul. If the theology of the church were as much like God as I believe you are, Mabel, then I could gladly receive it; but your principles do not agree with the dogmas of the church; nor is your theology that of the church to which you belong. The truth is, that should the dogmas of the church get into your heart, you would drive them out as you would a rattle-snake from your bed-room."

"I know my information is nothing when compared to yours, Harry. I suppose this is the reason that I don't trouble myself about these matters, as you do. I am glad I have the comfort of my religion; I am glad I love the blessed Jesus. But I am also glad I believe the people of heathen countries, who do the best they know how, are children of God, and go to heaven after death."

"I do not believe in eternal damnation, Sunshine, nor in the infallibility of the Scriptures; I do not believe in the vicarious atonement of Christ; I do not believe in a literal resurrection of the dead; I do not believe that any man, civilized or uncivilized, who lives, as he believes, an honorable and just life, will be damned; I do not believe that nations without the knowledge of Christ, are in a lost condition; I doubt that a direct revelation has ever been made from God to man; I doubt the bible which is exponential of the Christian religion, is, in any real sense, any more divine than the many other bibles which are exponential of the other great religions of the world; I doubt that the method by which man was first brought into being, was, in nature, different from that by which other animals were first brought into being,—that is, I doubt that man was specially created; I doubt very much that Jesus Christ was ever born, in a real sense, of a virgin,—that is I am inclined to believe he had a father and mother, as I myself had; I doubt that a miracle has ever been performed; I doubt that the future state is fixed and unalterable; I doubt a localized heaven; I doubt a localized hell; I doubt the existence of a personal devil. I could add more, but you have surely heard enough."

"Well, Harry, I do not know; but I suspect other scholarly ministers, if the truth were known, have about the same belief in regard to these things as yourself; but you must do what you think best. Mabel knows you will do what is right; and I am perfectly satisfied that God will never forsake you nor blame you for being honest to your own convictions of duty and truth."

"As to scholarly ministers, Mabel, they are few and far between. Our ministers are first-class at smoking cigars, and drinking wine; but as to any real thought, I assure you, they rarely descend below the surface of things. That God will forsake me, my darling, I can not for a moment think. I love Him, hunger and thirst for Him; and I pray with my whole soul, that I may never stray from the path wherein He would have me walk."

"Harry, is there any church whose principles you fully believe; any denomination whose teachings you wholly and unreservedly accept?"

"I do not know that there is, Mabel. My belief might be called simple theism, which is, and always has been, the religious faith of the most learned of every age. Of this statement I am certain enough. There are, it is true, many pretty pictures in our orthodox churches, which are very pleasing to the eyes of the many who worship there; but I assure you, it never has been proved that those pictures, however pleasing, ever had a real existence outside of the diseased or superstitious brain which originated them. I consider any and every religious principle not sanctioned by simple theism, to say the least, doubtful. Orthodoxy is a charming name; but when examined by the critical mind, it appears equivalent to the will of the party in power, whose interest it always is to enforce that will by every possible sanction. When I think of orthodoxy, I imagine a cow standing before me. The tail goes where the cow wills it; and orthodoxy has depended on the emperor's wish. I will here give you an example of this:

"'We, the three emperors, will that all our subjects follow the religion taught by St. Peter to the Romans, professed by those saintly prelates, Damascus, pontiff of Rome, and Peter, bishop of Alexandria, that we believe the one divinity of the Father, Son, and Holy Ghost, of majesty coequal, in the Holy Trinity. We will that all those who embrace this creed, be called catholic Christians; we brand all the senseless followers of other religions by the infamous name of heretics, and forbid their conventicles to assume the name of churches; we reserve their punishment to the vengeance of heaven, and to such measures as divine inspiration shall dictate to us.'

"This, Mabel, is the edict of Gratian, Valentinian II, and Theodosius, emperors of Rome, A. D. 380. Commenting on this edict, Dean Milman says, in his history of Christianity, 'Thus the religion of the whole Roman world was enacted by two feeble boys and a rude Spanish soldier.' It is certain, Mabel, that from the legislatures of the different countries, not a little of the prestige of the church has been derived. I remember myself when no one ever thought of calling the sectarian meeting-houses in England by the name of 'churches.' That name was exclusively applied to the Church of England, whose ministers were better known for their indolence, and fox-hunting tendencies, than for any spiritual power they may have possessed. Bishops and priests, more especially the former, have been more noted as warriors, and for laxity in life, than for their power of healing sin-sick souls. Says Lecky: 'In looking back, with our present experience, we are driven to the melancholy conclusion that, instead of diminishing the number of wars, ecclesiastical influence has actually and very seriously increased it.' He who really knows the history of orthodoxy, can be but little moved by its pretensions. I do not say, Mabel, that I have no faith at all in some of the dogmas peculiarly characteristic of orthodoxy; but I must say I have doubt concerning them. And it is because of these doubts that I wish to take a rest to ease my mind of the many disturbing forces which now so greatly agitate it."

"Your Mabel is greatly troubled for your sake, Harry. I do wish I could help you to clearly determine what you should do. We may at least both pray that God may lead you to decide for the best."

"Though faith in most of my childhood beliefs grows

weaker every day, Mabel, my faith in prayer, weakens not. To God as to a father I am constantly carrying my doubts and fears, and as constantly expecting from Him a solution. Between my desire to be true to the church, and my desire to be true to my own convictions, there is an irrepressible strife which makes even existence itself almost unbearable. In solving the questions which produce this strife, I wish to act slowly, but deliberately. I feel shut up as it were in a hollow sphere, as I was in my dream; and as then, so now, not able to liberate myself, I confidently expect that God will make an exit. Of one thing I am sure,—I wish the will of God done in me; for it is most reasonable to believe that a man had better a thousand times die, than live in opposition to his true and only real life; and God, in my opinion, is the true life of the human soul, apart from which it can but wither and die, as the tree must die, if up-rooted from its parent soil."

CHAPTER XXXI.

A PRIEST AND A PHYSICIAN ON ECCLESIASTICISM.

Vulgus ex veritate pauca, ex opinione multa æstimat—
The uneducated judges little from truth, much from sentiment.
(*Cicero.*)

MERTON had now given the highest proofs of his scholarship, having passed examinations, in leading universities, for no less than five degrees, the last examination having been for the degree of Doctor of Laws. He had found no difficulty in completing the studies leading to all of these degrees. Study was to him his great delight. He loved it for the sake of itself, but more especially as the means whereby he might either substantiate or disprove the faith of his childhood. He wanted the truth; for he knew well, as the blessed Christ says, that this only could make him free. After all his years of study and excessive labor, Merton found that his faith in exclusively Christian dogmas was wholly undermined, that his belief was untenable; but at the same time that his faith in God had taken deeper root. God alone was his hiding-place; and in that refuge of the tempest-tossed soul, Merton found security and rest.

It was while thinking on how great the change was that had passed over his belief, since the time he had knelt with his father in prayer, that Merton was visited by his friend, the learned Quaker physician.

"Well, my friend," he began, "I see I find you musing. I have thought much about you, since hearing your sermon of last Sunday: I really felt deeply for you, knowing the conflict raging within. You once told me that the pulpit was the best field for an able man; and I denied that it is. On the contrary, it is fitting such a mind as you speak of, only as a place to go to sleep in. When I see an able man in the pulpit, I pity him; when I hear him preach, I partly feel the lash that is held over him ; and when I hear him repeat the creed, I know his words assert one thing, while in his heart he believes another. But he is led from fear of the lash and its consequences, like a lamb to the slaughter. On the other hand, when I see one of your average idiots dosing a congregation with, 'thus saith the Lord,' and 'thus saith the church,' I feel as a part of nature so greatly offended at his almost blasphemous nonsense, that I curse myself for a fool for coming where priests are known to rave. If the average preacher could be only made to know with what indifference or contempt the man sitting in the seat before him, receives his thunderings, I feel confident that he would be ashamed thereafter to manufacture his lightnings again."

"I can not but sympathize with you, doctor, in your righteous indignation. I well remember hearing such sermons myself, and how they filled my very soul with contempt for those who preached them. It was certain that the preacher I listened to, was either educated or not educated. If educated, I could not believe that his head admitted the truth of his lips, and I therefore had a contempt for him because of his insincerity, and lack of manhood ; if uneducated, I could not think that he rightfully or worthily filled the position he held, and I therefore had a contempt for him because of his conceit and audacious pretension. It was a cruel thing for me in those days to hear such sermons ; for it really seemed a foretaste of the hell the preacher spoke of. I was certain that the character of the God I worshipped, did not agree with that of the being the preacher declared ; that, therefore, in a true sense, one of us had no God at all, was in fact an atheist ; for since God is one, He can not be apprehended by two persons who have contradictory notions concerning Him. It is true I went to church generally, and sat good-manneredly in my seat; but ten thousand needles and pins seemed to prick me, frequently turning the place of worship into one of martyrdom for me."

"We have all had such feelings, Mr. Merton. In these days, however, I rarely go to church, and therefore rarely expose myself to the martyrdom you speak of. I have noticed that the more ignorant the preacher, the more certain he is concerning those matters which nobody knows anything about; also the more groundless the dogma asserted, the more vehement is the preacher in insisting on its truth. When the foremost of the age turn their backs on a dogma as contradicted by the known facts of science, and the deliverance of the reason, it is then that the preacher rages, and utters his maledictions against the ungodly speculations of science. The higher reason lifts her head beyond the mists of superstition into the clear light of heaven, discovering the filth of priestly rags, the higher the preacher rises in his holy indignation, and, striking the desk in his rage, with one blow knocks the Humboldts and Darwins and Huxleys into hades. If I had any faith in the miracles of the New Testament, and wished to see a person possessed of the devil, as I go to a hospital to look for a sick man, so should I go to a church pulpit to look for a man possessed. What a logomachy the pulpit is! One insists on immersion, the other laughs at it; one insists on baptismal regeneration, the other scouts the idea; the Episcopalian denies the validity of the orders of the other great Protestant bodies, claiming that no man can rightfully and authoritatively perform the functions of a minister, unless he has received ordination from the hands of a bishop, and they wink at his claims. Finally the Roman Catholic denies the ministerial authority of any and all, unless received from a bishop in communion with the Pope of Rome; and even asserts the hopeless state of all who are not within the pale of the holy Church of Rome. At this a howl is heard from the Episcopalian officers, seeing their lines threatened with confusion, their generalship being held up to the ridicule of their enemies. What a great body of truth the church possesses! There never was such a many-headed, dubious monster speaking great things in a language which nobody understands. I am glad that the day of the church is passing, and that of reason coming. Ring out the old; ring in the new."

"The day of the church that is, my dear doctor", said Merton, "is most surely passing away; but like all other days of darkness, it must be followed by a time of preparation, before a brighter dawn. Note the long night that intervened between the passing away of the ancient cults and the establishment of a more agreeable faith. Faithful ones thought that their gods had forsaken them; that even Jove would nod his mighty head no more forever; that the night which had fallen upon them, would be one of eternal darkness. At last day broke, bringing with its roseate beams a religion more advanced, more adapted to the then existing civilization. A religion fitted for the present, becomes a superstition to those that shall follow. But superstitions die hard. They have their organizations, their drilled officers, their priests and ministers, their functionaries, all most vitally interested; these do not yield in a day. You must not expect a too early ringing out of the things that are, and a ringing in of the things that are to be."

"I wait patiently," replied the doctor; "but in the mean time I do my part to hasten in that glorious day, by acting an honest part, in joining the ranks of those who turn toward the light, and leaving the hosts of those who, for fear or favor, shroud themselves in darkness."

"Some may really believe, doctor, what they preach;

but such men are peculiarly constituted, being never given to examine seriously the principles of their faith. As infants eat, so they believe. The mother puts her infant to her breast, and it imbibes, whether the fluid be fit for food or not; thus with such men, they believe, without question, whatever they have received, and even seem happy and satisfied. But that a faith makes a man happy, is no sufficient reason for holding or adopting it. A man might have all confidence in his ship, although, unknown to him, she may be fast filling with water. As a rule, the faithful followers of any religion are contented and happy. I can assure you that the degree of happiness a religion may give a man, has nothing to do with its truth or falsity. But although I have known some ministers whose sincerity and truthfulness I have had no reason to doubt, I have known many more who were insincere and untruthful. Such ministers have spoken to me of their doubts concerning Christ's divinity, who yet in their sermons never breathe such doubts; have denied to me the Trinity, and afterwards in the pulpit affirmed their faith in it; have denied to me the personality of the devil, and afterwards before their people asserted their belief in it; denied eternal punishment, and in their public utterances affirmed it; denied the inspiration of the Scriptures, and on the very next Sunday affirmed their faith in it. All this I have known them to do; and the only excuse they give, is that a man should not give utterance in the pulpit to his private opinions. I tell you, doctor, I am sick of the insincerity and hypocrisy that I have witnessed among ministers. Some good and noble men there are; but, as I have said, I do not believe that the average minister is, in the true sense, a good and noble man."

"I have seen enough, indeed, to assure me that ministers, like others, are in general moved by a short-sighted selfishness which teaches, that the welfare of the body is more than that of the soul."

"And what good, indeed, do you suppose I could get by going to church? Suppose the minister be a good man; what then? He believes that his faith is true; I am satisfied that it is seriously to be questioned. What help or consolation could I receive from such a man? I answer, I could receive none whatever, but rather irritation. The justice and greatness of his god, is the injustice and littleness of mine. The blood of Calvary has a sweet-smelling savor to him; to me it represents an intentional and wilful homicide. The immaculate conception, the deity of Christ, vicarious atonement, the doctrine of election, eternal blessedness, eternal damnation, the call of Abraham, the resurrection of the body, the choice by God of the Jews and Christians, apostolic succession, — these are some of the beliefs which give him comfort; but these same beliefs cause me pain and disgust — they are an offence to me. If you ask me to believe in the immaculate conception, I am offended: you might as well ask me to walk on my head. In the latter case I would answer, it is not the natural mode of locomotion; in the former case I would answer, it is not a natural explanation. If you ask me to believe in the elect character of the Jews and Christians, I am disgusted and offended; you might as well ask me to believe that God is unjust and wicked. If you ask me to believe in vicarious atonement, eternal damnation, or the resurrection of the body, you ask what a reasonable man can not do: you might as well ask me to believe that there are more gods than one, or that the one God is self-contradictory. No, indeed, I am gone further than ever from such beliefs. I can not believe anything of God, which is contradicted by his visible works; I can not believe anything of the works of God, which is contradicted by every-day experience. Talking a few days ago with one of our ablest judges the other day, he said, "The fact is, my friend, the dogmas of the Christian church are absurd. It is my belief that in a few years they will be universally rejected. They are an insult to the thinking mind. Had it not been for the strenuous efforts of the parties interested, and the credulity of the ignorant, they would pass away in a generation. I believe, Merton, in one God who is the Father of all. This God has no elect. All religions come from him, as all warmth comes from the same sun. But as the sun's heat, although scattered equally in all directions, is not equally felt in all places, depending on our nearness to the sun, and the absence of intervening substances; so God's revelation of himself, though given to all and everywhere alike, is not equally felt, nor in the same manner expressed, by all, this depending on the character of the man, and his degree of cultivation. But all religions come from God; and all do good, in their time and place. The coarse and bloody religion is adapted to the coarse and bloody man. He who conceives of God as having human characteristics, will have such a religion as his own mind might be the author of. But as all flowers will not grow in the same soil, so such low, gross, and bloody conceptions of the Deity can find no acceptation with me. We all see with our own eyes; we all think with our own minds; and the ability to think correctly depends, of course, on the character and amount of our education. I am perfectly satisfied that neither the confidence a person has in his faith, nor the degree of happiness he derives from it, has anything to do with its truth or falsity. It is certain that base actions, and false ideas often give us most happiness; while noble actions, and correct ideas frequently bring us pain. I believe with you that the only test of a religion is its reasonableness. A reasonable religion may be false, I'll admit; but I am certain that an unreasonable one can not be true. For it is evident that, if anything unreasonable can come from God, He must remain unknowable to us, since we have only our reason whereby to know Him. If some one says: 'Not so; we have the Scriptures whereby to know Him.' I might answer: 'You receive the Scriptures only because you believe they are reasonable.' Thus there is no way to deny the fact, that reason remains the only power whereby we can know God; or that, if God be unreasonable, He must remain unknown to us. But since the Christian and most of the non-Christian world believe that God is known, they must admit his reasonable character. Therefore I say, as you said last Sunday in your sermon, that although all religions have their root in God, the unreasonable parts of them have their roots in foolish-minded humanity only, and that such parts are therefore false, and should be rejected by the thinking mind."

"In my opinion, doctor," replied Merton, "your conclusions are valid. But let me beg you to remember that although there is a lot of chaff in so-called religion, there is also not a little wheat. I am sorry to say that our conversation must now end, as I have some parish duties to perform."

Merton felt conscious that the words of the text of the sermon to which the doctor in his conversation had made reference, did not agree with his own belief, nor with the highest reason of the age. His views were daily broadening: he saw less and less of the miraculous; he was becoming more and more a child of nature. Yet, in the text referred to, he saw a beautiful truth conveyed, as it were, in a fairy tale. This truth he sought to apprehend; and as he believed he apprehended it, he declared it to his people, not only to direct them in religious matters, but also to guide them into truth; for without the latter, the former becomes but baneful superstition. Truth may be possessed without religion; but religion can not be possessed without truth. In his study Merton was ever confronted with the growing contradictions between science and religion; in his pulpit, between those of reason and dogma. Ministers and commentators he found bending the Old Testament to suit the requirements of the New; and having succeeded in this base work, bending the New to suit the exigencies of their respective creeds. Everywhere he cast his eyes, he beheld dogmas ready to break, and the ecclesiastics who were supported by them, patching them up. The inner-world, the reason, he saw at war with the outer-world, ecclesiastical dogma; and ecclesiastical dogmas, at war with one another. While the people of the parish were no better than others, no more honorable, dutiful, or charitable, he was still more troubled at knowing that the position he claimed, and the dogmas he asserted, could not be sustained with satisfactory credentials. The occurrences he asserted in the creed were stupendous; but the evidence upon which they were based, were puerile, absurd. He clearly saw that to ask a man to accept the creed on the usual interpretation, is no less unreasonable than to expect him to infer that a mountain has been in labor, to explain the existence of the progeny of a mouse. The more he looked for proof of the occurrences asserted in the creed, the further he found himself from the object of his search. Whatever he sought to solve by a supernatural explanation, he readily saw was much more reasonably solved by a natural one. In his mind he beheld Reason carrying a key with which she unlocked the doors that led by labyrinthian ways to the dark hiding-places of ecclesiastical dogmas. He saw her enter, and shed on their monstrous forms the blazing light of her own radiant countenance effulgent with light divine. As she approached, they cried: "What have we to do with thee? Art thou come hither to torment us before the time?" and, crouching in their lairs, sought to conceal themselves in still deeper darkness; but at her look they were filled with consternation, and at her touch were paralyzed. One by one, by the might of her own arm, did she drag them forth, and decapitate them, hurling their lifeless forms into the outer-darkness of superstition, where they first had received their life. There those many-headed giants lay, without hope of a resurrection. The priests of the world went in mourning; but Liberty and Truth clothed themselves in gorgeous apparel, singing: "Alleluia! for the Lord God Omnipotent reigneth."

With all his uncertainty and trembling, Merton yet hesitated to renounce his faith. He felt unwilling to grieve his friends. He knew that false as many of the dogmas were, he was yet accomplishing some good in the work he was doing; and he desired to search more fully into the foundations of his faith, before giving it up, lest too sudden action might bring him repentance:

Lasst uns auch diesmal doch nur die Mittelstrasse betreten!
Eile mit Weile! das war selbst Kaiser Augustus' Devise.
(Goethe: Her. and Dor. 81.)

CHAPTER XXXII.

ON THE RESURRECTION.

He that goeth down to the grave shall come up no more.
(*Job vii. 9*)

TO him who faithfully studies the origin of Christianity, and the work and position of the early Christian church, it will be apparent that the beginnings of Christianity were laid in strife, and that strife was the common heritage of all those who in early days labored to spread the new doctrine. The words put by Matthew into the mouth of Christ: "I came not to send peace but a sword," were certainly verified in the development of the early church. Husbands and wives were estranged, parents and children separated, brotherly ties broken, and friends made enemies. Such results must have followed, and must always follow, the renunciation of one's own religion for the sake of some new and untried faith. Fierce and long was the strife the teachers of the new religion waged, and strong was the opposition brought to bear against them, before Christianity can be said to have felt secure in its position. This time of felt security did not come before near the close of the second century. The great general, strategist, organizer, and dialectician, in this early strife, was Saul of Tarsus, or Paul. It is to this earnest, shrewd, and laborious worker that the Christian church owes a debt it can never pay; for without him it is doubtful if it could have held together, or even been established at all. As Prof. Pfleiderer of Berlin says, it was through Paul that Christianity became recognized as the universal, world religion; and this recognition was won only after a long and bitter strife with the Jewish body in the primitive church.

The dogmas of the early church were, as the dogmas of the church always will be, matters of contention; and among those that received, and must receive, the strongest opposition, is that of the resurrection of the dead.

The early opposition to this dogma is evident enough from what is recorded in St. Mark, the most trust worthy of all the gospels: "Then came unto him the Sadducees, which say there is no resurrection." The Sadducees were a Jewish sect, who held strictly and exclusively to the written Law. This written law, the Pentateuch, never mentions in any instance the doctrine of the resurrection of the dead. Not only does it not give a hope of a resurrection, but one may search its pages in vain for a single word teaching the immortality of the soul. If the great lawgiver himself believed in a resurrection, or even in the immortality of the soul, it is certain that he has left us no evidence of such belief; and in the answer which Christ is said to have given the Sadducees, nothing can be found clearly to establish belief in the resurrection. If Moses had taught this doctrine, surely Christ must be supposed to have known it, and knowing it, it can not be doubted that he would have quoted the strongest text possible. But the words which Christ is said to have spoken, can hardly be construed as giving any strong hopes of the resurrection, or as strengthening to any great extent our faith in that doctrine. What Christ says is at most only an inference which one might make, provided it be granted that the doctrine in question be true. The question itself was left by Christ where the Sadducees affirmed it had always been and was, namely, among the many suppositions which man labors to establish, but labors in vain.

That the infant church was at strife about this dogma, is evident enough from Paul's words to the early Christians: "How say some among you that there is no resurrection of the dead." That the best educated considered such doctrine without warrant, is certain from the manner in which Paul was received by them: "Then certain philosophers of the Epicureans and of the Stoics encountered him. And some said, what will this babbler say? other some, He seems to be a setter forth of strange gods: because he preached unto them Jesus and the resurrection. And as he thus spake, Festus said with a loud voice, Paul, thou art beside thyself; much learning doth make thee mad."

Disbelief in this dogma did not die through the efforts of Paul; for Clement, the first of the apostolic fathers, supposed to have been a disciple of Paul, found it necessary to strengthen the faith of his followers in the doctrine of the resurrection. The proofs, however, which this good father adduced for it, were not unlike those the church fathers adduced for other beliefs. To establish this doctrine Clement tells us that: "Day and night declare to us a resurrection. Let us," he says, "behold the fruits of the earth. The sower goes forth, and casts the seed into the ground; and the seed being thus scattered, though dry and naked when it fell upon the earth, is gradually dissolved. Then out of its dissolution the mighty power of the providence of the Lord raises it up again, and from one seed many arise and bring forth fruit. There is a certain bird which is called a phœnix. This is the only one of the kind and lives for a hundred years. When the time of its dissolution draws near, it builds itself a nest of frankincense and myrrh, and other spices, into which it enters, and dies. But as the flesh decays a certain kind of worm is produced, which, being nourished by the juices of the dead bird, brings forth feathers. Then when it has acquired strength, it takes up that nest in which are the bones of its parent, and bearing these it passes from the land of Arabia into

Egypt, to the city called Heliopolis. And in open day, flying in the sight of all men, it places them on the altar of the sun, and having done this hastens back to its former abode. Do we then deem it wonderful for the Maker of all things to raise up those again that have piously served Him, when even by a bird He shows us his power to fulfil his promise?" (Epistle I. 24, 25, 26). Such is the proof that this great Father gives us for the resurrection of the dead. It is hard to think that any man could be guilty of such folly; but not only, as we see, was Clement guilty of it; but Tertullian also, and others of the Fathers, give us similar arguments to substantiate this nature-contradicting dogma. In the return of day and night, the man of common sense sees nothing else than a necessary result of the earth's diurnal rotation; and in the growth of vegetation from the seed, it is well known that there is no death, and therefore no resurrection. Nothing will grow from a dead seed. At the time of sowing, the embryotic plant is alive. It needs only a little to enable its encased life to burst its barriers, and become a thing of beauty and usefulness; and this little it finds on being buried in the soil. Its transformation from seed to plant, is as simple and real, as is the growth of the chicken from the egg. In each case there is no break in life's continuity, no cessation of life's activities. With regard to what Clement says of the phoenix, it would be foolishness to say anything. His credulity must have been amazingly great to adduce a myth in proof of such a stupendous miracle. One cannot fail, however, to recognize the fact that the testimony of such writers must be received with the greatest caution.

A little after Clement, Polycarp speaks of the doctrine of the resurrection; but makes no attempt to adduce any proof by way of substantiating it. Another of the apostolic Fathers, Justin Martyr, who died near the end of the second century, found it necessary to write apologies for the doctrine of the resurrection of the dead. In these apologies Justin admits that even the resurrection of Christ was denied by some Christians: "And there are some," he says, "who maintain that even Jesus himself appeared only as spiritual, and not in flesh, but presented merely the appearance of flesh." After much useless argument, the only proof of the doctrine adduced by Justin, is the alleged resurrection of Christ, the actuality of which, as he admits but a moment before, was denied by many.

Another great church Father, Irenæus, who died about the end of the second century, endeavors to show the reasonableness of faith in the resurrection of the dead, in these words: "For if God does not vivify what is mortal, and does not bring back the corruptible to incorruption, He is not a God of power. Surely it is much more difficult and incredible from non-existent bones, and nerves, and veins, and the rest of man's organization, to make man an animated and rational creature, than to reintegrate again that which had been created and then afterwards decomposed into earth. Let them inform us, when they maintain the incapacity of the flesh to receive the life granted by God, whether they say these things as being living men and partakers of life, or acknowledge that having no part in life, they are at the present moment dead men." (Against Heresies III). In another place the same author speaks of the growth of the seed from the plant as showing the probability of the resurrection.

Tatian, one of the early church writers, while not attempting to give any reasons for his belief, states his faith in these words: "For just as, not existing before I was born, I know not who I was, and only existed in the potentiality of fleshly matter, but being born after a former state of nothingness, I have obtained through my birth a certainty of my existence; in the same way having been born, and through death existing no longer, I shall exist again. For God will restore the substance to its pristine condition."

Theophilus, another apologist for the resurrection, and writing about the close of the second century, bases his argument on the growth of seeds and fruits, and on the recovery of the body after sickness.

About the end of the second century, Athenagoras also wrote what is called by some a noble treatise on the resurrection. In this work he tells us that the resurrection is made probable because of the changes which occur in man's body during life; because judgment must have reference to the body as well as the soul; because without a resurrection man would be less favorably situated than the beast; because the resurrection of the body is necessary to man's perfection; because unless there be a resurrection, the same soul could not in any other way possess the same body.

Tertullian, who died about 220, and who states that for one to assert the resurrection of the body was to incur the risk of being stoned to death, gives us in his apology for the resurrection almost the same reasons as Clement. In his Address to the Nations he tells them that Christians take for granted a resurrection; and that hope in this resurrection amounts to a contempt of death. In his Address against Marcion, who denied the resurrection, Tertullian's chief work is to quote texts in proof that Marcion was a heretic; but he fails in every way to give the thoughtful Marcion any reasonable grounds for abjuring his heresy.

In the middle of the third century the famous Origen wrote on the resurrection against Celsus, who denied its possibility. In his argument Origen states that the doctrine of the resurrection is a great mystery, that it is a high and difficult doctrine, and one which more than others requires an advanced degree of wisdom; but he fails to make the mystery any more clear; or to give us any stronger reasons for believing in it.

Minucius Felix, writing about the middle of the third century, assures us that the resurrection is proved by the whole course of nature. Arnobius, who wrote at the end of the third century, says it is symbolized in Pluto's myth; and Methodius, who died early in the fourth century, declares it is even paralleled by the generation of man. In the Constitution of the Holy Apostles, an early Christian production, we are told that the sibylline books testify to a resurrection. Lactantius also, in his Divine Institutes written about the middle of the fourth century, refers to these books in proof of a resurrection. While referring thus to the sacred books of the people whose religion the Christians denounced, Lactantius, nevertheless, speaks more dogmatically than his predecessors, declaring that on the resurrection day, God will visit the unbeliever with the most awful punishments, while the believer is raised to everlasting blessedness; nor does he hesitate to set forth minutely the different ways in which the infinite and loving God will seek to avenge himself on the helpless but unbelieving creatures whom his own hands have made.

We have mentioned the chief church writers during the first four hundred years, and given their reasons for believing in the resurrection of the dead; but out of all these reasons we have been unable to find even one that gives us any reasonable ground for faith in the dogma of the resurrection. Most of these reasons are too childish to mention; the rest are partly mere repetitions of irrelative facts, and partly quotations whose truth remains unproved and unprovable. Why is it that after nineteen hundred years of preaching and threatening, the most enlightened minds of the world are unable really to believe in the doctrine of the resurrection? Is it because of wilful refusal? Is it because of a desire that the dogma should be false? Neither of these can possibly be the reason; for man is predisposed to faith in the resurrection.

The cause of this predisposition is not far to find; and the result of this predisposition enables the priest to sow his dogmatic seed on many a piece of fallow ground, that brings forth a thousand-fold. Man is a very self-conceited animal; and the labors of dogmatists, moralists, and psychologists, moved in general by the same motives of gain, or prevented from acting sincerely and boldly through the fear of estranging their friends, or of the loss of prestige, have greatly strengthened man in this conceit. In his studies, true enough, he is frequently brought face to face with the fact that zoology classifies him as a member of the animal kingdom, a single limb of a common tree, a branch of a common stock; but he is not a little offended at any attempt to subject him to the natural results of such a classification. His admission that he belongs to the animal world, is a mere lordly condescension, or an admitted relation which he feels he may at any time deny. Nor is such a feeling of superiority at all to be wondered at, as it is one which manifests itself, more or less, through every plane and sphere of life, and is undoubtedly coextensive with the whole animal world. With the increase of intelligence, we are sure, comes the decrease of this feeling of greatness; but rare indeed is he who is willing to admit either his own ignorance, or the insignificant part he plays in the world of being. Man is ever willing, as Cicero, to magnify the worth of his deeds, and to imagine that his name will be held in honor by the generations to come; that he will be called "wonderful counsellor," after the names and vain doings of his contemporaries shall have been lost in oblivion. No word in the English language is smaller than the pronoun, I; but on the other hand no other word is regarded by us as having such a precious content; and anything and everything which in our judgment tends to increase the value of this content, is eagerly accepted. We are in haste to find out the abode of a rich and influential relative; but we are more than willing to let the home of the poor and lowly one remain unknown to us. While a few of us may not seek to be flattered; all want to be praised, or regarded as superior to our own fellows. Having such a feeling of superiority, it is not at all strange that many are found willing to subscribe to the dogma of the resurrection, even though, at the same time, fearing that they really are but members of the animal world, they despair of the truth of the dogma; or that so many sit passively in their own pews while their ministers make their unproved and unprovable assertions, and fulminate their anathemas against unbelief and unbelievers.

Man is predisposed to believe in the resurrection also, because of a desire of a reunion after death. If the resurrection of the body were really necessary to a reunion after death with our departed friends, in the highest and truest sense, then I for one should be inclined at least to hope for it; but since it can not be shown that this reunion after death is at all conditioned on the resurrection of the body, I should certainly be foolish to entertain any such delusive hope against science and reason. Belief in the resurrection, however, based on the desire of again being with those we have so much loved, is at least founded on something else than conceit. Indeed, scarcely could a noble man be blamed for indulging such a hope, even though there were no vested priest, nor mitered bishop, and church bell had never tolled; for true love is not selfish, but seeks another's good. It labors not to sound the praise of self, nor to magnify one's own superiority. It is the fairest tree in the garden of God, but it is grafted on another; and all the flowers it bears, and the perfume it sheds, are used to beautify and make redolent the life of another. The beauty and worth of friendship can never be overestimated; it is a principle truly divine, full of solace, full of hope; yet, how much more praise-worthy and holy is that all-over-powering love which man feels for the woman in whom the forces of his being are centered. O woman, thou art God's true high-priest, his faithful prophet and teacher, and his most blessed angel! Without thee the sun does lose its potent heat, the earth its greenness, and the heart its buoyant hope. When moved by this holy force of love two noble hearts that have beaten together in joys and sorrows, are riven asunder by the strong arm of Death; when beauty, and hope, and consolation are taken away from man, is it any wonder that he should yield a willing assent to the dogma of the resurrection. Indeed, having such fallow ground and fruitful soil, the wonder is, not that the church should have succeeded in making so many believe in the doctrine, but rather that her success should be so limited, and the believers in the dogma so few. But the reader may contend that the believers in this dogma are not few; that multitudes assert their belief in it two or more times each week, by the repetition of the Creed. Our reply is, that repeating the Creed is not believing in it. A few months ago a lady, who was an Episcopalian and had been all her life, told me that though she had repeated the Creed year after year, she had never been able in her heart really to believe in it; and the writer knows that the acknowledged disagreement between the heart and lips of this woman was not peculiar to her, but is one that is most common to professors in general.

In showing the improbability of the resurrection of the dead, we may state first that—

Man is a Member of the Animal Kingdom.

A man comes to us with a report of having seen an aeronaut ascend to the height of two miles, using for his balloon a soap-bubble fifty feet in diameter. Such a report without doubt would be believed by many uncultivated, unintelligent, and unquestioning persons, especially if the reporter should state that the balloonist had received divine assistance; but by the intelligent it would be set down as a falsehood or a joke. No amount of testimony could make the educated man believe that a thin film of water having such a large surface exposed to unequal internal and external pressures, could possibly escape collapse under the strain necessary to effect the ascent reported. Nevertheless, that a man should have faith in such a report, is far more reasonable than that he should believe in the dogma of the resurrection. Believing in the former does not involve a violation of the known laws of nature; believing in the latter does. The soap-bubble, especially if filled with hydrogen, can certainly ascend with some weight, to some height, for some time; for this has been over and over demonstrated. In the report, therefore, there would be nothing absolutely contrary to established laws; although it would be a gross exaggeration of the force of a soap-bubble. On the other hand, to have faith in the dogma of the resurrection of the dead, is not to believe in a mere exaggeration, but in something absolutely at variance with all known universal laws. Man is a member of the animal kingdom. His generation differs in no respect from that of any other animal; and he is subject to the common laws that govern all animal life. There is not an atom in his physical organism that is peculiar to him, or produced in any way different from that in which those of any other animal are produced. In birth, in infancy, in maturity, in decline, in death, man only exemplifies animal life in general. During the period of gestation he assumes the forms and characteristics of various lower animals; and after birth, though his form is comparatively fixed, he manifests common animal propensities, and is governed by common animal necessities. It takes man about twenty-five years to pass from the egg to the perfect state; while it takes the cicada about seventeen years, and the bee only about twenty days. In the beginning, indeed, "all animals from the sponge to man, appear essentially alike;" and even after quite a little time has passed, it is yet impossible to determine whether the rudimentary form under investigation is that of a frog or a human being. "The gill-arches of fish originally exist exactly the same in man; and in the first months of development he possesses a real tail," (Haeckel), a remnant of which remains even in his perfect state. Indeed, at the age of four weeks the embryos of man and dog are almost exactly alike; and even when the human embryo is eight weeks old, it has a most striking resemblance to that of the dog at six. Every atom of man's frame is of the earth, earthy; and every atom after death returns to the earth from which it was derived. We lay the forms of our dear ones in their peaceful beds. In a few years, perhaps, a handful of dust remains; and in a few more, even that has become diffused, or incorporated in other animal and vegetable life; and the animals and vegetables thus produced become in time again incorporated in the living bodies of other living forms. Thus it is that the atoms forming our frames are, as it were, but given us for present use, afterwards inevitably to be handed over to the use of others. The real title to these atoms remains in the earth alone. She grants their use for a time to certain of her offspring, who after they become physically unable to make a profitable use of them, are forced to yield them up, and give them over to others who use them profitably. Thus in process of time much of the earth's surface will have been incorporated in living animals; and after countless years shall have rolled around, even in human frames. The same atom will thus have passed from one human frame into another an indefinite number of times. Since, therefore, the self-same atom enters into the formation of an indefinite number of individuals, the number of different atoms that have helped to form all the human beings that have ever lived, are very small indeed compared to that vast number which have hitherto entered into the formation of all mankind. Now, if the dead be raised at all, they must be raised having the identical atoms they had when living. That the spirit be clothed about with a similar body, is by no means a resurrection of the body that was laid in the grave. We affirm again that if the identical atom which enters into the body when living, be not raised after death in the resurrection, there is no resurrection of the dead; and that any assertion contrary to this statement will, in due time, be found to consist of empty words. Now, as the forms of energy are various, while the total amount of energy is invariable, and since it is impossible to make fifty pounds of flour out of one ounce of wheat; so, as we have seen, it is impossible to fashion out of atoms sufficient only for a million of bodies, a number sufficient for a million millions. Out of nothing, nothing comes. If the reader should hold that God Almighty can create atoms whenever necessary, we reply that even were such creation possible, it could not affect the impossibility just stated. Creation does not partake of the nature of resurrection. The one is the bringing into being, out of nothing, of that which has not been before; the other is simply the bringing back to being of that which has been before. The resurrection of the dead is conditioned on the bringing back to being of the bodies that have been; and it is this that we find impossible; since it is contrary to well-known universal laws,—to the law of the conservation of energy, to the fundamental law of equality, and to that of common sense, and every-day experience.

Another insurmountable objection to faith in the dogma of the resurrection, is found in the fact of the constant and incessant changes to which the body, during life, is subject. In order to understand the nature and amount of this change, one must have some knowledge of the basic elements of living organisms. As in the city there is nothing foreign to man, the city being only a multiplication of the individual, so in the human framework there is nothing foreign to the individual cells which compose it; but as by the association of individual men, the possibilities and latent powers of each are called forth and manifested in civic government, and in higher and more complex activity, so do the human body and its government show us, in a higher and more complex form, the forces and latent powers of the individual cells which compose the body. In size the cell ranges from one five-hundredth to one ten-thousandth of an inch in diameter; but "within their narrow boundaries are exhibited all the essential phenomena of life, growth, development, and reproduction". (Norton). It is as certain that every living organism originates in a cell, as that the house originates in a brick or stone; and that as a house is but a multiplication of the individual brick or stone, so is the adult organism only an aggregation of the individual cells. Not only is this true, but the same elementary phenomena of life are common to all cells alike, whether it be a unicellular organism, a cell of a plant, or one from the tissues of the highest animal. "The minutest cell", says Prof. Max

Verworn, "exhibits all the elementary phenomena of life. It breathes, and takes nourishment. It grows, and propagates itself. It moves, and reacts against stimuli". Furthermore, in lower animal life in general the waste resulting from the wear and tear of life is not so great as it is in the higher ones. In man this waste is very great indeed; for in him "the constituent cells live very fast, making much waste, and using much food". (Martin). Some idea of cell life may be had from the action of blood corpuscles. The colorless blood corpuscles act as if living animals. Each of these consists of a soft mass of protoplasm. They change their forms constantly and spontaneously, thrusting out one process, and retracting another. They are even seen to "creep across the field of the microscope; and they sometimes bore right through the capillaries, and creep about among the other tissues". (Martin). As they become chilled, after having been taken from the body, they get closer and closer together, as pigs on a cold day. Thus we see the elementary stones of the human temple are constantly crumbling into dust, and others take their places. The body, therefore, that we have at one moment, is not, in all of its elements, the body we have at the next; far less is the body we have to-day the body we shall have to-morrow. It is absolutely certain that the body even at the instant of the last breath of life, is not the same, in all respects, as that which is afterwards laid in the tomb; for even after we cease to breathe, many changes take place before all the vital forces cease to act. Since in life, therefore, we have really very many bodies, only one of which is dogmatically promised us in the resurrection, it follows that we can not hope that the body which we have at any particular moment can be raised from the dead; and therefore that we can not hope that the body can be raised at all. In this we have another reason for not believing in the absurd dogma of the resurrection of the dead.

For the truth of this dogma we have no positive evidence whatever. The changes which come over the larvæ of most insects in passing from their lowest to their perfect state, are held by some to be typical of the resurrection; but we find no reason whatever for such conclusion. "Man", says Norton, "is developed on the same general principles as the butterfly; but the transformations are concealed from view". The likeness of man's transformations to those of the butterfly, however, has reference exclusively to those transformations which occur on this side of the tomb. The organs of the larva do not change directly into those of the perfect insect, but develop gradually out of, as it were, formless matter; but the animal while in this intermediate state, is not dead. Shut up in silence, its living forces manifest the most wonderful activity, and cease not until the perfect insect is produced. In such transformations we find nothing like that from life to death. Indeed, in such we find no more appearance of death than in the case of a master-builder who, having determined to change the plans of his building, ceases not his labors, but sets more men than ever to work, to finish the structure according to the new design. All animal transformations are constructive; death is destructive. The one builds up; the other tears down. The one is conservation; the other is dissipation. The one is victor; the other is captive. The one is form; the other is chaos. The one is light; the other is darkness. In brief: the one is life; the other is death. We insist that the reasonable man can find nothing in animal transformations to strengthen his belief in the dogma of the resurrection. From such considerations as these, we are forced to conclude that nothing other than the common fate of animal organisms can await the human frame.

Concerning the character of the proof which we find in the New Testament for the truth of this dogma, we think sufficient has been said in "God and Man," and elsewhere in this volume. Mr. Fisher, writing in support of the New Testament miracles, but speaking of those which are said to have been wrought more especially by the medieval saints, says: "It can not be denied that pious fraud played a prominent part in the biographies of the saints. When positive trickery has not been practiced, circumstances have been concealed which, if known, would have stripped many a transaction of the miraculous aspect which it wore in the eyes of the ignorant. In order than an individual may be enrolled as a saint, and invoked in this character, it has been held to be indispensable that he should have wrought miracles. It is easy to conceive not only what a stimulus this theory must have afforded to the devout imagination, but also what conscious exaggeration and wilful invention must have sprung out of such a creed. A great number of ecclesiastical miracles can be explained by natural causes. Frequently natural events of no uncommon occurance are viewed as supernatural. The physical effects of vigils and fastings, were no doubt in many cases salutary. Heated imagination, ardent faith, confident hope, may produce extraordinary effects. A variety of nervous disorders are cured by sudden shocks." Mr. Fisher then admits that if the Gospel miracles were of the character of the ecclesiastical, "there might be no occasion for referring them to supernatural agency;" but he, of course, denies their similarity.

In reply we would say that in most ancient times, no less than in apostolic, men were predisposed to belief in the miraculous. Dreams were supernatural; comets were prophetic of dire calamity; prodigies announced every memorable event; sacrifices prevented divine wrath. Even Cicero assures us that no one ever heard of a nation that did not believe in divination, as was proved by the existence for so many ages of the temples and the oracles. This universal predisposition to faith in miracles, would naturally incline men to accept as true any reported wonder, and to unfit them for all critical investigation of the nature required. Belief in the marvelous has been in all ages the one string in the human instrument, on which priests and bishops have delighted most to play. "Their power has always grown, with the extinction of civil government, and the spread of superstition." (Bryce.) Apollonius of Tyana, whom the pagans declared superior to Christ, was said to have raised the dead, cast out devils, healed the sick, and to have performed countless other miracles equally wonderful. In like manner Porphyry was held to have exorcised evil spirits, and Iamblicus to have made himself appear, by praying, ten cubits tall, and to have drawn out of the waters the goddesses of rivers, and to have exhibited them in bodily form. Eleazer, a Jew, drew a devil through the nostrils of an afflicted person. That the followers of Christ should have believed that he possessed miraculous power, is only what might be expected; nor is it any more strange that the medieval saints should have professed to do what they believed their master did. According to Irenæus all Christians had the power to work miracles. He tells us that they prophesied, cast out devils, raised the dead, and healed the sick. Augustine assures us that many miracles were performed, some of which he had himself witnessed. The relics of saints gave sight to the blind, and expelled wicked spirits. In the sixth century the blood of St. Stephen is said to have been found upon the altar in Bordeau. In the diocese of Tours an altar had been raised near the grave of a supposed saint. To make himself sure of the character of the person who had been interred there, St. Martin stood upon the grave, and prayed that God would remove all doubt from his mind. Instantly a frightful-looking ghost is said to have appeared, saying, "I was a robber, and these are my bones." A finger of St. Celsus is reported not to have been in the least affected by the fiercest flames, even after long exposure; and a piece of linen with which Christ is said to have wiped the apostles' feet, could not, it is reported, be consumed by the fire. When Clovis sought to carry away a bone from the body of St. Dennis, the ecclesiastics tell us he was immediately struck with blindness. They also affirm that the relics of Saints Peter and Paul wrought most wonderful miracles, similar in character to those we have mentioned. Gregory the Great assures us that the bishop of Placentia wrote a letter to the river Po, when it had overflowed some church lands; and that when the letter was thrown into the waters, the river immediately fell back into its customary bed. The fame of Gregory Thaumaturgus as a wonder-worker was too world-wide to need mention. We have need only to say that for the genuineness of his miracles the ecclesiastics have produced a host of witnesses.

It is useless to reason with any man who holds that such miracles are, in their character, different from those reported in the New Testament. For our own part we can explain Mr. Fisher's position only on the grounds of the charge which he himself brings against the ecclesiastical miracles: his apology for the New Testament miracles should be regarded as made "in coincidence with a prevailing system, and for the furtherance of it." Not only are there a vast number of reported ecclesiastical miracles whose wonderful character is fully equal to that of any of those in the New Testament, but many of them are far better substantiated. The charge, however, which Mr. Fisher brings against the ecclesiastical miracles, is true; but the apology he makes for those of the New Testament, is utterly groundless. No reasonable man can found his faith or hope on miracles; for they can not be substantiated. It is impossible to remove the feeling that they may have originated in some way or other as Mr. Fisher and thousands of other able writers before him, have described. We can not, therefore, appeal to miracles in proof of the dogma of the resurrection.

So convinced was Merton of the absurdity of the dogma of the resurrection, that at the last Easter services he held in the Episcopal church, while declaring the power of Jesus to raise his followers out of a life of sinful indifference to a life of holy activity, he did not hesitate to state to his people that he did not believe the bodily resurrection of Jesus Christ had been sufficiently substantiated to remove honest doubt from the thoughtful and scholarly mind.

In conclusion, we can not too forcibly remind the reader that this chapter has not been written with the view of weakening his religious inclinations, but rather of strengthening them. We fully believe that God is no respecter of persons; that He has no favorites, no elect, no chosen people; that what He has done for any, He has done for all; and that what He has not done for all, He has not done for any. His laws are for all. His spirit is in and over all, transforming, purifying, sanctifying, and encouraging; and it is led by this spirit that humanity worships, adores, and glorifies the ever-living and only God and Father of all. There could be no greater miracle than that man who needs a miracle to convince him of his duty and privilege to adore his Creator, and chant the universal hymn of praise to God.

CHAPTER XXXIII.

THE HEAVENLY ADVERSARY.

(*Numbers* xxii. 22.)
(*A Sermon by Henry Merton.*)

"THERE is no subject which brings religion into such antagonism with science, as that of prayer. There are many ignorant, earnest Christians who fully believe in the power of prayer to move the Deity to act in their behalf. On the other hand, most scientists affirm that prayer is not only irrational, but that it partakes of the nature of irreverence, if not of blasphemy. Such men may find some reasonable hope of immortality; but they find no grounds whatever of hoping for an answer to prayer. Nor must it be supposed that only irreligious scientists and infidels thus deny the efficacy of prayer; for even some who are among the most religious take the same position. Says Eckhart: 'Thou needst not tell God what thou hast need of; he knows it all beforehand. If I pray for anything, I pray for that which is nothing. He who prays for anything besides God, prays for that which is an idol. The pure man does not pray; for every prayer is for some definite object, but the heart of the pure craves for nothing. God is not moved by our prayers. He has foreseen all things from eternity, including, therefore, our prayers; and he has from all eternity granted or refused them'.

"But if prayer has no other value, it is certainly of infinite value in its subjective influence. We should pray rather that God's will be done in us, than for any special object or favor.

"Near the close of Israel's wanderings, and on the eastern side of the Jordan, opposite Jericho, might have been seen two men, Balak and Balaam, the former being the king of

Moab, the latter his heathen priest. Balak saw what the chosen people had lately done to the Amorites, and fearful that his own subjects might be dispossessed of their country by these strange Israelites, who, he says, were sufficiently numerous to 'lick up all around about them as the ox licketh up the grass of the field,' besought Balaam to importune with God to rid him of the Israelitish immigrators.

"Whoever Balaam was, as a priest he stood high in the hearts of the people, and, without reasonable doubt, was in favor with God; for the king says: I know whom thou blessest, is blest; and whom thou cursest, is cursed. He therefore sent the elders of his people with gifts to his priest that he might intercede in his behalf, and turn Jehovah against the chosen race. As asked, Balaam prays, but is commanded not to curse whom the Lord hath blessed. Balak does not yet despair   He appeals to the pride of the priest by sending him princes as messengers bearing the promise of great promotion, and even of royal obedience, if only the priest come, and pray against the Israelites; but Balaam nobly says: If Balak would give me his house full of silver and gold, I can not go beyond the word of the Lord my God to do less or more. Again the word of the Lord is unfavorable to the king who once more importunes his priest to plead with God against the Israelites. Five times does this priest, by request of the king, seek to know if God will oppose the progress of the Israelites. After his second intercession with God, and on going to have a personal interview with the king, he is met on his way by the Angel of Jehovah who opposes his progress with drawn sword. The priest forthwith confesses his sins, but pleads his ignorance of having God for an adversary. On the whole the character of this heathen priest compares very favorably with that of the Christian priests of to-day; for the word that God put into his mouth, that would he speak, and none other, though his house were filled with silver and gold.

"In considering our very important subject, we shall seek to throw light upon the question, when may we expect to be opposed by the heavenly adversary.

"(I) : Rome is coming into prominence. The descendants of Romulus and Remus, though at first despised by the Carthaginians, are now getting to be treated with deference. Their merchant-ships frequent ports hitherto visited by the Carthaginians only. The city upon seven hills must be plowed up, if Carthage holds her sway. One of the bravest and most skilful generals that ever led armies to battle, is sworn by deadly oath never to sheathe his sword, till hated Rome be humbled. The foes have their priests who day by day plead with God for victory ; the generals and the soldiers gaze into the face of God for a sign. Heaven and earth are invoked by the hostile armies ; thousands upon thousands lie weltering in their blood ; the eternal city is threatened, but the tide turns. Rome sails out to sea a stately ship, and mistress of the world ; Carthage is thrown on shore a pitiable hulk, and left to be buried by the drifting sands of time. These countries were not Christian ; but who dares to say that no praying hearts were found among these people ? Could a man be the author of Cato Major, and never pray to God ? Could the heathen priests and temples receive from the people such lavish offerings, unless the people had faith in their worship ? We have every reason to believe that such people, without the knowledge of Christ, had a knowledge of the one God and Savior of all. They having not the law, were a law unto themselves, their consciences bearing witness unto the truth. Where there is a heart to pray according to the light given, there is there a God to bless. Rome grew, spreading her branches into every land ; scattering literature, arts and science into the darkness of heathendom ; opening the channels of communication by inculcating an harmonious and universal language ; and crowning all with a jurisprudence the growth of centuries, and the wonder of the then known world. Her noble minds are to be the vehicles of higher truths; her philosophy is to be given to the nations as the outward garb of righteousness,—even to distant Britain which, in the ages to come, was to develope a nobler freedom, and an intenser light for those sitting in darkness, and in the valley of the shadow of death. Carthage, with all her prayers and sacrifices, was to cease to be remembered : her cruel laws, her heartless oligarchy, her inhuman butchery, her stunted literature, her lack of an appreciative moral-sense, were all to pass away.

"France impelled forward by monk and friar, is not to rule the western world, but England is to enter in, and take possession. Her strong sense of justice, her love of principle, her sense of duty, her spirit of freedom, are marked qualities of the nation that God destined to be the educator of the world. The world writhes under the heels of Bonaparte, and liberty's blood sends up its cry from the ground of oppression. God hears the cry ; and Waterloo rescues humanity from the spirit of tyranny. Thousands of faithful prayers from cottage and temple had ascended for the success of the great general ; but God winked at them : freedom must extend her sway, and the truth must be preached, and the chariot of the true Christ move triumphantly on. France, powerful as she is, and pray as she does, in 1815, is not permitted to sway the nations.

"Mary is very ardent, zealous and prayerful for the Roman cause ; and bishops and priests, then as now, invoke the blessing of the Almighty upon her endeavor to extirpate the great schism and heresy. The machinery of the church— the sword, the pike and the faggot, are on hand in abundance, to add force to the prayers of the priests; but the blood of Latimer and Ridley is stronger than the papacy, and cries to God for vengeance from the Smithfield fires. This small but worthy sacrifice for truth and freedom was accepted; and Latimer and Ridley lit a candle in England that never can be put out. The blood of martyrs is the seed of truth. That seed has taken deep root with us. The prayers of the Bloody Queen, though fervent and faithful, availed not. She died, and the power of Romanism, in England, died with her.

"(II): A faithful mother bends over the fever-lit eyes of her dying son. It is her only boy, and her heart yearns over him. Already over the grave of her husband, whom she loved so dearly, is the grass growing green. How can this widowed heart give up her only support? Must the angel of death reap on such a blighted ground? Must the heart lose its last object of love, the eye its lustre, and the breast its hope? 'Take this bitter cup from me, O my Father,' she cries; 'oh, spare my boy, my only boy, that the springs of my life may not be altogether dried up!' Few prayers so fervent as this of the lonely and brokenhearted mother; but, alas! it availeth not. Her boy was laid in the cold, cold grave, by the side of her husband; and she is alone in the world, a miserable object of charity. Perhaps the son was taken from the evil to come. The tree had borne but little fruit; but had it been left in the garden, it might have become worm-eaten, and, thus cumbering the ground, been cut down, and cast into the fire.

"In a paternal mansion a happy gathering is seen. Faces are flushed with pride, spirits jubilant with joy; for another unit is to be added to the nation, a new family circle formed, a new centre of pleasure created. No heart-thrust can be received from the world, that may not now be healed by loving hands at home; for the twain shall be no longer two but one. No tears can flow, which may not now be wiped away; no woe endured, which is not gladly shared. Even here, into this union of hearts, does death make an entrance, and rive the bonds asunder. Without apparent aggravation or cause, the chariot and horsemen have taken the spirit of the fair one to the skies, leaving the bereaved to wither and die. What grief such soul endures! What woe now fills his breast! Can it be a pleasure to God, thus to afflict his children? It can not be. Our sky may never again be clear, the heart no more may feel its bliss; but with arid sands beneath, and a brazen sky above, we may be sure He doeth all things well. Our life, if lonely, is short; if the burden be heavy, we may lay it down to-morrow. Besides, our loss is our friend's infinite gain: the fever no more shall parch the lips, nor dethrone the mind; harrowing pain no more shall rack the body, nor disturb the soul's tranquility; no more temptation, nor bitter tears of repentance; the conflict with death is over, the eternal shore is gained.

"The apostles prayed, and their brethren through all ages have followed their example; yet thousands of those prayers have never been answered. The wise father on earth will refuse the petition of his child, if detrimental to the family's interests; so will our heavenly Father refuse to hear our prayers, if they be opposed to the well-being of his other children.

"(III): The great apostle of the Gentiles prayed three times that the thorn in his flesh might be removed; but God's ears were deaf to his cries. That his prayers should be granted, was very desirable to Paul; for whatever the thorn in his flesh may have been, it seemed a great impediment to his popularity as a preacher, and to his success as a master-builder in the great temple of God. But, in after years, Paul confessed it was good for him that God had been averse to his prayers. How many of us plead with

God for things which unmask our selfishness! How few resign self into the hands of our heavenly Father! He puts us into the furnace to burn away the dross, and we endeavor to resist; the adversary meets us on our way in our unrighteous ambition, and after a contest generally succeeds in driving us back into the valley of humility; but sometimes we parry so long with the sword of Jehovah that He sheathes it, allowing us to pass madly on in the road of pleasure, until we fall headlong into the gulf of ruin. Better for such had he died in his infancy, before the 'silver cord was loosed, or the pitcher broken at the fountain, or the wheel broken at the cistern, or the grasshopper became a burden, or his desire failed.'

"Job prays that God may forget the day of his birth, and that the people curse the night wherein he was born. He prayed for death as for hidden treasure, yet it came not. Day and night he complains of the heavy hand of God; still the Lord continues to visit him with affliction, until Job saw it was in love that God had smitten him. Few pray as this man prayed, yet the Lord refused to grant his wish.

"Far off in eastern lands, where every stream and river is a memorial of past greatness, where every zephyr falls on our ear as a requiem for the dead, I see an aged man toiling up a mountain side. For six-score years he has braved the sea of life, which has brought him every phase of human activity. The royal palace and the hovel have alike been his home; the court and the desert are alike familiar to him; he has been the greatest of legislators as well as the humblest of shepherds. But now, full of days, weary, wounded and worn, with his white locks falling upon his shoulders, leaning on his staff, he gazes into the distance, and beholds the object of his yearning spread out before his longing eyes,—the Promised Land, where his heart longs to beat, and his head to rest; but God will not listen to his cry. Here on lonely Nebo, without a friend to wipe the death-sweat from his brow, or pillow his fainting head; here on the threshold of his home must he fall down, and give up the ghost. Ah! it was a thorn in the flesh of Moses to be left for the birds of prey. I can see his face, in a halo of glory, turned pitifully to God, but Jehovah says: 'Thou shalt not go over thither.' He is dead; but did the birds of the air feed on his flesh? Oh! what a burial! what a sepulchre! what a funeral service! God was his priest, and cherubim and seraphim took care of the dead.

"Away yonder in lonely Gethsemene a sorrowful man is seen crushed with care and anxiety. He hath not where to lay his head; he is despised and rejected of men. He foresees the pricks of the spear, the wagging heads, the mocking multitude; he feels already the burning thirst, and the pains of death. With such a bitter cup to his lips, he cries: 'Father, if it be possible let this cup pass from me; nevertheless, not what I will, but what thou wilt.' The desire of his great human heart is not granted; the Father's will is done; the cup is quaffed, and Christ the Savior dies; but though he died, he lives, and lives forevermore, our exemplar, our master, and our guide.

"We have seen that prayers, however fervent, are frequently never answered; we, too, must therefore expect such disappointment. But to have the will of the Father done in us, is to have the best done for us. 'Not what I will, but what thou wilt,' was the submissive cry of Christ, and should be that of us.

"Whatever ye ask in prayer, it shall be given you, provided it be agreeable to God's will. Pray, and pray with your might; but do not seek to turn the heavenly adversary aside from guarding your way. Whether your prayer be answered or not, never cease to believe that God doeth all things well."

CHAPTER XXXIV.

HAPPINESS AND VIRTUE.

Two Sermons by Henry Merton.

"IN a world so full of toil, anxiety, uncertainty, sickness, and death, a discourse on happiness would seem but idle talk, and waste of time. But we have all been happy in our dreams, and even in moments of semi-consciousness, imagining ourselves again at the hearthstone of our parents. Such moments are as showers in times of dearth—they leave a blessing behind them.

"It can not be disputed that men have lived in all ages, under all civilizations, who have appeared at ease, while their neighbors have been restless; contented while their neighbors have been consumed with desire; discharging willingly their duties however lowly, while others have been subjects of grumbling and despair. As the bee makes honey out of the juices of insignificant plants, so some men appear to have the wisdom of extracting a blessing out of almost a curse. They seem to have a higher faculty of discrimination than their fellows. Should we, however, more critically examine the matter, we should probably find that their superior attainments were but the result of the use of those powers common to us all, but which in the case of some, are allowed to remain dormant.

"When Pericles was dying, and his friends stood around his bed lauding his great deeds, the dying man said, 'What I chiefly prize myself, you have not noticed: No Athenian ever wore mourning through me.' Pericles' estimation of what was good, differed from that of his friends.

"In discussing the subject of happiness we may say that the days when purity of heart and sadness of countenance were thought inseparable, are no doubt gone, and properly enough. Utilitarianism though perhaps to some extent an exaggeration, is yet more in conformity with human nature, than any system of ethics which teaches that pleasure is a barrier to the attainment of the highest manhood.

"In seeking a true polity for a people, we should first ask ourselves, what form of government will be the most agreeable, suitable, and enduring, and, at the same time, give them the highest benefits of social life. So in morals and religion, we must not, as many have done, make man to suit a preconstructed system, but the system to suit man as we find him,—the man of to-day as distinguished from the man of other ages, the being that inhabits this world of ours as distinguished from those who possibly dwell in more perfect worlds. We must seek what will perfect, develop, educate, all the powers of his varied nature. So far as any system fails in accomplishing this, so far is it a departure from the true method.

"As man is but a small part of the great whole, so is his nature a veritable copy of it. Nature does nothing in vain, and she is beautiful and happy. Incessant change characterizes her: frost and snow, sunshine and shade, cold and heat, summer and winter, storm and calm, abundance and want. So with man: his life is but a cycle of changes,— sorrow and gladness, pleasure and pain, the warmth of manhood's mid-day splendor, and the chilly air of life's setting sun. Yet throughout all these varied scenes he continually strives for happiness. This is but natural, and nature is but the garment in which God wraps himself, and all her ways are but manifestations of the operating Deity. To conform to nature, is therefore to conform to God's law; and to conform to this law, is to be godlike; and to be godlike, is to be continually striving for the perfection of our nature.

However varied his life, man is only consistent with nature, therefore with himself as a part of nature, when he makes happiness his end.

"We can lay down therefore as our first proposition, that happiness is the end of life. This I am not only willing to admit, but all teaching which denies it, I regard as illogical, or founded on imaginary premises. You and I are each seeking pleasure, enjoyment. Our working-days, our sleepless nights, our beating hearts, our aching heads, our days of suffering, our deeds of kindness, our deeds of hatred, are all the product of the one desire—the desire for happiness. That this is the end of all effort is evident; but why in seeking it, different men frequently pursue contradictory methods, is not so evident. We may say, however, that as nature in general is varied, so is human nature, and that this variety makes men pursue different courses in the pursuit of the one universal object — happiness. Moreover, when the nature is debased, it may make man pursue a course destructive of what he aims at. Those who fail to attain happiness, may frequently be said to labor under a false impression, or false apprehension, either through a perverted nature, or a lack of education, or both. There are those, for instance, who seeing the power of money, give themselves wholly to its acquisition. They are willing to shut up every avenue to their soul, except that of avarice; and to prevent the egress of any thought, except that which meditates on gold. The possession of money, the power of wealth, the flattery of parasites — these things appear to them radiant with beauty; and casting aside all scruples, disregarding all other claims and duties, they reach forward to the acquisition of worldly possessions, believing that once obtained, they will be to them a fountain of pleasure. I remember well in my boyhood four brothers, of whom one by report had said, 'I will make a fortune for my children, if I go to hell for it.' He had succeeded in acquiring about ten millions of dollars, when he received a visit from Death, and was informed that the time was at hand for giving an account of his stewardship. He piteously begged his visitor to depart, and offered his attendant physicians thousands of pounds, if they could force him from his presence. But notwithstanding the power of gold, they were compelled to leave him to his fate; for they knew they had no power with death. It is evident that something was wrong with this man; for it is most improbable that a man who had lived well, whether Christian or heathen, would object to nature drawing the curtain at the close of this life. Because, as in any other drama, so in the drama of life, such a man wishes to see the next scene.

"Some there are who fancy their happiness best obtained by becoming the heads of political circles. Already they imagine themselves sought after by corporations, and office-seekers. Power is what they want. They do not understand that happiness and great power are not inseparably connected; nor does the fatal mistake of Wolsey serve to correct their judgment.

"There are those who might say to me, it is ignoble to teach that man strives for his own happiness rather than his neighbor's. To such I reply that man in seeking his own happiness, most effectually accomplishes that of society. We do not deny that self-denial is a principle of the human constitution, and that it must be an ever-active one in that man who wishes to develope the highest manhood. Indeed, without any doubt, the power to restrain, to refuse to gratify, is not less necessary in the attainment of human happiness, than the power to accomplish. Passive energy is as necessary as active, in building up the perfect man. Nor should it ever be forgotten that one immoderate or unguarded act may work a greater injury than months of labor could repair; aye! it might mar or ruin the whole life. Yet, even in the committal of this one blasting act, the person was seeking what he thought was his own happiness.

"The non-use of anything, is its impotence; the excess of anything, is the evil thereof. The self-love which Christ condemned, while apparently self-love, is really self-destruction; and destruction is not life's end, but preservation. Therefore the short-sighted selfishness of the vulgar, is not productive of their happiness; for it is not true self-love. I can say without limitation that no unbridled, immoderate, excessive, or unreasonable, act ever produces individual good or happiness. In the words of Aristotle: 'Noble action and happiness are the same thing.' Nothing can be said truer than this; and we should govern ourselves accordingly.

"There are those who apparently labor contrary to all their own interests, and for so doing earn the names of heroes — in charity, in philanthropy, in the church, in politics, in state, or on the field of battle; but whether a man dies the death of Nelson, a Howard, a Savonarola, a Becket, or a Cook, it may safely be said that he died pursuing what he thought would most likely work out his own happiness. Great heroes have great souls, and great souls have good judgments, and good judgments look at final not less than immediate results. What to a short-sighted man may appear ruinous, to him who sees the end of things, may appear most desirable. But whether the judgment of the worker be correct or incorrect, I insist that the thing sought in the activity of every living being, is the laborer's own happiness. Nevertheless, it is certainly true that while all men aim at happiness, only the few succeed in reaching it. You say, 'but we can conceive a man or woman committing an act which they know must be ruinous to their own interests; and in that case, they can not be seeking their own happiness.' I reply you are mistaken. That they may be committing an act which, in your judgment, may be ruinous to their own interests, I am willing enough to admit; but I affirm that at the time they commit the act, however ruinous it may be, and however differently they might act in cooler moments, they are lost to all but the pleasure of the moment, and this pleasure appears just what they need. They can not see the deadly poison in the food they eat, nor the fatal fangs of the serpent they play with; rather do they say 'all is fair, all is beautiful.' But after a time, when the wickedness which was conceived is brought forth, they behold an evil-shaped monster, rather than the beautiful form they had imagined. That which promised to be their constant joy, turns out to be their corroding sorrow.

"Our blessed Lord was once asked, what is truth; and the multitude might ask him to-day, were he here, what is happiness. The one great proof of darkness within, is the fact that while we think we are partaking of some dainty morsel, we are not unfrequently found eating our own flesh. Not that we know we are acting thus foolishly, for no man would wilfully and knowingly injure himself; but by the fallaciousness of our judgment we may imagine the shadow to be the substance, or even destroy the very thing we are searching for. The sunken eye, the bloodless cheek, the tottering gait, the repulsive countenance, the ennui and lassitude, which characterize so many of our young men and young women, have their causes more frequently in dissipation than in any too severe mental labors. Your family physician knows the truth of this assertion.

"In judging what is for their own happiness, some are almost certain to be mistaken. Such mistake, when made, is not with all a sin; it may be only through a natural weakness.

If we have but one talent, God holds us not responsible for having ten. The nature with which the child is endowed is frequently but a bow strung with poisoned arrow aimed at the heart of the child. The instruments of death were prepared for him, without money and without price, in the laboratory of his parents. The sins of descent are cumulative; and because of this, man has an aggravated depravity, and is found everywhere deceived and deceiving. His appetites unbounded, his understanding narrow; his desires devouring, his judgment untrue; his passions a giant, his will a dwarf. Many a parent deserves no blessing from the child he has brought into being. We should be temperate in all things. Thus living, every house will be a church; in every heart, enduring joy; in every breast, immortal life."

VIRTUE.

A Sermon by Henry Merton.

"It was common among the Stoics to define virtue, as a certain quiet or rest of the perturbations and passions; but Aristotle was by no means satisfied with this definition. In one place he says that virtue is a habit or state of mind, which chooses between two extremes—excess and deficiency; in another, that it is the finding and pursuing the middle course. The power of finding and pursuing the middle course, lies in the reason. A virtuous man might therefore be defined as a man who lives in accordance with the dictates of the reason. But just as surely as Jesus Christ spoke the truth, when he said that there were but few entering into life, so true is it that there are but few living a life in accordance with reason.

"From the practice of virtue, says Aristotle, a man becomes virtuous; from the practice of justice, a man becomes just. So says St. John: He that doeth righteousness, is righteous. As the practice of virtue, justice, or righteousness, makes a man virtuous, just, or righteous; so he who does not practice justice, virtue, or righteousness, can never become a good man. The knowledge of what constitutes these noble, moral traits, is not sufficient: right theory and proper practice are each alike necessary to the development of a good man. In this, as in other arts or sciences, every man is not competent to theorize for himself; for virtue is as much the flower of reason, as the rose is the bloom of the rose-tree. Now all rose-trees are not alike: while some are so situated as to produce a perfect rose, others are not. And when we desire to know the nature of a rose, we never think of choosing a stunted and sickly tree; but we search until we find a perfect one. Thus when we search after the normal action, and proper uses, of the reason, we do not choose for examination a sickly, poorly endowed, badly educated mind; but one, as far as possible, properly educated, and harmoniously developed. Ever and anon such a man appears; and, like a star of the first magnitude, his path of life is a stream of light emanating from virtue. Such a soul is indeed a true light that lighteth every man that cometh into the world. In him only is seen the truly beautiful and good; and he only has that reason which may be taken as our guide. Such a man has meat and drink of which the multitude know nothing; and to him nature is responsive and the secret of happiness made known. To virtue nothing is beautiful but truth; for virtue seeks greatness of soul, and greatness of soul continually feeds on truth's immortal fruit. Virtue can never be fed on silver or gold, or any other external adornment; for in possession of all these, it would speedily sicken and die. Virtue lives and grows only through the right use of the reason; and reason hath its perfect work, only when building up a man immortal and divine. When we say that reason must be our guide, we mean the reason of the reasonable man. Reason other than this, is no more to be trusted as a guide, than the stunted, sickly rose can be used as a type of roses.

"Virtue is its own reward. In speaking of one of the elements of virtue, Solomon says: 'She shall give to thine head an ornament of peace; a crown of glory shall she deliver thee.' Kingdoms must rise and fall, nations live and perish; but the head that is decked with virtue's crown, remaineth king forever. How petty appear the objects of the vulgar man to that soul possessed of the quietude, and heavenward tendencies, of virtue! Every other possession is sought as a means; virtue only is sought for itself. Virtue is true life, soul-life; the absence of virtue is true death, soul-death. Soul-life is spiritual life, and spiritual life is divine energy, and divine energy is an emanation from the one Universal Spirit, God. He that dwelleth in virtue, therefore, dwelleth in God, and God in him. The possession of virtue gives peace, rest, trust, hope, courage and joy; the total lack of virtue leaves the soul in outer darkness, and deplorable misery; while the lack of it, in any degree, mars to that extent the sacred temple of God. From the petty jealousies and hatreds of neighbors to the armament of continents in universal strife, every thing destructive to human happiness, can be attributed to the lack of virtue. On the other hand, whatever happiness is found, blessings experienced, or peace possessed, may certainly be said to be the fruit of virtue. Well may virtue be its own reward; for with it, poverty is riches; without it, the millionaire is a beggar.

"Virtue we have said is soul-life. Now, soul-life depends for its existence on intercourse with the Deity, the Universal Soul. The virtuous man, therefore, is devout, and ever listening to the whisperings of the Infinite Spirit. Quiet within, he is not greatly disturbed by the distractions without; his peace flows like a river; his eye sparkles with celestial light; his heart beats in unison with the heart of nature; and he understandeth the words:

> 'Change and decay in all around I see;
> O Thou who changest not, abide with me.'

"How can such a soul, fanned by the gentle breezes of heaven, be content in a polluted atmosphere, or with a mere display of drapery! As day by day the feathers appear, the little nestling tries to leave its mother's home. Its latent powers are breaking into activity. It feels the stirrings of a new life; and longs to soar into yon azure skies. So with the virtuous man: he becomes conscious of latent powers; feels the stirrings of a higher life; longs after suitable companionship. Music from another clime breaks upon his ears; multitudes of the holy and the just seem exposed to his gaze, bathed in a flood of divine light; and he feels himself ascending, as he longs for their companionship.

"How such a soul pities the mass of mankind, as he sees them consumed in the hells of their own making! There they lie, without a drop of water to cool their burning tongues. Deceived and deceiving, they taste not the water of life, nor eat the fruit of blissful immortality.

"Let us choose that part which can not be taken from us, which will stand adversity and prosperity alike, which is hopeful in life, and confident in death; let us choose the part of virtue; and soon, as immortal flowers, we shall grow and bloom forever in the paradise of God."

CHAPTER XXXV.

DEATH AND IMMORTALITY.

Non censet lugendum esse mortem quem immortalitas consequatur—
He does not consider that death should be mourned, which immortality follows. (*Cicero*)

"Das Grab ist tief und stille,
Und schauderhaft sein Rand;
Es deckt mit schwartzer Huelle
Ein unbekanntes Land.

"Das Lied der Nachtigallen
Toent nicht in seinem Schoos;
Der Freundschaft Rosen fallen
Nur auf des Huegels Moos.

"Verlass'ne Braeute ringen
Umsonst die Haende wund;
Der Waise Klagen dringen
Nicht in der Tiefe Grund.

"Doch, sonst an keinem Orte,
Wohnt die erselinte Ruh;
Nur durch die dunkle Pforte
Geht man der Heimath zu.

"Das arme Hertz hienieden
Von manchem Sturm bewegt,
Erlangt den wahren Frieden
Nur wenn es nicht merh schlaegt."

(*Salis*)

MERTON and his wife had been visiting a parishoner very sick of cancer. It would be, perhaps, impossible to find stronger evidence of the vicissitudes of human affairs, than Merton received by this visit. But a year before, this patient had been in robust health, and surrounded with contentment and happiness. Now all was changed; and death was near. On leaving the residence of this sick person, they wandered in the cemetery for some time among the sleeping dead. Merton's wife moved among the graves like a drooping lily.

"Harry," she said, "before I knew you, and for some time afterwards, I was greatly troubled with the fear of death. Do you know that that fear has entirely left me now? How peacefully the dead sleep here! The flowers seem to put forth more beautiful hues, and shed a sweeter fragrance, blooming over such peaceful forms. It is said, 'God is not the God of the dead, but of the living.' I do not like that saying. I have no doubt that He is as much the God of the dead, as of the living. It may be the dead are even more alive than the living. Look at this tombstone, and at the inscription it bears: 'Sie schlaft in ruhe — she sleeps in peace.' How many German names are here! and how I love that language! What a blessing to think that God knoweth no nation as such! that all the sleeping dead, of whatever kindred or tongue, may rest in peace, watched over by Him! I know that it is taught that only he who dies in Jesus, may hope to rest in peace. But I believe none has lived so well as he might have lived, and none so wickedly ; and that it is not the believer in this or that dogma, of whom after death it may be said, he rests in peace. Rather may it be said of him who in this life stood at his post of duty, and did what he could for himself and others, according to his own consciousness of what was right. I love the blessed Jesus, but I can not but believe that every man in the world, who lives up to his own ideas of truth and right, will after death rest in peace. Surely, this is not the only world for rectifying our judgment! How ignorant are the wisest of us! how little our greatest strength! What contradictions exist in the different denominations! I thank God that I firmly believe that all Christians and heathens will be judged by the same rule of justice ; and that rule is, in my opinion, that we must do with our might what we believe we should do. If I believed anything less than this of the goodness and justice of God, I should be afraid to trust Him, afraid to die ; but I feel perfectly safe in trusting my body and soul to Him. If at any time I shall learn that I did wrong, wherein I thought I was right, I shall not be afraid, provided I can say, Dear Father, forgive me. I thought in doing what I did, I was doing thy will.

"This is a beautiful cemetery, Harry, sweetened by the fragrant breath of flowers. I like the thought of lying beside my people in my death ; but if I should die, I would like you to bury me here. It is a sweet place, and you and my children would be more likely to visit my grave. I want to live, darling Harry, for your sake ; but if I die, let me sleep in peace here."

"My lovely Mabel, I trust you will not wither away as yet. To die would be gain to you, my sweet one ; but your death would be a cost to me that I could never pay. I pray the dear Father for my sake to spare your precious life ; for without you I fear I can not live. Fight hard for health, dear Mabel, for my sake. Courage, you know, is half the battle."

"I will try to live, Harry, for your sake. I know you need me. But if I die, you must not give way. If God takes me from you, He will give you strength to do both your work and mine. He doeth all things well."

"I do not doubt the goodness of God, my darling Mabel, and that you know right well ; but I can not bear to hear you talk of leaving me. I know when you go away to that better land, your sun will rise to set no more forever ; but, O Mabel, my darling, mine will go down to rise no more. May God grant your translation may be long postponed. Thou art 'so conjunctive to my life and soul, that as the star moves not but in his sphere, I could not but by ' thee."

"Harry, do you believe the dead know what the living do? do you believe the one may aid the other?"

"Mabel, I have thought much on what you now ask. Concerning the future state we have no certain information. All we know is based on conjecture; but I have never been able to see any valid reason, why I should not answer your question in the affirmative. The living can certainly aid one another; and if the dead be not dead but living, I think it unreasonable to hold that the dead and the living are separated by an impassable gulf. The idea that they are, will not stand examination. There is no reason for believing that any other portion of infinite space is provided with a better place for heaven than the part we now occupy. The spirit after death might move a thousand times swifter than the earth in her orbit, and still, in all probability, move for millions of years through space filled with suns and planets, similar to those we know, all obeying the law of gravitation, a law which we have every reason to believe, is universal. There must be a limit to swiftness of motion; for a finite being can not be everywhere at once. It must, therefore, take a spirit some time to pass from one part of space to another; and, for my part, I do not like to think of the soul, after death, as making a long and lonely journey through the burning or frozen regions of limitless space. Such an idea of death is well set forth by the immortal bard:

> "Ay, but to die, and go we know not where,
> To lie in cold obstruction, and to rot;
> This sensible warm motion to become
> A kneaded clod; and the delighted spirit
> To bathe in fiery floods, or to reside
> In thrilling regions of thick ribbed ice;
> To be imprisoned in the viewless winds,

> And blown with restless violence round about
> The pendant world: or to be worse than worst
> Of those that lawless and uncertain thoughts
> Imagine howling, — 'tis too horrible.
> The weariest and most loathed worldly life
> That age, ache, penury, and imprisonment
> Can lay on nature, is a paradise
> To what we fear of death.' —[Measure for Measure.]

"The common idea is, that after death we pass somewhere beyond the stars. The nearest star to us is Alpha Centauri. To reach it a cannon-ball would require more than three million years; and light, which moves at the rate of one hundred and ninety-two thousand miles a second, requires three and a half years to pass from it to us. By this I mean that if God were to blot out Alpha Centauri, it would still appear shining to us for three and a half years. The double star 61 Cygni requires a period of nine and a quarter years to transmit its light to us; and Capella requires more than eight times the period of the latter; while light from Alcyone, in all probability, is not less than five hundred years in coming to us. Nor have we any reason for supposing that beyond these distant worlds there are not others rolling, whose distances are as great from these, as the distances of these worlds are from us. The universe, as far as reason teaches, has no limits; and throughout its awful depths reign law and order, and the whole is filled with worlds in all stages of perfection, ruling and ruled like our own. At what point of space between Alcyone and the earth shall we fix the place where the average orthodox believer locates his heaven? and why should we fix an asylum for the departed spirits, in such far off regions that light requires more than five hundred years to cross? Is it to find its God? I answer, I can not imagine any place more filled with deity than the space through which our earth now rolls. I conclude that there is no reason for supposing a

long and dreary journey, or a flight in angels' bosoms, for the
departed spirit, in order to find its place of rest. Heaven is
is as likely here as elsewhere. Just where it is, none but mad-
men has ever conjectured; but we can with as much reason
fix it near the point of space we now occupy, as in any
other. It is awful to think of a soul wending its way
through the dreary abyss of infinite space, to find its resting-
place. I rather like to think of the spirit-world as opening
to the eyes and ears of our departing friends, as the scenes
of this world disappear. Not to some far-off region do the
spirits of the departed fly, 'blown with restless violence
round about the pendant world;' but though hidden from
our gaze, they may yet continue near us; and if so, why
may they not aid us? why may we not aid them? I know
we have no positive knowledge concerning the future world;
but it is my faith that between the living and the dead there is
no impassable gulf, except in states of being. I, therefore,
pray for my departed dear ones, and I believe they pray for
me. If prayer be of any value, it is foolishness to suppose
that it avails nothing between the living and the dead. If
I should die, I should hope to be able to watch over you,
and inspire you with faith and trust; if you should die, I
should pray for you, as I believe you would continue to pray
for me. I will never believe that in death the soul eternally
dies; and while I believe the soul in death does not die, I
shall think it reasonable to believe that the dead know what
the living do, and may help them in various ways, more especially by inspiring them with high and noble thoughts.
But, my darling, while I believe all this, and hope it true, I
yet trust it will be many years before I shall have to exchange the positive blessings of this known existence, which
I now receive from your dear self, for the hoped-for blessings from a world unknown. Abide with me, Mabel, for

when thou art near, I fear no foe; thy presence turneth my darkness into light."

"Your Mabel will abide with you, darling, if she can; but I was going to say, some of the teachings of the church about the departed are very comforting to me; but others are not so. I do not like, for instance, the idea of a fixed state. It seems to me to be so unlike God, as manifested in his visible works."

"I hardly think, dear Mabel, that a judgment so mistaken and self-contradictory about things so easily known, can be considered of much value about things beyond the reach of human thought. The church whose ignorance and arrogance have led her to persecute, and put to death, the purest and best the world has ever known, can not be trusted to decide for us concerning the future. Not a little of her teachings is the laughing-stock of the world, at least of all rational-minded men; and her teachings with reference to the unknown world, are probably as true as they have been concerning physical science, witchcraft, and heresy. Think what we will, dear Mabel, about the future state, I do not believe the King of glory is any less merciful and good than any king of earth. When we live, let us trust Him; when we die, let us trust Him. He who watcheth the sparrow's fall, will not be unmindful of ours. I would not like to live without faith in the immortality of the soul, Sunshine. Here, I fancy, we scarcely begin to know, to love, or to do. We come into the world infants physically, and leave it infants mentally and spiritually. Few there are of those who have lived, who, before death, attained to anything like spiritual symmetry, or soundness; and I am sure that the wisest man that has ever lived, has felt, at the time of death, that all his learning seemed nothing, as he thought of the vast fields beyond, which he longed to explore. It takes a life-time to make a beginning in the world of knowledge. Is it possible that so fair and promising a flower must be cut off in its bud! Nature herself seems to say it cannot be so. Such a spirit as thine, Sunshine, I cannot believe will die; it could not have been made to die eternally, or sleep the sleep of death. Rather shall thy sun shine on, brighter and brighter, after all earthly suns have ceased to shed their light; for thou shalt have gone to be nearer to that One Infinite Sun, the Life, the Savior, and the Father of all."

Several months had passed away. Mrs. Merton lay upon her dying bed.

"Harry," she said, "I want to tell you that a few days ago, I destroyed all your love-letters to me. I am not willing that any eye but mine should see the expressions of your tender love. And I hope you will burn all the letters you received from me, before my marriage. What I wrote, I wrote for you. I want you to destroy them all. One thing more, darling, your Mabel has arranged everything in those drawers. You know they will want clean clothing, and such things. You can tell the ladies that they will find everything in those drawers.

"And now, Harry, I feel I am leaving you fast. Let me ask you to administer the holy communion."

In the celebration of this sacred rite, Merton was always most earnest and devout; for he believed it his duty and privilege to offer himself therein a living sacrifice unto the God whom he adored. In this holy sacrament he felt his fellowship with Jesus was perfected. He was his guide; and it was he who had said, "Do this in remembrance of me." So in this holy rite, Merton remembered him as a preacher of righteousness, as a savior of men, as a friend of sinners, as a son of God, and finally as laying down his life for the sake of the truth. So when Merton figuratively drank his blood or ate his flesh, he tried to offer unto God a real offering—his powers, his life, his all. This was his aim, and such was his resolution when he prepared to perform this office for his dying loved one. Mrs. Merton well knew his belief, and that he was trying not only to be calm in the presence of death, but also to drink the bitter cup he was offered. As Merton placed the element denoting the body, in the palm of her hand, and said, "The body of our Lord Jesus Christ which was given for thee," he knew she was offering herself then, that the offering had been received, that she was really disappearing from his view, in a few hours to be given over to the cold embrace of death. But his soul was comforted at the words, "preserve thy soul and body unto everlasting life." Death could take her from him, and hide her in the moldy chambers of the tomb; but it could not take away the hope, that in one of the many mansions the Father hath, he had a room for her, and some day would have one even for him, and that there he would see her again. True enough, as Kant teaches, Merton well knew that "the permanence of the soul beyond life remains undemonstrated, and undemonstrable;" but the belief in immortality was too strong in him to give up the hope of meeting his wife again. It was a solemn time; but one in which the hope was strong, that the spirit shall not die.

"Harry," she said, "I felt prepared before; but now everything has been done that is thought proper. Now go, and take care of yourself; look to your own health. Much will in the future depend on you. For the sake of our three little ones, you must bear up. The duty of mother and father must hereafter, dear Harry, fall on you. I know you will not fail; I am sure you will not be found wanting; and may God pity and help you, dear one, when Mabel shall be no more."

"Mabel," said Merton, "tell me, have you any fear of death?"

"I have no fear whatever," she answered. "The dear Father will take care of me. I think it would be wicked to be afraid of death. How could I so mistrust my God!"

"I am glad, Sunshine, to hear these words. And just think of it,—if you should leave us now, you will find your dear mother there waiting for you. She is forever free from pain and care. Neither winter's cold nor summer's heat will ever affect her again. She is at rest; and should you die, you will not leave her behind you to grieve in this vale of tears."

"Call your mother and our children," said the dying wife.

They stood around her bed. Tears were seen in her eyes, as she with difficulty said: "God bless you, dear Harry; God bless my little ones; God bless dear mother; God bless you all."

Merton knelt by the bedside. "Come nearer," she said; "come nearer. Let me have your hand in mine; I am passing away."

"Dear Sunshine," said Merton, "Tell me, is there any darkness where you are?"

"Darkness, Harry!" she replied. "There is no darkness where the Father is. He will lighten my path."

"Oh, Mabel, my darling, how great should be thy joy! Thou art going to see what the glorious future is. Oft hast thou heard me say how sweet such death must be! how sweet to know what heaven hath in store for us! and to join the company of the holy and the blessed! Oh, Mabel, my darling, do not forget me when thou art passed from scenes of pain. I shall be weary, fainting, broken-hearted, sighing for heaven and thee. Do not forget me, Mabel. I shall always pray for thee, and teach our little ones to do so. Help me, Mabel, from that better world, to live a pure and holy life, and to be strong for thine and mine."

"Blessed, blessed Jesus," she said, gasping for breath. These were her last words. For about three hours she lay in a comatose state, when her heart ceased to beat, and her breast to heave. Without a sigh or murmur she passed from Merton into the unseen world. The words of the beautiful hymn that she so much loved, were as balm to Merton's wounded spirit:

"My God, my Father, while I stray
Far from my home, on life's rough way,
O teach me from my heart to say
Thy will be done.

"Though dark my path, and sad my lot,
Let me be still and murmur not,
And breathe the prayer divinely taught,
Thy will be done.

"What though in lonely grief I sigh
For friends beloved no longer nigh,
Submissive still would I reply,
Thy will be done.

"If thou shouldst call me to resign
What most I love, it ne'er was mine;
I only yield thee what is thine—
Thy will be done.

"Renew my will from day to day,
Blend it with thine, and take away
All that now makes it hard to say,
Thy will be done.

"Let but my fainting heart be blest
With thy sweet Spirit for its guest,
My God, to thee I leave the rest;
Thy will be done.

The body was dressed for the grave by loving hands; and the next morning it was placed in the coffin, which was covered with black broadcloth. On its cover it had a plate, in the form of a cross, on which had been engraved the name of her whom Merton had so greatly loved.

"Oh, my loved one!" said Merton, "no more shalt thou tremble in the presence of death, or at wading the dismal flood. No more shall earth's troubles disturb thee, nor the words of unkind ones tear thy tender breast. Henceforth thou shalt live a higher life; and dressed in garments whiter than snow, join in songs of praise to Him, the only God and Father of all. The courts of the temple of the higher Jerusalem are now open to thee. Enter thou into the holy of holies. Fields of brighter glory are now open to thy view. Rejoice and be exceeding glad; death hath no sting for thee, nor the grave dominion: through death hast thou entered into life."

The funeral service was preached by the bishop, and the long procession was on its way to the cemetery. Many a mourning heart was there, in addition to Merton's; but as the body of the departed one was borne along over the road which Merton and Sunshine had so often trodden together, his soul was heavy and his spirits sank within him; for every step was full of memories of the dead. There is the house they lived in, when first they came to the city. There is the beautiful evergreen whose shade the departed wife had so often sought. There is the walk she had so often travelled, making music in Merton's ears, as her feet moved over its surface. There is the gate her blessed hand had so oftened opened, sanctifying the catch she touched. There is the beautiful grove, still singing its wierd music; there the short walk through the pines and evergreens, which she so oft had taken. Here is the gate that opened at her approach, when visiting the sick with cancer, and the last through which her beloved body shall ever pass; for it leads to the chambers of the dead, where the wicked cease from troubling, and the weary are at rest. Here are the graves among which she moved, and the epitaphs she read; and there a grave newly made, beside the carriage-way. The hearse stands still: this grave is for the body of Sunshine. The service was continued; the coffin lowered; the body given to the forces of destruction; the grave made redolent with flowers; the Gloria in in Excelsis sung. They hid the coffin from Merton's gaze, deeply covering it with new-born earth. The body of his loved one slept alone; and from that day, its sleep hath been unbroken; and never again, though the earth stand green forever, and the heavens pass not away, shall the lovely form of Mabel be seen among the living. It was then that Merton thus poured forth his poetic soul:

"Wave your branches, ye lofty pines, and chant your dolorous music. Ye feathered songsters that warble over her resting-place, sing me now a funeral dirge accordant with my soul. Thou glorious sun, vail thy proud face at the sorrows of humanity; and thou pale moon, pour down thy lambent beams on this our weeping earth. Ye stars, that gaze out of the illimitable depths of time and space, give but a flickering light; boast not your power, your splendor, your magnitude, your eternity, in the presence of a broken heart. Ye weeping-willows, bend low your branches, bathe the earth in tears, and let the mournful vapor rise to heaven, wrapping the globes in mourning-weeds. Ye sweet forget-me-nots, cease not to bloom on the grave of her who sleeps, nor to remind the living of the lovely dead."

As being among the forces that greatly affected Merton's religious conceptions, it is fitting, perhaps, that we should say here, that Merton had been twice married. His first wife was one of those beautiful and loving creatures born to inspire man with courage and hope, by making him conscious, in her every step, that all her happiness is centered in him. In this beautiful woman, for a brief period, Merton found every desire and expectation realized. She then gave up her youthful life as a sacrifice for the continuance of the race, the child following its mother to the grave, after the brief period of three months.

At the loss of his first wife, it were vain to attempt a description of Merton's suffering. Suffice it to say, that it was that soul-felt agony experienced by every noble man, of high education and most sensitive nature, when forced to let his wife, to him the image of all perfection, pass into that shadowy realm where Death holds supreme dominion. Bitter was the cup which Merton drank, and bitter were its dregs. O earth, earth, earth, what is life when the heart is dead! As a tree when struck by lightning, as a dying world that rolls through sunless space, so is man upon whom the beams of love no longer fall.

But life is real, and its duties are urgent; and man must either strive to overcome by adjusting himself to his circumstances, or yield himself up a prey to his adversaries.

The influence of a good wife is of inestimable advantage to a man in the ministry. The pastor's relation to his congregation, especially to the female part of it, is of a most delicate nature; and no unmarried minister is able, in the judgment of a man of cool, calculating, practical sense, to take himself wholly out of the plane of suspicion. It was this knowledge, added to his desire to be made more efficient, that led Merton, who was yet but a young man, to take to himself his second wife. It was a happy choice. She was young, beautiful, and of a most happy disposition; and although Merton had never ceased to keep in his soul a holy memory of his first wife, his heart was fully satisfied, and his happiness complete, with his second. Their union had also been blessed with three of the loveliest children, and strengthened by more than six years of happy, wedded life. It was this beautiful wife, and holy mother, that the grave had just claimed from Merton.

After the burial rites Merton returned to the parsonage. It seemed an empty nest. The air seemed chilly; the rooms seemed vacant; the house appeared strange,—love had flown. The chamber Mrs. Merton had occupied, was full of mournful memories; and the bed upon which she lay, and where she breathed her youthful life away, became to him a thing of pain, and not the place of rest. The sound of every foot-fall created expectations, but to blast them as they rose. Oft he called to Mabel, but she answered him not; oft he sought her presence, but failed to see her form. Oft he turned to speak to her, to be mocked by empty space. The light of the house no more did shine, the warmth of the hearthstone no more was felt; no more was he influenced by the attractions of life. The house was not home; for home itself was dead.

Soon Merton visited the grave in company with his little children. Nothing had disturbed the lost one's resting-place: she still slept; and the odor of fresh flowers perfumed the grave. The beautiful lily, though, had drooped its head, and died, as if of grief for her that slept. In love and sorrow they bent their knees; and there Merton made for the children the following prayer, as well that they might be reminded of their mother, as because of the promise he had made her:

"O Lord God Almighty, give rest and felicity to our dear mamma in thy eternal kingdom; and cause the light of thy countenance to shine upon her, through Jesus Christ, our Lord." From that time, in their daily prayers, they never failed to use these words. Thus the memory of their mother was kept ever green in their minds; and thus is made possible the realization of the hope of spirit-communion.

Merton had been brought up to believe that everything which happened to him, occurred by God's appointment; and he knew well that this belief was supposed to be held by Christians in general. At the same time he knew what he had lost, and what he was suffering as the result of that loss. He also knew that one might say, as some one frequently did, that such suffering or chastisement was good for him; but he could not be satisfied with such an explanation. What had he done to be thus afflicted? All around him he saw multitudes of men whose lives were a shame to themselves and their friends; yet they lived and prospered, and enjoyed the good things of this world, their dear ones being with them. Riches, honor, and love seemed abundantly possessed by them who lived without a thought of God, or a care for their future state. They lived in fine houses, and possessed many sheep; but Merton though having but one little lamb, was in his wretchedness deprived even of that, and permitted to live disconsolate. He who had been but a bruised reed, was now broken, but suffered to live with his head in the dust; he who had been but smoking flax, was now made more ready for the flames, by the friction of pain and grief. The knowledge of these things made it hard for Merton to recognize what is called the providence of God. He knew he had prayed and, so far as he could see, prayed in vain; he knew he had knocked and, so far as he could see, knocked in vain; he knew he had asked and, so far as he could see, asked in vain. Yet would he often endeavor to answer himself by saying: "God's ways are not my ways. He knowing all things, wisely arrangeth them with a view to my eternal welfare." But if this be true, at what a cost was he redeemed! Without his wife, his life seemed a vacancy, with her, a fulness; without his wife, his life seemed chaos, with her, order and beauty; without his wife he seemed weak and destitute, with her he seemed strong and completely furnished. With his wife he had much to be thankful for: her companionship sanctified his life, and made it rich and full, indeed, a foretaste of heaven; without his wife, the reason for thankfulness seemed taken away; for her absence robbed him of the beauty of life, and made it beggarly and empty, indeed, a fore-taste of hell. At what a cost, then, was he redeemed! At what a cost obtained he his salvation, were it true that what had happened to him had occurred by God's appointment, for the working out of his eternal good! Merton could not but think that an almighty being, full of love and wisdom, might have found some method for the accomplishment of this, which would have been less painful to him.

We have no doubt that the suffering Merton endured in those days, instead of adding to the faith of his childhood, greatly detracted from it, by lessening his faith in what is termed the providence of God, and in supernatural interferences. He never could believe that the death of his wife was by the will of God; he always did believe it was the result of unwise treatment, improper management, and insufficient care. So in the case of the death of a little son he had lost: Merton believed that it was not a result in accordance with the will of God, but of injudicious treatment or nursing.

By their death Merton was made more practical, more realistic, more skeptical; less visionary, less superstitious, less credulous; more a child of reason, less a slave of dogma.

Easter, Easter, glorious Easter! how I love thy glorious time!
Alleluia! heaven's echoes fill my soul with hope divine;
And the earth, her icy garments casting off, from nature's bed,
Brings with joy her new creation, leaping, bursting from the dead.

Easter, Easter, heavenly Easter! lays to thee divine I'll sing,
When thy Son, the Lamb of Calvary warms my wintry soul with spring;
When the yearning hope within me, for a power from death to save,
Rises clad with exultation at the Christ who bursts the grave.

Easter, Easter! saints and angels, all creation's wide domain,
Bring to thee their alleluias; and we join their sweet refrain:
Alleluias to the Father, alleluias to the Son,
Alleluias to Jehovah, to the great Eternal One.

Easter, Easter, joyful Easter! O, what human tongue can tell
What a comfort thou dost bring us, ever here with us to dwell:
What a radiant light thou pourest on this palsied soul of mine,
What a glory all-transcendent; aye! I feel its power divine.

O my soul! thy jubilations make thee tremulous with praise,
And thy being, thrilled with rapture tuned to all creation's lays,
Bursting with its glad TeDeums for the Christ who came to save,
Now peals forth the song triumphant: Christ is risen from the grave.

Easter, Easter, day triumphant, day of God's redeeming love,
When the mortal spirit vibrates with the harmony above;
When the cerement, which confines me, scarce prevents the upward flight
Of my soul redeemed, victorious, from the shadowy realms of night.

Aye! my soul now rides the billows swelling from sepulchral gloom
Surging o'er the blasted nations, sweeping 'fore it death's dark doom;
Rising to the throne eternal, bathing Chaos' wide domain,—
Hark! I hear the whole creation chanting loud this Easter strain:

Alleluia to the Father, alleluia to the Son,
Alleluia to the Spirit, God eternal, Three in One;
Alleluia to the Victor leading Death in captive's chain;
Alleluia, alleluia! Christ the Lord is come to reign.

H. T. B.

CHAPTER XXXVI.

AN INQUISITIVE VISITOR.

Neque decipitur ratio, nec decipit nunquam—
Reason is never deceived, nor does it ever deceive.
(*Cicero.*)

Moneo ut agentem te ratio ducat, non fortuna—
I advise thee that in thy action reason not fortune may be thy guide. (*Livy.*)

MERTON was sitting one evening in his study, when he fell into a reverie. While in this state he imagined that the air of his room became redolent with the most heavenly fragrance, and that he heard a voice saying:

"Thou earnest seeker after the truth, thou so greatly tossed on the ocean of doubt and uncertainty, look up; for he in whom thou so greatly delightest, is present with thee."

In his mind Merton raised his head from his study-table. There stood before him a being of most surpassing majesty, whose eyes shone like most resplendent suns. In his hand he carried a shining sword with hilt bestudded with precious gems, and on which was written, in letters of gold, "The sword of truth."

"Who art thou?" asked Merton in his reverie; "and what is thy mission, thou most glorious being? Surely thou art one of the immortals, whom death toucheth not. Yea, thou appearest as one of the gods who take counsel with the Father, and know the secrets of nature."

"I am Reason," he answered, "sent forth by the Father of the gods to commune with thee. Thou recognizest me not, because of the outward form which I now assume; although I have often come to thine aid before. I am now present to commune with thee, as if mortal with mortal, about the groundwork of thy faith and work. I have many matters to discuss with you; but they are all so important that I regard it immaterial whether I state the first last, or the last first. I see you have the Hebrew bible in your hands. Do you prefer the original to the translations?"

"I always make it a practice, Reason, to read the Hebrew bible every day. I have read it through nearly three times; and as in reading it one can more clearly see the true or radical meaning of the words, I prefer the Hebrew to any translation."

"I am glad you are so well acquainted with the Hebrew. It certainly enables you to escape many of the errors of the accepted version; but your interpretation would be much more exact, had you a lexicon prepared by some one without Christian or Jewish bias. The bible, as you know, stands upon the lectern of your church, as the very word of God; and from what the people hear their ministers say about it, and its conspicuous position in the church, they naturally enough regard it as proceeding from the very mouth of God. Have you yourself no doubts about its inspiration?"

"I believe the bible, Reason, is a holy book, full of eternal truth, and as such fit to be your guide."

"That is not an answer to my question. Do you to-day, as you did in times past, believe that those who wrote the bible, did so under the immediate guidance of God?"

"In my childhood, O Reason, I regarded the bible as divine and infallible; but, I am sorry to say, since I have learned what I have from you, although I accept it as containing much of holy truth, I do not, and can not, regard it any longer as literally inspired."

"With regard to such a book, it is nonsense, if not wicked, to talk of literal inspiration. I am glad you have given up that idea. That ministers deceive the people as they do, is not a difficult fact for me to explain; but it is one which heaps disgrace on them. I have often smiled on hearing them read the twentieth chapter of Exodus, how that God with his finger wrote the ten commandments, and gave them to Moses. I have told you, as I have tried to tell them, that the ten commandments know no such origin; nor from my knowledge of the history of the Jewish religion, and the many other religions of the world, can I admit that Moses was ever their author. I can not tell you exactly what the work of Moses was; but I do emphatically deny that he was really the author of the ten commandments. Moses was a wise, shrewd and great character. He was a Hebrew of the tribe of Levi, who in the natural course of events had received the benefit of a thorough Egyptian education, and the standing of the ruling caste in that country. But though indebted to Egypt for his education and social standing, he felt still greater obligations to his own kindred; and when he saw them, once free men of the plains, now serfs of their Egyptian lords, he determined on their deliverance, and, with this object in view, set himself at their head. Having had all the benefits of a learned Egyptian education, he was well acquainted with Egyptian cosmogony, theology, and such sacred writings as were extant, and known to the priests of that religious country. I am willing to admit that Moses may have formed a kind of digest out of the materials known to him on the subject; that he may have purified and simplified the modes, forms, and ceremonies, of religious worship; that from his superior mind stored with the varied learning of the times, he may have made some original contributions to such digest; that assisted by his father-in-law, Jethro, a priest of Sinai, he may have given the Israelites their national god, Jahve; but that there was anything miraculous about the work of Moses, or about the origin of the ten commandments, I emphatically deny; and I insist that it is very wrong in ministers to teach that there is. Ministers are too fond of either not stating known facts at all, or, which is about as bad, of only half stating them. They give the people to understand that the first five books of the bible were written by Moses; yet they know, or should know, that they were not. The so-called books of Moses were written hundreds of years after he had passed away; and their substance had been handed down by tradition and legend."

"Then you teach, O Reason, that the Jahve of the Israelites was only one god among the many who were, in those days, thought to rule over the affairs of men."

"I have said, sir, that Moses may have given the Israelites their national god, Jahve. This is only what he would have been expected to do, since in those days every people had their national god. The name he chose for the god of the Israelites was Jahve, a word not of Hebrew origin, when taken in the sense in which Christians use it. Jethro, priest of Sinai, and father-in-law of Moses, may have been Moses' advisor in choosing this name; or he may have given the word to Moses independently, as an appropriate name for the god of the people over whom Moses, his son-in-law, was to rule as priest, and king, and legislator.

"I can not tell you exactly who are the authors of the different books of the Old Testament, any more than I can tell you for certain who are the authors of all those of the New Testament. The learned Spinoza, you remember, held that the writings of the Old Testament were not produced until the time of Ezra. So much I can say: the writings of the Old Testament grew as the sacred writings of other peoples; and they contain, as all other such writings, much that is good, and much that is evil. I should find no fault, if ministers would tell the people the truth about the bible. It is not a miraculous book. The bible, as all other similar books, is largely the product of traditions and legends, and treats of the rise and progress of a people, of their warriors, priests, prophets, morals, cosmogony, and theology. The historical books of the Old Testament were for the first time subjected to a comprehensive revision during the Babylonian exile. Says Prof. Carl Heinrich, an orthodox theologian of the University of Koenigsburg, speaking of the books of the Pentateuch: 'Not before the exodus from Egypt can we speak in a strict sense of a history of the people of Israel. All that lies before this point of time, may be characterized as prehistoric. Even if we regard Moses as the author of the five books which bear his name, yet concerning this remote epoch, separated from its own by a series of centuries, Moses himself would have had to resort to oral tradition. It was impossible for him to report these things as eye-witness. But it is now generally conceded that Moses can not possibly be the author of the books named after him. These books originated from the comprehensive digestion of a whole series of independent written sources, of which the oldest can not be older than King Solomon, nor yet much later, and written consequently between 900 and 850. Any comprehensive and coherent work earlier than 900 can not be proved. The material contents, the ingredients of these narrations, must be regarded from the point of view of popular tradition, or legend. It remains utterly impossible to state precisely and positively of what the work of Moses really consisted; since, however unwelcome the truth may be, not even the ten commandments may be regarded as actually formulated by Moses. We have here only an inverted conclusion from effect to cause.' In theological discussion the average minister invents illogical issues, to inflame the minds of his hearers. Denying a special revelation, I am charged with denying the sacred character of the Scriptures; denying the deity of Christ, I am charged with denying the usefulness and beauty of his life. Reason must ever revere the sacred impressions which the infinite Spirit hath made, and is making, on the mind and the heart of man, in awakening in him a sense of his Creator's will; nor less acknowledge the leadership of him who is first among the Lord's begotten. I would for the sake of truth that the whole bible were subjected to-day to a thorough purging. It is a good book; but it might be made a much better one, if its absurdities, contradictions, immoralities, and even obscenities, were purged away. That ignorant people should claim God as its immediate author, we should of course expect, as similar claims are made for all the different bibles of the world. But when I see men who professedly have sat under my instructions in schools and seminaries, making such claims, I feel offended as well as ashamed,—offended because of my love for the truth, and ashamed because of their real ignorance or insincerity. Let others do as they will; you, I hope, will not claim God as the author of a book which, to a large extent, might be greatly improved by the revision of a good man; and which, in no sense, calls for any other origin than a purely human and natural one."

"My acquaintance with you, O Reason, has led me to refuse my assent to anything as having a miraculous origin for which a natural one may be reasonably inferred; and to refuse my assent to the genuineness of a reported miracle, unless substantiated by evidence whose nature is like that which it is claimed to substantiate,—that is, unless the so-called miracle be substantiated by supernatural evidence. I do not believe that a miracle has ever occurred. I find a full and sufficient cause in man, nursed as he naturally is by the fostering care of God, for all that the bible contains. I claim the bible to be a holy book, because it deals with that which is most sacred and dear to the human heart; but I find in man, as I have said, a sufficient and reasonable cause for whatever I find therein. I fully agree with you, O Reason, that there is nothing miraculous or supernatural about the origin of the ten commandments, nor any other portion of the bible; nor do I teach my people that there is."

"Your conduct meets my approbation; but I fear your brethren of the clergy will suspect you of trying to steal away their household gods, and your bishop of trying to remove the strongest sanction for his proud and superstitious claims."

"Of that, O Reason, I can not speak. But painful as it may be, I will follow your guidance, and leave the results with God,—not the god Jahve of whom you have been speaking, but with God, the one and only Universal Father of all nations and worlds."

"During almost every church service, you say: 'God spake these words and said, Thou shalt have no other gods before me.' If, as you say, you do not believe that the ten commandments were given directly by God to Moses, do you not feel some hesitation, some conscientious scruples, when you utter these words?"

"I confess, O Reason, that I do. But since as often and fully as possible I give the people to understand my belief concerning these matters, I comfort myself with the thought that I can not be justly charged with hypocrisy. Perhaps you would say that I am at least guilty of idly using the name of God; but I do not think you would, if you thoroughly considered the matter."

"To take the name of God in vain, is certainly a great sin; but when I say this, as I do not mean the god of the superstitious Greek, so do I not mean the god of the superstitious Israelite. The Israelitish conception of God, was but little if any different from that of the other uncivilized nations of those days. Their god gave Moses the ten commandments; in like manner did the god of the Greeks give his decrees to

Rhadamanthus. If Moses had a difficult problem to solve he sought the aid of his god; in like manner did Minos repair to his deity, and ask his advice, when in similar difficulties. When Moses wished to converse with his god, he went to the top of Mount Sinai; so with the Greeks,—the home of their god, who was the father of the gods and men, was the cloud-enveloped Mount Olympus. The heathen gods were mighty in battle; in like manner was the god of the Jews a man of war. As the various heathen gods were rivals, and actuated by jealousy, so was it with the god of the Israelites, who said, 'Thou shalt not have any other gods before me.' It were impossible that such a command could come from the one infinite and eternal God who knows, as no finite being can, that He is God alone. The gods of the heathens were sometimes overcome; so with the god of the Israelites, whose most sacred dwelling-place, the ark, was captured, and who could not drive out the inhabitants of the valley, because they had chariots of iron. They were also at times outwitted; so with the god of the Israelites, of whom it is said, the devil having succeeded in destroying his plans, 'It repented the Lord that he had made man on the earth, and it grieved him at his heart.' The gods of the heathens used to plot and deceive; so with the god of the Israelites, who could purposely harden Pharoah's heart, send a lying spirit to deceive Ahab the king, and, at another time, to deceive a prophet. As the heathen gods were supposed to enjoy the smell of sacrifices, and the sight of the victim's blood, so with the god of the Israelites, who smells a sweet savor, and around whose altar the blood of the victim is sprinkled; for 'without the shedding of blood, there is no remission of sins.' As the heathen gods were often at war one with another, so with the god of the Jews,—'And there was war in heaven; Michael and his angels fought against the dragon.' The Israelitish conception of God was that which was commonly held in those times, no better, no worse; but it was infinitely inferior to that afterwards held by the noble minds of the Greeks and Romans.

"But when you say in the service, 'God spake these words and said,' although in these words there is no literal truth whatever; yet, since you convey to the audience the idea that the one and only God gave the ten commandments directly to Moses, it would be speaking his name in vain, unless you gave the people to understand your belief in the matter. But, having done this, it would not be taking God's name in vain, to read these words, though you disbelieve in their literal truth. However, to say with the lips one thing, and in the heart believe another, is a most dangerous practice, and one which can not be too strongly condemned. It is hard to see how one who does not believe in the literal truth of these words, can consistently utter them. Here there is good reason for your hesitation, your conscientious scruples. I advise you to act with great care in the matter, lest in trying to save a little, you waste much."

"Since you first began to visit me, O Reason, and ask me your searching questions, I have wished over and over I had never seen the work of the ministry; but having entered it, it is hard to turn aside,—hard because of the difficulty experienced in falling readily into new lines of work, hard because of disavowing openly what you have as openly avowed, and hard because there are some holy things connected with such a life. In my heart I long for a pure and simple theology,—a theology rid of all the grossly anthropomorphic conceptions which prevail in all the churches of orthodoxy. I sometimes hope to see that day when the churches will shake off the filth of dark ages, and clothe themselves about with a more glorious clothing; when priestly vestments will be no longer soaked in the blood of a vicarious sufferer, nor a soul be cast into hell because he does not recognize in a human form the all-prevailing and infinite God. God have mercy on me, and direct my ways! They are dubious and dark; yet I will go along trusting in Him, to bring me into the way wherein I should go. Surely, O Reason, you can not think me worthy of censure."

"Considering all things I do not. I recognize your difficult position, and can not but sympathize with you. Do not be discouraged. If you are honest, and continue to search after the truth, the way will appear more and more plain to you. The theology you speak of, will not be long in coming; but I fear its coming will not be in your day. The interests of powerful organizations are opposed to such a change. These vast bodies will hold their ground as long as possible, but little by little will they be forced to yield; and finally, pressed on all sides, they shall flee from the field, and truth shall claim the victory. It is natural enough that the priests of Christendom should teach their people that Christianity is the only divine religion, and that it will continue forever; for the priests of all other religions do likewise. It is to their interests thus to act. Christianity, like all the other great religions, is only a stepping-stone, a stage, a scaffolding, upon which, if the earnest and thoughtful man stand, he is better enabled to reach after pure theism. God leads the minds of men, step by step, into a simple and pure theology. Believe me, all religions are, in a measure, useful for the time and place; they all vary as the minds of their adherents become enlightened; they all have earnest, though deluded, priests and bishops; and what is best of all, they all have something of good mixed with much that is evil. They all, though in a bloody and most repulsive way, offer a road to life; they all serve, in a measure, to strengthen the weak and despairing; and they give their adherents the hope of rejoining their friends after death. They all come professedly with a blessing for their followers, and at times a real blessing is received; though not unfrequently the value of the blessing received, is more than outweighed by the attendant and consequent evils. To him who has no taste, the bitter is as the sweet; so to the unenlightened mind, the greatest of errors may appear the profoundest of truth. It is to the ignorant, therefore, that the religions of the day appear dressed in such attractive clothing; the thoughtful soul can find in them but little attraction for him. Indeed, the prevailing religions are painful to him. He sees the cunning and hypocrisy of those who sell the wares, as well as the worthlessness of most of the wares that are sold. Therefore he does not invest. It is because of this that the really great and pure souls stand alone in the world: they have but little sympathy from the age they live in. This is as true of Socrates as of Christ; as true of one age as of another. By his accusers Socrates was thought an infidel; so in all probability was Christ. What was true of them, has been, and will be, true of their noble and pure-minded brethren. Truly enough may it be said of such, they are not of this world; yet on them do the hopes of this world hang. You remember the passage, 'In the beginning was the Word and the Word was God.' Here we have a good example of how shamefully and wickedly translators do bend the sense of the original to suit their own crooked minds. It should read, In the beginning was reason and reason was God. In such a rendering of the original, we would have a positive truth. God is reason; and, therefore, let me advise you to live a reasonable life. As much as possible seek a reason for all you say and do: for all your faith, your hope, and your fears. Follow after reason, let her not depart out of thy sight; and the Infinite Reason shall shine forth more and more, making thy night bright as the day.

"I have said all I will for the present. When I come

again to question you, I hope that I may find you still more ready to receive me, and listen to my advice. In all your ways, be thoughtful, studious, honest, truthful, and sincere. He who thus lives, lives most religiously, and, in due time, becomes most like God."

As this noble visitor left him, Merton could not but admit, in his mind, the beauty, simplicity, harmony, and reasonableness of his visitor's remarks; and he determined, by God's help, to follow more fully than ever the advice he had received.

> Before the gods had yet been born,
>   When Chaos ruled and Night;
> Before creation had its form,
>   Its harmony and right;
> When law was not, nor time, nor season
>   Alone was universal Reason.
>
> Throughout the wide unbounded tomb,
>   Was hid naught from thy sight;
> Thou didst arise, dispel the gloom
>   With thy all-searching light;
> For God thou wert, and God was Reason,
>   And by thee all was made in season.
>
> **(H. T. B.)**

CHAPTER XXXVII.

GOD AND THE WORLD.

Credebas dormienti haec tibi confecturos deos?—
Terence: Adel. 693.

We are children of a day; mankind the offspring of untold ages. Humanity is one and all preceding generations are our parents. To these, therefore, we should go for whatever instruction they may be able to give us; and few indeed are the questions on which the master-minds of old can shed no light.

Somewhere about 2,500 years B. C. a conquering people were migrating southward, coming from along the waters of the Oxus, in north-western Asia. They were Sanscrit-speaking Aryans, and of the stock from which we have sprung. As with their descendants of to-day, so with them—ruin and death marked their path. They robbed, dispossessed, and killed; and in time founded the peoples of Persia, Greece, and Rome. Many of them settled in India. The earliest account we have of them is found in the Rig-Veda. Varuna was the all-encompassing Deity, upholding earth and sky, omnipresent, omniscient, the serene, universal majesty. Two other but inferior deities were Indra and Agni, the former being the god of beneficence and the latter the god of fire. Marriage was sacred, women highly respected, the forces of nature adored, and the doctrine of immortality taught. Long after this, somewhere about a thousand years, these invaders had planted themselves firmly along the banks of the Ganges, and the caste system had sprung up. The Supreme Being is called Brahma, forth from whom the universe forever flows. All nature is animated. The doctrine of metempsychosis is taught; and he who dies in sin, is doomed to repeated incarnations, until he shall have atoned for his wrong-doing, and arrived at that state of perfection which fits him for union with Brahma, where only eternal bliss is found.

Not knowing in what form of life the re-incarnated spirit might take up its abode, a deep and abiding love for all creatures was earnestly inculcated, and a close union between man and the rest of nature was consciously felt. Thus, although among the earliest of our forefathers of whom we have any trust-worthy account, these people do not leave us in doubt as to their ideas concerning the relation of God to the world. In Vedic literature the universe is everywhere said to be substantially flowing out of the Divine Essence itself.

Somewhere about 1,000 B. C. flourished Zarathustra, the founder, or great reformer, of the Persian religion. His teaching is modified Brahminism. About all we know of him is contained in the Zendavesta. With him there are two eternal principles, that of good, Ormuzd, and that of evil, Ahriman. Originally man was holy, but through the wiles of Ahriman he fell, and thus became a wanderer from God. For all wrong-doing the wicked must make their own atonement. Prayer and adoration are everywhere enforced, and pure morals inculcated. Truthfulness is especially enjoined, and every form of deception condemned as most wicked and debasing. The Zarathustrans have been said by some to be worshippers of fire; but this is not true, for every one of his true followers abhor the very name of fire-worshippers. It is probable that in fire, cleansing as it does everything it touches, they see something truly symbolic of Ormuzd, the Divine Presence itself: Πέρσαι γὰρ θεὸν νομίζουσι εἶναι πῦρ [The Persians say that God is fire, (Herod. iii. 16)] but this is no more worshipping fire than the Catholic worships the crucifix, when he bows before it.

Buddha flourished about 550 B. C. He asserts that the original essence of all things is one and spiritual. He would have little to do with cosmology or theology. His aim was to find a cure for the woes of man. The moral code of Buddha is one of the purest possible. Its four great principles are: existence is to be deplored; all misery results from passion, or unsatisfied desire; passion and desire should be eradicated; Nirvana should be obtained. Imperfection must be overcome by repeated incarnations, for the law of Karma assures every one that whatever he sows, he must reap. When perfection is attained, identity is lost, and Nirvana gained, the soul being merged in the infinite Self. As generally understood, immortality is not taught in Buddhism; but its moral code is one of the noblest, teaching patience, and compassion and efficient help for all in need of succor. So lofty are its precepts that Buddha might well be called the universal friend.

The Greek mind was naturally philosophical. Their early poets lived in the company of gods and goddesses, and were always prone to discuss the origin of existence and the destiny of man. These and the theologians of Aristotle's time taught that what is highest and best in the development of the world, was subsequent, and not first, in the order of time; while others, standing between the poets and the theologians, placed the best as first. Among the poets Hesiod says that Chaos was first of all, then wide-extending Gaea; and Acusilaus tells us that from Chaos sprang black Erebus and Night; while Homer makes Oceanus the origin of all. (Hom. Il. XIV., 201, 246.)

The highest conception of deity among the Greeks culminated in that of Zeus. He is all eyes, all ears, ever guarding, ever protecting, ever the object of adoration and prayer, ever just to all and partial to none.

Thales (640 B. C.) the founder of the Ionic school, taught that the original source of all things is water, and that the divine spirit is diffused throughout the whole creation. Nothing is dead; even the stone has soul within it.

Anaximander (611 B. C.) calls the original substance "the arche." This first substance is undetermined in character, and infinite in quantity. He also calls it "apeiron." In this infinite, undetermined body or apeiron there exist all power, all possibilities, whether of mind or matter; and independent of it, other causes cannot exist; for, in the words of Aristotle, Anaximander declares this apeiron to be God. (Phys. iii. 4, 9.) In the eternal motion of this apeiron there arise elementary contraries, such as warm and cold, moist and dry; and finally, by universal condensation, worlds and divinities. The earth, as well as all forms of life, is the result of evolution. Land life was preceded by water life. As all living existences have arisen by evolution out of one common substance, the infinite and undifferentiated apeiron (Aris. Phys. i. 4, 2), so of necessity shall all return to their common origin, and lose their individualities, God being once again alone in the awful stillness of boundless space. As with Buddha, so with Anaximander—individual existence results from some injustice or imperfection, and can only be atoned for by final extinction.

Pythagoras (582 B. C.) taught that all nature moves in cycles. Forms perish only afterwards to reappear. He taught the doctrine of metempsychosis, which he is supposed to have learned from the Egyptians, whom Herodotus tells us he had visited. (ii. 81, 123.) Moderation in attire, frugality in diet, rigorous self-examination were enjoined on all the followers of Pythagoras; and if animal food were eaten at all, it could be used only sparingly.

Xenophanes (569 B. C.) taught that earth and water were the two original elements. But even these have their real being in the universal Deity, for he declares God to be the one and only true existence. (Aris. Met. i. 5, 12.) "Over all gods and men," he says, "there is one Supreme Deity, who in form and thought is in no respect like unto mortals." No matter where he turned his gaze, Xenophanes saw in nature's infinite variety one universal unity, the very embodiment of God himself.

Anaximines (528 B. C.) taught that the original substance was an aeriform body. Out of this all other bodies have been evolved by condensation and rarifaction. This original substance was boundless and animated, and in character the highest and best. Our souls are of the nature of this substance, and by it the earth and the other worlds are kept in position.

Heraclitus (506 B. C.) considers the original substance to be animated and divine, knowing and directing all things, a fire self-kindling and self-extinguishing. The soul is immortal, and the universe is the Deity dispersed. Out of this divine fire individualities come into existence by "going the downward way," and after a time lose their existence, and return to the original and divine fire by "going the upward way." Thus do the life and death of creation move forever in cycles, existence and non-existence being only as the ebb and flow of the tide. All things are in a perpetual flux. The present state of man is not the best: while we live our souls are dead and buried within us; when we die, our souls truly begin to live.

Empedocles (500 B. C.) taught that there are four original elements—earth, water, air, and fire. These he called the roots of all things. (Aris.: De Gen. i. 1.) In these original forms there are two forces ever working. Of these the ruling force is Love, the divine mind itself; the other is Hatred. In dominion the one of these gives way in turn to the other. Love during some unguarded moment, or unsuspicious of its adversary, finds itself in conflict and surrounded by traitors. It is overcome, and Hatred now assumes dominion; but ere long with blasted ambition, and energies expended, it gladly gives way to the only true source of life, divine Love. Thus is the world destroyed and again renewed, and these cycles continue forever. To Empedocles nature is a living whole. Nothing really comes into being, nothing really loses its being. Man is a result of evolution. Plants have feeling and desire. In the development of life the vegetable kingdom first manifested itself, then the animal. All higher forms arise out of lower. Says Empedocles: "I myself have already been boy and girl, plant and bird, and the swift-gliding fish of the sea." The doctrines of this philosopher differ but little from those of Oken, Lamarck, and Darwin.

Anaxagoras (500 B. C.) believed in an indefinite number of elements, and in the divine mind as immanent in the substance of the universe. Matter is inert; mind alone moves, acts, and shapes. There is no chance, no fate, all is moved and guided by the divine presence. All living things have souls; even plants have their joys and sorrows.

Melissus (475 B. C.) taught the unity of the universe, and the eternal nature of its substance. The original element is continuous, and neither matter nor mind, but the common plasma out of which all things have been formed.

Democritus (465 B. C.) held that there is in space an infinite number of atoms. The union of these, by necessity, brings all possible forms into existence. The atoms as well as their motions are eternal, and their magnitude as well as their weight varies. This difference forced some elements downward, others upward, bringing about a rotary motion, which extended farther and farther, bringing together homogeneous elements, and finally forming the worlds, not as the result of divine guidance, but of natural necessity.

Diogenes of Apollonia, who flourished in the fifth century B. C., agrees with Anaximines in making an aeriform body the original substance. As a strong proof of the oneness of creation, Diogenes adduced the fact of the assimilation of inorganic matter by vegetables, and of vegetable matter by animals.

Socrates (471 B. C.) was the son of Sophroniscus and Phaenarete. He received such education as Athens afforded the children of its best citizens. This philosopher believed that creation is moved and guided by the divine presence. Material possessions do not really enrich man. To desire nothing is truly divine; to desire the least brings one nearest to divine perfection. The virtuous man is always the subject of divine guidance, and constantly hears the voice of God. Socrates was tried by about five hundred judges, and was condemned to death in the year 400 B. C. by a majority of more than eighty. He was accused of corrupting the youth, and teaching a new religion. He was a great and pure soul, and has had great influence in shaping the thought of the world.

Euclid of Megara (435 B. C.) held that the good is one, call it by what name we will, reason, intelligence, or God; and that evil has no essential existence.

Plato was born 427 B. C., and was highly educated, having had among his teachers such as Dionysius, Aristo, and Draco. He is said to have been present at the trial of Socrates, of whom he was a most faithful disciple. Plato taught that matter is eternal, and that in the beginning it was chaos. Then comes the Deity, who is perfect goodness and beauty, and works upon it, first forming out of two opposite elements a third element; and of these three, the soul of the world, to which he afterwards joined the body. The Deity, being perfect in all his attributes, it follows that the world is the best possible. The soul of man is similar in origin and nature to that of the world, and is deathless. Plato taught the doctrine of metempsychosis, the future punishment of the wicked, and the final bliss of the righteous.

Aristotle was born 384 B. C. His paternal ancestors were all physicians back to Asclepius. He was twenty years a student of Plato. So great was his learning that he was sought after as an instructor of princes, such as Hermias, Philip, and Alexander. Matter, he says, is passive, unable to move itself. Motion implies a mover. In the universe we find that which is perpetually moved, and that which both moves and is moved. There is, therefore, a third force—pure actuality, absolute spirit, God—loved by all, and the divine life and support of all existence. There is only one heaven, and this is eternal and perfect, and God fills the whole. (De Coelo, i. 9, 13; De Gen. ii. 10, 11.) The world is not infinite but bounded, and God acts upon it from without. Reason is prior in existence, and comes into the body from without. In its nature and origin it is divine. (De Gen. An. ii. 3, 10, 11.) There is no special creation. The world-mind acts upon matter according to fixed and immutable laws; and thus by a gradual process brings forth the various forms of life, first the lower, then the more perfect.

Epicurus (341 B. C.) taught that matter exists from all eternity. The earth with the stars is only one of an infinite number of worlds. Man is a result of evolution. Language has been acquired after long and constant attempts to express sensation and desire. Man's ideas of right and wrong are not innate, but an outgrowth of experience and development. While we live, death does not come to us; when we die, we cease to be. Death should, therefore, be of no concern to us whatever.

On the rise of Christianity man's mind was occupied either in theological disputation, or in an attempt to harmonize the thought of the past with the dogmas and principles of ecclesiasticism. Cicero, the orator, died near the eve of this period (43 B. C.). This writer affirms that if thought may be predicated of anything, it surely must be of the universe itself.

Plotinus (204 A. D.) taught that God is at once nothing and all things; everywhere and nowhere. Matter has no real existence, being only an image of the true ousia.

Porphyry (233 A. D.) held that matter is eternal. This writer was much occupied in refuting some Christian teaching. Ecclesiastics have taken care that his works should be lost.

John Scotus (805) held reason superior to faith; that God is the substance of all things; that the life of finite beings is simply God living in them; that all created things must finally return into God, and lose their individual existence.

Alfgarabi (820), Avicenna (980), Averroes (1126), Amalrich of Bena (1140 cir.), and David of Dinant (1160 cir.) differed but little in their teachings, holding that God is identical with the universe, and that the Deity is the only active intelligence, from whom all things emanate. By order of the church council at Paris (1209) several adherents of these men were committed to the flames. Even the bones of Amalrich were burned.

Spinoza (1632) affirmed that nature is one in essence, and identical with God, who is the only substance; that the human mind as far as it knows anything truly, is a part of the divine intellect. Leibnitz (1646) taught that God is the substance of creation. Diderot (1713) held that matter is sentient, and that the universe is God. Kant (1724) admitted the probability of the oneness of the substance of the universe, and the possibility that matter itself is thinking being, the signs of whose thoughts we see in its phenomena. Lichtenberg (1742) believed that matter and force are identical. Schelling (1775) called matter extinct mind. Herbart (1776) believed in a common substance. Lammenais (1782) held that matter is only God realized externally; Schopenhauer (1788), that the universe is only objectified will, and that man's body is but his will brought into the sphere of cognition. Sir William Hamilton (1788) says: "When God is said to create, we construe this as meaning that he evolves existence out of himself." Lotze (1817) regards the Deity as the universal monad, and the elements as spiritual existences. Bain (1818) declares that the arguments for two substances have lost their value. Tyndall (1820) and

Huxley (1825) each alike hold to a common and universal substance. Richter says: "The fundamental deduction necessarily resulting from the law of periodicity is, that the various elements must be aggregations or condensations of the one and same primordial substance. (Inor. Chem. 251.)

Man is a product of the living forces in creation, and there is nothing in him foreign to the forces that brought him forth. Intellectually and morally, with all his hopes and fears, his joys and sorrows, his design and forethought, his adoration and praise, his artistic and inventive skill, his music and harmony, man is but a mode of the infinite thought, an expression of the infinite Presence, a voice in the wilderness trying to echo the voice of God. In ancient days gold was not so firmly enthroned in the temple of man's heart as to-day, and there was a deeper sense of God's nearness to man. Said Pliny: "Non possum dicere aliud tunc mihi quam deos adfuisse—I can only say that I believe God was my support;" and Cyrus affirms that God took care of him, and revealed the things that were to occur. (Herod. i. 209.) Perhaps it was this deeper sense of God's nearness to man that gave rise in ancient days to belief in the possibility of Divine conception, and the many stories relating thereto. Homer (Il. xvi. 150, 522, 568), Aristotle (Hist. An. vii. 4, 13), Aeschylus (Suppl. 18), Aristophanes (Aves. 695), Herodotus and others, all give evidence of the prevalence of this belief: Φασί . . τὸν θεὸν αὐτὸν φοιτᾶν τε ἐς τὸν νηὸν καί ἀμπαύεσθαι ἐπὶ τῆς κλίνης . . καὶ γάρ δὴ ἐκεῖθι κοιμᾶται . . γυνή . . ἀνδρῶν οὐδαμῶν ἐς ὁμιλίην φοιτᾶν . . ἡ πρόμαντις τοῦ θεοῦ, ἐπεάν γένηται.

ὁ δὲ Ἆπις οὗτος γίνεται μόσχος ἐκ βοὸς ἥτις οὐκέτι οἵη τε γίνεται ἐς γαστέρα ἄλλον βάλλεσθαι γόνον . . λέγουσι σέλας ἐπὶ τὴν βοῦν ἐκ τοῦ οὐρανοῦ κατίσχειν, καὶ ἐκ τούτου τίκτειν τὸν Ἆπιν.— They say that God himself comes to the temple, and reposes on the couch, where also sleeps a woman who has never had sexual converse with man, and that when the child is born it is regarded as the chief priestess. . . . This Apis is a calf from a cow which could not possibly have conceived in the natural manner. They say that a bright beam of light from heaven enters into the cow, and that from this she conceives the Apis. (Herod. i. 182; iii. 28.)

We may have no faith in divine conceptions, in special interposition of Providence, in the miracles by which the different systems of faith attempt to establish their divine or exclusive authority; but we may not doubt the truth of Cicero's words, that "the world is the common habitation of men and gods." Even the atom is a domicile of Deity. Every point of force may be a center of divine consciousness, and the universe itself the objectified, infinite Presence. As a diseased blood-cell in man loses its vitality and gives way to a healthful one, so globe after globe, in the glorious body of God, dies only to become more fitted for its own activity. All parts of the universal body, as in our own, are subject to change; but as we preserve our personality from year to year, so the universe, the divine personality, changeth not, but abideth the same forever and ever. The heavenly bodies do not move without nor around, but really within the body of nature, as the atom or physiological unit moves within the organism, or the atom of silicon within the block of granite. Nature is a solid living whole. Its parts are subject to change, we among them; but the body itself remains unchanged and immovable from age to age. In the universe there is really no hap, no chance, no miracles. However hidden the relation, there is in every manifested force an expression of the one universal and immutable cause. Acting upon the elementary, original essence, and upon being in each and every stage of development, this divine, immanent, immutable, and universal cause brings forth and sustains every material and mental existence; and independent of it such existences could neither continue to be, nor be conceived.

In reading the pages of the earth's biography, we find faith in divine guidance standing forth more clearly than any other record. This is reasonable and natural. The divine Being acting in all things, and revealing himself in the harmonious operations of the universal whole, acts upon the inner being of man. Listening to his voice, recognizing the Father's touch, and yielding to the divine pressure man becomes a subject of divine guidance. We must listen that we may hear, and yield that we may be guided. He that is void of passion, without beginning or end of days, has the universe for his only-begotten, and every atom in it alike dear to him. "Being is unbegotten, indestructible, whole, eternally one, immovable, and infinite. With it there is no was nor shall be; the whole is forever now, one and continuous." (Parmenides.) Our work as that of an atom in our own body is to adjust ourselves to the requirements of the divine whole, of which we are a part. It is our privilege to become one with the eternal.

In conclusion, with reference to the great souls of the past, we would use the eulogy passed on Spinoza by Schleiermacher: "Offer reverentially with me a lock to the manes of the holy. *They were* filled with the lofty world spirit; the infinite was *their* beginning and end; the universe *their* only and eternal love. In holy innocence and deep humility *they* saw *themselves* in the mirror of the eternal world, and saw how *they*, too, *were* its most lovely mirror; full of religion *were they*, and full of holy spirit, and hence *they* stand there alone and unrivalled."

Serit arbores quae alteri seculo prosient.—Cicero.

CHAPTER XXXVIII.

REASON PREVAILS.

Eadem ratio, cum est in hominis mente confirmata et confecta, lex est. (*Cicero.*)

And that same reason when once it is confirmed and perfected in man's mind, becomes law—

IT soon became evident that Merton's controversy with the Roman missioner widened the breach already existing between him and his diocesan. Merton's nature appeared to be undergoing as it were the throes of parturition, in its efforts to burst the barriers which confined him, and bring him forth to the light.

While in this mental agony, Merton received a visit from Reason. "I am sorry" said Reason, "to find you in so great distress of mind; but pain and pleasure are very near related. The highest enjoyment is ever preceded by the acutest pain. The mother drains her cup of pain, before she tastes her cup of bliss. To him who is born and educated in superstition, it must be said to-day, as of old, 'Ye must be born again.' You must break through the barriers which confine you, and drop the load of superstition which crushes you. Either enjoy the benefits of a child of Superstition, by a faithful performance of those duties which the dark monster imposes on you, or as a true child of Nature, follow the dictates of universal reason, leaving the consequence with God. This is undoubtedly hard for you to do. In the occupation you follow, you are a member of a powerful corporation actuated by common interests; and while you are true to those interests, you can not fail to get bread to eat and clothing to wear. On the other hand, should you refuse to uphold those interests, that 'Corporate Animal' will cut you off from its fleshly self, and if possible trample you under its cloven feet, and leave your mangled remains as food for the vultures. But what then? Does life consist of food and raiment? Is this dark and painful existence the end of all activity? The highest duty of a true man, is first of all to be true to himself — to his own convictions of right, as impressed on him by the Infinite Mind urging him onward to a more exalted life. You must choose between reason and superstition: 'you can not serve God and mammon.' Let your decision be determined by motives of personal interests, and be a follower of mammon; or let your decision be determined by your consciousness of duty, and be a follower of righteousness and God. You are not the one to enjoy deceiving or being deceived. A short time ago, you remember, you were visited by three clergymen who, for more than an hour, argued in favor of the deity of Christ, and the literal inspiration of the Scriptures, and asserted the doctrine that the man who rejects the deity of Christ, must be eternally damned. You remember it was but a few days after this, when one of these same clergymen wrote you a letter, confessing his disbelief in the deity of Christ, and in the exclusive inspiration of the Scriptures, at the same time praying you to keep to yourself this confession, on the ground that he would suffer, should it become known. There are very many thousands who would readily acknowlege their disbelief, were they not afraid of the consequences; but I say unto you again, 'Ye can not serve two masters,— ye can not serve God and mammon.' I know there is a superstitious feeling which makes you hesitate to leave the church in which you were born; but the church should receive the obedience of the reasonable man, not in proportion to its assumptions and claims, but in proportion to the amount of unquestionable truth it possesses. Now, that which the church declares is the most exact symbol of its faith, is the Nicene Creed; and it is to this creed that it professes authority for demanding the obedience of the whole world.

Now, it is evident that the reasonableness of this demand, must depend on two things:

"1: On the reasonableness of the creed it would impose;

"2: On the power of the church to discriminate between truth and error.

"When we come to the examination of the Nicene Creed, the great symbol of orthodoxy, we find that only the first clause, which refers exclusively to God the Father, has ever received, or does receive, universal assent. It will be admitted that if the balance of this creed be believed at all, it must be by Christians exclusively. A slight examination of the origin and growth of this creed, will better enable us to understand its value as a symbol of faith

"The original Nicene Creed was formulated at Nice, A. D. 325, by three hundred and eighteen bishops convened at the summons of the Emperor Constantine. In this council there were not less than three antagonistic parties, — the homoousian, the homoiousian, and the Origenian. The homoousian, which to-day represents the orthodox party, in this council was in a decided minority The majority of the bishops headed by Eusebius of Caesarea, followed the lead of Origen who represented the liberal party, while not a few were homoiousians, or followers of Arius, who represented the more radical party. The result of this council was a victory for the homoousians. This victory was brought about through the influence of the presiding emperor, the oratory of Athanasius, and the fear, on the part of many, of deposition, or of giving offence to the emperor. Only three were brave enough to refuse subscription to this creed of Nice,—Arius, Theonas, and Secundus; and these, for their refusal, were exiled into Illyria.

"Thus the Nicene Creed is a child of force, political influence, and oratorical persuasion.

"But even this creed was not unreasonable enough to satisfy the ghostly minds of the one hundred and fifty bishops who formed the Second General Council of Constantinople. This council, which convened A. D. 381, both added to, and took from, the Nicene Creed. The words, 'God of God,' they took out of the Creed; and they added the formula consisting of the words, 'the Lord and Giver of Life, Who proceedeth from the Father, Who with the Father and the Son together is worshipped and glorified.' These words were added to show the equality of the Holy Ghost with the Father and the Son.

"But not even this creed of Constantinople was so repugnant to reason as that which you confess, and call the Nicene Creed. For neither the Nicene nor the Constantinopolitan asserted the procession of the Holy Ghost from the Son. This second addition to the genuine Nicene Creed is uncertain in origin; but its first undisputed appearance is in the creed of the Third Council of Toledo, A. D. 589. It is this addition to the Creed of Constantinople, thus made by a provincial and obscure council, which caused, in 1054, the great schism between the Eastern and Western Churches, and fills them to-day with mutual bitterness; and it is through the confession of this addition, called the 'filioque clause,' that the Eastern Church charges the Western with heresy. So the creed you confess should be called the creed of the ghostly fathers who assembled at Toledo, A. D. 589. It is certainly not the genuine Nicene Creed; it certainly is not the genuine Constantinopolitan; and certainly its first undisputed confession was made by the Council of Toledo in 589. Is it possible that such a creed as you confess, should be stamped with the seal of eternal truth! The fact that it was the result of long-continued and most bitter strife, beginning in the very earliest ages of the church, and ending as we have said above, is most conclusive proof of the lack in those days of Christian unanimity; and the fact of the existence to-day of Unitarianism, and other unorthodox faiths, is the most conclusive proof of existing lack of Christian unanimity. So then, the creed which you profess, with the exception of that part which refers exclusively to God the Father, not only does not receive the assent of humanity in general, but not even that of the general Christian church. As the controversies through which this creed has passed, is conclusive proof that, at its different stages, it was not in general regarded as a reasonable document; so is its present contents such as no reasonable man can give hearty assent to.

"The church being thus unable to expect the obedience of the reasonable man, on the ground of the confession of faith which she offers him, has she the right to expect his obedience, on the ground of her reliability as a judge of the truth? That she has not this right, is sufficiently evident from the contradictory judgments of the different communions which form the Christian church. The Eastern Church charges the Western with the guilt of schism and heresy, and the Western Church charges the Eastern with the guilt of schism. The Roman Church charges the whole Anglican Communion with the guilt of schism, and denies the validity of its orders; and the Anglican Communion charges the Roman Church with corruption and heresy, and affirms that it alone is the cause of the disrupted and schismatic state of the Christian church in general; and it also charges the various Protestant bodies with schism, or heresy, or both. Thus there is not a Christian body whose judgment is unreservedly received by another.

"The treatment the church has given the great scientists of the world, is well known to every reader of history. It was the church which could accuse of magic and heresy the most learned man of the Middle Ages, Roger Bacon, and keep him shut up within prison walls, for the most of his life. It was the church which, in 1615, could summon Galileo before the bar of the Inquisition, and force him to renounce truths that are now generally accepted ; it was the church which, in 1633, could cite the same philosopher, now aged and infirm, before the same cruel Inquisition, and through its agency, utter the following decree :

"' By the desire of His Holiness and of the most eminent Lord Cardinals of this supreme and universal Inquisition, the two propositions of the stability of the sun and the motion of the earth, were qualified by the theological qualifiers as follows :

"'1: The proposition that the sun is the centre of the world, and immoveable from its place, is absurd, philosophically false, and formally heretical ; because it is expressly contrary to Holy Scripture.

"'2: The proposition that the earth is not the centre of the world, nor immoveable ; but that it moves and also with a diurnal motion, is absurd, philosophically false, and theologically considered, at least erroneous.

"'We decree that the book of the dialogues of Galileo Galilei, be prohibited by edict; we condemn you to the prison of this office during our pleasure ; we order you for the next three years to recite once a week the seven penitential psalms.'

"And it was the church which, then and there, could wring from the old and withered philosopher the following confession, though it perjured him in the eyes of the world:

"'With a sincere heart and unfeigned faith I abjure, curse, and detest, the said errors and heresies (viz., that the earth moves, etc.) I swear that I will never in future say or assert anything verbally, or in writing, which may give rise to a similar suspicion against me.

"'I Galileo Galilei have abjured as above with my own hand.'

"It was the church which, on the conclusion of this trial, could conduct the terrified old man from his place of judgment to the prison of the Inquisition, and keep him virtually a prisoner the remainder of his life. It was the church which could bury the broken-hearted philosopher's body in an obscure corner of the grave-yard, and refuse his friends permission to erect a monument over his grave.

"It is safe to say that with the known facts of history before us, no reasonable man can admit that the church should be obeyed, on the plea of the reliability of her judgment; for these facts unquestionably prove that no judge ever sat on a bench, whose judgment was more fraught with error than the judgment of the Christian church has been.

"I say again, 'Ye can not serve two masters, ye can not serve God and mammon.' If you would be a follower of righteousness and God, you must break through the barriers which confine you, and speak the thoughts of your soul, as impressed on you by the God of nature, revealing himself in every movement of the cosmos. He who would be true to God and man, must first of all be true to himself. I must leave you now. My parting word is: do what in your soul you believe to be right, and leave the consequences with God."

"One question, O Reason, before you leave. If during the last eighteen years you have had such influence over me, why during the last eighteen hundred have you not had more over the church? Surely you are not unknown to the different parts of it!"

"It is true I am not an entire stranger to the church; but my presence in it is almost as unwilling, as unwillingly received. At times it apparently receives my instructions; but it immediately proceeds to distort and change them to suit its own desires and ends. In a few instances I have found ready minds, and willing hearts, and the seed I have sown in them, have brought forth abundantly ; but even in such cases they are generally cut down by the scythes of the bishops, before they have yielded a tithe of what they might have produced. Ever since the order of priests and medicine-men has been established, you can with as much safety touch the scorpion's tail, as the interests of a bishop. They are so deeply pledged, and their interests are so wholly dependent on the dogmas they inculcate, that they strive as zealously to secure their safety as the heathen to secure the safety of his penates, or the drowning man to get air to breathe. Dogma and Superstition are the sovereign ecclesiastical powers ; Reason is offered in the church only a subordinate position, and such I can not accept. Bacon expresses a partial truth when he says : 'If I proceed to treat of theology, I shall step out of the bark of human reason, and enter the ship of the church. Neither will the stars of philosophy, which have hitherto so nobly shone on us, any longer give us their light.' There is a fallacy, however, in this saying of Bacon ; for however dark the heavens over the head of the average theologian, theology can only flourish when the stars of philosophy shine most brightly on it. Theology is without prejudice or sordid interest, theologians are prompted by both.

"I have answered your question. You are an apt pupil, yet I must leave you. As Kreeshna said to Arjoon, so say I unto thee: 'Let the motive be in the deed, and not in the event. Be free from duplicity, and stand firm in the path of truth. Be not one whose motive for action is the hope of reward. Let not thy life be spent in inactivity. Perform thy duty, and abandon all thoughts of the consequence.' "

" With all the pain you have given me, O Reason, I can

not be other than thankful to you for what you have done for me. You have opened my eyes to see in a finer light the God of love; and my ears to hear more harmonious and heavenly sounds than the dissonant clangors of superstition. I intend to follow your advice: I will break through the barriers which confine me, and drop the load of superstition which crushes me, and leave the consequences with my God."

Notwithstanding the firmness of his resolution, Merton's soul was so heavy, and his mind so troubled at the thought of the many evils which he would have to undergo, resulting from ecclesiastical action, that he was driven to seek comfort from the Fountain of strength, and thus to address the Father and Savior of all:

"Thee, thou Universal Spirit, will I adore. Thou only art holy, and from Thee alone, as from a bottomless and boundless ocean, does eternal truth forever flow. Oh, as that stream of virtue flows freely from thy adorable Self, may I drink forever; and as I drink, may my desire for Thee forever increase. O Thou unapproachable and most glorious Deity, transcendently holy and good, who changest not, who fillest the boundless depths of space, and movest the whole with thy immanent Spirit, to whom the whole and every part are dear; Thou who art well pleased with righteousness, and seekest to restore the erring,—move, O righteous Being, the tremulous soul of man, with thy pure breath of life. Thou who art decked with majesty, whose diadem is the boundless universe, show thy glory to every longing eye; give quiet to the troubled spirit, and comfort to the broken-hearted; and whether from the Red-man's wigwam or Parsee fire, from Indian temple or Mohammedan shrine, from the disciples of Confucius or the followers of Jesus,—O hear the cry of him who calls for light and truth.

"Pass me not by, O my God. As Thou art Father of the whole, and all are dear to Thee, so let me be thy child. O my God, I look to Thee, I trust in Thee. Strengthen my mind, purify my heart, sanctify my soul, and make me able to feel thy influence, and ready to obey thy voice; and let me live in Thee, that when my life thus spent is over, I still may rest in hope."

On the Death of Merton's Little Son:

> A ray of light coming out of the gloom,
> A bud of life springing out of the tomb,
> We saw thee, though but for a day;
> A spark of fire falling down from above,
> A burst of joy from the Ocean of Love,
> Appearing, it passes away.
>
> A garden of flowers which bloom all the year,
> And trees of sweet fragrance which give the soul cheer,
> We loved thee, and found in thee rest;
> A wandering star sent forth by His might,
> A world all arranged out of chaos and night,
> Shone brightly, then died in the west.
>
> The darkness of death which has fallen on thee,
> Shall hide thee from perils most painful to me,—
> The heart finds peace in the tomb;
> Where the body of Sunshine, thy mother, finds rest,
> There, deep in the darkness, thou'rt near to the breast
> Whose spirit shall lighten the gloom.
>
> A gift from heaven, and my heart's first delight,
> An image of God, though effaced in a night,
> My child, thou shalt never grow old;
> The eye of the Father shall show thee the way,
> The love of Jehovah may bring thee some day,
> To meet me, a lamb of the fold.

(H. T. B.)

CHAPTER XXXIX.

THE BARRIERS ARE BROKEN.

Deus ipse faces animumque ministrat—
God himself will give us light and courage.
            (*Vergil: Aen. v, 640.*)
Ich thue recht und scheue keinen Feind.
Wer gar zu viel bedenkt, wird wenig leisten—
I do right, and fear no enemy.
Who hesitates too long, will accomplish little. (*Schiller.*)

MERTON greatly loved the forms and ceremonies of his church. They were, as he believed, of much educational value, apart from their worth in developing religious knowledge, and devotional strength. But as much good is frequently found in connection with far more abundant evil; so in the case of good resulting from Merton's adherence to the creed of his church,—it was more than neutralized by the accompanying evils.

Matters incapable of proof, were represented as certain; statements evidently of human origin, were asserted to be divine; rational and beautiful sayings were found sparsely scattered among assertions absurd and nature-contradicting. The links of his creed Merton knew were, for the most part, of a very frangible material, and welded together by superstitious hands, in days when Darkness ruled. Here and there he found a link of fine material and great strength; but Merton was sure the chain of his creed was unutterably weak.

It was in those days that Merton received the following letter from his bishop:

"My dear Dr. Merton: I feel very thankful to you for sending me back to my books again, as I have been absent from them for many years; but feeling that it is the deeply felt conviction of the very large majority of all Christian people that the Christian religion is supernatural in origin and life, as no other religion ever was, or is to be, except the Patriarchal, and the Jewish, which it has succeeded and absorbed, I am pained that you have allowed yourself to speak of the Christian miracles so slightingly, or to press so unduly the natural as against the supernatural. And Bibliolatry has so far forgotten the genesis and history of The Book that in reminding men of their forgetfulness, and giving corrections to their errors, you have allowed yourself to go to the other extreme of exaggerating the uncertainties connected with it. Natural science does not include all science. Do not uphold scientists in their narrowness. For instance, Huxley and Tyndall are always narrow; Darwin never.

"You are in danger of injuring souls in your intellectual work—in weakening their faith (justly and reasonably founded as the vast majority of Church people are convinced it is) in the Divinity of the Blessed Master, and in the special inspiration of the Holy Scriptures.

"May I lovingly request you to be on your guard. Intellectually restrain yourself from making statements which may weaken the faith of listening ears. And for the sake of the Blessed Master and his cause in His Church, and the hearts of the souls connected with your charge, give heed to the building them up in the faith, rather than explicitly to dissecting and analyzing and destroying by reason of exaggerated truths.

"In your utterances from the pulpit, in all thanks for earnestness and faithfulness, I ask you to avoid those things that may give hurt to faithful souls of plain Church views.

"May God bless you in all the good you are doing, and overrule by His Holy Spirit's grace what error you are allowing yourself to commit, is the prayer

Of your loving bishop,

W. V. DUMMKOPF."

What could Merton reply to a man who had acknowledged that he had been many years away from his books? who could show his holiness and sanctity rather by the use, in his letters, of an archaic language, and a foolish display of capital letters, than by earnestly seeking after and discovering the real truth of the Infinite God, and teaching it to the deluded souls of his bishopric? What could he reply to a man who had asserted the broadness of Darwin, and the narrowness of Huxley? "Darwin," said he, "is never narrow." True he was not; but Darwin, unlike the bishop, was wide enough to see the greatness and broadness of Huxley. No man was ever more admired by another than Huxley was by Darwin. In a letter to Huxley, Sept. 30th, 1871, Darwin even quoted approvingly what he had heard Hooker say of Huxley: "When I read Huxley, I feel quite infantile in intellect." "Darwin is never narrow," said the bishop. Very true; but it was Darwin who said, in 1876: "By such reflections as these, I gradually came to disbelieve in Christianity as a divine revelation. This disbelief crept over me at a very slow rate, but was at last complete." "Darwin," said the bishop, "is never narrow." Very true; but it was Darwin who wrote to Lyell, "I conceive you might crush a leaden-headed old Don, as a Don, with more safety, than touch the finger of that Corporate Animal, the Clergy." "Darwin," said the bishop, "is never narrow." Very true; but it was Darwin who wrote to Spencer, "Every one with eyes to see and ears to hear, ought to bow their knees to you, and I for one do." And yet this same Spencer to whom Darwin thus did homage, has done more to tear to fragments the gigantic fabric of superstition in which the bishop worships, than any living man. The bishop, it must be admitted, called a very damaging witness in the person of Charles Darwin; although he was one of the most capable and best the world has ever known.

In reply Merton said but little except to call the bishop's attention to the dangerous admissions he had made. In his letter the bishop had pleaded for the divinity of Christ, and the special inspiration of the Scriptures; and it was but natural: a bishop is a lord, though his reason is enslaved. In such a case it is to be expected that he would make a strong plea for those principles on which his bodily comforts depend. If he should once admit his unbelief in the superstitions on which his office is founded, he would be forced instantly to vacate his residence, and lose a substantial income. This a man like Merton's bishop, could not be expected willingly to do.

The correspondence did not tend to unite them in friendship, but rather to increase their mutual antipathy. It was more than sixteen months from that time, before they again penned a line to each other.

When Merton came to execute his determination, he found it so unutterably painful as to surpass all powers of description. What was he about to do? His action would separate him from the church of his birth, and from the friends he so dearly loved. Even those of his own blood, called after the name of his father, would censure and upbraid him, and even accuse him of sin in doing the act he contemplated. The Bible which had long since ceased to be thought of by the most learned theologians of all lands, as a literally inspired book, was regarded by those most dear to him as the very autographic work of God. But though Merton believed that a much better bible than ours could be made by sifting the precious wheat out of the abundance of chaff contained in the many different bibles of the world, he yet felt convinced that those nearest to his soul would cry aloud, "thou reprobate!" So great was his suffering that he determined to strain his sense of duty, by writing his bishop the following letter:

"Right Rev. Sir: From my youth up I have done scarcely anything else than study; and since 1867 I have always shaped my studies for the better preparation for the ministry. My mind is now much disturbed. All men are more or less superstitious, often founding mountains of fear upon imaginary foundations. From my infancy Christ has been my meat and drink. Why should I now hesitate to turn aside from a work not at all desirable? My intelligence says, 'go;' but the web which my life's activities have woven about me, is hard, yes, painful to break. But, God helping me, around whom may my little world ever move, I feel I must break through it. That I should have much disquietude in ceasing to publish the theme of Calvary, seems childish, or at least superstitious; for seeking after God on purely Platonic grounds, I should be confident of beautifying my life's temple, and of fitting it for the hoped-for future life. Thus while intellectually confident that the door to God is every point in space, and that earnestly seeking after Him, whatever may be the seeker's creed or belief, brings a resulting, divine knowledge; yet this web of being, so persistent in holding me down to my youthful thoughts, tends to put great limitations upon my intellectual freedom.

"I do, as you know, belong to the extreme wing of the Broad-church party. My interpretation of Scripture and ritual is conducted on rationalistic grounds that I may avoid blaspheming Him whom I have always worshipped. In other words, instead of subjecting reason to the teachings of alleged revelation or of accepted dogmas, I insist most strenuously at all times on subjecting all teachings whatever to the decision of the reason, whether such teachings be that of alleged revelation, tradition, or ritual practice. I do this that I may be one with science, and one with myself. He who does not this, is not one with science; nor is he any more one with himself.

"The extreme Broad Church has but little representation in the United States; and the principles of my late book will bring me but little sympathy from any other party. It is far from a pleasure to me to dissever all my relations with the Episcopal Church, for I have received much loving kindness therein; and I can never forget to my dying day the dear ones to whom I have ministered. Even in this painful letter, the saddest of my life, I pray for them, and hope to meet them, not again in the Episcopal Church, but in a better land where none shall be forced to choose between yielding up the most sacred things of his life, or doing violence to reason and known facts. I am as fully convinced that the usual method of Scripture interpretation is false, as I am of my own existence; and I am equally convinced that the rational method is true. In this belief I am not alone; rather am I in the company of the brightest minds of all ages before and after Christ. Every distinguishing doctrine of the church has passed through seas of blood; and frequently a belief has become enthroned against the reason by acquiescence through fear of further opposition, — for few are they who will not yield to threats of excommunication, exile, social ostracism, or death.

"It is with much pain that I take the action I now take; but after years of consideration, I am fully persuaded that I owe it to the world, and most of all to myself.

(1): "I do not believe in a complete, local, exclusive, or infallible revelation.

(2): "I can not believe in the doctrine of special creation.

(3): "I do not accept the story of the fall of man.

(4): "I do not believe in the doctrine of vicarious atonement.

(5): "I do not believe in the doctrine of eternal punishment, nor in that of a fixed state after death.

(6): "I do not believe that Christians possess an exclusively divine revelation, or that their Scriptures are perfect or complete,

(7): "I do not believe in the dogma of the resurrection of the dead.

(8): "I protest against making belief in the deity of Christ an essential part of faith.

(9): "I believe that all mankind are alike dear to God, alike cared for, alike provided with means necessary for their good. I believe in a continuous and universal revelation whereby God has revealed, and does reveal, himself through various channels of the reason to all mankind; and that all local revelations are but parts of a grand whole; and that while their differences may be, and probably are, useful, as being the natural outcomes of the minds professing such differences, they are, on the other hand, no essential parts of saving faith in God.

(10): "I have a reasonable, a well-grounded hope, in the immortality of the soul.

(11): "I believe that for every wrong committed we must all pay the penalty, must make our own atonement, either in this world or that to come.

(12): "I believe that the present age witnesses a higher revelation of God than any preceding age. This is the substance of my faith.

"If you think there is work in your diocese for a man with principles as broad as I profess, I am ready to continue in it; if you think there is not, I will seek work of some kind elsewhere.

"I have written you confidingly and candidly; **and I ask of you an equally open and candid answer.**

"I am greatly delighted with Plato. I think there are but few living Christians who might not be made much more virtuous, and much wiser, by an attentive study of his gospel:

'ουκ αρα του δικαιου βλαπτειν εργον, ουτε φιλου ουτε αλλου ουδενα, αλλα του εναντιου του αδικου·' (Repub. I. c. IX.)

"Adieu, dear sir. May God Almighty help us all to do our duty, until we meet where the weary are at rest.

"Very respectfully,

"Henry Merton."

To this letter Merton received the following reply:

"My dear Doctor Merton,—Yours of the 1st inst. is received.

"I thank you for writing me so frankly and for asking of me a candid answer.

"Candidly, therefore, I do not think that any place will open in this diocese for usefulness for you in discharge of your duties as a clergyman, while you hold your present opinions. Faithfully yours, W. V. Dummkopf."

After fifteen days of indescribable agony, Merton resolved to strive no longer with himself against his convictions of duty, but to break the bonds that bound him, and lay his burden down, by writing a letter to his bishop, asking that all his relations with the Episcopal Church might be immediately severed. Merton's request was granted by his diocesan; for he was one of those bishops who are so holy, that they can either fry their opponents in the "dry-pan and gradual fire," roast them at the stake, or hang them up by the heels, and smoke them; and such a man could not be expected willingly to be classed with heathen characters like Plato, who taught that it is far better to receive injustice than to do it; that the just man never does an injury, not even to his enemy.

At the time of Merton's ordination to the priesthood,

he wrote, in his Hebrew Bible, the following sentence:
"Ηιπτω ενωπιον του θεου και προσκυνω τον κυριον ὁς πεποιηκε με πρεσβυτερον και δουλον του χριστου του Σωτηρος εμου.—I fall down before God, and worship the Lord, who has made me a priest and slave of Christ, my Savior." These words flowed from a most earnest and devoted heart; and the literal characters were not the mere scratches of a pen, but the true imprint of a soul. As Merton read them at the time he ceased to act as a priest in the Episcopal Church, a solemn question arose in his breast: "Have you been true to the promise contained in these words? Have you been true to the God and Lord before whom you fell down and worshipped?" Merton answered himself thus: If a man promises to live faithful to all the injunctions of the Koran, is he morally and rightfully bound to keep his promises, in regard to those injunctions which he afterwards discovers to be neither useful nor true? Do Latimer, Luther, and Ridley fasten upon themselves the charge of moral turpitude, because they broke their ordination vows? All that a man can rightfully mean in his ordination vows, is that he will be faithful in the discharge of what he believes to be his duty. No person can possibly be faithful to God, who is not first of all faithful to his own convictions of right and truth. The highest obligation a man can have, is the discharge of what he believes to be his duty, as day by day, in his eventful and progressing life, he is called on to determine what his hands and heart shall do. There can be no virtue or moral worth belonging to an act that is not done in accordance with the convictions of duty, it matters not how remunerative or apparently successful such an act may be. He who would fall down before God and worship Him, must take care to do so, first of all and more than all, in his own heart, the place where God delights to dwell, and where He most reveals himself. Merton had

kept the vows of his soul: he had been true to his convictions of duty, however much the pain he had suffered in discharging the same. When he read the above words, therefore, he did not feel he had been unfaithful; but he did feel pained at the thought that the narrowness and darkness of the church he gave his life to, denied him the privilege of falling down and worshipping his God, within her walls, or of completing the work which reverently and fearfully he had undertaken to perform. In the best and truest sense Merton had kept his promise; but when his expanding and rising soul was refused a little space within the walls of superstition, he was compelled to seek a temple whose chancel has never been polluted, nor altar desecrated, either by the hollow mockery of proud and designing bishops, or the false-hearted worship of poorly educated and hypocritical priests,—the temple whose doors are never closed, whose lights are ever burning, whose walls are subject to no decay; and where, entering into her portals, a refuge from superstition, bigotry, and tyranny, the best and greatest have ever found closest communion with their God,—the temple of Reason.

"*Liber captinos auis ferae consimilis est:
Simul fugiundi si datast occasio,
Satis est: post illam nunquam possis prendre.*"
(*Plaut. Capt. 116.*)

Thus it was with Merton: the barriers were broken, and he went forth free; and as his soul inhaled the breath of heaven, he felt, as it were, a new birth. His shackles were loosened; and as the chains so strongly wrought by the powerful arm of Priestcraft, were snapped asunder, he felt as never before the meaning of the cry: Give me liberty or death.

Now he could speak his thoughts—the thoughts of an honest heart beating for union with God and with good-will toward mankind, and have no fear of those rolling and bloody eyes, and that lolling tongue, of the many-headed monster, Superstition. Now he could follow after righteousness, and hear and obey the whisperings of the Infinite Soul as He reveals himself in the onward movement of the age.

Go forth, ye tear-wrought pages, take wings, O love-wrought book,
Go, tell the Christian savage, God hath no bloody look.
Say to the mitred bishop, to sacrificing priest:
Leave Superstition's banquet for Reason's royal feast.

She hath no votive Victim, no chalice for his blood;
Nor blood-besprinkled altar, nor martyred flesh for food:
She hath no angry Father, no sacrificial Son;
Her God is good forever, she knows He favors none.

Go to our ice-girt neighbor, where lofty pines do wave,
Where Earth is great with mineral, and rich in Sunshine's grave;
Speak out to ancient China, to India, Afric's land,
To Europe blessed with science: ye all are Holy Land.

Go to the sun-burnt millions, where golden grain e'er shines,
And to their sallow brethren pent up in deep, dark mines;
To crowded cities peopled with Want and cold Neglect,
And bid them all take courage, for all are God's elect.
Say to the noble-hearted, when crushed with toil and pain:
Be brave, for God, my brother, and duty still remain.

(H. T. B.)

CHAPTER XL.

THOUGHTS ON THE OLD AND THE NEW.

Schon weicht die tiefe Nacht. (Goethe: Faust 4506.)
Ja, wahrlich! Ein Regenbogen mitten in der Nacht.
(Schiller: Will. Tell 975.)

IT was only a vision in which I had been attending a meeting of so-called liberal ministers. All around me I saw portraits, images, statues, of the leading religionists, and moralists of the world. Buddha, Chreshna, Zoroaster, Moses, Confucius, Mencius, Plato, Aristotle, and numerous others, occupied honorable niches, indicating the sources from which the assembled divines drew their inspiration and strength. As I gazed at those images, I perceived, to my astonishment, that they became more and more indistinct, until finally their outlines seemed scarcely discernible.

A little to my right began to assume form a beautiful, marble statue representing Judgment. It was looking in the direction of the figures whose outlines had become so obscure. Words can not describe the sublime beauty of this wonderful piece of marble; and my soul was on fire with admiration. It was an ideal work. The eyes seemed piercing every obscurity; the nose was Grecian; the lips were closed; the chin, prominent; the brow, lofty; and over the whole countenance there seemed spread that firm resolution as well as that lofty seriousness so characteristic of Pallas Athene. I approached the figure, touched it with my hand: it was but stone. "O Judgment," I cried, "thou art indeed beautiful, perfect in outline, lovely in form, glorious in appearance; but thy touch is cold. Solace beams not in thy eyes, thy bosom heaves not with compassion, comfort falls not from thy lips. Thou searchest, inquirest, discoverest, judgest; but I long for the touch of a friendly hand, listen in agony for words of comfort, hope in vain for love or mercy. Oh, Judgment, turn thy gaze in the other direction; look into the face of the pitiful, merciful Christ. His lips give comfort, his word assurance, his arm strength; his bosom heaves with compassion, and his heart is bursting with sympathy.

The glorious image, to my amazement, turned on her high pedestal, cast for a moment her large, piercing eyes on me, and then fixed them on the statue of Jesus, which stood at the back of the statue of Judgment, and in a less conspicuous part of the room.

"Is this, then, thy God?" she asked.

"Oh, no," I replied, "I ask thee not, O mighty Judgment, to look on him as thy God or mine, but to recognize in him the great fountain of my comfort and hope, the great solace of my despairing soul, and the balm of my broken heart. I ask thee not to worship him as thy God, but to see in him the bright ray out of the deep darkness, the sweet voice out of deathlike silence, solace for the despairing, hope for the dying."

Tears were gushing from my eyes, my heart was wildly beating, when, behold, I saw a soft and most glorious light surround the beautiful statue. The beautiful form appeared to be alive. A look of compassion passed over her countenance; and crystal tears dropped from her eyes, causing white roses instantly to come into bloom, filling with their fragrance the whole assembly room.

"Thou hast well said," she replied. "None should disparage the works of the great moral and religious leaders of the world; and since they were and are, each and all, co-workers in the building up in humanity the kingdom of God, they are all duly to be honored and reverenced.

But the lion roams not in company with the polar bear; the orange blooms not among the pines of Norway; this flower dies, where that flower blooms. So with different nations,—what is mental and moral food for one, is mental and moral poison for another. For thyself and thy kind, no voice can ever sound so sweet as that of Jesus; no word be so inspiring, no gospel so full of hope, as that which comes from his dear lips. Man may turn my gaze on other forms, and I look on them with pleasure; but only when I contemplate the face of him whom thou so greatly lovest, do I become warm, and feel the breath of life within me. As the moral and religious leader of thy race, and of the nations who have followed him for so many centuries, he can not be supplanted, and need not be. Though thy manhood sees not in him the god of thy youth, thou canst yet find in him the great burden-bearer and comfort-giver of suffering humanity. So, weary soul, cast thy burdens on him, and he will help thee; imitate his life, and thou shalt find his strength in thy death."

My vision passed away. It was early morning; and I was so much affected that I have been led to pen these lines on the present religious unbelief, or on the old and the new.

I am no more a believer in visions than in dreams; and I have no more faith in dreams than in a universal and invariable revelation. Dreams are but faint echoes, under unconscious conditions, of the soul's cries under conscious activity. True enough, there was more poetry, more imagery, in my dream-thought, than in my waking; but the substance of my vision was but the conviction of my soul in my most thoughtful moments. The assembly of preachers shows the general dissatisfaction with existing, religious conditions, and the unrest of clergy and people, and a desire on the part of the clergy to find a remedy.

With reference to faith, mankind may be divided into four classes,—Scholars with ecclesiastical duties and obligations, Scientific scholars, Men of average education whose reading consists chiefly of current, cheap literature, and the Ignorant classes. Of the first class it may be said that their duties and obligations have such a restraining influence over their tongue and pen, as to dwarf, or kill, the growth of honest skepticism, or to lead them to make known to the world those thoughts only which give least offence to their church superiors or relations. Of the second class it is not too much to say, that it is wholly composed of infidels (considered from an orthodox standpoint), agnostics, and skeptics. The third class is made up in general of men wholly indifferent to church and creed, though for the sake of appearances they may sometimes be found in comfortable pews. The fourth class contains the men and women of simple and unquestioning faith; and from this class the rank and file of the greatest of all orthodox churches are recruited. Such are those, we are told, who heard the Lord in the beginning; and such are they who will be found following his banner, when all others have fallen out of the ranks.

Some may insist that I have no right to hold that those who fill ecclesiastical positions, or are in any way under ecclesiastical obligations, are in such servitude as I have here stated; but such objectors I am sure have not the scholarly qualifications requisite for criticizing my assertion, or else have but a very slight knowledge of human nature, or of the results of ecclesiastical ostracism. It is only a short time ago that a leading minister, in one of the foremost cities of the country, told me he had no faith in the deity of Christ, and that his wife was an infidel; yet this minister could preach a rousing Methodist sermon. Another equally high in standing, but of a different denomination, said that "a man dares not preach as he believes; congregations have troubles enough without having to carry those of their ministers." Should it be objected that my judgment of the attitude of scientific scholars, is an erroneous one, I have only to refer the objector to the writings of scientists dead and living.

It may be asked, what is the cause of this general unrest. We reply—philosophical inquiry, scientific discoveries, and the general scientific spirit. Science has completely shattered much of what for ages has been held, without question, to be the indestructible work of God himself. The biblical account of the creation of the world, the special creation of man, the story of the garden of Eden, the fall of man, the placing of all animal life in the ark by Noah, casting out devils, blowing down walls with trumpets, resurrections from the dead, virginal parturition, the stories of the Annunciation and Ascension, and other miracles of every description,—these are some of the so-called facts of the Bible, which Geology, Astronomy, Anthropology, History, and the critical spirit in general, have made it utterly impossible for the thoughtful and independent mind any longer to believe. The popular publication of the writings of the ante-Nicene Fathers, and the whole-sale biblical criticism of the age, have done their share in filling the average breast with unrest and skepticism. I must admit that nothing had a more damaging effect on my boyhood faith than my acquaintance with these ante-Nicene writings of the church. The absurd, gross, revolting, and disgusting assertions contained in these writings, vouched for by those holy men, are sufficient to prepare any man to expect similar absurdities from writers contemporaneous or almost so,—for instance, from the writers of the New Testaments.

Having spoken of the present religious unrest indicated by the meeting of the preachers in my vision, we might ask, can any remedy be found? Is there any balm in Gilead?

The immortality of the soul, and the existence of a personal God, remain in the judgment of the leading thinkers of all ages undemonstrated and undemonstrable. Even philosophers most friendly to the religious spirit, have willingly or unwillingly admitted this. Now, while it is, as Kant teaches, utterly impossible to demonstrate the soul's immortality, or the existence of a personal God, it is not true, as some would-be philosophers of the present day affirm, that man is as contented with belief in the immortality of his moral influence upon the soul of the race to come, as in his own personal immortality; and with belief in universal nature as his impersonal, unconscious god, as in that of the God of Jesus, who is represented as ever ready to hear his children's cry, and provide for their wants. Mankind clings to the hope of personal immortality, and longs for it, whether the hope or longing can be ever realized or not; and man naturally prays to what he imagines to be a living, personal, conscious God, whether such a being be existent or not. Man as man loves whom he imagines to be God, and is prone to seek help and comfort from Him, when he despairs of getting aid from any other source. Nor does any man live, in my judgment, who hates God. A few days ago there appeared, in a leading paper, the assertion that a certain, widely known, popular lecturer hates God and the Democratic party. Such foolish, and most unjust assertions are common in newspapers; but they are no less untrue than they are common. The lecturer may hate the god of the person who wrote the article, but I am sure he does not hate the Being whom he himself imagines to be God. It is evident enough, therefore, that if a remedy is not at hand for the existent, religious unbelief, it is not that mankind is unwilling to receive one. Man is ever ready to hear a word from heaven, or to receive divine consolation; but he has been humbugged so many hundreds, thousands, of years, that he is no longer the ready tool of ecclesiastics.

Is the remedy for the present unbelief a restoration of faith in the god of the Old Testament, or in the god of Jewish conception?

My answer to this question is, that whether or not such a restoration would constitute a remedy for the present unbelief, all attempts at applying this remedy must surely fail; because mankind, unless it retrogrades, can never again conceive of God under the dark and bloody character ascribed to Him in the ancient Jewish religion. No refined mind can believe in a god who delights in burnt offerings, bloody sacrifices; who sniffs with pleasure the smoke from the burning victim; who orders the massacre of every man and woman, but the preservation of virgins for the purposes of lust; who hardens men's hearts, to punish them the more cruelly; who sends a lying spirit into the heart of man, for the purposes of deception; who fears that man may attain equal power with deity; who seeks vengeance on the innocent for the crimes of the guilty; who creates that he may destroy; who makes one for the purpose of honor and life, and another for the purpose of dishonor and death; who teaches his favorites the art of war; who with fury and hatred exterminates nations for the happy settlement of his chosen people; who writes with his fingers, and talks with humanity as man to man; who visits the sins of fathers upon their children. All these unjust and wicked acts are ascribed to the god of the Old Testament, and a thousand others equally shameful; and such are the acts that make it impossible for any refined mind to believe in the god of the Jews. God writes not his laws with his fingers on tables of stone. As Goethe well says:

> "*Sie reden nur durch unser Hertz zu uns—*
> God speaks to us only through our heart." (*Iph. auf Tau.*)

We do not say that faith in the Jewish god was not good and proper for the Jews of ancient times; nor that the character of their god, Javeh, was not better than that ascribed to the gods of many other ancient peoples. The gods of ancient times could not have been, and the gods of present time can not be, other than the embodiment of the ideals of those who worshipped or worship them. The truth of this statement no one will attempt to combat. It is therefore not reasonable to suppose that the god worshipped by a people of one civilization, can receive the faith of a people of another and different civilization. As a people advances, so does the character of their god become more and more exalted. We hold, therefore, that a restoration of faith in the Jewish god is wholly impossible; and that even if it could be accomplished, such restoration would result, of necessity, in the deterioration of present civilization. We next ask—

Is there a Remedy in Moral, Philanthropical, and Sociological Work?

To this we reply: What physician talks of an epidermic disease, when his attention is called to a case of tuberculosis? The foolishness of such a course on the part of a physician, would be no more apparent, than is the folly of those who offer, as a remedy for religious unbelief, a moral, sociological, or philanthropical cure. Men may illogically, sophistically, or basely use the term, "religion," when in the general judgment of mankind, they mean only morality, or a life conformable to nature; for there is no way of forcing on writers candor or perspicuity. But the efforts of such men to pass themselves off for doctors of religion, when every troubled soul knows they are evident quacks and impostors, will be most surely in vain. Morality and religion are no more one, than are night and day. True enough, night and day make one revolution of the earth on her axis, and the highest morals and truest religion enter into the making of a perfect human character; but as night means the time of rest and day the time for activity, so morality means man's relation to man, and religion his relation to God. It is not enough that by lexicology we can show an apparent right to the use of a given word in any given case. We should ask ourselves, if such a word will convey a false impression, or if such a word is the one generally used in the given case. If it will convey an ambiguous meaning, or to the general reader a meaning other than the writer intends, then no honest or careful writer will make use of such word. The word "religion," it matters not what its derivation may be, has been used such a vast number of years exclusively to show man's duty or obligation to God, that it can not be correctly used to-day to convey any other meaning. Every fair-minded man must look with contempt on the actions of those who use the word "religion," when the content of the word, according to its received meaning, never enters into their hearts, in the use of it.

We most emphatically hold that man is a religious being, and that therefore no merely moral, sociological, or philanthropical food can ever appease his longing for Him after whom he gropes in the darkness, whom he believes to be a living, conscious, personal God, and in whom he hopes for comfort and peace. Man prays, but not to a mere force; man hopes, but not in mere universal law; man trusts, but not in the "survival of the fittest," true as the law undoubtedly is. Nor can man cease to hope, and trust, and pray; and, therefore, he will ever be a religious being, hoping and trusting in, and praying confidently to, a living, personal God, to whom in distress he naturally cries: "Father, if it be possible, let this cup pass from me."

Man may lose all faith in church and priest, in forms and ceremonies, in surplices and stoles, in patens and chalices, in altars and sacrifices; but in the darkness he will still feel after Him, for whom his heart and his flesh cry out; nor will he cease searching after and trusting in God, while life shall last. Man asks for a fish, will you give him a stone? Play not with man's sacred feelings thus. But this is what is done by him who seeks to cure the present religious unbelief by applying moral, sociological, or philanthropical remedies. We therefore conclude that such efforts can have no remedial effect on the the evil in question. We may look on Buddha, Confucius, Mencius, or any others of their kind whom our fathers never knew; but great and noble as they all were and are, our countenances will not shine, our poor dead hearts will not pulsate with warmth and life from the reading of their moral or philanthropical precepts. They move us only so far as they speak to us religiously; and since our civilization can not be made to recognize in them the fountains from which we draw our religious inspiration, we hold there is no remedy for existing religious unbelief, in pointing burdened souls to them.

A Proposed Remedy:

In geological study, nothing is more evident than that in the evolution of vegetable and animal life, certain forms have had their culmination during certain epochs of the earth's history. In some cases this is so evident that their fossils are characteristic of the age. Reptiles and mollusks culminated in the Mesozoic age, and Trilobites and Brachiopods in the Paleozoic. Says Dana: "Living species are always adapted to some special climate or condition of the globe; and when this climate or condition has been passed in the earth's progress, the tribes fitted for it no longer exist." I should rather say that the forms of life are true though slow results of the earth's geological, physical, and climatic conditions; and that, therefore, they change of necessity as their conditions change. Notwithstanding the fact that in Devonian times the seas were swarming with fishes most formidably armed for offensive as well as defensive warfare, of all the species, genera, and even families then existing, not one to day remains. Le Conte says that the mammals of Tertiary times are now wholly extinct; and Dana tells us that all the fishes, reptiles, birds, and mammals of that same period, are extinct species. (Manual of Geology, 518). The statement that all mammalian life of the Tertiary period has passed off the earth's surface, I consider far from substantiated; but I have given the words of authorities more to prove the general fact of the constant change of living forms than to show the extinction or continuance of any particular species.

Now, as animal forms are the results of peculiar geological, physical, and climatic conditions, which cause the culmination of different forms at different times; so it appears to me are mental forms surely and certainly the products of evolution, though the factors causing mental changes are more obscure, and therefore less easily recognized. Certain mental types appear to have their culmination, and then to pass away, never again to return; or if ever they return, it can be only after man has passed through a preparatory period similar to that which preceded their first coming. A man honored at one age as an apostle of God, is at another cast into prison as a disturber of the peace, or put to death as a malefactor. To-day over the people, a man has almost miraculous power, and unlimited influence; while sometime in the past or future, he would have been, or would be, received by the same people with shouts of derision. A god at one time, is a deranged person or an impostor at another. The same forces which evolve the prophet or reformer, evolve also the receptivity of the masses. This is the natural order. When this order of nature is departed from, as it sometimes is, as in the cases of retrogression and monstrosities, if the prophet is at hand, the people will not believe him; and if the people are at hand, they seek the prophet in vain.

About two thousand years ago the Jewish people had been passing through those experiences that in their very nature resulted in the expectation of a political and spiritual reformer or savior; and the customs of the people had for ages been such as naturally resulted in the culmination of the prophetic type. It is not unfrequent that persons appear to-day claiming to be prophets and saints; but they are sporadic characters, whose professions and powers are soon scoffed at, and disproved by the critical spirit of the age. Such characters generally appear among ignorant people, and within their narrow sphere become celebrated or worshipped; but they can not pass beyond the bounderies of superstition. Science and skepticism set up an effectual barrier. Many of these pretenders would have flourished, or become universally famous, had they appeared during the ages of credulity; and many of those who have been universally celebrated, would never be known beyond their own superstitious circle, if they made their appearance to-day. In olden times an infectious disease had open way, and therefore cut down the people as a scythe the grass; but to-day sanitary science and disinfectants confine the disease, prevent its progress, and cut off its sway. Thus it is with the class of saviors and prophets: their times are passed, and the rule of science and critical inquiry has set in. It matters not how great a professed reformer and savior appeared to-day, in a scientific country he would not be received except as a disturber of the peace; but as time blunts the edge of criticism, and weaves about the persons of ancient days garments of sancity, authority, and devotion, it is not easy to destroy the faith of people in their idols, nor is it at all apparent that it would be wise to do so.

Jesus Christ, supposing him to be an historical character, was a great Jewish reformer, who was naturally enough denounced and persecuted by those whose offices he sought to change, or whose ways he labored to alter. Such characters were opposed to him chiefly on the grounds of self-interest, and not from any adherence to science or from the fact that they were governed by the scientific spirit; for the mantle of superstition was almost universally spread. Few men there were of scientific turn of mind, and such only smiled when they heard of the wonderful works of the great Jewish reformer; but these were foreigners, or outside of synagogue and indifferent to temple. The great majority of every land had been born, rocked, and raised, in superstition; and such heard the reformer gladly, and very many followed him. He preached to the poor, and loved them; while he burned with indignation at the idleness, selfishness, and sordidness, of the rich, giving the latter a place in hell, and the former a place in heaven. He was a lover of truth, justice, and righteousness; and had a sublime and unlimited faith in God and his providence. He brought God as near to man, as Socrates brought philosophy. He was filled with one idea—the completion of what he believed was his conscious mission. Neither the threats of his persecutors, nor suffering, nor penury, nor death could deter him from denouncing the transgressor, and hurling his maledictions on the hypocrite; any more than they could from blessing the poor in spirit who were lovers of God and man.

It is this Jesus, this Jewish reformer, that alone holds any sway, as a religious leader, over the more enlightened nations of the world; and although by men of scientific mind and education, whose bread comes not from the offerings of the faithful, he is almost without exception regarded as only human, it is safe to say that they admire and love him, and indignantly resent any attempt to dethrone him, or to put another in his place. They may admire other great world-reformers, acknowledge the great good they have done, and see in them the Christs and saviors of their respective peoples, but for them, skeptics as they are, there is only one Jesus, and his glory and leadership they will not give to another. To them his name is dearer, his word more cheering, his presence more hopeful than that of any other leader who has ever lived. It is therefore safe to say that whatever remedy we seek to use for the existing religious unbelief, it must be given, if at all, under the leadership of Jesus; and this is said not on the grounds of any absurd or monstrous claims of his being God-man, or having been born of a virgin, but solely on the grounds that, having as clear a right and title to this headship as any other claimant, and having been in quiet and peaceful possession of this headship for nearly 2,000 years, he can not be supplanted by another, or in legal language, ousted from his occupancy.

Having shown that under the conditions of our present moral and spiritual enlightenment, no other leadership than that of Jesus is possible, it now remains to ask whether a symbol of faith is necessary, and if so what must be its form and substance.

All true men are more or less patriotic; but in cases of actual warfare it has ever been deemed useful, if not necessary, to have some symbol, banner, or standard to fight under. Such a symbol reminds one of his country, his wife, and his children; and serves as a rallying centre or point, and fills the spirit with those qualities so requisite for the battle-field. The symbol makes possible unity of thought and act, and enables each soldier to know that he is fighting under the direction of one common commander or general. In addition to this, it serves to distinguish the forces of one's country from those of the enemy,—a work of no little importance in times of warfare.

Now, the work of a church must be carried on, if at all, in a manner similar to that in which a battle is waged. Church-work is supposed to be a battle against wrong-doing of every description. Sin and immorality are to be overcome, and righteousness and good morals built up. The pastor is the commander, and the other church officers are his assistants in this battle which is supposed to be waged for God and humanity. Every reason urged for the necessity of a symbol in secular warfare, may be equalled with similar reasons for the use of a symbol in spiritual battles. The principles for which one fights, should be clearly understood; the will of the commander should be known; there should be a rallying centre or point; the forces for and against should be distinguished; and there should be an object from the sight or contemplation of which, courage or zeal might be derived. As we do not believe that success can follow the movements of a bannerless army, so do we not believe that success can attend the labors of a symbolless church. In other words, a creed is necessary to the existence of a conquering church. No banner, no army; no creed, no church.

Admitting there must be a creed in order that a church may have a successful existence, our last question is, what must be its form and substance.

A creed of no words is despair, and a creed of many words superstition. Of these two evils some may prefer the one, others may prefer the other; but neither the one nor the other can finally hold the heart of humanity. In form a creed should be simple to understand, grand in expression, concise in statement, and sufficiently long to attract and hold the thought of a worshipping assembly. The custom of repeating the so-called Apostle's Creed by Episcopal congregations is of incalculable value to that church itself, and has a striking effect on strangers that happen to visit it. Its length is but little if any too great for the end desired; and in grandeur, and conciseness it is everything that could be wished for. Nor in our judgment does it fall short in clearness and simplicity. The logomachy that so often occurs over it, is rather the result of forced constructions than of any ambiguity in meaning. We admit the beauty in form of that creed, but we can not yield our assent to its substance; and from many years of ministerial experience in that church, we do not believe we ever knew a single male communicant who had no doubts of the truth of that creed in its entirety. Nor can this be wondered at; for men in general inhale the air of a scientific atmosphere, and are therefore prone to regard with grave suspicions all assertions which in their very nature are subversive of universal law, order, and experience. It is therefore first of all and most of all necessary that in substance a creed should be at one with universal law, order, and experience, that it receive the assent of men of independent thought and liberal education,—in other words, of the scientific world.

It may be regarded as highly presumptuous in the author, in daring to express his opinion as to what the substance of a creed should be; but we believe that there are but few men of our civilization who would not give their hearty assent to, or at least hope for the truth of, a creed something like the following:

I believe in God the Father Almighty, Creator of heaven and earth; and in Jesus Christ his Prophet our Leader and

Head, who suffered under Pontius Pilate, was crucified, dead, and buried; but is alive with God forevermore.

I believe in God as the Savior and Sanctifier; the communion of saints; the forgiveness of sins; the brotherhood of man; and the life everlasting. Amen.

We would assist in establishing a religion broad as humanity, deep as God's love; and in the establishment of a church whose creed every religious person, of whatever name or nation, could heartily repeat. We do not believe in establishing, nor would we wish to join, a creedless church; nor do we believe that the heart of humanity could ever find rest in such a body. But the clauses in the creed of the church that we would assist in establishing, would be few indeed—the fewer the better; for the strength of a creed is not in its length. A long and closely defined creed may be a string of subtilely woven falsehoods; whereas a creed of not more than a single clause, might be a truth upon which humanity could build forever. The God of such a creed, however, although immanent in, would not be thought of as synonymous with, nature, nor nature's laws; but as the Being in whom nature has its existence, and its laws their source.

Some may imagine that our work has been destructive; but such would be an unwarranted inference. We wish to tear down only what is crumbling and dangerous, that we may the more firmly establish what is solid and abiding. We would break down falsehood, boasting, hypocrisy, pretence; we would build up truthfulness, humility, sincerity, candor.

As a parting word the author would say that he has aimed to set before the reader the footprints of a soul searching after truth and righteousness; and in the person of a most scholarly and conscientious priest, to exemplify the strife existing in the mind between reason and dogma. This strife exists in all thoughtful souls; but so deep and intense is it in the minds of the most scholarly, that they can not any longer fall down before the idols of their youth—the absurdities of old. They therefore look earnestly for a faith that shall be consonant with reason, at one with nature, and at the same time comforting to the heart. Let us not deceive ourselves with boasting of our great knowledge of God: the conscious ignorance of the true scholar precludes all dogmatism. So much we know: he that most doeth justice, most loveth mercy, walketh most humbly,—he it is who is made most in the image of God.

> "*Das Alte stuerzt, es aendert sich die Zeit,*
> *Und neues Leben bluehet aus den Ruinen—*
> The ancient powers and customs fall,
> The age itself is changing;
> Behold a new and youthful life
> From out the ruins springing."
> (*Schiller: Wilhelm Tell, 2425.*)

A "TE DEUM," OR HYMN TO GOD
BY
CLEANTHES.
(Born about 300 B. C., at Assos in Troas.)

Most glorious of the Immortals, many-named, Almighty forever!
Zeus, ruler of Nature, that governest all things with law,
Hail! for lawful it is that all mortals should address Thee.
For we are thy offspring,taking the image only of thy voice,as many
Mortal things as live and move upon the earth.
Therefore will I hymn Thee,and sing thy might forever; for Thee doth
All this universe that circles round the earth obey,moving whithersoever
Thou leadest, and is gladly swayed by Thee. Such a minister hast
Thou in thine invincible hands:the two-edged,blazing,imperishable
Thunderbolt. For under its stroke all Nature shuddereth,and by it
Thou guidest aright the Universal Reason, that roams through all
Things, mingling itself with the greater and the lesser lights, till
It has grown so great, and become supreme king over all.
Nor is aught done on the earth without Thee, O God, nor in the divine
Sphere of the heavens,nor in the sea,save the works that evil men
Do in their folly. Yea, but Thou knowest even to find a place for
Superfluous things,and to order that which is disorderly,and things
not dear to men are dear to Thee.
Thus dost Thou harmonize into One all good and evil things,that
there should be one everlasting Reason of them all.
And this the evil among mortal men avoid and heed not; wretched, ever
Desiring to possess the good,yet they nor see nor hear the universal
Law of God, which obeying with all their heart,their life would be well.
But they rush graceless each to his own aim, some cherishing lust for
Fame, the nurse of evil strife, some bent on monstrous gain, some
Turned to folly and the sweet works of the flesh hastening, indeed,
to bring the very contrary to these things to pass.
But Thou, O Zeus, the All-Giver,Dweller in the darkness of cloud,
Lord of thunder,save Thou men from their unhappy folly,which do
Thou, O Father, scatter from their souls; and give them to discover that
Wisdom in whose assurance Thou governest all things with justice;
So that being honored, they may pay Thee honor, hymning thy
Works continually, as it beseems a mortal man.
Since there can be no greater glory for men or gods than this,
Duly to praise forever the Universal Law.

INDEX.

Adam:
>date of his creation, 204; fall of, 180.

Affliction and faith, 38.

Agathon on the coward, 176.

Augustine:
>and Pelagius, 223; on Adam, 224; on moral freedom, 224; the first to anthropomorphize God, 232.

Ante-Nicene Fathers, 422.

Appointment of ministers, 102, 110.

Aristotle:
>on development of character, 167; on manliness, 175; on the city, 282; as a philosopher, 294; on virtue, 352.

Bacon, Roger, 401.

Bacon, Lord, on theology, 404.

Belief saves nobody, 224.

Bible:
>considered as a whole, 232; should be purged, 379; how regarded by scholars, 410.

Bill, Wild, 82.

Bishop:
>powers of dispensation, 162; a suspected, 179; unseemly action of a, 185; a dishonorable, 200.

Bishopric, how sought after, 198.

Blood-atonement, 265, 313.

Blossom:
>Merton meets Mrs., 81; as Job's comforter, 82; his excuse, 83.

Buddha, life and death of, 243.

Business is business, 122.

Buttolph:
>his hard experience, 87; on guarantees, 88; on faith, 88.

"Call:"
>Mr. Pascoe's proof of a, 47; on "calls" in general, 48; of Mr. Carter, 62, 68, 69; more fully discussed, 63, 69.

Calvin, 284.

Carter:
>his "call," 62, 68; subject of his thesis, 67.

Castles in the air, 51.

Cause and effect, 161.

Calf, divinely conceived, 394.

Change, all subject to, 180.

Christ:
>concerning his divinity, 221, 234, 253, 270, 335; concerning his deity, 222, 225, 235, 237, 253, 260, 269, 278, 413; Celsus on, 255; and blood-atonement, 265; his teachings, 274; is supreme, 431.

Christian civilization:
>and heathen, 124, 383.

Christianity, 383.

Church:
>and science, 402; and creed, 432.

Churches all at variance, 401.

Churchmembers:
>Inhospitality of, 77; lives of, 124; first duty of, 140.

Church-officers:
>a trio of, 130; Loveright on, 153.

Church-buildings, 182.

Cicero:
>on reason, 374; on happiness, 158; on justice, 184, 191; on the universe, 202; on philosophy, 294.

Clergy, how restrained, 421.

Communion:
>Scene at, 189; meaning of, 363.

Conception, divine:
    Homer on, 233; commonly believed in, 236, 242, 259; of Christ, 241, 259.
Conduct, dishonorable:
    no excuse for, 196.
Consciences, men's, 79.
Contraction and temperature, 212.
Creed, 327, 399, 407, 431.
Creation:
    Song of, 163; of the world, 203; date of, 204; special, 412.
Croquet, a game of, 105.
Day, a happy, 91.
Darwin:
    on the clergy, 397, 409; the bishop on, 409.
Death:
    of Merton's father, 24; must not fear, 174, 175; should not rashly seek, 174; of Mrs. Merton, 366; the gate to life, 356, 365.
Death-bed repentance, 173.
Deity, how only established, 237.
Democritus, 45.
Denominations, setting up, 85.
Disappointments, are common, 180.
Divinity of Christ:
    not satisfactorily proved, 237; and that of Buddha, 252; Mr. Pomposity on, 259; Merton on, 273.
Dogmas:
    the churches seek, 58; and science, 59; and reason, 190, 225, 248, 303, 434; leading astray, 223.
Dogmatists:
    escaping the question, 59; banners of, 59.
Dreams, 420.
Drunkard, a typical, 105.
Duty:
    doing our, 115, 415; must perform our, 172, 174, 415; Kreeshna on, 262.
Earth:
    a child of the sun, 216, 217; age of, 216, 218; past history of, 217, internal heat of, 217; beginning of the life of, 218; different ages of, 218; how long occupied by man, 219; glacial epoch of, 219; losing its heat, 218.
Easter, poem on, 372.
Ecclesiastics:
    and justice, 283; and legislation, 287; Lecky on, 306; and truth, 421.
Elder, the, breaking promises, 72.
Energy:
    conservation of, 211; amount of, invariable, 330.
Episcopal Bishop, Merton and the, 100.
Evangelist, an, calls for prayer, 151.
Evil-speaking, Merton on, 131.
Evolution:
    generally received, 180, 205; of living forms, 219, 427, 428; of mental forms, 428.
Faith:
    the best, 125; and works, 125, 141, 261; salvation by, 157; a reasonable, 433; and truth, 279, 312, 314; in the churches, 401.
Faiths:
    thoughts on religious, 56; Tennyson on, 181.
Fall, on the, 180, 412.
Fisher on miracles, 334, 336.
Fixed State:
    doctrine of, 159; no evidence of a, 161.
Fraudulent, Mr.:
    Mr. Smalleyes on, 112; visits Mr. Longshanks, 120; Mr. Longshanks on, 123; Mr. Loveright on, 153.
Friend, Merton loses a, 24.
Friendship, 327.
Galileo, 402.
Genesis, on creation, 210, 220.
God:
    many-named but one, 299; has no favorites, 275, 301,

314, 337, 405, 413; formless and unbounded, 269; and natural order, 65; and reason, 384, 385; and nature, 66, 434; Mr. Carter on, 69; anthropomorphization of, 70, 314, 382, 424; doeth all things well, 84, 365; and human affairs, 96; sons of with daughters of men, 119; sons of, 235; a child of, 140; just and good, 161; man accountable to, 165; how revealed, 165, 340; infallible, 166, 203; deceives not, 203; his revelation, 220, 263, 301; his fatherhood, 235, 301, 423; only one, 265; man's true life, 307; Israelitish conception of, 381, 424.

Godspeed, Mr., kindness of, 152.

Globes, collision of, 216.

Goethe:
a love poem, 145; on the church, 293; on the power of gold, 201; on revelation, 425; on the words of the gods, 231; on God's works, 267; on deliberation, 317, on the character of the gods, 281; on priests, 293.

Gold, the power of, 198, 199, 201.

Gospels:
dead and living, 123; Mill on the, 222; when critically examined, 226; the authors of the, 230

Geology, as a science, 218.

Grasshoppers, a shower of, 92.

Happiness, on, 179, 348, 350.

Harnack on Augustine, 232.

Headstrong, Mr.:
speaks at a revival, 116; Longshanks offends, 117; Mr. Squareman on, 129, 131; Merton calls on, 137; on book-learning, 138; advises Merton, 140; Mr. Loveright on, 148.

Heaven and earth, meaning of, 204.

Heine, quotation from, 258.

Heat: a mode of motion, 210; loss of by the earth, 218.

Hell, located by the Fathers, 218.

Heresy, not so bad as deception, 169.

Holiness, personal, 58.

Holy Ghost, impressions from, 64, 68.

Honor:
the highest possession, 191; how characterized, 191; and priests, 195, 196; a reward of virtue, 157.

Homer, 87, 104, 114, 126, 240.

Huxley, Darwin on, 409.

Hypocrite:
a typical, 98; in the pulpit, 169, 183, 197; in the congregation, 327.

Immaculate conceptions, 241, 313.

Immortality:
Mr. Gray on, 233; Mr. Judex on, 246; man longs for, 326, 423; Merton on, 362; Kant on, 364; leading thinkers on, 423.

Imputed Righteousness, 125, 158.

Infidel, Merton meets an, 38.

Insincerity, 175.

Insurance, Headstrong on, 138.

Jesus:
persecuted by the church, 60; a martyr for the truth, 242, 430; incredible stories about, 242; and Buddha, 243; Celsus on his divinity, 255; on his deity, 269, 270, 274, 278, 419; on his teachings, 274, 430; prayers to, 277, 278; the one sweet voice, 419; Judgment on, 420; is supreme, 430, 431.

Jordan, crossing a, 80.

Judgment-day, not far off, 161.

Justice, practice of, makes just, 157.

Kansas:

Merton invited to, 71, a beautiful view in, 72.
Kant on immortality, 364.
Kindness: a paying investment, 108; power of, 135.
Knowledge, key of, 239.
Kreeshna:
on immortality, 261; on duty, 262.
Lady, a hospitable, 73.
Laplace, on the original nebula, 208.
Larva, 333.
Law, sources of the, 283.
Letter to the bishop, 411.
Life:
thoughts on the phases of, 54; must not rashly sacrifice, 176.
Locke:
on miracles, 238; on reason, 156.
Longshanks, Mr.:
Merton visits, 114; on religion, 115, 117; on preachers' visits, 115; on Mr. Smalleyes, 119; on Mr. Fraudulent, 123.
Luke, Gospel of:
nothing known of its author, 229; not an apostle, 229; not an eye-witness, 229; statements of, 229.
Lyell, Sir Charles:
as a geologist, 218.
Man:
affected by accidents, 160; unequally endowed, 161; a child of error, 166; an animal, 328; fossil man, 219; how long on earth, 219; self-conceited, 325; desires immortality, 326, 423; his love for woman, 327; foetal life of, 329; his conception of God, 425; must pray, 426; should be true to self, 398.
Mark, Gospel of:
little known of, 227; ours not the original, 227; not an eye-witness, 228; a disciple of Peter, 228; statements of, 228.
Marcus Aurelius:
on mental improvement, 30; on studious attention, 53; on doing our duty, 110; on preparation for death, 115.
Masters, serving two, 398, 403.
Matthew, Gospel of:
original work lost, 226; translation of questionable, 226, 227.
Meekface, Mr., on Mr. Squareman, 132, 134
Megalauchus, Mr., goes a fishing, 195.
Men after God's own heart, 231.
Merton:
his parents, 24, 29; and the professor, 27; his religious experience, 26, 39; how impressed in youth, 33-35; and "sloping," 36; his early doubts, 39; takes his first degree, 40; and Mr. Tubbs, 42; in the great city, 53; his hopes not realized, 55; takes his second degree, 62, 71; vain hopes of, 60; on nature, 66; on prayer, 66; uncertainty of, 39, 40, 68; his first charge, 75; a perilous journey, 84; pursued by wolves, 93; offends Mr. Soulless, 95; accepts a new appointment, 100; receives advice, 102; and Mrs. Woundedheart, 107; advises Mr. Meekface, 135; leaves Methodism, 155; and the examiner, 167; and Mr. Insanitas, 187; and Mr. Megalauchus, 192; receives his third degree, 283; takes his fourth and fifth degrees, 308.
Ministers:
young, how favored, 24; as students, 25, 27, 28; young, great professions of, 25; young, characters of, 31; the marks they leave, 82; giving

advice, 101; Mrs. Merton on, 102; tobacco-chewing, 106; and the Holy Ghost, 149; plotting, 172, 180; their labors, 181, 182; the actions of certain, 190; hypocrisy of, 201, 421; skeptical, 223, 421; illogical, 254, 378; duping their followers, 245; an assembly of, 420.
Mill on the authority of the Gospels, 230.
Miracles:
impossible to prove, 48, 273; how the credulous assume, 50, 335, 395; not admissible, 205, 316, 336, 379; New Testament, 238, 241, 253, 273; not essential, 260; improbability of, 272; non-occurrence of, 379.
Missionaries and salvation, 301.
Moses and the Pentateuch, 378.
Murderer and Murdered, 158.
Nirvana, 388.
Nature:
bond of sympathy in, 51; differently impressed by, 52; and God, 52, 347; a divine organism, 66; ever changing, 347.
Nebular Hypothesis:
generally accepted, 206, 207, 209.
Nicene Creed, 398.
Noble, the, how distinguished, 191.
Opinion, should not readily give up, 167.
Ordination, little required for, 162.
Organs, Headstrong on, 133
Origen, excommunication of, 256.
Orthodoxy:
dogmas of, unproved, 222, 305; and the facts of science, 222; its followers, 421.
Ovid, quotation from, 92.
Pascoe, Mr., proof of his call, 47.
Pericles, 346.

Physician, heal thyself, 128.
Plato: 268, 247, 276, 282, 295, 414.
Plautus on freedom, 416.
Poems:
39, 40, 163, 164, 372, 385, 406, 417.
Pope, the:
and English Church, 285; and John Calvin, 284.
"Power," the:
Mr. Headstrong on, 138; experiencing, 140; and ministers, 148.
Prayer:
proper use and end of, 66, 338, 342, 345; for the dead, 370; a natural cry, 234, 307, 426.
Preserve, a rare, 89.
Priests:
scheming, 181; and honor, 191, 195, 197; going around the world, 193; and information, 197; and love of gold, 199; and hypocrisy, 199, 200, 201; and unbelief, 240; Mr. Judex on, 248; and power, 284, 285, 291; and politics, 283, 285, 293; teaching and practice of, 290; and philanthropy, 292, 341; and science, 310; and pulpit, 309.
Pulpit, the:
its true work, 164, 188; kind of men filling it, 188; as it is, 309.
Profession, vain, 123.
Professor, the, and the shoe, 28.
Protestantism, 395.
Providence, Headstrong on, 138.
Reason:
man's glory, 165; Cicero on, 374; Livy on, 374; Few live a life of, 352; a poem on, 385; in the churches, 403; the temple of, 416; the gift of God, 63; Locke on, 156.
Religious Experience, untrustworthy, 32.
Religion and Science, 59.
Religious Principles, how de-

veloped, 33.
Religion:
  a central fact, 245, 301, 426; should be purified, 264; common to humanity, 264; fundamentally true, 263; sources of, 283; and politics, 284, 285; and truth, 316; what, 425.
Richter, 394.
Revelation:
  fitted to man's growth, 239, 420; not infallible nor complete, 263; not direct, 304; and natural order, 313, 411; universal, 301, 379; not special, 378, 412.
Revivals:
  results of, 29, 116; Mr. Loveright on, 147; a scene at, 149.
Revivalists, 116, 147.
Resurrection, 328, 333, 337.
Ride, a, for life, 94.
Righteousness, personal and imputed, 58.
Ritterhaus on the true wife, 177.
Sacraments, save not, 173.
Saint, a, with seven devils, 134.
Salis, 356.
Salvation:
  by faith, 157; by works, 260, 302.
Sanctification:
  Merton professes, 25; meetings for, 28.
Sanctity, Father:
  his speech, 42; his prayer, 43; his hypocrisy, 44.
Savigny, 282.
Saws, ten thousand, 89.
Science:
  and religion, 59; and miracles, 205; and orthodoxy, 222, 402, and theology, 225; and revelation, 411.
Sincerity:
  nothing so desirable, 169, 170; lack of in the pulpit, 183, 312; necessary, 397.
Slanderers:
  Mrs. Merton on, 111, 123; examples of, 133.
Slander: Mr. Squareman on, 127.
Smalleyes, Mr., on slander, 112
Solar System:
  one of many, 206; age of, 206.
Soulless, Mr.:
  a crabbed old fellow, 87; a Shylock, 95; Merton leaves, 96; Mr. Smith on, 97.
Shakspere, 70, 142, 170, 221.
Schiller, 52, 164, 197, 435.
Skepticism:
  among ministers, 183, 312; among the learned, 284.
Spencer, Herbert, and superstition, 409.
Squash, a load for quarterage, 82.
Subscriptions, Longshanks on church, 118.
Suffering, results of, 372.
Stewards:
  stealing timber, 121; plotting against one another, 122.
Substance, one and divine, 388.
Sun:
  Helmholtz on, 206; Tyndall on, 206; Youmans on, 207; a star, 209; origin of, 210; its heat, 211; contraction of, 212, 214; existence of prior to the earth, 212; present condition of, 213, 214; age of, 215, 216.
Teacher:
  character of his work, 182.
Testament, Old, its teachings, 231.
Testament, New, fruit of many trees, 232.
Temperature and Contraction, 213.
Te Deum, 436.
Theologians:
  how characterized, 44; what they seek, 57; their great error, 232; Lord Bacon on, 404.
Theological Schools:
  their character, 45, 46, 65.

INDEX.

Theological Professors:
how restrained, 45; repairing the breaches, 46.
Thoughts, Emerson on, 183.
Thunderstorm, a, 85.
Tobacco, foul uses of, 92.
Town, a strange, 104.
Trustees:
Mrs. Woundedheart on, 109; yet not trusted, 113.
Truth:
alone saves, 57, 224; what, 115; and faith, 181, 279, 312; and religion, 316.
Truthful, Mr.:
hospitality of, 75, 76; anxiety of, 90.
Truthseeker, Mr., meets Merton, 142.
Unbelief, causes of, 422.
Universe:
subject to decay and death, 205; not created in fact, 205, 208, 212, 220.
Vergil, 39, 71, 98, 99.
Vicarious Atonement, 313; evil results of faith in, 125; no faith in, 413.
Virgin, conception by, 238, 240, 241, 313.
Virgin Mary: a lawful wife, 257.
Virtue:
definition of, 352; a result, 353; its own reward, 354;

brings peace, 354.
Virtuous Acts, what constitutes, 166.
Visions, 420.
Visit, Merton makes a, 104.
Votaries, religious, 286.
Walk:
a long, 79, 81; a perilous, 84.
Wheat, Mr., and his call, 149.
Wife:
"a rum one," 85; dearer than all, 92, 144; good, the gift of God, 177; husband's love for, 327, 369.
Woman:
beautiful, power of, 78; beautiful and good, 88; with the serpent's sting, 107; Mr. Headstrong on, 137; man's love for, 327.
Workandpray Mr.:
on divine forgiveness, 143; on Mrs. Squareman, 143.
Work:
unproductive, 111; and faith, 141.
World, creation of, 203.
Worldly Men and Churchmembers, 124; Sunshine on, 144.
Worship, must be sincere, 415.
Woundedheart, Mrs.:
on the church-officers, 107; Merton's appeal to, 108.
Zoroaster on God, 263.

A GREAT WORK BY THE SAME AUTHOR

"GOD AND MAN"

OR

"A PHILOSOPHICAL INQUIRY INTO THE PRINCIPLES OF RELIGION."

Where Agents are not, Sent to any Address, Post-paid for $2.50.

WHAT THE PRESS SAYS OF IT:

"The more I read it, the more I like it. It is a pleasure to open the pages of a book so scholarly, candid, fearless, and positive. The earnest, able and patient author and thinker comes out into a clear field."—*The Rev. Dr. Thomas, Chicago.*

"I greatly prize your book."—*The Rev. Prof. Swing, Chicago.*

"No more able and comprehensive work on religious questions has appeared in America."—*St. Louis Republic.*

"The product of a scholar with a masterful grasp of a profound subject."—*Evening News, Newark, N. J.*

"A grand, good book."—*Editor American Microscopic Journal.*

"It is wonderfully erudite."—*New Ideal, Boston.*

"The work of a learned man."—*Atlantic Monthly.*

"We commend the work most heartily."—*Quarterly Journal of Inebriety, Hartford, Conn.*

"A learned view of religion."—*Brooklyn Eagle.*

"Its tone is excellent; its style simple and clear. Will well repay perusal."—*Science, New York.*

"We gladly commend the work.'—*Boston Globe.*

"The use made of his large knowledge is judicious and effective."—*The Religio-Philosophical Journal, Chicago.*

"The work will commend itself."—*St. Louis Spectator.*

"The work teems with scholarship."—*Standard, Bridgeport, Conn.*

"A surprising book; a brave and learned one."—*Freethought, San Francisco, Cal.*

"Here are pages of thorough scholarship."—*Gazette, Davenport, Ia.*

"A work constructed with great breadth of view."—*Evening Wisconsin, Milwaukee.*

"A scholarly and commanding treatise."—*Record-Union, Sacramento, Cal.*

ADDRESS: THE TRURO PUBLISHING COMPANY,

CHICAGO, ILL.